through Herakles back to Zeus, set out into the world from Argos. They came to Upper Macedonia and at first entered the service of the local king. Later, however, the brothers were dismissed and exiled, and they took refuge in the region around the so-called Gardens of Midas at the foot of the Bermion mountain range. There they remained and conquered bit by bit the other regions of Macedonia. Perdikkas then became the founder of the royal line.[3] Justin, who wrote a school book in the third century A.D., relates another story, which springs from the similarity between the name of the capital, Aigai, and the Greek word *aiges* (goats). In this version the goatherd Caranus gained control of the town Edessa, which was then renamed Aigai because of his goats. Perdikkas was supposed to be the first successor to Caranus.[4]

These stories provide little historical information. However, two conclusions can be drawn. First, the original home of the Argeadai was situated in the valley of the Haliakmon, probably at modern Verghina, where spectacular graves were found, which strongly suggest a royal burial place. Second, Herodotos' early legend discloses a desire to link the early history of the Argeadai with the legends of the Greek world; and both legends established the claim that the origins of the Macedonians and their kings were Greek. This claim was already made by Alexander I, who wished to participate as a runner in the Olympic Games, which apparently no Macedonian before him had done. But because participation was traditionally restricted to Greeks, Alexander had to prove his Greek ancestry, which he was able to do brilliantly with the tale of the Argive origins of his family. That the Macedonians and their kings did in fact speak a dialect of Greek and bore Greek names may be regarded nowadays as certain. The Macedonian dialect made use of many loan words from the languages of their Illyrian and Thracian neighbours, a circumstance that does not surprise modern philologists but provided ancient opponents of Macedonia with "proof" that they could not be Greeks. The question of the actual racial origins of the ancient Macedonians cannot be answered adequately on the basis of the language or of social and religious customs in historical times. It is, however, historically an unprofitable question, which has only gained in importance in modern times because it has been taken up by nationalists of all kinds in the Balkans and elsewhere and exploited, according to the answer, in the service of territorial and other claims.

Ancient allegations that the Macedonians were non-Greeks all had their origin in Athens at the time of the struggle with Philip II. Then as now, a political struggle created the prejudice. The orator Aischines once even found it necessary, in order to counteract the prejudice vigorously fomented by his opponents, to defend Philip on this issue and describe him at a meeting of the Athenian Popular Assembly as being "entirely Greek."[5] Demosthenes' allegations were lent an appearance of credibility by the fact, apparent to every observer, that the life-style of the Macedonians, being determined by specific geographical and historical conditions, was different from that of a Greek city-state. This alien way of life was, however, common to the western Greeks in Epeiros, Akarnania and Aitolia, as well as to the Macedonians, and their fundamental Greek nationality was never doubted. Only as a consequence of the political disagreement with Macedonia was the question raised at all.

Most Greeks lived in relatively small, self-governing city-states (*poleis*), which normally contained an urban settlement that served as the political centre of the state and as the seat of the administration of the territory belonging to the state and its citizens. By contrast Macedonia was a relatively large, centralized territorial state with a royal capital as the centre of power. The population lived mainly on the land in villages. Larger villages may indeed have reached the size of a small town but had (insofar as we can tell for the early period) at first no self-administrative function. The territory of the state appears to have been administered, if at all, by local nobles, who, depending on their distance from the capital, represented the interests of the state or merely their own. The areas where the local lords and barons acknowledged the Argead monarchy were ruled solely by the king, who in principle enjoyed a total power that was otherwise only familiar to the Greeks from non-Greek peoples such as the Thracians, Illyrians or Persians. Here as well a large difference from the political structure of the majority of Greek states could be observed. Among the larger city-states at the beginning of the fifth century B.C. only

Sparta still had a hereditary monarchy, and even there it was formally restricted in its powers.

Whether the Macedonian monarchy was in practice as independent of other power blocks within the state as it appears to have been is disputed. There are good reasons for assuming that powerful barons could exert influence on more important affairs of state—for example, on decisions about war and peace or about the succession to the throne. It would have made no sense for the king to make decisions his followers were not prepared to carry out. The most influential lords and barons at any one time thus constituted an informal council of state. The sources offer, however, no grounds for the assumption that there was ever a formal assembly of the whole people. At the same time it would have been possible for chance groupings of, say, the inhabitants of the capital or those eligible for military service to exert pressure occasionally on the king or to express a group opinion. The practical administration may have lain in the hands of the king and his retinue, but the viability of his decisions and his administrative regulations depended entirely on the readiness of the barons (perhaps sworn in an oath at the accession) to acknowledge his position.[6]

This primitive state structure was alien to the Greeks of the city-states in the fifth century B.C. Moreover, the size of the territory to which the Macedonian king laid claim revealed quite another dimension, even when those claims could not always be realized, particularly in the mountainous Upper Macedonian principalities in the west. The geographical core of ancient Macedonia comprised the water cachement areas of the river Haliakmon and the southerly course of the Axios (Vardar); on the lower Haliakmon near Verghina lay Aigai, the original residence of the Argeadai. In connection with the events of 429 Thukydides gives details of the gradual expansion of the Argead state before the Peloponnesian War: "The Lynkestians and Elimiots also belong to the Macedonians, as well as other up-country peoples; they are indeed allies and subjects of the Macedonians, but each has its own monarchy. Alexander, the father of Perdikkas, and his ancestors, who were originally Temenidai from Argos, were the first to occupy the region by the sea now called Macedonia, and they ruled

here as kings after driving out the Pierians from Pieria in a battle . . . and the Bottians from what is called Bottia. . . . Along the
Axios they took a narrow strip of Paionia stretching from the
mountains as far as Pella and the sea; east of the Axios, between
it and the river Strymon, they drove out the Edonians and took
over the area called Mygdonia. From the land now called Eordia
they drove out the Eordians . . . and the Almopians out of Almopia. These Macedonians also gained control of the land of
other peoples, which they still rule today: Anthemous, Krestonia,
Bisaltia and much of the land of the Macedonians themselves."[7]

This inventory unfortunately offers no clue to a chronological
ordering of the expansion. Thukydides appears to give promi-
nence to Alexander, but probably only because he was the father
of the reigning king Perdikkas, and it seems fairly certain that
Alexander was only responsible personally for the last phase. According to Thukydides, the first step was the conquest of the
coastal region Pieria, lying immediately to the east of Aigai, and
the expulsion of its population. Access to the sea and control over
the rich agricultural land of Pieria would have been the prime
consideration for this expansion. Similar considerations doubtless
made desirable the taking over of Bottia, the plain between the
Haliakmon and Axios bordering on Pieria, and the strip of the
Axios valley itself (Amphaxitis). Krestonia, Mygdonia, Bisaltia and
Anthemous were geographical neighbours, but it is probable that
these regions were first added to Macedonia as a result of the
disbanding of the Persian satrapy (province) in Thrace after the
abortive Greek campaign of Xerxes in 480/79. The sources give
no evidence for dating the acquisition of the other areas of Lower
Macedonia referred to by Thukydides. It is unlikely, however,
that they all were under the control of the house of the Argeadai
before the Persian War.

In Upper Macedonia the development is even more difficult to
follow. Eordia, which according to Thukydides was not originally
Macedonian, probably fell victim early to the ruling ambitions of
the Argeadai. The Macedonian tribes of Upper Macedonia retained their own hereditary lords, or *basileis*, who claimed a certain measure of independence and, because of the relative weakness of the house of the Argeadai, also exercised it. Thukydides

defines them as "allies and subjects" in an attempt to make clear the hardly definable and constantly changing relationship between the *basileis* of Upper Macedonia and the *basileus* of the Argeadai. Relations between the barons of the wild mountainous country and the Argeadai of the more gentle coastal plains, who nevertheless claimed sovereignty over the whole of Macedonia, must always have been somewhat tense. Before the reign of Philip II the Argeadai were not generally able to establish their claim on a long-term basis that would allow them to exert regular control.[8]

Thus at the beginning of the fifth century B.C. the Macedonian state was a loose construction of regions that more or less voluntarily, according to their geographical position and the political inclinations of their lords, gave their allegiance to the Argead king, who resided at Aigai. To the outside world the Argead king certainly represented the Macedonian state, even though, to lend the necessary conviction to an international treaty, some of the most powerful lords and barons were occasionally also required to swear the oath.[9] It also appears that they were required to affirm their recognition of a new king when he succeeded to the throne—normally an adult son designated as successor by his father, the ruling king (the oldest son when there were several). In cases of dispute the influence of the lords and barons must have been decisive.

We have little concrete knowledge of the economic structure of Macedonia in the fifth century B.C. Agriculturally the country was probably self-supporting since the climate of Macedonia, the Mediterranean climate of the coast as well as the pure continental climate of the interior regions, was more suitable for cereal crops and for horse and sheep breeding than that of many other regions of Greece. If Arrian's description, mentioned above, has any validity, then even in the fourth century B.C. many Macedonians lived as shepherds in the mountains of Upper Macedonia. Macedonian horsemen together with those of their Thessalian neighbours were later regarded as the best in Greece, a fact from which extensive horse breeding can be inferred. Macedonia was also heavily forested, and one community was even named Xylopolis, or Timber Town. Timber was mainly exported for ship building. It is unclear how this trade was transacted, but it is possible that the forests, or large portions of them, were royal possessions. At any rate the king was certainly in a position to control the timber exports.[10]

Macedonia also commanded silver and gold deposits, although the most abundant source for precious metals in the North Aegean area, the Pangaion range, lay beyond the frontiers of the Macedonian state until the reign of Philip II. Kallisthenes, the historian of Alexander the Great, whose commission and style were to present Macedonian affairs in the context of Greek mythology, wrote that the Phrygian king Midas, famous for his wealth, drew his riches from the Bermion mountains. However, this statement probably refers to the iron-ore there, as in modern times no silver or lead deposits are known. The river Echedoros ("gift bringer") was famous for the gold contained in its waters, and at the time of Alexander I mines on Mount Dysoron to the east of the Axios produced large amounts of silver. It is not possible to establish whether Dysoron became Macedonian before or after the withdrawal of the Persians, who, at least in theory, ruled the region until 479. But once this rich mine came into Macedonian possession, it was placed directly under the administration of the crown.[11]

2. BEFORE THE PELOPONNESIAN WAR

Macedonia first becomes accessible to the historian when Dareios, the Persian king, set out to conquer the regions of Europe bordering on his Asian empire. Since the collapse of the kingdom of Lydia around 546 the Persians had controlled western Asia Minor including the numerous Greek city-states, but an expansion into continental Europe did not occur until about 512 when Dareios led a campaign against the Skythians north of the Danube. This campaign came to a halt in the steppes of southern Russia, and after some months Dareios was forced to retreat across the Danube. To gain any advantage at all from the expensive expedition, Dareios decided to leave an army behind in Europe with orders to conquer Thrace. According to the account of Herodotos, the commander Megabazos did indeed succeed in subjugating the coastal strip. Only at Perinthos on the Sea of Marmara and from the Paionians in the Strymon valley did he meet with much resistance. But there he was finally able to assert himself, and the Paionians of the valley and the hinterland as far as Lake Prasias were subjugated and even transported to Asia. A Persian satrapy does not, however, appear to have been established.[1]

These events did not affect Macedonia directly. One passage in Herodotos indicates that contact was made with King Amyntas, but Amyntas did not yield to the Persians. The contact was not necessarily unfriendly. Macedonia certainly profited from the weakening of the Paionians, and it may have been at about this period that Amyntas annexed to Macedonia the Amphaxitis (at least part of which was held to be Paionian) and the adjoining coastal strip on the Thermaic gulf. He was at any rate able to offer refuge in Anthemous to the exiled Athenian tyrant Hippias in 506.[2] This offer sheds light on relations between Macedonia and the Greek city-states. At around this time Amyntas' son Alexander participated as an athlete in the Olympic Games, perhaps more than once.[3] The Olympic Games were far more than just a religious festival with sporting and cultural events. They offered the still mainly noble participants, all leading figures in their own states, a regular, if only occasional, opportunity to get to know one another personally. This aspect must have been important to the son of the Macedonian king, the future ruler of the largest territorial state bordering on the Greek world. Such acquaintanceships could indeed have political consequences. In 480 Alexander was described as *proxenos* (guest friend of the state) and benefactor of the Athenians, an honorary title only conferred for concrete acts of beneficence.[4]

What his acts were is not known, but they could perhaps have been the delivery of ship-building timber for the expansion of the Athenian fleet. The title might also have been inherited from his father Amyntas, a friend of the Athenian tyrants, and so be an indication of long-term good relations between the two states, despite the expulsion of the tyrants. In any event, the Olympic Games made it easy to establish and maintain such relations.

At the time of Amyntas' death ca. 497–496 storm signals were hoisted in Aegean politics. The first phase of the rebellion of the Ionian cities against the Persians in Asia Minor had already proved abortive. After the battle of Lade and the Persian reconquest of Miletos in 494, the uprising was finally put down. A reconstruction of the Persian administrative structure in Asia Minor followed, which inevitably exposed their weakness in the North Aegean. That the Eretrians and Athenians had given assistance to the Ionians provided an additional impulse to the intention, already implicit in the instructions given by Dareios to Megabazos in 512, to absorb the European Greeks into the Persian empire. Until then Macedonia had been affected by the previous Persian activities in Thrace only positively. It could not, however, remain unaffected by a systematic execution of the new plans to establish a satrapy in Europe. At first the objective was no doubt simply to consolidate Persian interests in the North Aegean region, but this activity was certainly also the first step to an extensive and long-term expansion of Persian interests into the Balkan peninsula. In 492 Mardonios, the nephew and son-in-law of the Great King, Dareios, was commanded to "conquer as many as possible of the Greek cities." Mardonios achieved that goal: "With the fleet they subjected the Thasians without meeting opposition; with the army they added the Macedonians to the subjects of the Persians. All peoples who lived east of the Macedonians had in fact already been made into Persian subjects."[5]

The campaign, however, was not a complete success. A large part of the fleet was lost in the attempt to round Athos, and Mardonios himself was wounded in a Thracian night attack on his camp "in Macedonia." The Persians therefore did not reach Eretria and Athens. The Persian subjects in the North Aegean now included the Macedonians, and they were organized as a satrapy. The Macedonian king Alexander met with flattering special treatment, as he was allowed to marry his sister Gygaia to Boubares, the son of Megabazos, the conquerer of Thrace, who possibly now himself took office as the satrap of the new satrapy.[6] For this reason it is unlikely that Alexander considered his relations with the Persians to be a particular burden. The Persian presence in Thrace brought definite advantages to the Macedonians, which could be exploited through the connection with Boubares. Most important for Macedonia was the pacification of its Thracian neighbours. As long as they remained under Persian sovereignty, it would be difficult for them to disturb Macedonia. Alexander's recognition by the Persian great power must also have increased his standing internally, particularly in those regions Amyntas had recently annexed. His close relationship to the Persians did not, however, prevent his maintaining friendly relations with Athens. In 480 his titles as *proxenos* and benefactor were not divested from him, despite the conflict of interests.

Two years later Dareios attempted to reach Eretria and Athens by way of the Kyklades with his fleet, but after destroying Eretria he was routed by bitter Athenian resistance at Marathon. As a result of this failure Mardonios' route through Thrace came into its own again, but further preparations were prevented by the death of Dareios. His son and successor Xerxes continued with the Greek schemes of his father but was unable to make concrete preparations until 484. Within the new European satrapy large supply depots were established in Thrace and Macedonia, and to eliminate the danger in which Mardonios had found himself in 493 on Athos, a canal was excavated across the neck of the peninsula, the work being carried out under the supervision of Boubares, who had local knowledge, and Artachaes.[7] When Xerxes finally set foot on European soil in 480, he found preparations for his advance as far as Therme in Macedonia entirely satisfactory. Apart from one or two difficulties with the water supply, the transport of the fleet and the army functioned with complete efficiency. The integration of Macedonia in the Persian war machine had proved worthwhile.

Alexander continued to be reliable. When the united Greek army took up positions at the pass of Tempe—the narrowest but easiest and, above all, shortest route between Macedonia and Thessaly—Alexander was able to dislodge them rapidly by informing them that they would have no chance there against Xerxes. Herodotos himself thought that they withdrew because they had learned of other routes, and Xerxes did indeed make use of other passes because of the extreme narrowness of Tempe. However, there is no doubt that Alexander had smoothed and simplified the way into Thessaly for the Persian army. There was also certainly a strong, purely Macedonian interest that the vast Persian army should remove itself as rapidly as possible from Macedonian soil. Alexander's influence with the Greeks was also utilized in the later stages of the war. After the dramatic defeat of the Persians at Salamis in September 480 and Xerxes' withdrawal to Sardis, Mardonios, who remained behind as Persian commander, attempted to split the labile alliance of the Greeks. Through the offices of the Athenian *proxenos* and benefactor King Alexander he made the Athenians a capitulation offer that seemed advantageous, but in spite of his own recommendation Alexander was not able to persuade them to accept it.[8]

After the second Persian defeat at Plataiai in 479, the remainder of the army of the Great King retreated into Asia Minor. Only two garrisons remained behind in Europe, in the forts of Eion and Doriskos, but the European satrapy could no longer survive. Alexander appears to have seized the chance to annex the mountainous areas of Mygdonia, Krestonia and Bisaltia, lying between the Amphaxitis and the Strymon in the immediate hinterland of Macedonia. By this move he gained much more than land and people. Of great importance were the silver deposits on Mount Dysoron, which yielded as much as one talent of silver daily and made it possible for him, as first Macedonian king, to strike his own coins.[9] A formal break with the Persians, however, does not appear to have taken place. It is at any rate known that Alexander's nephew, the son of Boubares and his sister Gygaia, was appointed by the Persians to be administrator of the Karian town of Alabanda.[10]

In future Alexander had to get along with the victorious Greeks. After the Persian withdrawal he dedicated a golden statue of himself at Delphi, seen by Herodotos. The financial means for this dedication were, according to his account, part of the plunder taken from the Persians, by which he must certainly have meant from one of the territories he had taken over from them.[11] He also went to trouble in other ways to present his actions during the war as having been of help to the Greeks. Of this view he had the good fortune to convince Herodotos, the most influential historian of the Persian War, probably during a visit of his to Macedonia. Alexander's father Amyntas was blamed for the first recognition of Persian sovereignty, and Alexander recounted how he had tried as a boy to save Macedonian honour by causing the Persian ambassadors to be kidnapped and murdered.[12] Later, in his report about the events of 480/79, Herodotos emphasizes Alexander's friendly intentions towards the Greeks when he recounts the advice he gave at Tempe, as well as the friendship shown to Athens when he represented the interests of Mardonios there in the following winter. In Boiotia he had allegedly helped save some cities, and it was asserted that in a cloak-and-dagger action on the eve of the battle of Plataiai he gave the Greeks the information that the next day would be decisive.[13] Herodotos appears to have incorporated quite happily the entire *interpretatio Macedonica* in his history, thereby giving one of his readers in the hellenistic period a reason for dubbing Alexander with the soubriquet Philhellene, to distinguish him from his descendant of the same name, Alexander the Great. Alexander's image-polishing campaign thus met with good success.[14]

The actual facts were more modest. Alexander must inevitably have had contacts with the victorious Greeks. It is fairly certain that Macedonian timber, as well as tar and pitch, continued as before to find a good buyer in the Athenian fleet and that economic necessity lent Alexander's self-portrayal a certain credibility among the Greeks after the event. However, after the withdrawal of the Persians Macedonia declined again for the Greeks into a political backwater. It did not become a member of the alliance of the Greeks under Athenian leadership (the Delian League), which had adopted as its aim the expulsion of the Persians from the regions of Greek settlement. Military activities of the league also took place in the North Aegean, where at least in Eion and Doriskos Persian garrisons still held out after 479. Herodotos relates the heroic defence and despairing self-annihilation of Boges, the Persian commander in Eion, but he knows nothing of Macedonian participation, either on the Greek side or on the Persian side.[15] The Macedonian king seems to have looked on without taking action when Athens attempted to found a colony in the lower Strymon valley around 476 and when Thracian resistance brought this attempt to a bloody end at Drabeskos.[16]

Not until about ten years later is Alexander mentioned again in connection with the activities of Athens and its allies. In the meantime the Persians had been expelled from the Aegean area, and most of the islands and coastal towns of northern Greece and Asia Minor had become members of the league, whose sphere of activities was increasingly defined by Athenian interests.[17] In the North Aegean region these were certainly economic. Athens must have laid great value on obtaining direct control of deliveries of ship-building timber, but the mineral resources of Mount Pangaion to the east of the Strymon, the richest gold and silver deposits in the whole Aegean basin, must have provided the main attraction. These reserves of precious metals had been exploited until then mainly by the local Thracian tribes, but the island city of Thasos, a member of the league, had also been able to pursue important economic interests in the region. Around 465 the Athenians turned against the Thasians, who were forced to relinquish their mainland possessions to Athens. At that time, too, plans for a settlement in the lower Strymon valley, which had already failed once, were resumed, and the Athenians dispatched a larger group of settlers (the number ten thousand is recorded) to Ennea Hodoi ("the Nine Ways"). But the Thracians again offered bitter resistance, and when the Athenians attempted to penetrate into the interior they lost so many of their settlers in a fight that they were forced to give up the attempt.[18]

The prospect that Athens, which in the meantime had become the largest and most expansionist power in the Aegean region, should wish to settle so many colonists from the states of the league immediately on his frontiers cannot have pleased the Macedonian king. There seem to have been certain contacts with the Athenian general Kimon. After the failure of Ennea Hodoi, Kimon was accused by political opponents in Athens of letting himself be bribed by Alexander to refrain from attacking Macedonia and acquiring territories there for Athens, although it would easily have been possible. Kimon was acquitted.[19] This report is not very concrete, but it allows the conclusion that already in the 460s there were circles in Athens that were not afraid to make propaganda for an offensive war against Macedonia. The desire does not appear to have been strong, but a certain logic cannot be denied. The Greek coastal towns in the immediate neighbourhood of Macedonia, in the Chalkidike and in Thrace were already members of the league, and the control of Mount Pangaion was a clear aim, so that it is easy to imagine that the main objective of the Athenians in the Macedonian region was the mines in Bisaltia.

The collapse of the settlement at Ennea Hodoi made these plans seem no longer feasible. Moreover, the 450s allowed Athens no possibility of realizing its North Aegean dream. Because of Athenian political neglect there is no record of events in Macedonia during these years. It doubtless continued to play its modest traditional economic role as supplier of raw materials. At the time when evidence is again available, Alexander was already dead.

3. THE PERIOD OF THE PELOPONNESIAN WAR

Alexander I died in the 450s without having adequately prepared for his succession. His death therefore introduced a period of internal instability such as almost always offered interested external powers the opportunity for interference and destroyed much of his constructive work. He left behind five sons, of whom Perdikkas, probably the eldest, was recognized as successor. There is no evidence for the modern view that Alexander formally divided the kingdom among his five sons.[1] Two of Perdikkas' brothers, however, Philippos and Alketas, obtained locally limited areas of power (*archai*)—Philippos even in the central Amphaxitis. A third brother, Menelaos, also retained some kind of function in the leadership of the state, and only the fourth, Amyntas, appears to have retired to his lands and taken no part in the exercise of power.[2]

It is unclear how this situation came about. Perhaps the most likely development is the transfer to the sons of large estates with associated administrative functions that, with the passing of time, turned into local bases of power within the Macedonian state. The nature of that state during the reign of Perdikkas is illuminated by an international treaty with Athens. The inscription was found in Athens but is badly damaged and cannot be exactly dated, though much speaks for a dating in the 440s.[3] The list of those who swore the oath on behalf of the Macedonian state allows several conclusions to be drawn. Listed are members of the royal house: Perdikkas, Alketas, Menelaos, perhaps also Philippos and Amyntas, Archelaos, the son of Perdikkas (as designated heir to the throne, probably still very young but nevertheless listed after his uncle Alketas) and sons of Alketas. Then comes a list of people otherwise unknown to us, certainly all barons from Lower Macedonia, but among these there is also a son of Philippos. Towards the end of the extant part of the text are names that probably come from Upper Macedonia: Arrhabaios (from Lynkestis), with whom the Athenians had made a special agreement, Derdas (from Elimiotis) as well as Antiochos (from Orestis) and another man whose name has not been preserved, all of whom bear the title *basileus*, (which in accordance with Macedonian custom was not given to Perdikkas himself).[4] The Athenians, negotiating from a position of strength, would appear to have demanded that the entire nobility of the Macedonian state witness the oath—an indication of the relative weakness of the central power and the strength of the local lords and barons.

The treaty not only allows us to perceive the relative weakness of Perdikkas; it also bears witness to the fundamental solidarity of the most influential magnates with the Macedonian state, probably a political achievement of Alexander's. The treaty probably dates from the early years of Perdikkas' reign before the initiatives towards unity had been squandered, from a time when the crown prince Archelaos was still so young that royal protocol placed him after his uncle Alketas. Thukydides also records an initial friendship between Perdikkas and Athens, which by 433 had been terminated by the Athenians, when they gave support to two opponents of Perdikkas, his brother Philippos and Derdas, the local prince of Elimiotis.[5]

The reasons for the break are not known, but Athenian policy in the North Aegean had not remained static after the failure of Ennea Hodoi ca. 465. Already during the 450s Argilos, a small town on the Bisaltic coast, became a paying member of the Athenian League. The Bisaltic lands, above all the mining area in the central Strymon valley, had been claimed by Macedonia ever since the withdrawal of the Persians, but an old Greek coastal city may have been able to maintain an exceptional position. The membership of Berge, situated in the interior, which is first attested in 451, and Perikles' sending of some thousand Athenian settlers into the Bisaltic lands around 450 were much more dangerous developments. Subsequently, during the 440s, an Athenian colony was established at Brea, whose locality is not exactly known but which probably lay in the Strymon valley, followed in 437 by the foundation under Athenian leadership of Amphipolis on the lower Strymon, whereby the long-term Athenian plans for taking possession of and settling this area were finally fulfilled.[6] There are also some uncertain indications that the Macedonian state apparatus may have had difficulty in asserting itself in the Bisaltic area. For reasons unknown, Perdikkas struck only small coins (*tetroboloi*), more suitable for local commerce than for trade. A partial explanation might be that for a period he had lost control over the Bisaltic silver deposits.[7] We know too little about the silver market, however, to be certain since not all the silver produced need necessarily have been converted into coin by the producer. It is, though, easy to imagine that this state of affairs might tempt the Athenians to aim at acquiring direct influence in Macedonia.

After the foundation of Amphipolis the Athenians raised the amount of tribute to be paid by some of the paying members of the Athenian League. The records of tribute payments are by no means fully preserved, but enough still exist for us to be able to establish that several increases were levied in the Chalkidike, in the immediate hinterland of the Macedonian territory Anthemous. The largest were at Potidaia, from six talents in 434 to fifteen in 432, and at Torone, from eight hundred drachmae in 434 to three thousand in 433. Also among the Bottiaians, the payment at Spartolos was increased from two talents to three talents and five hundred drachmae, and in the interior the payment at Chedrolos was raised from five hundred drachmae to one thousand drachmae, each from 434 to 433.[8] A consolidation of Athenian control in the North Aegean area can clearly be recognized. At about this period Methone on the coast of Pieria also became a paying member of the Athenian empire, but it is unfortunately not clear whether this happened before or after Athens' break with Perdikkas, whether before or after the start of the Peloponnesian War in 431.

The lust for power that Athens radiated during these years under the leadership of Perikles and that found its expression, among other things, in the lavish embellishment of the Athenian city centre with expensive temples and other extravagant public buildings, which served to boost Athenian self-confidence, led Athens to become arrogant in its dealings with other states and finally to underestimate its own vulnerability. This result can be most clearly seen in its dealings with Sparta and Sparta's allies. Although Athens cannot be made directly and indubitably responsible for the outbreak of war in 431, it is indisputable that its lack of readiness to compromise and the hard line taken on issues of marginal importance did not exactly contribute to preventing the war. The challenge to the Spartan allies occurred in part on the Chalkidike, where Athens' provocation of Perdikkas proved in the long run to be disastrous.

As a result of tensions between Athens and Korinth, which led to a serious dispute over Kerkyra in 435, the Athenians demanded in autumn 433 that Potidaia, the largest town in the Chalkidike and a Korinthian foundation, should raze part of its town walls and break off contact with Korinth. Potidaia refused and appealed to Korinth. Perdikkas saw here a chance to win allies against Athens and addressed himself to Sparta, at first to no avail; but in Korinth, where feeling against Athens was already running high, his application was received positively. He also attempted to instigate a secessionist movement among disaffected Athenian allies on the Chalkidike. To some of the smaller coastal communities he offered land in Mygdonia and around Lake Bolbe and urged that during the course of a war against Athens they should find refuge with the Olynthians. Some accepted the offer, and the secessionist movement away from Athens led to founding a new federal state of the Chalkidians with its capital at Olynthos.[9]

The general weakness of the Macedonian monarchy, internally as well as in foreign affairs, is evident from the events of the first years of the Peloponnesian War. Perdikkas had set himself two modest aims: first, to maintain his own rule in Macedonia, and second, to protect the territorial integrity of his country. When threatened by Athens in 432, he sought protection from Sparta and Korinth; and when some years later Spartan influence seemed more menacing, he attached himself again to Athens, only to ally himself once more with Sparta a couple of years later. His dealings make clear his fear for the survival of the Macedonian kingdom, should a major southern Greek power establish itself firmly on his frontiers. It is characteristic of him that his policy was a tactical steering through the shoals of the conflicting interests of Athens and Sparta. In this way Perdikkas became notorious for his unreliability and his disloyalty to allies. Fundamentally, however, Macedonia needed neither Athens nor Sparta, and when their dispute posed a threat to Macedonia, which had become involved in the war through Athenian actions, not through its own, then no treaty partner could reasonably blame Perdikkas for acting in his own interest, as indeed did Athens and Sparta themselves.

The events of the war allow an insight into Athenian attitudes towards Macedonia, which remained consistent, as far as circumstances allowed, for the whole period up to the time of Philip II. The basic principle was to keep Macedonia weak but as friendly as possible, so that the Athenians could pursue undisturbed their interests in the North Aegean, which concerned above all access to the reserves of ship-building timber, to the mining areas and to the trade routes. The method of achieving this objective was extremely simple: it was to support Macedonian opponents of the king, so long as Athenian interests could be maintained thereby. Thus Athens gave support to Perdikkas' opponents Derdas and Philippos; the purpose was served by the Athenian presence in the Chalkidike and later by the existence of states there and on the coast of Pieria friendly to Athens; and a third element was a friendly relationship to, or an alliance with, the non-Greek neighbours of Macedonia, above all the Thracians of the Odrysian kingdom. This last element also served the security of Athenian possessions—the members of the Athenian League—on the coasts of the North Aegean. Sparta, however, had no permanent interests in the North Aegean region not directly connected with the war with Athens.

These considerations determined the course of the war. In spring 432 the Athenians were supported by Philippos and a brother of Derdas in taking Therme and laying siege to Pydna. When news arrived of Korinthian support for Potidaia, the Athenians concluded a temporary agreement with Perdikkas allowing them to enter the Chalkidike by the land route from Pieria. Perdikkas assented because it was in his own interests that the Athenians should leave Macedonian territory. The agreement had no long-term implication: immediately afterwards Perdikkas allowed himself to be elected commander of the cavalry by his Chalkidian allies, but he does not appear to have done much.[10] Long before the Athenians took Potidaia in winter 430/29, it had become clear to him that he had supported the weaker of the two combatants, and in summer 431 he made an alliance with Athens. The Athenians were prepared to return Therme to him, and he subsequently took part in operations in the Chalkidike in accordance with his treaty.[11]

What appeared to be a reconciliation was for each side no more than an alliance based on mutual interest. Perdikkas seems to have asserted himself against Philippos and Derdas, the rebels supported by Athens. But in spite of the treaty the Athenians changed horses. They now laid their money on Perdikkas' external enemies in the east, the Thracians of the Odrysian kingdom, who had given asylum to Amyntas, the son of Philippos, before 429. Sitalkes, the current king of the Odrysians, ruled a loosely connected empire that stretched from the Aegean to the Danube and from the Sea of Marmara to the Strymon valley. An influential citizen of Abdera, Nymphodoros, whose sister Sitalkes had married, negotiated first an alliance between Sitalkes and Athens (Athens hoped to employ the Thracians on the Chalkidike and against Perdikkas) and then the alliance already referred to between Perdikkas and Athens.[12]

Only after the fall of Potidaia did Sitalkes move against Perdikkas. In the negotiations of 431 Perdikkas had made promises (their nature unknown to us) to Sitalkes, which he did not keep. Sitalkes had promised for his part not to give assistance to Philippos. In the meantime Philippos was dead, but his son Amyntas was a refugee at the Odrysian court. Relations were strained. In 429 Sitalkes marched with a large army into the Axios valley, where Philippos had ruled and Amyntas must have inherited his father's contacts. Sitalkes marched plundering across the country before entering the Chalkidike, as provided for in his alliance with Athens. The Athenians, however, had ceased to believe in the realization of the campaign they had agreed on two years previously and had not sent their fleet. Supplies became scarce, and a short campaign ravaging the area in revolt satisfied the terms of the treaty. The army of Sitalkes withdrew within a month.[13]

At about this time Athens admitted Methone to the alliance. This act was clearly part of its policy against Perdikkas. Perhaps in 430, certainly during the siege of Potidaia, the Athenian Assembly decided for the second time to reduce the tribute from Methone, as well as to send envoys to Perdikkas to inform him that he must allow Methone access to the sea and freedom to trade with the interior and not lead an army through the territory of Methone without its explicit permission. In case of a dispute Methone and Perdikkas should send representatives to Athens and, in addition, it would favourably influence the attitude of Athens towards Perdikkas if the soldiers in Potidaia should have a good opinion of him.[14] This implied threat was a clear attempt to keep Perdikkas in line. That Athenian doubts as to his reliability were not entirely unfounded is demonstrated by his secret help to Sparta in western Greece in 429.[15] Three years later Methone laid a complaint against Perdikkas in Athens, which led to activity by at least two groups of Athenian envoys. At the same time the Athenians resolved that Methone should be allowed to import grain from Byzantion, a decision that implies some sort of chicanery on the part of Perdikkas.[16]

Under the circumstances Perdikkas' reaction is understandable. If the Athenian comedy writer Hermippos had already presented the Athenians, probably in the same year (426), with a verse about the "shiploads of lies" Perdikkas dispatched to Athens, recent events could hardly have improved the Athenian reputation in Macedonia.[17] Athenian actions and aggressive Athenian attitudes inevitably clouded the mutual relationship. On the Chalkidike the Athenians remained aggressive even after the fall of Potidaia; they sent one thousand settlers there and continually tried to push their old allies back into the Athenian League. In spite of the current alliance with Athens it therefore clearly lay in Macedonia's interest to involve Sparta also in the affairs of the North Aegean as long as the Athenian war with Sparta continued. According to the conservative tradition and the entire ethos of the Spartan state, the danger could be considered minimal that Sparta would wish to establish long-term dominance in an area far away from the Peloponnese. But it was correspondingly more difficult to persuade Sparta to concern itself with the situation in the north at all.

Not until 424 did Perdikkas and the Chalkidians succeed, by means of an offer to share the costs, in winning those responsible in Sparta for a campaign in the north. Even then a certain halfheartedness is apparent. The expeditionary corps, under the command of Brasidas, was far from being well manned, as only seven hundred helots outfitted as hoplites (heavily armed infantry soldiers) and one thousand Peloponnesian volunteers were assigned to him. The Spartans did indeed hope that they would be able to damage the Athenians sufficiently to force them to put an end to their devastations in the Peloponnese. At first, however, Brasidas was the servant of two paymasters. On his arrival in Pieria Perdikkas put him into action against Arrhabaios of Lynkestis, one of the barons of Upper Macedonia, but the Athenians guessed the actual aims of Brasidas and revoked their alliance with Perdikkas.[18]

The enterprise brought Perdikkas nothing but trouble. Brasidas saw in Arrhabaios a potential ally against Athens and was unwilling to fight him, and the Chalkidians—who after all provided half the money, and that for a war against Athens—were furious about this private campaign of Perdikkas. Arrhabaios declared at the first meeting that he would accept Brasidas as arbitrator in his dispute with Perdikkas. At this Brasidas withdrew his army and accepted the consequences of the anger of Perdikkas, who immediately cut his contribution to one-third of the costs. The Spartans went into the Chalkidike, where Brasidas could satisfy the anti-Athenian interests of both his Chalkidian employers and the Spartans. There he achieved many successes, including the taking of Amphipolis in winter 424/23. Perdikkas was impressed and immediately showed himself cooperative again; the Macedonian army was present when the small neighbouring towns of Myrkinos, Galepsos and Oisyme were captured.

Perdikkas' flirtation with Sparta came rapidly to an ignominious end. During a cease-fire between Athens and Sparta in 423, Perdikkas talked Brasidas into campaigning against Arrhabaios once more; but disputes between the commanders, combined with Macedonian incompetence, resulted in a debacle. When Brasidas and the Spartans returned to Perdikkas' territory, they plundered and laid waste the lands.[19] This action marked the end of Perdikkas' expensive attempt to use the conflict of the Greek great powers to serve internal Macedonian purposes. He was now regarded as an enemy by both sides. However, on account of Brasidas' successes in the Chalkidike, the Athenians were again prepared to accept a new offer of a pact, as a result of which Perdikkas prevented the passage of reinforcements for Brasidas and in the following year received an appeal from the Athenian general Kleon to support him in an attack on Amphipolis.[20] Before Perdikkas had reacted to this appeal, both Brasidas and Kleon had fallen in the struggle for Amphipolis. The great powers then began negotiations, which led to the cessation of hostilities (the so-called Peace of Nikias, 422/21).

The Peace of Nikias regulated very arbitrarily just the main points at issue between Athens and Sparta.[21] Athens was given practically a free hand in the north. The main problem was Amphipolis. Its inhabitants refused to rejoin Athens, as was stipulated in the treaty, and Athens was not able to gain control of the town again. By contrast, Bormiskos in Mygdonia and Trailos in Bisaltia, as well as Heraklieion in southern Pieria, are listed in the so-called Kleon assessment of the Athenian empire in 425/24 and again in the assessment of 422/21.[22] All three belonged to the immediate sovereign area of the Macedonian king, who can hardly have been happy with this result of the war. At about this time Athens also made treaties of alliance with some of the towns of the Bottiaians on the Chalkidike.[23] Hence Athens, even after the Peace of Nikias, continued to be the strongest foreign power in the north and was free to build up the empire again, insofar as it was able to assert the claims recognized by Sparta against the resistance of those affected.

Perdikkas was obliged under his treaty to give assistance to the Athenians. To what extent he complied is not clear. Athens maintained armed forces in the Thracian area in 418/17 and 417/16 but did not regain Amphipolis.[24] Perdikkas, however, was clearly worried and in 418/17 he accepted the Spartan invitation to enter into an alliance with Sparta and Argos. For this he reaped an Athenian complaint that he had brought about the failure of a planned action.[25] As a result the Athenians attempted to exert pressure on Macedonia by mounting a sea blockade, but this action against an economically self-sufficient country was a failure. A year later Macedonian refugees arriving in Methone received Athenian help, just as Philippos and Derdas had received assistance twenty years earlier. Perdikkas received no support from his new treaty partners.[26] As in 423 after the collapse of his agreement with Brasidas, he again made his peace with Athens. In 414 he took part in an attack on Amphipolis launched by the Athenian Euetion.[27]

Perdikkas was forced to make his lifework the steering of a safe course through the conflicting interests of the great powers. When his relationship with Sparta again collapsed because of Spartan reluctance to act, he had no alternative to getting on with Athens. Recognition of this fact seems to have become general in Macedonia by the time of his death in 413. His son and successor Archelaos certainly oriented himself exclusively to Athens, though he was confronted with a different set of circumstances. After 413 Athens was no longer in a position to dominate the Aegean as it had previously because of the enormous losses it had incurred in the recent abortive attack on Syrakuse. Athens nevertheless continued to be the most important external power to show permanent interest in the North Aegean region. This fact was recognized by Archelaos when in 411, while the four hundred oligarchic insurgents were in control in Athens, he delivered timber for oars to the democratic Athenian fleet on Samos. The delivery was arranged by the Athenian exile Andokides, who related his contribution proudly before an Athenian court in 408 in a plea for his restoration to Athens; he added that his family was on terms of guest friendship with that of Archelaos.[28] He clearly would not have wished to boast of this relationship if Archelaos had not been persona grata in Athens.

Other clues point in the same direction. In 410 Archelaos received the assistance of an Athenian squadron for the siege of Pydna, which had seceded from Macedonia and made itself independent.[29] That the readiness to provide assistance was mutual is apparent from a fragmentary decree of the Athenian people, probably dating from 408/7. The extant part of the text contains the words "from Macedonia," "transport," "to Athens," "army" and "oar"; and because the unique importance of the North Aegean region for the supply of ship-building timber is well known, it seems reasonable to construe the inscription as praising someone for securing the transport of ships and timber from Macedonia. Even if the person being praised was not Archelaos (the name is missing on the stone), the inscription still offers proof of close cooperation between Athens and Macedonia.[30]

The stabilizing of the relationship to Athens, encouraged by the inevitable weakening of Athens' domination over its allies, brought advantages to the Macedonian state. That Archelaos had

already been designated for the succession by about 440, the time
of the alliance between Macedonia and Athens, can be deduced
from the protocol order of the listed names.[31] Even if he was the
son of a slave, as is maliciously asserted in Plato's *Gorgias*,[32] he
was recognized for more than twenty years before his accession
as the chosen successor of his father Perdikkas. This man, about
forty-five years old in 414, had had ample time to admire his
father's policy towards the Greek great powers—perhaps even to
have influenced it himself—and to draw the lesson that it was
crucial to get along with the only great power of importance for
Macedonia. He also appears to have reached important and influential conclusions for internal Macedonian affairs from his experiences of the past. It was alleged that at the beginning of his
reign he ordered the murder of his uncle Alketas; Alexandros,
Alketas' son; and a seven-year-old boy, the last son of Perdikkas
by a Macedonian noblewoman, Kleopatra.[33] It is impossible to
ascertain if the allegation is true, but it is certainly not impossible.
Perdikkas had had great difficulties with his brothers, particularly
Philippos, and Archelaos may well have drawn the consequential,
if brutal, lesson from a past that he had shared, deciding, as did
Alexander the Great three generations later, that the stability of
his regime demanded the sacrifice of possible contenders within
the family, so that as king of the Argeadai he would have a monopoly of influence on the barons of the country.

Archelaos also drew conclusions from the military weakness of
Macedonia. The measures that he took, above all for the military
infrastructure of the country, won the admiration of Thukydides,
who may have known Archelaos personally. In a passage already
cited, he affirms that Archelaos did more in this area than his
eight predecessors put together.[34] He refers to the building of
straight roads, probably in conjunction with military forts and
supply points.[35] In addition came the provision of "horses, armour and other weapons." These measures, cursorily mentioned
by Thukydides, must have brought a lot of people into close contact with the central power of the kingdom. They imply an organization that must have reached into the most remote regions
of the Macedonian countryside. The word *roads* is certainly not
to be understood to mean fully surfaced roadways such as the
Romans built, but instead well-constructed paths through forests

and swamps that made possible the rapid transfer of soldiers and equipment from one area to another. The provision of horses and armaments also implies a royal ordnance organization, royal depots and studs for horse breeding, which cannot have existed previously on this scale.

The decision to elevate Pella to be the royal capital served to strengthen the central power of the regime as well as improve communications. In antiquity Pella had direct access to the sea by way of the river Lydias (though the bay has long since silted up). It was also in general much better sited than Aigai as the communications centre of a kingdom that no longer consisted only of Pieria and the Haliakmon valley but wished to realize its claim to sovereignty in all lands between the Pindos mountains and the Strymon. Not much is known about this change of capital, but Archelaos clearly endeavoured to create a representative capital to gain cultural entrée to the world of the city-states. The imposing buildings that have been uncovered by excavations all belong to considerably later periods, but it is known that the famous painter Zeuxis of Herakleia was engaged for the decoration of the new palace.[36] Poets as well came to Pella, and the most famous, the Athenian Euripides, died in 406 at the court of Archelaos. In honour of his royal host he wrote a mythical drama entitled *Archelaos*, celebrating the origins of the Argeadai in Peloponnesian Argos. His famous play *The Bacchae* is also supposed to have been written under the influence of his Macedonian experiences. But Euripides was not alone. The Athenian tragic poet Agathon also visited Pella, as did two Ionians, the epic writer Choerilos of Samos and the writer of choral lyrics, Timotheus of Miletos.[37]

Cultural activities were not confined to the capital and the court as Archelaos founded a new festival with the ambitious name Olympia. It was held at Dion in Pieria, below the massive heights of Mount Olympos, and took the form of a national Macedonian festival, run on the well-established Greek pattern. Archelaos had had personal experience of the importance of such festivals when, probably as a youth, he had achieved victory in the four-horse chariot races at Delphi and Olympia.[38] His activities make plain his concern not only to get on politically with Athens but also to forge cultural links with the Greek states of the south (again with Athens above all), which must have improved the political climate.

The general conditions of international political life in the Aegean region abruptly changed in 405. The war between Athens and Sparta, which with only short breaks had affected all the inhabitants of the Greek world since 431, came to a sudden and unexpected end. The Athenian fleet was annihilated by the Spartans under Lysander at Aigospotamoi on the Hellespont, and in the following year Athens had to agree to humiliating peace terms. Destroyed with the fleet was Athenian dominance at sea, which had been maintained until then, despite some damaging blows. For the Macedonians, in spite of their recent friendship, it can in fact only have been an advantage to have the strongest foreign power in the North Aegean area removed. Perhaps the time had finally come when Archelaos could consolidate his internal state organization and assert his dominion in the border areas of his kingdom without the burdensome interference of external powers.

4. ON THE EDGE OF THE WORLD

For twenty years after the end of the Peloponnesian War the main stream of events in the Greek world flowed past Macedonia. Athens was no longer able to interfere in the north, and Sparta had no wish to. The Macedonians were therefore left to themselves. Archelaos seems to have been confronted with increasing problems during the years before his death in 399. A war is reported by Aristotle "against Sirrhas and Arrhabaios." Arrhabaios probably came from Lynkestis, like his namesake of the 420s—if he was not indeed the same man—and Sirrhas appears also to have been a baron from Upper Macedonia, possibly also from Lynkestis. To gain a free hand for this war, Archelaos married one of his daughters to Derdas, the local ruler of the Elimiotis. The result of the war is unknown, but the pressure of the central government on the border areas is clear, and we can also recognize in the case of Derdas the attempt to bind noble provincial families to the royal house. Unfortunately, this war cannot be dated exactly.[1]

Archelaos also appears to have looked beyond Macedonia towards the south. The intensity and intention of his interference in the affairs of Larissa, the leading town in Thessaly, are not certain. When civil war broke out there, Archelaos intervened in the interests of a group that had turned to him for assistance, but this action did not lead to his taking permanent possession. Some refugees or hostages seem to have been received in Pella.[2]

Archelaos died a violent death. Aristotle, who resided at the Macedonian court about sixty years later and was able to learn and transmit the local tradition, speaks of murder.[3] The crime was committed by a certain Krataios, either because he had been sexually abused by the king or because he had not been given the already promised daughter of the king as his bride. (Aristotle relates both traditions.) At any rate he did not act alone: Hellenokrates of Larissa is imputed with similar private motives, and a third man, Dekamnichos, had once been flogged because he had accused Euripides of having bad breath. That the brutal life-style of the Macedonian king could so offend the pride of young nobles that they set out to murder him makes here its first appearance in Macedonian tradition, but in the light of later events it does not seem at all incredible. The complicity of the man from Larissa is certainly not to be viewed as a "foreign-policy incident"; Hellenokrates may have been a refugee or a hostage, and there is no reason to doubt the personal nature of his motives. A coup d'état had not been planned.[4]

The new king was Orestes, son of Archelaos and Kleopatra, still a minor and under the guardianship of his uncle Aeropos. Three years later Aeropos formally took over the kingdom, but whether he had murdered Orestes, as reported by Diodoros, or whether in the interim he had simply won the support of the most important nobles is uncertain. Stability could at any rate have been expected under Aeropos, but he fell ill and died in summer 394. His son Pausanias then took over as his successor.[5]

It is astonishing that this succession to the throne seems to have taken place without problems. It did not, however, last long. Two other members of the royal family put in their own claims—Amyntas, son of Arrhidaios, grandson of Perdikkas' brother Amyntas and so, like Pausanias, a great-grandson of the first Alexander; and another Amyntas, also a great-grandson of Alexander, a son of Archelaos, nicknamed "the Little," perhaps only to distinguish him from his older contemporary.[6] Much is uncertain here, but Amyntas "the Little" appears to have been first to assert his claim against Pausanias and for chronological reasons must be considered as ruling at the same time. The only evidence from the short period when he and Pausanias were both in power (which occurred in 394/93) is a few coins, but these are so strikingly similar that one could be tempted to regard the two kings not as rivals but as partners.[7]

After one year, at any rate, both had been removed. Aristotle relates that Derdas murdered "Little Amyntas" for personal motives; and Pausanias had been murdered, according to Diodoros, by Amyntas, son of Arrhidaios.[8] Derdas, the ruler of the Elimiotis, is known some years later to have assisted King Amyntas, son of Arrhidaios, and it seems reasonable to assume cooperation at the time of the double murder. If this Derdas was also the son-in-law of Archelaos, then his action shows a split among the heirs of Archelaos in favour of Amyntas, son of Arrhidaios.[9]

It was lucky for Macedonia that it was spared interference by the Greek great powers during these years. Apart from an abortive attempt by Aeropos to prevent the passage of the Spartan king Agesilaos through his territory in summer 394, nothing is known.[10] But the rapid changes of ruler and the resulting instability were far from being without danger for Macedonia. It is therefore surprising that after the succession of Amyntas, son of Arrhidaios, major internal political problems seem no longer to have been particularly important. He had won over Derdas of Elimiotis, and the largest internal Macedonian problem, the relationship to the Lynkestians, seems to have been completely solved through the politic marriage of Amyntas with Eurydike, the daughter of the local prince Sirrhas.[11]

The exact date of the marriage is not known, but it may have taken place because of pressure from the Illyrians on Lynkestis. The Illyrian empire, under the leadership of Bardylis, seems to have expanded massively during the 390s from its base apparently around Kosovo towards the south and to have threatened the northwestern parts of Macedonia. Particularly endangered were the Lynkestians because Bardylis probably already ruled the area around Lake Ochrid, and for this reason they may well have wished to strengthen their ties with the Argeadai.[12] But it was not only the Lynkestians who were threatened. For 393–392 Diodoros records: "In Macedonia Amyntas, the father of Philip, was driven from the country when the Illyrians invaded Macedonia. Despairing of his kingdom, he presented the Olynthians with a piece of territory bordering their own. At that time he did indeed lose his kingdom, but shortly thereafter he was brought back by the Thessalians, recovered his throne, and ruled for twenty-four years. Some say, however, that after Amyntas had been expelled, Argaios ruled the Macedonians for two years, and only afterwards did Amyntas recover the kingdom."[13] All the main problems of the Macedonian kingdom are mentioned here: the Illyrians, Olynthos as the leading city of the Chalkidian League, the Thessalians, the neighbours to the south and an internal rival for power.

Further information is scarce. The Illyrians under Bardylis overran Macedonia but seem to have wanted in the main just to rob and plunder. Yet the chronological connection with the competing claim of Argaios suggests that Bardylis may have supported him. The report that Amyntas undertook to pay regular tribute to the Illyrians perhaps also belongs to this period;[14] it could have been the price for future good treatment of Macedonia and the abandonment of Argaios. In any case, no more reports have come down of Illyrian attacks or of pretenders to the throne before the death of Amyntas in 369.[15]

The two neighbouring Greek states were not at first as dangerous. Archelaos, perhaps following an established pattern, had fostered good relations with the Thessalians, particularly with the most powerful clan of the largest city, the Aleuadai of Larissa; but the Thessalians were divided among themselves. It had already come to actual war in 404 between Pherai, under the tyrant Lykophron, and other Thessalian cities. The conflict continued until at least 395, when Medeios of Larissa received help from the anti-Spartan coalition of the southern Greeks. It must certainly have been this Medeios or his predecessor who asked Archelaos for help in about 400, and it was presumably the same Larissans who helped Amyntas in 393/92.[16] The fostering of good relations with the Argeadai indeed accorded with the self-interest of Larissa. It could not suit them that a protégé of Bardylis, even if he were a son of Archelaos, should rule in the labile neighbouring state, particularly in view of the tense situation in Thessaly.

The Chalkidian League was a creation of the Peloponnesian War. Perdikkas had given powerful impulses to its development by making over stretches of land to the league "for the duration of the war with Athens" and by encouraging the capital Olynthos to strengthen itself.[17] After the Peace of Nikias the league no longer played an important part in the war, and after the peace settlement of 404 the Chalkidike, like Macedonia, was largely ignored by the southern great powers and left to its own devices. Around 393 Amyntas relinquished to the Olynthians a border area—probably Anthemous—in an attempt to win over Olynthos and the Chalkidian League. The Chalkidians, like the Thessalians, can have had no interest in having as neighbour a Macedonian state under the protection of Bardylis. Macedonia should remain weak but still be strong enough to act as a bulwark against the Illyrians.

A treaty was also concluded between the Chalkidians and Amyntas. It falls into two parts, which were negotiated at different times.[18] The first part, which may well have been directly connected with the threat posed by Bardylis, provides for mutual assistance against attack by a third party for fifty years. The second part regulates two areas favourably for the Chalkidians: (1) The export of pitch, building and ship-building timber (including the particularly suitable white fir, insofar as it served the public needs of the league) is guaranteed under payment of normal customs duties and fees; additionally, free trade in other goods between the Chalkidians and the Macedonians is agreed on under the same conditions; (2) Friendship with Amphipolis, the Bottiaians, Akanthos and Mende may not be arranged by either partner without the agreement of the other. Although the text is only partially extant, the second part seems to indicate a relatively stronger position for the Chalkidians than the first. It would, as an extension of the first part, fit very well into the period directly after the return of Amyntas, when he had to struggle hard to assert his position within Macedonia and planned to retain the good will of his neighbours by means of these economic and political favours.

Amyntas established his position in Macedonia after his return.[19] To his advantage were his friendship with the Thessalians, concessions to the Illyrians and the Chalkidians, the expulsion of Argaios, his marriage alliance with the Lynkestians and his friendship with Derdas of Elimiotis. He also cultivated the Thracians in the east. The Athenian Iphikrates, mercenary leader and son-in-law of the Thracian king Kotys, was adopted by Amyntas sometime after 386.[20]

Already before 382 Amyntas felt himself firmly enough in the saddle to risk a conflict with the Chalkidians and demanded the return of the border area ceded to them in 393.[21] His justification is dubious; the sole source, Diodoros, speaks explicitly of a "gift," which should be plain enough. But the legal question was a side issue. The Chalkidians reacted strongly. They were not prepared to give up the area in question; instead they took the offensive and proclaimed also for Macedonia the much-overused slogan of the times, "Freedom for the cities." They did not have much success in the dependent Macedonian towns, but they were able to demonstrate their current military superiority by capturing Pella and chasing Amyntas out of his capital for a time.[22]

Then in autumn 383 Amyntas appealed in his despair over Olynthos to Sparta, the only power that could possibly have an interest in preventing further growth of the Chalkidian League.[23] At almost the same time envoys arrived in Sparta from Akanthos and Apollonia, two smaller Chalkidian cities, which felt themselves threatened by Olynthos. According to Xenophon, they described the major threat to peace posed by Olynthos. They not only complained about the enormous extension of the league but also mentioned that Sparta's rivals in central Greece, Thebes and Athens, were currently negotiating with Olynthos. This news convinced Sparta.

In spring 382 an army of two thousand men under Eudamidas set out for the north, where it immediately took possession of Potidaia.[24] The Spartans did not find their task an easy one, even though they received reinforcements from home and cavalry support from Amyntas and Derdas. Not until 380 did they succeed in closing a ring of siege works around Olynthos, and they finally took the town in 379. Nothing is recorded of Macedonian participation in the siege actions of 380 and 379, and the capitulation conditions give no indication that Macedonian interests were taken into account. The Olynthians undertook to share the friends and enemies of Sparta, be its ally and give military assistance, but the Chalkidian League seems to have been dissolved.[25] The Spartans had achieved their aim, the prevention of a great power evolving in the north, but the costs were tremendous: a king and the brother of a king were among the fallen, and not everyone was pleased that Sparta was advocating the interests of the absolute ruler Amyntas at the expense of the Greek cities. The Athenian Isokrates had already made use of this argument during the siege to raise feelings against Sparta.[26] In fact Amyntas probably came out as the main winner. He was certainly now in a position to regain possession of the disputed Anthemous; the Chalkidian League had been dissolved; and from Sparta itself he had nothing to fear because the excessively long and expensive war against Olynthos had made the expansionist policies of King Agesilaos unpopular even in Sparta.

Events in central Greece led in 377 to founding a new treaty organization under Athenian leadership, the Second Athenian Confederacy, with the aim of fighting Sparta in the cause of freedom for the city-states. The military events of the war did not impinge on the north at all, although the Thracian coastal towns one after the other became members of the confederacy, and it is even possible that a refounded, but much smaller, league on the Chalkidike joined in.[27] Amyntas did not join the confederacy, although an expansion of the Athenian fleet, a precondition of the confederacy, created an immediate demand for ship-building timber that could be most easily satisfied in Macedonia. It is probable that the fragmentary inscription of a treaty between Athens and Amyntas belongs to this time.[28] Unfortunately, nothing survives on the stone except formalities, but the mere existence of a treaty made during the years of the war between Athens and Sparta indicates, whatever its content, that Amyntas had changed course in his foreign policy and that he considered it yet again more important for Macedonia to stand on a friendly footing with Athens than with Sparta. It was probably this consideration that lay behind his recognizing the Athenian claim to Amphipolis, which was presented at the peace congress in Sparta in 371.[29]

A further treaty, also of unknown content, with Jason, the tyrant of the Thessalian city of Pherai, must have been concluded during this period.[30] Jason's policy was to make the league of cities in Thessaly militarily and politically more efficient by abolishing the aristocratic governments in the cities. The Macedonian king, who from personal inclination and in view of the Macedonian aristocratic tradition would certainly have preferred to co-operate with his aristocratic friends in Larissa, had to recognize as a pragmatic politician that Jason's success had made him a very powerful neighbour, and for this reason he must have concluded the treaty with him. From this period we also have an arbitration decision of Amyntas over a border dispute between Elimiotis and the Perrhaibic town of Doliche. An arbitration ruling is no proof of a bid for control, but it presupposes the acceptability of the arbitrator to both sides. The good relations between Amyntas and Derdas of Elimiotis are well known, and the arbitration ruling bears witness to a friendly relationship with this northern border region of Thessaly.[31]

When Amyntas died in 370/69, after twenty-four years of rule, another comprehensive overturn of the power relationships of the Greek cities to one another had just taken place, similar in scope to the change in the balance of power in 404. This time it was the Spartans whose dominion came to a sudden end. On the bat-tlefield of Leuktra in Boiotia in 371 the army of the Boiotian League, under the leadership of Thebes, defeated the entire force of Sparta and thus destroyed the military basis of Spartan su-premacy.[32] It remained to be seen whether the Thebans would be in a position to fill the suddenly opened gap in the power struc-ture.

II

The European Great Power

1. THE SUCCESSION IN THE ROYAL HOUSE OF AMYNTAS

When Amyntas III died in 370 B.C., none of his contemporaries could have foreseen that his grandson would turn Macedonia into the ruling power in the whole of the eastern Mediterranean. The necessary preconditions seemed to be completely lacking. Only thanks to great efforts and a goodly measure of luck had Amyntas been able to give his country a certain stability. On his death the whole traditional kindling pile of problems, ranging from interference from outside to internal disputes at court over the succession, sparked once again into flame.

At first these dangers remained more or less latent. Alexander, the eldest of the three sons born of the politically conciliatory marriage of Amyntas to Eurydike, was about twenty years old when he succeeded his father. Only a short time later he felt secure enough to give assistance in Thessaly to the Aleuadai of Larissa against the current tyrant of Pherai, Alexandros. He took the urban area of Larissa, and shortly afterwards, Krannon. Macedonian occupation troops moved into both towns.[1] In his absence, however, his opponents in Macedonia staged a rebellion against him and presented Ptolemaios of Aloros as their candidate for the throne. Ptolemaios, an older relative of the king, who had married Alexander's full sister Eurynoe, was a man of experience. Whether he also had a love affair with Eurydike, the queen mother, as part of the tradition states, cannot be ascertained, but it seems probable that he had her support.

The occupation troops in Thessaly were not able to hold out for long. At about the same time as the Aleuadai had appealed to Alexander, another group of Thessalians had called for help on Thebes, the new great power of central Greece. In answer to this

appeal Pelopidas, one of the influential statesmen who had mas-
terminded the Boiotian rise in power and had already at the time
of Jason cultivated contacts in Thessaly, led an army into Thessaly and took over from the Macedonians. Shortly afterwards he
was called in to arbitrate in the internal Macedonian dispute,
which involved in practice the recognition of a certain Theban
patronage over Macedonia. Hence it is not surprising that Alexander had to send thirty hostages, including his youngest brother
Philip, to Thebes and that Ptolemaios even had to remain un-
punished. A short time later the young king was murdered. It
was said that Ptolemaios, or even his evil-minded mother Eurydike, had ordered the murder. Ptolemaios was at any rate the
main gainer, and he was recognized as regent for the two younger
sons of Amyntas, Perdikkas and Philip, both still minors. However, without Thebes a permanent settlement could not be found.
The adherents of the murdered king, probably mainly the relatives of the hostages, appealed immediately to Pelopidas. This
time he confirmed Ptolemaios as regent and took fifty extra hostages, including Ptolemaios' son Philoxenos. At about the same
time a certain Pausanias, also related in some way to the royal
house, attempted to conquer Macedonia from the Chalkidike with
Thracian help, but he was stopped by the intervention of the
Athenian general Iphikrates.[2]

The Macedonian stability so laboriously fostered by Amyntas
seemed to be shattered. No ruler could assert himself against his
internal opponents without external help, and Thebes, Thessaly,
Athens, the Thracian king Kotys and probably the Olynthians as
well had all tried to influence the government crisis in Macedonia.
It was inevitable that the murder of Ptolemaios by the young Perdikkas in 365 should instigate further foreign intervention, but
this time not by the Thebans.[3] After they had not been able to
intervene immediately, the death of Pelopidas in the following
year led to the abandonment of the Boiotian policies in the north,
which he had personally conceived and executed. It was the Athenians who leaped into the breach, and their interference was at
least potentially more dangerous for Macedonia, as they had concrete aims in the north: they wanted to recapture Amphipolis,
which had been lost to them in 424 and ever since had conducted

bitter resistance, and reestablish their influence in the Chalkidike. Their influence in Macedonia was initially strong enough for them to be able to persuade Perdikkas to participate in operations under Timotheus against Amphipolis as well as against Potidaia and other Chalkidian towns in 364/65 and 363/62.[4] But Perdikkas' defeat by the Athenian general Kallisthenes in 362/61 implies a change of policy that must somehow have been connected with Amphipolis, which had been occupied by a Macedonian garrison sometime before 359. Timotheus' conquest of the Macedonian coastal towns Methone and Pydna (perhaps in 360/59) may well have been a part of the Athenian reaction.[5]

Countering the threat from Athens could not be the first priority for Perdikkas in the years 360 and 359. Upper Macedonia was in danger of being overrun by old Bardylis. The region of Orestis, or part of it, had perhaps already joined with its westerly neighbours, the Molossians.[6] But even this step cannot have brought security since the Molossian ruler Arybbas had his hands full protecting even the central lands of his people against the Illyrians.[7] In spring 359 Perdikkas marched out to engage the Illyrian king. It was an utter disaster. He himself and more than four thousand of his soldiers fell in battle.[8]

The death of the third king within ten years of the demise of Amyntas seems to have been generally received as a sign of the underlying weakness of the Macedonian monarchy. Although the third son of Amyntas and Eurydike was rapidly acknowledged as king by the most influential nobles,[9] the accession of the twenty-four-year-old Philip gave rise to no great expections—why should he fare any better than his elder brothers? The Illyrians under Bardylis were firmly in possession of Upper Macedonia; the Paionians of the Axios valley took the favourable opportunity of staging attacks on neighbouring areas of Macedonia; and no less than three pretenders to the throne, at least two with foreign support, were staking their claims. The situation closely resembled that of the 390s. At that time Philip's father had also had problems with the Illyrians and had bought himself the breathing space he needed to establish himself by the payment of tribute. That the payments had been broken off by Perdikkas only a short time before may well have provoked the latest attack. But the principle of keeping opponents quiet with money payments could be reintroduced, even if not against the Illyrians, and in this tactic Philip showed himself to be an astute successor to his wily father.

The Illyrians remained for the time being in Upper Macedonia. Philip first turned his attention to the Paionians nearer to him; as Diodoros wrote, "He corrupted some of them with presents; others he convinced with generous promises," so that a fragile peace was rapidly reestablished in the Axios valley.[10] In a similar manner he was able to conciliate "with gifts" the greedy Thracian king Berisades, who had supported a pretender to the throne, Pausanias. Nothing more is heard of Pausanias, and Berisades can be assumed to have behaved peaceably at least in the short term. Two other pretenders were potentially more dangerous. One was Philip's eldest half-brother Archelaos, from Amyntas' first marriage to Gygaia. Exactly what took place is not known, but the extent of the danger can be deduced from the violent death of Archelaos and from the fact that even ten years later Philip was still pursuing his two other half-brothers.[11]

When Perdikkas died, Macedonia stood on a war footing with Athens. It is therefore not surprising that Athens attempted to look to its own interests in the matter of the succession. A king set on the throne with Athenian help would immediately have been in a position to realize the Athenian dream of recovering Amphipolis since Macedonian soldiers currently occupied the town. The Athenians found an acceptable candidate in old Argaios, who much earlier had caused difficulties for Philip's father Amyntas. He had been living since then in exile, probably in Athens, and was at the service of the Athenians. They transported him together with three thousand soldiers to Methone, and he set out with this escort on the short journey to Aigai. He had hoped for a ready reception by the inhabitants of the old capital, but no one came to greet him, and there was no rising against Philip. Without any real hope, Argaios now attempted the return to Methone, but on the way he encountered Philip with an army, which defeated his mercenaries. Many prisoners were taken, and we hear no more of Argaios. It was not going to be so easy for the Athenians to regain Amphipolis after all. But Philip had already recognized the problem. To extricate himself from Athenian pressure, he had already withdrawn his garrison from Amphipolis before encountering Argaios—he could not be forced to relinquish what he did not possess. An independent Amphipolis was less of a threat to Macedonia than one occupied by Athens. As a gesture of conciliation, however, he released the Athenian prisoners without ransom and made an offer of peace that Athens was unable to refuse. Negotiations even took place for an alliance.[12]

These first acts of Philip show the unfurling of an unusual political talent. On the death of Perdikkas the vultures had gathered to plunder and divide up the land, yet only six months later all rivals for the throne had been dismissed from the field, and apart from the Illyrians all Philip's dangerous neighbours had been conciliated. In so doing, the young king had demonstrated a happy combination of diplomacy and military strength that was to become his outstanding hallmark. It seems clear that he was immediately acceptable to the circles that counted in Macedonia. For this reason he was able to settle with Archelaos and banish his other two half-brothers; moreover, the inhabitants of Aigai had shown no enthusiasm for Argaios. There is a report of a royal tour of the country with speeches to the people,[13] which must have contributed to a consolidation of his regime within the land. The Illyrian occupation of large areas of Upper Macedonia was a case of fortune in adversity. Under these circumstances no danger was to be anticipated from the barons of Upper Macedonia, who were dependent on the central regime if they were ever going to rid themselves of the Illyrians. Philip, as son of the Lynkestian Eurydike, would have to come to grips with the problem sooner or later, but luckily Bardylis remained where he was after his victory and so allowed him a breathing space. After all, luck was, in the opinion of the ancients, one of the attributes of a successful general and king.

In his dealings with his neighbours Philip also revealed a sixth sense for their weaknesses. The Paionian desire for plunder could be placated by money payments. The same held true for the Thracian king Berisades. Since Athens wanted Amphipolis, his first step was to withdraw his occupation troops to relieve Athenian pressure, a good piece of propaganda that could not be criticized in principle by the "freedom-loving" Athenians. His second step was to defeat Argaios and his accompanying Athenian army and then display generosity. Afterwards a formal peace treaty was con-

cluded, and talks about an alliance were initiated. Talking cost
little and gained time. They got to know one another.

2. SECURITY IN THE WEST

The presentation of events in the remainder of this chapter will
not be chronological but instead will be geographical. Additionally, no break will be made at the time of the change of rule from
Philip II to Alexander III (the Great) in 336. The treatment of each
geographical area will be continuous until the death of Alexander
(June 323) or until the end of the Lamian War (summer 322) to
emphasize the fundamental continuity in the different European
interests of the Macedonian state. Within each geographical section events will be treated chronologically. The reasons for this
division of the material lie, on the one hand, in the conviction
that the European interests of Macedonia under Philip II and
Alexander III were so closely related that in this area the death
of Philip marked no significant change and, on the other hand,
in an attempt to identify the priorities of the Macedonian state,
which otherwise become obscured in the mists of the Athenian-centred ancient tradition.

Philip used the breathing space he had won to train a new
army. The sources tell of frequent exercises and new weapons he
supplied to the army.[1] Exactly what is meant is not certain, but
the new weapons were probably the sarissa, an approximately
sixteen-foot thrusting spear that became the characteristic weapon
of the new Macedonian army. It must have been possible to obtain
the materials for this inexpensive innovation relatively quickly
from the royal forests and mines. The necessity of army exercises
for military success must certainly have been a lesson learnt during the last years from the Greeks, where the effectiveness of the
regularly drilled army of the Boiotians under Pelopidas and Epaminondas had impressed all opponents and observers. Philip
himself had spent three years as hostage in Thebes, as had other
young Macedonians, and must have observed exercises there. Still
more innovations were revealed in the spring. Not only did the
infantry march out in a relatively well disciplined phalanx formation, armed with the new long sarissa, but also the cavalry had
been allocated a new and largely attacking role on the flanks, a

role which must have been regularly practised in the course of the winter.

The emergency measures were sufficient. Before his decisive battle with the Illyrians Philip campaigned against the Paionians, whose king Agis had just died. The campaign was conducted like a military exercise, and his comprehensive victory so humiliated the Paionians that in future their land could almost be regarded as a northern province of Macedonia. Immediately thereafter Philip marched into Upper Macedonia, rejected the offer to negotiate made by the wholly unprepared Bardylis and defeated the Illyrians so comprehensively that they were forced to evacuate Upper Macedonia. It is reported that more than seven thousand Illyrians were killed.[2] This unexpected victory not only drove out the Illyrians and liberated the Upper Macedonian principalities but also made the dominance of the central power in the kingdom so clear that Diodoros was able to write that Philip had "subjugated all the inhabitants of the region up to Lake Lychnidos [Ochrid]."[3] The local barons had not succeeded on their own in freeing themselves from the Illyrians, and the credit could be ascribed solely to their king Philip, who had come to their assistance from Pella with his reorganized army. In consequence the undisputed power base of the monarchy was extended, and Upper Macedonian aspirations to independence, which had so troubled many of Philip's predecessors, could be expected to be effectively at an end. Philip's interest in the western areas of his country by no means subsided after his victory over Bardylis, and he recognized the opportunity he had created to integrate the western principalities, above all Lynkestis, Pelagonia, Orestis and Tymphaia, much more closely than ever before into the Macedonian state. Hardly any details of developments during the next years are reported, as the Greek writers who are our sources regarded the region as barbarous and therefore of little interest, but we can nevertheless perceive that much was achieved.

The most important precondition for this integration was the continuing interest of the king and his unflagging readiness to invest time, energy and money in Upper Macedonia. He took the threat from Illyria seriously. His first move towards safeguarding future security there was his marriage to Audata, the daughter of an Illyrian noble, the first in a series of political marriages with non-Macedonians. A daughter, Kynnane, was born of the marriage.[4] But this move still did not produce peace with the Illyrian tribes, and two years later (356) Philip's general Parmenio fought a further battle against the Illyrians, this time against Grabos.[5] Again the resulting victory benefitted above all the Upper Macedonians. In the following years Philip continued to operate in the western border areas, with the result that in 346 the Athenian Isokrates could write—with good reason, even if somewhat exaggerating—that Philip ruled over all the Illyrians apart from the inhabitants of the Adriatic coast.[6] This dominion was, however, by no means stable. Further campaigns against Illyrians (exactly which tribes were involved is not known) took place between 445 and 443,[7] and directly following the death of Philip, Alexander was forced in 335 to counter an Illyrian rebellion led by Kleitos, son of Bardylis. Yet again, after Alexander's death in 323, some Illyrians joined with the rebellious Greeks "because of their hatred of the Macedonians."[8] But although the agglomeration of Illyrian peoples, with their ever-changing loyalties to one another as well as to their non-Illyrian neighbours, continued to be a worry and nuisance to the Macedonians, it is clear that the danger never became so acute that the current king could not cope with it. The violence in the border areas was never stopped, but it was reduced to an acceptable level.

This circumstance had not been achieved merely through regular campaigns and swift military response to threats. The patent determination of the central government to gain peace in the region must have been equally decisive. This determination showed itself in extensive building and settlement measures in the border area. Already in 351 Demosthenes spoke of the fortification of towns in the Illyrian area, and a statement of Justin, which cannot be precisely dated, refers to population exchanges in the border region as well as to the settlement of prisoners of war there to strengthen the towns. These statements indicate that Philip was fairly systematic in settling the border area with reliable people. For example, he made grants of land, which served, among other things, to bind the recipients to the king, fortified existing market communities and built forts at strategic points.[9] Much no doubt was accomplished by these measures, which were supported by a regular military presence that lent credibility to the king's read-

iness to regard Upper Macedonia as an integral part of his kingdom.

The regions of Upper Macedonia were not disbanded as political entities but were firmly embedded in the state system. This
can best be illustrated concretely in military affairs. In the army
of Alexander some of the infantry units, or *taxeis*, were organized
by provinces, and *taxeis* from Elimiotis, Tymphaia and Orestis-
Lynkestis are specifically referred to.[10] Moreover, the old nobility,
which had failed miserably against the Illyrians, was incorporated
in the central military service of the state. Nothing much is known
of this arrangement during Philip's lifetime, but several officers
from Upper Macedonia are known to have served under Alexander, at least some of whom must also have served under Philip,
such as Krateros and Perdikkas from Orestis and Polyperchon
from Tymphaia.[11] Aristocratic young men were assembled at the
court in a sort of corps of pages, and members of the noble families of Upper Macedonia were also included.[12] Absolute security
certainly could not be achieved. Not every member of a former
royal house was content with his new role or remained above
suspicion, as is shown by the fate of the three sons of Aeropos
of Lynkestis, two of whom Alexander ordered to be killed as soon
as he came to power. A certain regionalism undoubtedly remained, even though we cannot always recognize it.[13] Nevertheless, Philip appears to have achieved peace in the west, and no
more serious threats to the unity of the state from this region are
known.

The second pillar of Philip's defence strategy in the west lay
in his relations with the Molossians. The Molossians were the
strongest and, decisive for Macedonia, most easterly of the three
most important Epeirot tribes, which, like Macedonia but unlike
the Thesprotians and the Chaonians, still retained their monarchy.
They were Greeks, spoke a similar dialect to that of Macedonia,
suffered just as much from the depredations of the Illyrians and
were in principle the natural partners for a Macedonian king who
wished to tackle the Illyrian problem at its roots. Philip seems to
have appreciated this common interest at an early stage, and already in 357 he married Olympias, a niece of the Molossian king
Arybbas. Olympias' sister Troas was already married to Arybbas
himself. In summer 356, when Olympias gave birth to a son Alex-

ander, whom Philip recognized as his heir, this connection became of even greater significance.[14]

The function of the Epeirot connection was not merely to produce royal progeny. Olympias' brother Alexandros was to assume a crucial political role. In the middle of the 350s, while he was still a youth, Olympias brought him to Pella, where he rapidly won the confidence and trust of his brother-in-law. When he was twenty years old, in about 350, he received Macedonian military assistance for the overthrow of Arybbas, who was forced to go into exile. Alexandros, the faithful friend of Philip (there were rumours of a love affair), furthered in exemplary fashion the cooperation between the two states, a service well rewarded by Philip. In 343, for example, he added to the possessions of his brother-in-law and rounded them off with the acquisition by force of the four small towns in Kassopeia.[15] There are also indications that during the lifetime of Alexandros the formal state influence of the Molossian king was extended to cover the Thesprotians. By around 330 a state had been created that, at least abroad, could be called Epeiros, and Macedonian influence must have been decisive for this development.[16]

In 337 a serious rift occurred between Philip and Olympias. Philip, now in his mid-forties, married the young Macedonian noblewoman Kleopatra, and Olympias, herself over forty and fearing to be relegated to the status of a second wife, left to take refuge with her brother. Alexandros, however, was not prepared to let his good relationship with Philip be spoilt just on account of an offended sister, and his loyalty was rewarded at once by his receiving as wife his niece Kleopatra, the daughter of Philip and Olympias. The importance of the family connection between the royal houses of the two neighbouring states continued into the second generation, despite Philip's murder during the wedding celebrations. But the conditions changed radically when both kings undertook distant campaigns—the Molossian Alexandros in Italy, where he was killed in 331/30, and the Macedonian Alexander in Asia, where he died in 323, in Babylon, and left their lands in the care of deputies. Personal rivalries also occurred when after 334 Olympias tried to interfere in Macedonian affairs under Alexander's deputy Antipatros and then finally returned to Molossis because she could no longer bear her situation in Pella.

Her return caused problems in Molossis because Kleopatra, after the death of her husband in Italy, could not assert herself against her mother, who had been born a Molossian princess, and Kleopatra returned to Pella. But despite the disputes of the women, good state relations were maintained between Macedonia and Molossis (or Epeiros) for as long as Alexander of Macedonia was alive, no matter how far away he was from home.[17]

3. THE EAST

Although the crisis of 359 first made itself felt in western Macedonia, the Macedonian state was also continually under threat from the east. The main dangers were presented by the Greeks of the Chalkidike, under the leadership of Olynthos, and by the Thracian tribal states beyond the Strymon. But Athens also had interests to pursue there and had recently served notice of them by the resuscitation of the old claims to Amphipolis and the capture of Pydna and Methone, as well as by sending colonists to Potidaia. When Philip came to power, Athens and the neighbouring Thracian king, perhaps also Olynthos, again supported pretenders to the throne. Philip's objective, the prevention of further interference, demanded as a consequence that the Athenians should be driven out of their new possessions and made to give up hope of a new power base in the North Aegean. As far as the Chalkidike was concerned, systematic thinking could lead to only one ideal solution, that of incorporating the region directly into the territory of the Macedonian state. This was exactly the course taken with Mygdonia and Bisaltia more than a hundred years before by Alexander I when he established the Macedonian frontier along the Strymon. And Anthemous had already established a precedent for the Chalkidike.

In comparison, the problem with the Thracians was much more complicated. The people whom the Greeks called Thracians consisted of a number of more or less independent tribes settled between the Aegean and the Danube. Of these only the most southerly, the Odrysians, had created a recognizable state system.[1] It was this kingdom of the Odrysians, with which Athens, for example, always attempted to maintain friendly relations, that gave Macedonia the most trouble. There was one possible approach.

For some time the Odrysians were no longer organized into a single kingdom but constituted three smaller ones, whose kings, despite blood relationship, got on badly with one another. Macedonia's immediate neighbour was Berisades, who ruled over the territory between the rivers Strymon and Nestos; next came Amadokos, who ruled as far as Maroneia or perhaps even the Hebros; and the original home area of the Odrysians to the east of the Hebros belonged to Kersebleptes. An advance against any one of these rulers would not necessarily be regarded as a provocation by the others. The elimination of Berisades, the supporter of Pausanias, and perhaps even the incorporation of his lands within Macedonia, would surely be possible for the army and king that had been capable of defeating Bardylis. This idea was attractive not only for reasons of security but also because Berisades controlled Mount Pangaion, the most important source of precious metals in the whole Aegean area.

After his victory over the Illyrians Philip set out to deal with Macedonia's weaknesses in the east. His brother Perdikkas had already made a start by breaking off relations with Athens and installing Macedonian occupation troops in Amphipolis, which controlled the lowermost bridge over the Strymon. Philip had at first withdrawn these troops so as not to provoke Athens further,[2] but in consideration of the help given by Berisades to Pausanias, control over Amphipolis again became a high, perhaps the highest, priority. The conqueror of the Illyrians had little to fear from the Athenians, who in any case only constituted a danger in the north on account of the manoeuvrability of their fleet.

In 357 Philip undertook his first moves. The time was extraordinarily favourable for a sudden attack because of disunity among the Amphipolitans themselves, because of Athens' distraction by a breakaway movement among members of the confederacy and because of the death of Berisades. A group of Amphipolitans did indeed send two envoys, Hierax and Stratokles, to Athens in the expectation of help. However, they achieved nothing, and by autumn Philip's siege had met with success. The fundamental weakness of the Athenians in the North Aegean could hardly have been more effectively demonstrated. They were not even able to take possession of Amphipolis, to which they had laid claim for more than sixty years, when invited to do so by some of the most influential Amphipolitans. Amphipolis was forced to conduct its resistance to Philip alone and unaided, and the "friend of Athens," Stratokles, found himself an exile as a logical consequence of Philip's victory.[3] Philip had quickly perceived that the Athenians would rather negotiate than take action; during the siege he let it be known that he was conquering Amphipolis for Athens, and immediately after it he received Athenian envoys, who hinted at the possibility of exchanging Amphipolis for Pydna. Their offer, however, merely revealed that Athens was not resolved to hang on to Pydna at all costs, and so Philip did not delay in taking Pydna as well.[4]

The Athenians declared war but otherwise did nothing. The Olynthians, made uneasy by Philip's successes, sent a deputation to Athens, just as the Amphipolitans had done before them, but their envoys too returned home disappointed. Their search for allies resulted in a treaty with the Illyrian chief Grabos, but Philip torpedoed it through generous promises, which he immediately made good.[5] He restored to Olynthos the disputed frontier territory of Anthemous and, much more important, helped expel the Athenian presence in Potidaia, a mere two miles from Olynthos. After the siege he enslaved the local population but dispatched the Athenian settlers back to Athens. Olynthos received possession of the land (356).[6] By this means the Chalkidians not only became treaty partners; they also, because of Potidaia, were embroiled in the war against Athens. Athens' chances of exerting influence in the north were diminishing rapidly; only Methone remained as a base.

In the same year an irresistible opportunity offered itself in Thrace, which led perforce to ever-greater Macedonian involvement there. Berisades, the Thracian ruler of the Pangaion mining area, died in 357, and his children split up his kingdom among themselves. A dispute arose immediately between Ketriporis and the flourishing Greek gold-mining town of Krenides, and the population of Krenides appealed to Philip. Successful cooperation with Krenides could bring control over the highly desirable deposits of precious metals, but only if Krenides were not left as an island in the middle of hostile Thracian territory. Free access to Mount Pangaion was essential to successful economic activity. Effective aid for Krenides thus implied satisfying this precondition, which in the present situation could only be met by Macedonian control of the entire Pangaion region. Such control meant, at least in the long term, the abandonment of the Strymon as the state frontier and made it necessary to establish a new natural frontier. The only alternative was the Nestos, which until now had formed the eastern frontier of the kingdom of Berisades and his sons. All things considered, effective help for Krenides entailed the complete conquest of Thrace up to the Nestos.

Philip executed his programme of aid for Krenides with his usual uncompromising persistence. He drove Ketriporis out of Krenides, brought in new settlers and, to emphasize that the new city was a royal foundation, renamed it Philippoi. There is no extant account of the further measures that must have been necessary, such as draining and settling the marshy plain of Philippoi and conquering the lands up to the Nestos, but these ventures must have been easy to finance from the annual income of one thousand talents yielded by the mines. Under Alexander the city territory was in some way augmented or reorganized, a sign of a successful development.[7] Although in summer 356 Ketriporis allied himself with Athens, the Illyrian Grabos and the Paionian Lyppeios, he never regained Krenides, in spite of its recapture being specifically mentioned in the treaty, and it appears that he must have acknowledged the sovereignty of the Macedonian king.[8] In the following year (355) Philip finally took Methone. This last Athenian base fell after a siege, in the course of which Philip lost his right eye. In revenge for the bitter resistance offered, and perhaps also for the lost eye, Methone was razed to the ground, and the inhabitants were allowed to leave with only the clothes on their backs. The town territory was divided among deserving Macedonians.[9]

The direct financial gains accruing from the takeover of Krenides flowed straight into the Macedonian state treasury. They made it possible for Philip to relieve his citizen militia with mercenaries. The newly won territories between Strymon and Nestos were allocated to Macedonians and to those who wished to become Macedonians.[10] Ketriporis' prompt capitulation did not, however, mean the end of the Thracian problem. Athens had traditionally cultivated good relations with the Odrysian kings on account of the importance of the two straits, the Bosporos and the Hellespont (Dardanelles), for the import of grain from southern Russia, on which Athens was dependent. Neapolis, Abdera, Maroneia and Ainos, the most important of the Greek coastal towns, were also dependent on good relations with their Thracian neighbours for the sake of their own security. Because of their exposed locations they were all members of the Athenian confederacy, as was Thasos. Two treaties illustrate Athens' relations with the Thracians. One belongs to the period before the death of Berisades, in about 358, and was concluded among the three Thracian kings of the time. The aim was to safeguard their respective interests in regard to the Greek towns, which were to remain "free and autonomous" as long as they paid their tribute to the Thracians and to Athens.[11] The other treaty was concluded in 356, this time with Ketriporis and his brothers, and the same aims are apparent. The Athenians now selected Neapolis, only ten miles away from Philippoi and the natural harbour of the region, as base for their fleet, thus effectively preventing Philip from bringing supplies by sea into his new royal foundation.[12]

But above all it was their immediate Thracian neighbour Amadokos who gave the Macedonians grounds for alarm. In 353 he refused Philip's demand for free passage for his Theban friend Pammenes, who was on his way to Asia Minor with five thousand Boiotian soldiers even though Kersebleptes, who ruled beyond the Hebros, had already given his permission. Philip vented his anger by laying waste the territories of Maroneia and Abdera.[13] A suitable opportunity to hit back at an uncooperative and dangerous neighbour offered itself in autumn 352. Amadokos had fallen out with Kersebleptes and received support from the two largest Greek towns in Kersebleptes' kingdom, Byzantion and Perinthos. Kersebleptes was also under pressure from Athens, one of whose generals, Chares, had just reconquered Sestos, an earlier Athenian possession on the Dardanelles, with spectacular brutality; he had had all the men killed and the women and children sold into slavery. By summer 352 Athenian settlers had been brought into the deserted town to secure this important base on the grain route. Impressed by this violent demonstration of power, Kersebleptes made over his previous income from the Chersonnesos, with the exception of Kardia, to Athens.[14]

The threat to the whole Pangaion region should Amadokos win his war against Kersebleptes could already be foreseen. Kersebleptes promised to be a more suitable client of Macedonia, al-

though his enforced flirtation with Athens laid him open to suspicion as well. Philip hastened into the area; he arrived in
November at Heraion Teichos on the Marmara coast and put an
end to the war. Kersebleptes was forced to withdraw from the
disputed territory and leave his son behind as hostage with Philip;
but of Amadokos nothing more is heard, which suggests that he
must have been deposed and replaced by his son Teres. In this
way Philip gained two weak kings as his clients and was able to
guarantee the security of his newly acquired territories.[15]

Now only one region was left on the traditional frontiers of
Macedonia, a region that had always presented a danger in the
past and where Philip had not yet fundamentally altered the situation—the Chalkidike. Only a short time earlier the Olynthians
had again demonstrated how insensitive they were to Macedonian
interests, and therefore to their own, by concluding on their own
initiative a peace with the Athenians, in spite of a moral (because
of Potidaia and Anthemous) and contractual obligation to Philip
not to do so unilaterally. That the leading political figures in Olynthos then committed the double stupidity not only of granting
asylum to Philip's two half-brothers, who were on the run, but
also of then refusing to extradite them, makes it clear that they
had utterly failed to realize that the balance of power between
them and the Macedonians had radically altered and that they
could no longer treat Philip as they had treated his father Amyntas.[16]

However brave their decision may have seemed to be, the times
when the Chalkidians could exert consultative or even initiatory
influence in the succession to the Macedonian throne were irrevocably over. The only practical possibility for Olynthos and the
Chalkidians in the immediate future would have been to accept
a form of client status. Philip had at first worked towards this
end. He had shown himself generous, making grants of territories, and thereby won over influential politicians and cemented
their friendship with expensive presents. But it was Olynthian
illusions of being a great power, and not Philip's friends, that
determined the future course of events. It is a matter for speculation whether Philip would have annexed the Chalkidike to Macedonia even if Olynthos had not acted contrary to Macedonian
interests; but it is certain that Olynthian actions were a decisive

factor in determining the timing and the uncompromising execution of the Macedonian attack. Freedom-loving Athens had just
demonstrated in Sestos how a Greek state whose orators on occasion accused Philip of being a barbarian could, to satisfy its own
exclusive interests, destroy another Greek state with merciless
brutality. Philip could not behave worse, but he could be just as
single-minded and uncompromising.

Olynthos was the only town of the Chalkidian League to offer
any resistance worth mentioning. Philip's investment in clients
paid dividends, even when the client-status solution no longer
came into question. The largest town on the Chalkidike was taken
and sacked in late summer 348 and its population sold into slavery. Olynthos no longer existed, and the Chalkidian League, of
which Olynthos had been the capital, was disbanded. As in all
the new territories conquered by Philip, Macedonians were settled
also on the Chalkidike. For the Macedonian state, it was of great
importance for the future not only that the danger from the Chalkidike had been finally eradicated but also that this rich agricultural region, so close to the traditional Macedonian homelands,
would now be part of the nucleus of the Macedonian state.[17]

Philip had a right to be pleased with his achievements in the
immediate frontier regions. The security of the Macedonian state
territories or of crucial state interests, as in Krenides-Philippoi,
always took first priority. He pursued these interests offensively
in the west against the Illyrians, Molossians and Paionians and
in the east against the Thracians, Chalkidians and Athenians.
However, the dividing line between offensive security policy and
open building of a position of domination is grey and blurred;
the one fades easily into the other without the actors or their
victims necessarily recognizing it at first. This uncertainty makes
it difficult for the historian to assess the development and establish where a genuine threat provided the motivation for action or
where a danger was invented as an excuse for expansion.

The problem arises directly in connection with the further development of Macedonian relations to the peoples and rulers of
Thrace. The Macedonians, and above all their king, were after
ten years accustomed to military success. Following generations
in which their frontier areas had been subject to repeated attack
from all their neighbours, their delight in victory and their self-

satisfaction came about not only because these threats would not soon rise again but also because the fate of those who in the past had caused Macedonia so much trouble now lay in Macedonian hands. It quickly becomes apparent that above all the peoples and lands of Thrace and the Greek towns in the region came to be regarded by the Macedonians as an exercise area for satisfying their lust for power and as a source of booty. The Thracians were now to be made to suffer themselves what they had done to the Macedonians over centuries. This attitude was not exclusive to the Macedonians: even the Athenians seem to have felt in Sestos that other standards applied in the north. Certainly here, as in all state dealings, important considerations of state played a part: the quieter the unruly neighbours were kept, the more subservient were their lords and kings; and the wider the buffer zone between enemy and homelands, the more secure were the state frontiers. In addition tribute could be demanded and perhaps even some form of permanent control could be established. In one way or another the state expanded and developed broader and more complicated interests, which finally far exceeded the original need for security; the state grew and profited, whatever the motives for the expansion may have been.

The Athens-centred sources at our disposal do not allow a detailed analysis of this development. We know, however, that by spring 346 Philip was so displeased with Kersebleptes that he found a further campaign necessary. His advance was directed against a number of fortified settlements as far as the Sea of Marmara. Serrion, Serrhaion Teichos, Doriskos, Ergiske, Ganos and Hieron Oros are mentioned, and at least two of these, Serrhaion Teichos and Hieron Oros, were occupied by Athenian troops, which Philip expelled. It is not known whether Kersebleptes, whose son still served as a hostage in Macedonia, had done anything more than perhaps cooperate under pressure with the local Athenian commander, Chares. But he had astute political friends in Athens, who immediately tried to have him included in the current peace negotiations with Philip as a member of the Athenian confederacy, which he was not. However, Philip's spring excursion with military escort put an end to this project.[18] The real aim, though, was to underline the permanence of Macedonian interest in eastern Thrace. The Athenian Chares dramatically described Philip's intervention to the Athenians and from the Athenian point of view as "Kersebleptes' loss of his land,"[19] but in fact Kersebleptes remained king for four more years. From the Macedonian point of view the relationship envisaged since 352 had been restored. Kersebleptes certainly lost his freedom of political manoeuvre, but Philip's view was that this freedom was one that he had had no right to since 352.

For reasons that must lie largely in the Macedonian lust for conquest, Thrace between the Danube and the Aegean was the main field of action of the royal Macedonian army for the four years after 342. There must certainly have been concrete grounds that served as an excuse each time and can be regarded as measures taken in the interests of Macedonian friends and allies. However, they all clearly served the expansion of Macedonian control to cover the whole region previously ruled or claimed by the Odrysians, from the Strymon to the Sea of Marmara and from the Aegean coast to the Haimos (Balkan mountains). That in addition Philip advanced as far as the Danube may be taken as an indication that not even the Haimos was considered the final frontier of the new Macedonian empire.

But the centre of activity was clearly in Odrysian territory. Kersebleptes and Teres were finally deposed and their former subjects forced to pay tribute to the Macedonians.[20] The payment of tribute presupposes a machinery for collecting and controlling the payments. The Odrysian kings must have had some sort of primitive administrative apparatus, but tribute collecting by the kings ceased with the monarchy. An alternative was to use town administrations. Philip founded a number of towns in the heart of Odrysian territory: Philippopolis (Plovdiv) in the Hebros valley; Kabyle on a tributary; possibly also in this area Beroia and the otherwise unknown Bine or Binai; and in 340 Alexandropolis in the territory of the Maidoi, founded by the king's son, Alexander.[21] These new foundations served first to secure Macedonian possessions and thus fulfilled primarily a military-political function, according to the tested pattern of the frontier areas in the west. However, even in Macedonia larger communities could not exist without a minimum of administrative apparatus, and the assumption can be made that these towns formed the nucleus of a royal administrative system and that tribute payments from the areas around them were processed by the respective town administrations. A few years later there is evidence of a royal functionary for Thrace with the military title of *strategos*, or general.[22] That such a controller was appointed already by Philip, perhaps on his withdrawal in 339, is not proven but nevertheless is very probable. It must have taken some years before the new system ran smoothly and the new towns became properly established.

The abolition of the Odrysian kingdom and the setting up of a Macedonian administration also had consequences for the Greek towns on the coast. The Greek towns had paid tribute to the Thracians probably in inverse proportion to the size and strength of each town and its relationship to the local Thracians. This formula applied particularly to the small towns on the Black Sea coast. At least one, Apollonia, appears to have established relations with Philip at that time,[23] and it is certainly possible that Philip claimed to represent the interests of the Greek towns against the Thracians, just as he had defended Krenides against Ketriporis, and then developed the town, or had in 352 supported Kardia against Kersebleptes (and Athens!).

The Greek cities, including those that were members of the Athenian rump confederacy, such as Abdera, Neapolis, Maroneia and Ainos cannot at first have been displeased at the weakening influence of the Thracian kings.[24] But when the Macedonians set about not only to weaken the Thracians but also to take their place, the attitude of the Greeks changed. Some of them conformed, and the towns of the North Aegean may have abandoned Athens and submitted to the new power. Kardia, caught in a strategic position between Athenian possessions and a friendly Philip, obviously remained true to Philip. But a matter of principle arose for the two largest towns of the region, Perinthos and Byzantion, which so far had supported Philip against Kersebleptes. The Thracians appear never to have attempted to exert influence on the general economic and foreign policy of "their" Greek cities; but now when Philip set out on a thorough reform of Thracian affairs, even the major cities were affected. In addition, the Athenians became increasingly convinced by the arguments of their war-mongering politicians, and by 340 it had become plain that the peace they had concluded with Philip in 346 could not be maintained.[25]

Diopeithes, an Athenian mercenary leader, had already in 341 ravaged Kardia and neighbouring parts of Thrace from a base in the Chersonnesos and had been covered by the Athenians.[26] Perinthos and Byzantion, both trading towns, were dependent among other things on their trade with Athens and would be forced to take sides should it come to war between Macedonia and Athens. Moreover, they had certainly perceived that Philip set no high value on the freedom of action of cities within his sphere of influence. In contrast to the Odrysian kings, he would wish to exert influence on decision-making processes. Perinthos and Byzantion—perhaps also Selymbria—decided to withstand Philip, and despite great Macedonian efforts they were successful because of assistance from Athens and other mercantile Greek states as well as from the Persians. It seems barely to have occurred to the Persian satrap of Hellespontine Phrygia that his new European neighbour would introduce a completely new and incalculable factor into the hitherto comfortable situation on the Sea of Marmara, the Bosporos and the Hellespont, should he gain control of the most important harbour towns there, and that because he was so incalculable, he must be kept as far away as possible.[27] The assistance given by the Athenians and the Persians lent a new dimension to Philip's painful defeat and pointed the future course of events. The two Greek towns were not essential to the security of his other Thracian conquests, but it was becoming clear that Macedonian activity in Thrace also affected other and greater powers than those immediately involved.

Philip paid not the least attention to this factor. In autumn 340, in a bravura response to the provocative despoliations of Diopeithes, he captured the entire Athenian grain fleet as it assembled into a convoy at Hieron before the entrance to the narrows of the Bosporos. Basically this was nothing but a piece of expensive and provocative piracy, yet it was received as a serious act of war by the infuriated Athenians, whose favourite orators liked to overvalue the Athenian dimension of Philip's enterprises in Thrace and misinterpret them as being wholly directed against Athens itself. The stone slab on which the terms of the Peace of Philokrates in 346 had been inscribed was overturned, and the Athenians once again declared war.[28] This war, which ended with the battle of Chaironeia in August 338, was not directly concerned with the north, and the northern Greeks took no part in it.[29] However, the defeat of the Athenians and Thebans and the other few southern Greeks who were involved certainly had its consequences in the north. The North Aegean Greek cities that had not already joined Macedonia now did so. It was now also possible to take Byzantion and probably Perinthos; Byzantion served Alexander in 335 as a base for his fleet when he crossed the Danube and perhaps also provided him with ships.[30] The Athenian defeat robbed the northern Greeks of their only potential support.

In 340, however, this all lay in the future. Philip did not throw himself immediately into the new war with Athens. First he wanted to exhaust the possibilities in Thrace and planned an advance through the Dobruja. While the Macedonians had been operating in the Haimos area in 342/41, they had forged contacts with some of the rulers between the Haimos and the Danube. Kothelas, chief of the Getai, sealed his friendship with Philip with the hand of his daughter Meda, and the old Skythian king Atheas called on Philip for assistance against the Greeks of Histria and hinted at the possibility of recognizing him as his heir; Philip sent some soldiers. During the siege of Byzantion Philip for his part asked for help, but it was refused him. The refusal was unacceptable, either because he genuinely felt that it compromised his security or, more probably, because he considered that his army needed a straightforward victory again. He achieved that victory. Atheas fell, and massive booty was collected; twenty thousand women and children were enslaved, and the Macedonians were able to take with them large herds of animals, including twenty thousand mares. But none of this arrived in Macedonia, since the Triballians, a Thracian tribe not yet subjugated by the Macedonians, attacked them with such vigour during their passage over the Haimos that they were lucky to get home at all.[31]

Philip had thus by no means made vassals of all the peoples between the Aegean and the Danube. The Triballians are a clear case. They reacted so tempestuously to the news of Philip's death in 336 that Alexander's first military action was to conduct a campaign against them. But it was not only the Triballians who refused to acknowledge Macedonian sovereignty. On his way across the Haimos Alexander had to struggle against "autonomous Thracians" who blocked his way over an important pass. It was in this region that Antipatros and Parmenion had fought against the Tetrachoritai, the "inhabitants of the four districts," in 340. It seems that the Macedonians had not found it easy to establish themselves on the Haimos in 342 and 341.[32] The Triballians were more important, however, as they were reputed to be the wildest and fiercest of all the Balkan tribes. In earlier times they had made plundering forays as far as the Aegean and into the Dobruja, and they were still capable of causing serious difficulties for the Macedonians in Thrace. Alexander's endeavours were crowned with success; after a victory over the Triballian army, he negotiated conditions with King Syrmos that secured him the participation of up to two thousand Triballian soldiers in his expeditionary army for Asia Minor.[33] The soldiers serving abroad were in a sense hostages for the good behaviour of the Triballians at home. All peoples up to the Danube had now formally acknowledged Macedonian dominion. Alexander's thirst for adventure even caused him to cross the Danube briefly and provoke a skirmish with the Getai on the north bank, but this episode remained without long-term consequences.[34]

Philip's policy for securing the Macedonian frontier areas had resulted, particularly in the east, in a formidable expansion of the territories claimed by the Macedonian crown. In other regions the local barons or the existing administrative systems were utilized to meet Macedonian needs and requirements, as with the Illyrians of Bardylis, whose son Kleitos was now tribal leader, with the Molossians, the Paionians and Agrianians, and with the Triballians. Only in the former Odrysian territories, for about fifteen years after the deposition of Kersebleptes and Teres in 342, is there no record of native rulers assuming positions of responsibility. Their place was taken by the Macedonian governor and the newly founded towns. The Odrysian royal house had not, however, been exterminated; one member of it, Sitalkes, commanded the unit of Thracians conscripted into the army of Alexander, and another member, Rhebulas, son of Seuthes, received honours, perhaps even citizenship in Athens in 330. Kotys, his brother, was also known in Athens, and a certain Seuthes, possibly the father of the Rhebulas honoured in Athens, was able, on the death of

the current Macedonian governor Zopyrion in about 325, to organize a rebellion that caused severe difficulties for Lysimachos,
the Macedonian governor of Thrace after the death of Alexander.[35]

Thus from the beginning the Thracians of the Odrysian kingdom were treated differently from the inhabitants of the other
frontier areas. The region up to the Nestos was fully integrated
into the Macedonian state territory; the Odrysian monarchy was
abolished and replaced by Macedonian military governors; towns
were founded at strategic points, and a Macedonian population,
perhaps including criminals from the prisons, was settled in them.
Land was allocated to the settlers, just as on the Chalkidike and
in the area around Amphipolis. Philip and Alexander seem to
have striven for a very close relationship between Macedonia and
the former Odrysian kingdom, at least in the area up to the Haimos.

It is idle to speculate as to whether the country would have
been completely integrated into the Macedonian state had Alexander not been driven by love of adventure and the thrill of victory as far away as the Punjab. As it happened, it never developed
into more than a territory under Macedonian administration. During the reign of Alexander three governors of Thrace are known
by name. The first was Alexandros of Lynkestis, son-in-law of
Antipatros, a scion of the Lynkestian royal house. On the death
of Philip he found himself in political difficulties, but in contrast
to his two brothers, who were promptly executed by Alexander,
he was saved by his own loyal behaviour (he was the first to greet
Alexander as king) and by his relationship to Antipatros.[36] In 334
he accompanied Alexander to Asia Minor and was replaced in
Thrace by Memnon. Both he and his successor Zopyrion appear
to have experimented with the possibility of expanding their province, which until recently had still been an independent kingdom.
The king himself was far away in Asia, and his deputy Antipatros
did not command the same regal authority. Memnon, with the
support of the native Thracians, appears to have challenged his
power. Antipatros marched with his entire army into Thrace.
Troubles in the Peloponnese forced him to abandon his plans and
come to terms with Memnon, but the potential danger posed by
the position of the *strategos* of Thrace is clear enough. In assuming

the duties of the native kings, he also inherited their opportunities.

Memnon does not seem to have sought complete independence. In 327/26 he did not refuse the king's command to set out on the long road to India with five thousand Thracian cavalry, which Alexander needed as reinforcements.[37] His successor Zopyrion was also characterized by dash and aggressiveness, which took the form of an insatiable lust for conquest almost equal to that of his king. But not as effective! Zopyrion crossed the Danube with a large army and reportedly advanced as far as Olbia before he and his entire army were massacred by the Skythians he had come to conquer. He had irresponsibly neglected his duties in his province, and his defeat damaged the reputation of the Macedonians in Thrace to such an extent that shortly afterwards Seuthes, a member of the Odrysian royal family, was able to shake severely the Macedonian position in Thrace that had been established at such great pains by Philip and Alexander. Alexander himself did not get round to designating a successor to Zopyrion, and not until after his death in 323 was Lysimachos entrusted with the province. By that time a state of general revolt under the leadership of Seuthes had had time to develop.[38]

4. THESSALY

When Philip came to power in Macedonia in 359, a state of war prevailed among his southerly neighbours, the Thessalians. Tensions between the Thessalian League, whose largest city, Larissa, had always maintained good relations with Macedonia, and the member city of Pherai, which had tried under several different dictators, or tyrants, to take over the leadership of the league, had continued without a break since the 370s. At that time Jason had succeeded in having himself acknowledged as leader (*tagos* or *archon*) of the league. But the league, which was traditionally led by the most powerful clan of Larissa, the Aleuadai, was generally considered to be a factor contributing to the stability of northern Greece because of its strongly aristocratic structure; it rejected the leadership claims of Jason's successors. It received assistance both from Macedonia, in 369 under Alexander II, and,

until 364, from Thebes.[1] Aid was also provided for in a treaty with
Athens.[2] To the Macedonians, however, their southern frontier,
despite the natural barrier of the Olympus range, must have
seemed increasingly insecure as a result of the tense situation in
Thessaly. When in 358, following Philip's victories over the pretenders, the Paionians and, most spectacularly, the Illyrians, the
Aleuadai appealed to him for help, the young king, whose attraction to the horse-loving aristocrats of Larissa must have had
both political and personal aspects, saw advantages for himself.
He seems at that time not to have undertaken much in the way
of military action against Pherai. However, the cultivation of personal contacts, a cornerstone of Greek politics, particularly for the
aristocrats, should not be undervalued in its importance for interstate relations. Even Philip's well-known and eventually notorious weakness for beautiful women played its part in cultivating contacts. From his affair with the Thessalian Philinna, which
probably belongs to this time, was born a son, Arrhidaios, who
in 323 was recognized by the Macedonians as king.[3]

Probably not until 355 did the leading Aleuadai feel compelled
to call again on Philip for help against Pherai, now led by Lykophron. He went immediately. This time he put pressure on the
Pheraians and "regained freedom for the cities and demonstrated
his great goodwill towards the Thessalians."[4] Goodwill (*eunoia*)
must have been the most important aspect of the whole enterprise
for Philip. Relations between Macedonia and her southerly neighbours had always been kept well tended through repeated dem-
onstrations of mutual goodwill.

In the meantime developments had taken place in the south
that were to have a great influence on the Thessalians. The Thessalians and their *perioikoi* (semidependent neighbours) controlled
half of the twenty-four votes in the international supervisory
board of the sanctuary at Delphi, the Delphic Amphiktyony. By
means of these votes the Boiotians, old friends of the league,
caused sacred war to be declared against their neighbours, the
Phokians, in whose territory the sanctuary lay. Sacred war could
be declared (though in practice it happened only rarely) by the
Amphiktyony to protect the interests of the god Apollo. The Amphiktyony, however, had become increasingly politicized over the

course of the fourth century B.C. and was used to advance the interests of the most powerful member, at that time Boiotia. This abuse was the cause of the war. Disputes had occurred between Phokis and the Boiotians and Lokrians over money fines levied not only against individual Phokians but also against Sparta during the period of Theban dominance in central Greece. In summer 356 the Phokians reacted impetuously by occupying the temple precinct at Delphi and offering armed resistance to the Boiotians and Lokrians. A year later the Sacred War was declared. It rapidly became apparent that the Phokians could expect no practical assistance from their sympathizers (most important Athens and Sparta, the political opponents of Thebes), so that they took for themselves a loan from the temple treasury and hired a large mercenary army.[5]

Military victory for the Phokians could not, however, in itself bring the Sacred War to an end. To do so, a new resolution had to be passed by the Amphiktyony, and because the Thessalians controlled half the votes, the key to a settlement clearly lay in Thessaly. But those Thessalians loyal to the league, the opponents of Pherai, had helped to carry the decision for war. The votes the Phokians needed could therefore only be obtained through a fundamental shift in power within Thessaly. Lykophron of Pherai saw here his chance of obtaining outside help and appealed to the Phokian leader Onomarchos, who saw in Pheraian dominance in Thessaly possibilities for ending the Sacred War to his own advantage. In 353 the Phokian mercenaries engaged the army of the league and their Macedonian allies in Thessaly, and Philip was beaten by Onomarchos, with heavy losses. Should political changes succeed the military victory, a very dangerous situation would develop for the Macedonians. Dominance of Pherai in Thessaly would mean the rule of forces hostile to Macedonia and thus have grave consequences for the security of Macedonia's southern frontier regions. Philip therefore marched out again against Onomarchos and Pherai in the following year. This time he did not make the mistake of underestimating his opponent. In a mighty battle on the Crocus Field the Macedonians and Thessalians, decked out with laurel crowns of Apollo, defeated the mercenary army of Onomarchos. Onomarchos' corpse was crucified for his blasphemy, and the Phokian soldiers who fell were punished as desecraters of the temple and their bodies were thrown into the sea.[6]

The role played by Philip as protagonist in the Sacred War is certainly an indication of the extent to which he had adopted the ideas and motives of his friends in the Thessalian League. He did not merely represent himself as a friend and ally but also, at least formally, identified himself with the ideological aims of the league. This novelty must have been well considered. The abolition of the tyrants of Pherai and the ending of the civil war in Thessaly (the Pheraians surrendered shortly after the battle, and the harbour town of Pagasai was taken by Philip after a short siege)[7] immediately raised the question of how the Thessalians could be neutralized or even made submissive to the future requirements of Macedonia. Without the threat posed by Pherai the Aleuadai would have had difficulty in maintaining permanently their claim to leadership in Larissa, as even in regard to Pherai not all members of the league were of the same opinion. Krannon and Pelinna, and perhaps Trikka and Pharkedon, appear to have defected to Onomarchos and the Pheraians.[8] Peace thus threatened to bring with it further uncertainties for Macedonia, but the proclaimed identification of Macedonian and Thessalian interests, first apparent on the Crocus Field, indicated the solution of the problem for Philip and the Aleuadai: Philip should be elected archon, leader for life, of the Thessalian League. The election appears to have taken place in summer 352.[9] The Aleuadai probably exerted pressure in favour of Philip on their friends within the league, but the impression made by the Macedonian victory in the Thessalian interest as well as the continuing presence of the victorious army in their country must have made an effective contribution to the election of Philip, king of Macedonia, to be archon of the Thessalian League.

Both rights and duties were associated with the appointment. The archon was traditionally commander of the league army. As a result he exercised responsibility for conscription and the federal finances and had even more direct power of disposal over the *perioikoi* of the league, whose tribute payments and conscription he controlled directly. In practice the extent to which these rights could be exercised depended on the current power of the archon, but he was always in a strong position straight after his election. As leader of the league he represented common interests, both internally and in foreign policy. Internally he had to concern himself with the promotion of peace among the notoriously and (particularly recently) deeply divided city-states of the league.[10] This last duty seemed specially created for the new archon, who as a Macedonian had only interested himself in Thessaly because of these troubles and uncertainties. The settlement of the conflicts between the league members indeed served Macedonian security in the south, and it is hardly surprising that at first Philip concerned himself mainly with this problem. Garrison troops moved into Pherai and Pagasai, and in Magnesia, also previously ruled by the Pheraians, several forts were built.[11] In other places he sought to reach settlements and establish friendships. A statement of the late writer Polyainos bears witness to his efforts. Polyainos refers to the entire span of Philip's relations with Thessaly, not just to this early period, but the principles of his policy can be clearly seen: he neither destroyed nor disarmed the defeated, nor did he raze their town walls; he concerned himself with the weak and weakened the strong; he was the friend of the common people (*demoi*) in the cities and encouraged their spokesmen.[12]

Philip's efforts to treat the Thessalians not as conquered people but as friends were made in the Macedonian interest. In contrast to the Chalkidike, for instance, there is no evidence of settlement by Macedonian settlers or resettlement by Thessalians. Instead the archon of the league took trouble over his friends and supporters in the cities, seeking to win influence, and where he had no traditional contacts or ties he created new ones by wooing the *demoi*, or lower classes. His love affair with a girl from Pherai, which resulted in a daughter—Thessalonike, or "Thessalian victory"—must certainly have helped him establish good relations with certain classes of the conquered town.[13]

Hence the rights and duties of the archon within Thessaly served in the long term the Macedonian state interest. This was not the case with the foreign-policy reason for Philip's election. At first this affair did not impinge on any vital traditional Macedonian concerns. The Sacred War had been begun without Macedonia, as Macedonia was not a member of the Amphiktyony, and would doubtless somehow have come to an end without Macedonian intervention. But not without Thessaly. On his election as archon Philip became automatically the leader of a region that controlled twelve of the twenty-four votes in the Amphiktyony. Should he wish to make his influence felt, he could reckon on controlling those votes, which had been crucial in the declaration of the Sacred War. The Sacred War therefore was in practice a continuing responsibility of the archon that in the end he could not avoid meeting. Philip had quickly grasped the significance of the war for the Thessalians, as is evidenced by his sending his soldiers into battle adorned with laurel wreaths and by his treating Onomarchos and his mercenaries as defilers of the temple. But he showed no deep and permanent interest in continuing the war against the Phokians. The most important thing for him was to secure his influence in Thessaly, though this depended on his not disappointing too greatly the hopes vested in him.

Had Philip advanced against Phokis immediately after the battle of the Crocus Field, he would almost certainly have been able to end the war in the interests of his allies within weeks, if not days. That he did not do so shows his order of priorities. Philip had only become involved in the Sacred War because Onomarchos supported the Pheraians. Diodoros specifically states that the "liberation" of Pherai and other actions in Thessaly were the immediate consequences of the battle.[14] Only when Philip became the archon of the Thessalian League did he undertake, duty bound, anything more against the Phokians, but even then he did not do much. The Phokians took advantage of the time gained to mobilize their allies—Spartans, Athenians and Achaians—and an Athenian contingent got into position at the right time at Thermopylae. When Philip heard of these preparations during his advance, he made no attempt to go farther. The Athenians celebrated their easy success as a victory over Macedonian imperialism, but Philip was probably content.[15] He showed no inclination in 352 to perceive Macedonian interests of any kind in central Greece, no inclination to embroil himself in the barren tangle of petty politics among the southern Greek states. Clear evidence of this disinclination is the fact that from 352 until 346 he undertook no military action whatever against the Phokians, although this neglect of his duty gave rise to great discontent among the Thessalians. One school of thought among historians asserts that Philip exploited this war to further his own imperialistic ambitions over the states of central Greece and that he had now won a toehold there to expand Macedonian dominion towards the south. Such an interpretation, however, takes into account neither the priorities of the Macedonian state at that time nor the instability of its rule in the areas immediately beyond its frontiers and merely adopts the later, prejudiced *interpretatio atheniensis* of Demosthenes. At Thermopylae in 352 Philip was representing in the main the interests not of Macedonia but of Thessaly.

Philip's election as archon marked the beginning of a formal, permanent relationship between the king of Macedonia and the Thessalian League since the archon was elected for life. It was not always easy for him to do justice to this double function, particularly as his Thessalian office was inevitably of secondary importance to him. Thessalian foreign affairs, above all the Sacred War, were at first badly neglected, and Philip's order of priorities emerges clearly from Macedonian military activities during the next years in Thrace and on the Chalkidike, in Illyria and in Epeiros. Already in 349 the Thessalians began to show signs of discontent. The Macedonians continued to occupy Pagasai, the former harbour town of the tyrants of Pherai, and also built some fortifications in Magnesia. Some of the Thessalians took exception to the treatment of this region almost as though it were a Macedonian possession. In addition, Philip was accused of appropriating Thessalian funds, apparently the federal share of the harbour and market dues of the member cities, for his own purposes.[16] On this account Philip may have been forced to intervene again in Pherai;[17] but it is unlikely that he did anything else until in 346, at a time convenient to himself, he was able to bring the Sacred War to a quick end without bloodshed. The mere threat posed by his army was by then sufficient to make the Phokians surrender. The Boiotian towns they had taken were returned to Thebes; the two votes in the Amphiktyonic Council that had been theirs for centuries were transferred to Philip personally; reparation payments were demanded from Phokis, and its settlement structure was altered. The Phokian allies, above all Athens, could do nothing but watch with gritted teeth when in autumn 346 Philip even presided over the Pythian Games. In the end he had done his duty splendidly as archon of the Thessalian League.[18]

Just as in foreign affairs Philip, as archon of Thessaly, was inclined to neglect even the most important matters and postpone them in favour of Macedonian concerns, his internal policy was rigidly trimmed to the requirements of Macedonia. The Perrhaibians, who bordered on Macedonia and had the status of *perioikoi*, were placed under the direct administration of one of Philip's new Thessalian friends, Agathokles, before 346.[19] Since something similar had been done with Magnesia in 352, this action meant, even if it was intended to be only for a few years, that the areas of Thessaly bordering on Macedonia were directly controlled by Macedonia. Polyainos reported that the increase in Philip's influence was due to his cultivation of friendships. Pharsalos is a good example. In 346 the harbour town Halos, traditionally dependent on Pharsalos, became refractory and even offered Philip resistance, in the hope of receiving help from Athens. Philip acted entirely in the interest of Pharsalos by laying siege to Halos and handing it back to Pharsalos.[20]

The promotion of Pharsalos probably went hand in hand with discord in Larissa, where Eudikos and Simos, who had been responsible for Philip's position in Thessaly, were dropped by him. Aristotle also refers to the downfall of the Aleuad government under Simos as an example of a divided oligarchy, and it is easy to assume that these events were connected with Philip's taking direct control of Perrhaibia through Agathokles, which had previously been controlled partly from Larissa, and with his supporting the *demoi*, as Polyainos says, against the aristocracy.[21] He appears to have experienced difficulties in Pherai again in about 344. Diodoros relates that "he banished the tyrants from the cities and won over the Thessalians by his benevolent actions." The events in Larissa might certainly be included among these actions, but in fact other sources indicate continuing discontent and the presence of Macedonian garrisons. In particular it is recorded that at some point the people of Pherai refused to serve in the army under Philip.[22] Even from this very fragmentary evidence a crisis in the relationship between the Thessalians and their Macedonian archon can be recognized, which appears to have reached its critical stage after the conclusion of the Sacred War. It is not difficult to see why this should have been so. Philip had been elected, under pressure from the Aleuad leadership in Larissa, at a time when his election seemed to offer the possibility of an early end to the war. Accordingly it must have been expected that on the conclusion of the war he would regard the archonship more as an honorary position and carry out his duties in the interests of his friends in Larissa. To their surprise they were forced to recognize that Philip perceived concrete advantages for Macedonia in his Thessalian office, particularly the possibility it offered of maintaining Thessaly as a peaceful buffer region on Macedonia's southern frontier, as his treatment of Pagasai, Magnesia and Perrhaibia shows. The question of the future relationship became much more urgent after 346 when it became clear that Philip had not the slightest intention of either relinquishing his advantages or leaving them unexploited. Grave differences of opinion arose at least in Pherai and Larissa, and these culminated in the occupation of Pherai and the overthrow of Simos in Larissa, events stylized by Diodoros' source as the banishment of tyrants.

In Polyainos' opinion the new men in power in the cities were no longer the old aristocratic families but people such as Agathokles, who owed everything to Philip. A shift in the balance of power also followed within the Thessalian League to the advantage of Pharsalos, who was to play a leading role in the league in subsequent years. Philip was not, however, content with the structure of the league of cities. Thessaly was traditionally divided into four main regions, or tetrarchies—Hestiaiotis, Pelasgiotis, Thessaliotis and Phthiotis—each of which provided a unit in the army of the league and for this purpose was led by a tetrarch, more recently called polemarch, or war leader. The tetrarchies functioned as a sort of intermediary organization between the league and the individual cities, and the polemarchs were elected annually. Philip appears to have altered the appointment procedures for the polemarchs. He reintroduced the old title of tetrarch, possibly extended its powers and himself appointed (probably as archon) the leaders of the tetrarchies.[23] It is unclear what concrete results were brought about by these changes. Philip's opponents berated him for having enslaved the Thessalians; but every measure of control was presented in this way in the undifferentiated rhetoric of the Athenian warmongers, even when basically directed against the power of the old Thessalian landed aristocracy, and the charge cannot be taken seriously. It is, however, certain that the internal political changes and organizational measures in Thessaly served above all the interests of Macedonia and that it was the new reliable friends of Macedonia in Thessaly who profited from the development. The reorganization of 344–342 enabled Philip to use the archonship more efficiently, even when he himself was not in the country, as he in effect created deputies for himself, although they were formally not envisaged, out of the traditional office of tetrarch. Two of the new tetrarchs, the Pharsalians Daochos and Thrasidaios, belonged to the group of Greek politicians whom Demosthenes, from his standpoint, regarded as traitors to the Greeks. They must therefore have served Philip loyally in the performance of their duties.[24]

The sources reveal little for Thessaly after 342. The chairman of the Amphiktyonic Council, Kottyphos of Pharsalos, and the other Thessalian members were instrumental in the assertion of Philip's interests in 339, when sacred war was again declared, this time against Amphissa. The war offered Philip the opportunity once more of taking an army into central Greece in the service of Apollo just when Athens had again declared war on Macedonia.[25] The Thessalian tetrarchs Daochos and Thrasidaios accompanied Philip's envoys on their unsuccessful attempt to dissuade Thebes from taking up arms as an ally of Athens,[26] and it can be assumed, though it is not explicitly attested, that a contingent of Thessalian cavalry was attached to the army of Philip that in August 338 at Chaironeia defeated the Athenians, the Thebans and their allies.

When Alexander set out for Asia Minor in 334, he took with him a contingent of eighteen hundred Thessalian cavalry, the only sizable Greek contingent.[27] His reliance on the Thessalian cavalry was based on the secure organization built up by Philip. The office of Thessalian archon passed without problems to Alexander on Philip's death.[28] In addition, Thessaly must have been a member of the Korinthian League founded by Philip in 338, an organization for guaranteeing the common peace that provided the formal framework for the planned campaign against the Persians. The number of votes carried by the member states may even have depended in some way on their military strength, and if so, the membership of Thessaly must have been correspondingly weighty.[29]

The Thessalian cavalry remained with Alexander all the time that he was fighting Dareios, and it took part in an exposed position in all the major battles. On the homefront relations between Macedonia and Thessaly also appear to have been untroubled during this period, even though Demosthenes in 330 claimed to have discovered elements of discontent.[30] In 330 the Thessalian participants in the expedition, together with the other contingents levied from the Korinthian League, were honourably discharged. However, when Alexander advanced even further east, neglecting his duties as Thessalian archon as well as the chain of personal relationships meticulously fostered by Philip, and when Antipatros, acting in his name, behaved in an increasingly authoritarian fashion, the Thessalians clearly felt the loss of their privileged position and therefore an increasing affinity to the southern Greeks. The result was that when in summer 323 the news arrived of Alexander's death in Babylon and many Greek cities under the leadership of the Athenian Leosthenes revolted against Macedonian rule, they were joined in the revolt by all the Thessalian cities with the exception of Pelinna. From the *perioikoi* the Achaians, with the exception of Phthiotic Thebes, also joined the insurrection. Indeed Thessaly contributed two thousand cavalrymen, who earned a large part of the credit for the initial successes of the Greeks against Antipatros in this so-called Lamian War.[31] On the death of Leosthenes in winter 323/22, Menon of Pharsalos, a member of the traditional ruling clan of the city, was appointed as one of the two commanders of the allied forces, and after the final defeat of the allies on Thessalian soil near Krannon in summer 322, each of the Thessalian cities had to be taken separately by Antipatros and Krateros.[32] Menon was able to escape to Aitolia, where the Aitolians continued their resistance successfully, even after the defeat at Krannon; in 320 he still exerted sufficient influence to raise Thessalian enthusiasm for a revolt in alliance with the Aitolians during the absence of Antipatros in Asia Minor. Thessaly became peaceful again only after his death in battle against Antipatros' deputy, Polyperchon.[33] These are the last independent Thessalian actions that we know of for more than a century.

The history of the relationship between Macedonia and Thessaly during the reigns of Philip II and Alexander III is the history of an attempt to influence and rule that gradually became more authoritarian. From the controlled partnership established by Philip in 352 and further formalized about ten years later, which in the country at large was either actively desired or freely accepted, evolved the direct exertion of power by the Macedonians after the Lamian War. The war itself and the fact that the majority of the Thessalians took part in the bitter resistance against Antipatros must have been the reason for the authoritarian treatment of the Thessalians after the war. But even more crucial were the attitudes that emanated from Macedonia and provoked the resistance in the first place, not only among the Thessalians, who on Alexander's death lost their institutional tie to Macedonia, which his Thessalian archonship had created. The king's many-year absence allowed his European deputy Antipatros a freedom of action that he was only capable of using in authoritarian fashion. Alexander himself had become acquainted in Asia with the authoritarian ruling methods of the Persians, and one consequence of his string of military successes was the conviction that it was unnecessary to show forbearance with opponents or inferiors when in a position of military strength. Alexander became increasingly intolerant and unwilling to differentiate even between Greeks and Asians. For the Thessalians this intolerance led to an erosion of their earlier privileged position among the Greeks, who found themselves treated more and more as though they were Asians. It can therefore scarcely have been a surprise when on the death of the archon, and with it the termination of their institutional ties to the Macedonian king, the Thessalians reacted in the same way as the other Greeks.

5. THE SOUTHERN GREEK STATES

When Philip II acceded to the throne of Macedonia the history of central and southern Greece had been characterized for more than 150 years by the imperial ambitions of one or the other of the three great powers of Greece. Sparta ruled in the Peloponnese, Thebes in Boiotia and central Greece, and Athens, thanks to its fleet, in the islands and coastal communities. These spheres of power were by no means exclusive to one another, and apart from short periods there was no recognition of the advantages to be obtained from a balance of power. After the Peloponnesian War a struggle for the general hegemony had taken place, first led by Sparta, then tentatively by Athens and finally by Thebes. This strife led only to a general weakening of all powers, even within their respective traditional areas of influence. Most strongly evident was the weakening of Sparta in the Peloponnese, where an independence movement supported by Thebes shattered a power structure that had existed for two hundred years. Xenophon, the contemporary historian, whose thinking remained set in the pattern of the conventional power structures, ended his history of the Greeks (*Hellenika*) after the battle of Mantineia in 362, in which both the Spartans and their Theban opponents suffered heavy losses, with the dejected conclusion that "there was even more uncertainty and confusion among the Greeks after the battle than there had been before it."[1]

This battle had practically put an end to Sparta as a great power. In the Peloponnese, however, in the newly independent states of Messenia and Arkadia, fear of Sparta's great past remained a dominant factor, and it was not at first fully credited that Sparta would never again be able to treat the Peloponnese as its own possession. But after the death of Epaminondas in the battle Thebes withdrew and restricted itself again to central Greece, and its friends in Thessaly and also in the Peloponnese had to make do without Theban help. The neighbours of Thebes, above all the Phokians, soon came to feel this intensive preoccupation with central Greece when they were driven into the Sacred War instigated by Thebes in 356. Only Athens remained largely immune to this loss of power, although it had participated in the battle as an ally of Sparta. Because the fleet had not been involved, the modest power base Athens had laboriously built up during the 380s remained for the time being unaffected. However, Athens had never been able to compete alone against Sparta and Thebes since its defeat in the Peloponnesian War, even though dreams of a restoration of former glory lent wings to the imagination of some of its politicians, and the fleet enabled it to maintain at all times the vital grain route from the Black Sea. But in actual fact the position as leading Greek power that Athens appeared to occupy after the battle of Mantineia was merely a symptom of the general military weakness of the three Greek states that until then had set the tone for the whole Aegean region.

The historical significance of the struggle with Athens in the extension of Macedonian dominion is greatly exaggerated in the majority of modern historical accounts. The reason is easily found: almost all the extant sources relating to the extension of Macedonian influence among the states of southern Greece are Athenian and consist for the most part of contemporary speeches by politicians rabidly opposed in principle to Philip, such as Demosthenes and his friends, or by more moderate politicians such as Aeschines. The main characteristic of these speeches, apart from their animosity towards Macedonia, is in the nature of things a concentration of attention on Athens because for the speakers before the Athenian Popular Assembly or an Athenian court of law, Athens inevitably constituted the hub of the world. Everything was interpreted from the Athenian standpoint, in particular according to each speaker's partisan view of current Athenian interests.

This attitude is especially crass in the case of Demosthenes, the chief warmonger of the late 340s, who does not even flinch from distorting, or perhaps even inventing, facts to imbue the Athenians with his own hatred of Philip. He denounces his opponents, whether in Athens or in other states, as traitors and as the paid puppets of the Macedonian king, and rigorously dismisses the possibility that there could be any honourable course of action other than the one he urges. Such is the nature of fanatical political speeches, and it makes them utterly unreliable as historical sources, at least insofar as they concern the motives of those viewed as opponents and possibly also in regard to cited "facts." The opinion of Polybios, however, who protested energetically against this condemnation of "the most distinguished of the Greeks" and in particular defended the Peloponnesians for having chosen Philip as the true protector of their states against Sparta, demonstrates that not everybody regarded those friendly to Philip as traitors to their country.[2] Polybios wrote two hundred years after the event, but there is no reason to doubt that his view reflects that of a large number of contemporaries. These were mainly citizens of the smaller states, who finally sensed the long-hoped-for possibility of freeing themselves from the dominion of the Athenians, Spartans and Thebans. Surely characteristic of these views is the statement of one such politician, Kleochares of

Chalkis, who declared in connection with the negotiations that led to the Peace of Philokrates between Philip and Athens in 346 that the small states feared the secret diplomacy of the great powers.[3]

The development of the relationship between the Macedonian state under Philip and Alexander and the cities of southern Greece thus presents a thorny field for the historian who is not content merely to accept the viewpoint of a Demosthenes. It is certain that at first there were no reasons affecting Macedonian security that would have justified aggressive measures on the part of the king south of Thessaly. Although Macedonia, like many other Greek states, had suffered in the past from the imperial ambitions of Athens, Sparta and, recently, Thebes, there is no sign of any retaliation beyond that necessary to achieve the territorial integrity of the Macedonian homelands and the security of the borders. All Philip's activity in the north, including the destruction of Olynthos and the incorporation of the Chalkidike within the Macedonian state, can be explained as exclusively serving Macedonian interests. These measures were not primarily directed against Athens, with whom a state of war theoretically existed since the taking of Potidaia in 357; neither was Philip's activity in Thrace, although the mere thought that he might gain a position from which to influence traffic through the Dardanelles and the Bosporos terrified the Athenians.

But events in Thessaly in particular convinced some Athenians that Philip harboured serious intentions against them. In the Sacred War the Athenians took the side of the Phokians, and when in 352 Philip, as newly appointed archon of Thessaly, sought to end the war in the interests of the Thessalians by a quick advance through Thermopylae, the Athenians promptly sent their troops to block the pass. On Philip's retreat the Athenians, convinced that Philip wished to wage a serious war against them, congratulated themselves on having won a victory. But nothing of the sort had happened. To the annoyance of his friends in Thessaly he placed no priority on the Sacred War; it was not until six years later that he again appeared as "sacred warrior" in Thessaly, by which time conditions had so changed that he was able to reorganize the affairs of the Amphiktyony without meeting any resistance, even though in the interim no Macedonian troops had been seen south of Thessaly. There could be no question of a deliberate attempt to gain power in Greece in that region.[4]

This attitude was a sharp contrast to that of the leading city-states. A constant element in the policies of the larger Greek cities was the unconcealed aspiration for influence, hegemony and dominion, even though many a smaller state willingly, according to the given circumstances, cast its lot with one or the other great power for protection against its enemies. It was the boundlessness of this desire to dominate, this wanting more (*pleonexia*) that had characterized Greek politics since the time of the Athenian Empire in the fifth century B.C., even though limits were set to its implementation. The novelty of the current situation was that clear possibilities remained unexploited and that the affairs of the Chalkidians, Thracians, Illyrians or the Molossians could seem more important than the concerns of the Delphic Apollo and all that was connected with it. The southern Greeks found it startling that the Macedonians should regard them as only of fringe importance. They considered Philip's attitude problematical and increasingly suspicious. Already in the 350s some politicians in the centres of power smelled a plot that they could not define exactly and began to conjure up nonexistent threats and create a climate of mistrust, in which all adverse events were blamed on Philip.[5]

In the smaller states, however, some of the more astute leaders saw a possibility emerging of protecting themselves, without much risk, against the old Greek great powers, whose claims to power had become burdensome. It was not new for a smaller state to rely on a distant great power to protect it in a struggle with a third party. One can assume that at least some politicians were impressed by the success of the Thessalian League against Pherai, and attempts were made from the late 350s on to interest Philip in the affairs of southern Greece.[6] In spring 346 envoys "from almost the whole Greek world" assembled in Pella.[7] Their ears were pricked for news of the peace negotiations with Athens, and the small states aired their fear that the great powers might come to secret agreements over their heads. This massive diplomatic descent on Pella does, however, lead to the presumption that the small states also expected something more from Philip than a settlement of the disputes among the great powers. Each state acted separately in its own interests and hoped for, or expected, sympathy from Philip. Thus by the year 346—whether it wanted it or not, whether on its own initiative or not—Macedonia had become at least diplomatically an important factor in the considerations of the southern Greeks, particularly in those of the smaller states.

The question is idle whether in this situation it would have been possible to avoid an increase in influence and therefore in responsibility, which inevitably must culminate in claims for hegemony such as the Greeks expected. A state run by calculating civil servants or a functioning democracy might have been able to show petitioners the door, but the Macedonian monarchy was too strongly conditioned by the personality of the king to be able to calculate coldly all the time, and Philip clearly enjoyed having his court suddenly transformed into a hub of the Greek world. He liked to be courted and enjoyed consorting with the versatile men from the south. He welcomed his guests with lavish presents and gave everyone the impression that he was ready to be a friend and perhaps an ally. In the political sphere—hard to distinguish from the personal one in such a state, where the two are interdependent—he wanted to be accepted as a partner by the existing major powers and gain recognition for his own Macedonian sphere of power, which in any case impinged only in a few places on that of Athens and in even fewer on that of Thebes.

However, Philip had not reckoned with the expansionist dreams of certain Athenian politicians. These developed disastrously and resulted in such a hardening of the fronts that in the end the Greeks were made subjects, instead of partners, of the Macedonians. It was this development that determined the future pattern of the interests of the Macedonian state in the south, a pattern that could have been quite different. In the first years of his disagreements with Athens Philip did little more than destroy hopes and expose dreams as illusions. Methone, Pydna and Potidaia had been acquired by Athens only shortly before Philip took them; Amphipolis had not been Athenian since 424; and Olynthos only allied itself to Athens when a struggle with Philip appeared unavoidable. Although Philip had indeed prevented the reestablishment of an area ruled by the Athenians on the frontiers of Macedonia, it is in any case dubious that Athens could have held on there indefinitely without the intervention of Philip.

Nevertheless, the Athenians considered themselves to have been gravely injured, and much reluctance had to be overcome before they were prepared to consider seriously Philip's offer of peace negotiations, an offer first made in 348.[8] The treaty, the Peace of Philokrates, was not finally accepted by both sides and the oaths sworn until early summer 346. It was based on mutual recognition of the current possessions of each party, and an alliance was also concluded.[9] The agreement came about under the tacit threat of Philip's military preparations for bringing the Sacred War to an end, and it seems clear that Philip, had he wanted to, could have won more far-reaching concessions. But he was satisfied with the form agreed—mutual recognition and a contractual partnership—which also left Athens with what remained of the confederacy. By this means Philip had fulfilled his aims with respect to Athens.

On the formal level Philip had brought his relationships with the most important of the southern Greek states into a certain order in 346. Athens was bound to partnership by the peace treaty. As a result of the Sacred War, which had been concluded without bloodshed, Philip now had the majority of votes in the Amphiktyonic Council at his disposal and so proclaimed his permanent interest in the Delphic sanctuary. However, all this had not happened wholly voluntarily nor without considerable misgivings on the Greek side. The Boiotians, under the leadership of Thebes, had instigated the Sacred War because they thought they could establish their power in central Greece at the cost of the Phokians. In the end they had gained nothing except the recovery of what they had lost in the war, and they now knew for certain that they would never again be able to manipulate the Amphiktyonic Council to their own ends, as they had done in the recent past. In addition, Nikaia, which controlled the pass of Thermopylae, had been assigned to the Thessalians. Never again would the Boiotians be able as a last resort to use the pass for military purposes as a quick route into southern Thessaly, and pessimists would doubtless remark that the possibility had now been lost of blocking the pass to Philip.

The Athenians were also loath to show their new partner the respect due him. Neither against Athens nor against Sparta was action taken to punish them for their support of the sacrilegious

Phokians, and this leniency must have been Philip's wish. Nevertheless, the Athenians only reluctantly recognized Philip's voting rights in the Amphiktyonic Council and sent no delegates to the Pythian festival at which the victory was celebrated. Formally all was peace and partnership, but the mutual trust that would have brought the partnership to life was denied Philip. The major Greek powers, each in its own way, refused to recognize fully the formal partnership. They simply could not believe that the Macedonian king would be content with such recognition and that he would not take full advantage of his military superiority, as they themselves would have done in his place. For the Greeks, it was a catastrophic miscalculation, which in the end brought about the very situation they had feared at the beginning and so seemed subsequently to justify their suspicious misconception.

During the following years, until 340, the Macedonians undertook nothing that might have jeopardized the agreements. In the northeast, the northwest and Thessaly Philip conquered and ruled in the interests of Macedonia. In Greece, south of Thessaly, he dutifully participated through delegates in the regular meetings of the Amphiktyonic Council and developed extensive diplomatic activity in reaction to the requests and demands of different Greek states and their politicians, but he gave no indication that he was in any way dissatisfied with the status quo established in 346. It would certainly be naive to assume that this diplomatic activity did not increase the standing and influence of Macedonia among the Greeks and not to recognize that with the assumption of the Phokian rights in the Amphiktyony by a major power a new, irreversible phase in Greek politics had been inaugurated. The petitioners from minor states, who had formerly made their requests to Athens, Sparta or Thebes, now had the comfortable possibility of turning to Macedonia. To do so it was not even necessary to go first to Pella, as initial contacts could be made through Philip's representatives in the Amphiktyonic Council. A typical case was that of Kallias from Chalkis in Euboia, whose political aim was to found a league of the Euboian cities that the other towns on the island were reluctant to accept. He turned first to Philip for help and received personal friendship but not the necessary active support that he had hoped for, and then to Thebes, which was also deaf to his wishes. Only then did he

approach Athens, where he finally received the support of Demosthenes.[10]

Not all received a refusal from Philip. In the Peloponnese, for
example, the new states Messenia and Arkadia, recently founded
under Theban auspices, as well as others, feared that after the
withdrawal of the Thebans the Spartans would revive their claims
to power. In this case the small states were given a sympathetic
hearing in Macedonia but received at first only diplomatic help.[11]
The temptation to interest the friendly new member of the Amphiktyony in local affairs in which it was felt that the traditional
powers were not to be trusted was understandably great, and
many minor powers were glad of the new possibility. The gulf in
interests between small state and major power becomes apparent
in such cases, and there was correspondingly little response to
the attempt by some Athenian politicians to form an alliance
against Philip in the south. The proposed opponent seemed to
many to be more friendly and trustworthy than Athens itself.
Even after almost two hundred years of Macedonian rule Polybios
felt able to defend those leading men in the small states who had
seen the salvation of their countries in an alignment with Macedonia against the vituperations of Demosthenes, who accused all
who did not agree with him of being traitors.[12] The interests of
all the Greeks were simply not identical with the opinions of the
power-hungry Athenians. More attention should have been paid
to Polybios' protest.

The history of Greece, as far as it is known for the six years
following the Peace of Philokrates, is necessarily dominated by
Athens because all the surviving sources come from it or are influenced by it; and Athenian history is dominated by the campaign of the political faction led by Demosthenes to gain influence
and establish a policy hostile to Macedonia. It is not possible to
reconstruct all the phases of the development. The surviving
speeches of Demosthenes give only momentary insights but still
transmit a picture of provocative rejections of offers to negotiate,
of baseless accusations, of the twisting of facts, and of a fomented
hatred that could only be stilled, if at all, by a call to arms. Hatred
became the hallmark of Athenian politics, as the group led by
Demosthenes gained in influence and finally was able to persuade
the majority in the Popular Assembly to adopt Demosthenes' ver-

dict on Philip. The details of this internal Athenian development
have been related often enough and do not belong in a history
of Macedonia.[13] It is important to note that the rapid gain in influence of Demosthenes' faction quickly destroyed all hopes that
Philip had associated with the Peace of Philokrates. It soon became evident that nothing would come of the sought-after partnership with mutually recognized interests. The Athenians could
not rest content with the peace treaty. Demosthenes and his com-
rades stirred up the disappointment and dissatisfaction that had
dominated Athens since it had formally relinquished its traditional
claims in the north and practically surrendered the Phokians.
These people did not really want improved peace terms. In 344
Philip tried to counter the increasingly adverse mood in Athens
and encourage the supporters of the peace by asking for sugges-
tions for its improvement. In response Hegesippos, the friend of
Demosthenes, arranged for a resolution of the Popular Assembly
in which the Athenians demanded that Philip hand over Amphipolis and other places in the north to Athens. This demand for
revision of one of the main clauses of the peace treaty amounted
in practice to torpedoing the negotiations. Philip did not, however, give up immediately, because there were indeed in Athens
supporters of the peace who might still gain in influence; hope
flared in 343 when Aeschines was exonerated, though only just,
of Demosthenes' accusations that he had deceived and betrayed
his country by his part in the delegation that had negotiated the
peace, although Philokrates himself had earlier been condemned
to death. Still another offer to negotiate was risked, but it also,
in 343, was attacked by Hegesippos in a speech so loaded with
hatred that the negotiations had to be abandoned as hopeless.[14]

It is hard to make sense of this warmongering. Desire for revenge cannot always be explained in rational terms and does not
necessarily depend on prospects of success. The decisive motives
are of another kind, grounded in injured self-esteem in a manner
that often leaves the historian unable to do more than make a
guess. Demosthenes and his friends poked at the open wounds
of the injured pride of the Athenian people; and the lost glory
and power of the past, monuments to which in Athens kept mem-
ories alive, were much more influential than any of the prosaic
visions of the future that realistic supporters of the peace could

forecast from friendly cooperation with Macedonia. These people, however, seem to have lacked the political imagination that might have created a more positive attitude towards future cooperation and coexistence with Macedonia. The warmongers gained the initiative at the time of the Phokian defeat in 346 and retained it, apart from some brief moments, until the catastrophe.

Athens was militarily in a weak position for a war against Macedonia. Even had the Popular Assembly been prepared to allow the necessary, enormous budget for wages, its great fleet would not have been able to accomplish anything decisive against the Macedonian land forces. For this reason the orators confined themselves initially to attempts to poison the political climate not only in Athens but also in all other states where they thought they saw possibilities. These were not many—only the states of the rump Athenian confederacy and Euboia, where the Athenians had assisted Kallias in founding his new league of cities. Most of the states of the Peloponnese preferred to put themselves under the protection of distant Macedonia rather than nearby Athens. In the north, Athenian settlers (*klerouchoi*) were firmly in position on the Chersonnese; Lemnos and Imbros belonged to Athens, and Thasos remained faithful to the Athenians. These positions on the grain route from the Black Sea were the only areas remaining subject to Athens abroad, but even there the Athenians were reluctant to invest militarily. In 342 an adventurer named Diopeithes was sent as a mercenary leader with new settlers to the Chersonnese but was not given adequate financial backing. Diopeithes knew how to help himself and conducted plundering forays into neighbouring Thrace, which in the meantime belonged to Philip, and thereby earned in Athens solid support, first from Demosthenes and then from the Athenian people.[15]

This and a number of other grievances were listed by Philip in 340 in a form of bill of indictment against Athens. This document is clear proof that Philip had abandoned hope that the Athenians might adopt a more cooperative attitude.[16] It was not in itself a declaration of war, but it closed with a threat: "I shall defend myself against you with justice on my side, and I call the gods to witness that I shall bring my dispute with you to a decision."[17] His previous tolerant consideration for exaggerated Athenian sensibilities was now abandoned. The Athenians were to be made aware, as coming events show, of the concrete advantages they had enjoyed under the peace settlement, which were now being lost because of the attitude of the war party.

Philip was occupied with the first phase of the siege of Perinthos when he dispatched his note to Athens. The Athenians did not involve themselves directly in the defence of the town, but their allies, the Byzantines and the Persians, with whom Athens had recently opened negotiations that were continuing, came to the aid of the Perinthians.[18] When a few weeks later Philip began to lay siege to Byzantion as well, he found a perfect opportunity to demonstrate to the Athenians the seriousness of their position. On account of the tense situation the Athenian grain ships were to be escorted through the straits in convoy by a naval contingent commanded by Chares. While the loaded ships were assembling at Hieron, near the mouth of the Bosporos, they were attacked by the Macedonians, and all 230 ships were captured.[19] This action took place without a declaration of war and must have been meant as a warning shot across the bows of the Athenian war party, as a serious indication that even the large war fleet would not be able to guarantee the grain supplies to the city, should Philip make war against Athens. But even this last attempt to demonstrate to the Athenians how futile were the policies of the war party failed completely in its object. The Athenian answer was plain. The reaction was one of neither despondency nor reconsideration but fury, and the warmongers seized this favourable opportunity to declare that the peace was at an end.[20]

This decision marked the beginning of a new phase in the relationship between Macedonia and the southern Greeks. The attempt to establish partnerships with the major powers by demonstrating tolerance and moderation had failed. This failure was most apparent in Athens, but discontent was also in the air in Thebes, where the Thebans still could not come to terms with the fact that Philip's voice now dominated in the Amphiktyony. In 339 leading hotheads took the action of despair: they ejected the small garrison Philip had left occupying Nikaia and took over the little town, which controlled the pass of Thermopylae, from the Thessalians.[21] The distinction, until now strictly adhered to because of differing Macedonian needs, between Philip's treatment of the classical cities of the south—with which he kept in contact, even though with difficulty, simply through diplomatic means—and the entire north, including Thessaly, where from the beginning force of arms had been decisive, now had to be abandoned. The Athenians, and in the end also the Thebans, by refusing to acknowledge that this distinction existed, had lost their big chance of gaining influence over Philip and working towards a treatment of the Greek cities of the north different from that meted out to the Thracians and Illyrians. But their narrow-minded politicians could think solely in terms of their traditional claims to power and thus saw in Macedonia merely a competitor instead of a new political dimension.

On account of his position in the Amphiktyony and his only recently reestablished dominion in Thrace Philip could not afford simply to ignore the war preparations in central Greece. When even the astute businessmen of Athens either failed to recognize or chose to ignore the futility of a war, it was impossible to predict how many other states would suffer the same delusion. Philip can certainly never have had doubts as to his military superiority. The tragedy lay in the fact that even after a victory he would have lost his best chance of ever being accepted during his lifetime by the leaders of political opinion among the southern Greeks. In 346 he had won wars without even having to fight a battle, but despite these victories he had already then lost the peace. This time the silk gloves had to be pulled off. The use of military force against Athens and Thebes inevitably brought with it a certain political assimilation of those Greek communities in the north that were already ruled directly by the Macedonians; the result of a war engineered in this way would have to be a much more severe attitude than that of 346. Even had Philip thought differently, his advisers could hardly have agreed to further special treatment of any kind for Athens and Thebes. The mere fact of the war's taking place would inevitably expand and increase the complexity of the area ruled by the Macedonian state.

Philip was slow in reacting to the new situation in southern Greece. Not until late autumn 339, after his campaign against the Danube Skythians, did he take an army into central Greece, and then it was as the authorized representative of the Amphiktyony. His main task had nothing to do with Athens and Thebes but with misdemeanours committed by the Lokrian town Amphissa

against the interests of the Delphic Apollo. Philip brought the
Macedonian army first to Elateia in Phokis, skilfully avoiding
Thermopylae and the Theban garrison in Nikaia so as not to provoke an immediate engagement with Thebes; but the Athenians
were misled by Demosthenes into immediately interpreting this
as an action against themselves and rapidly opened a successful
diplomatic offensive to win over their old enemies, the Thebans,
as allies. Straight afterwards military units from Athens and
Thebes occupied the passes from Elateia to Amphissa and in the
direction of Boiotia. Philip attempted to negotiate with both
Thebes and Athens,[22] but his diplomacy could achieve nothing
against the doctrinaire convictions of his opponents. Even the
successful conclusion of the Amphiktyonic dispute with Amphissa
that made necessary the withdrawal of the Greek forces to positions near Chaironeia could not break the will of the majority in
the two cities.[23]

By August 338 Philip had irrevocably abandoned his hopes of
a peaceful solution to the conflict and taken up a position opposite
the Greeks near Chaironeia. The majority of the Greek force of
about thirty thousand men were Athenians and Boiotians, but
they also included some allies and clients: Korinthians and Achaians from the Peloponnese; Euboians and representatives of the
Athenian Confederacy from the islands; and some Phokians, Me-
garians and a few Akarnanians from central Greece. The Macedonians and their allied forces were probably numerically about
equally matched, but the battle-hardened Macedonians finally
gained the upper hand in the engagement. By the evening one
thousand Athenian citizens had fallen, and two thousand had
been taken prisoner; losses of the other contingents must have
been in proportion. The unnecessary war was over.[24]

The victory gave encouragement to those Macedonians who
favoured a uniform treatment of the conquered, on the Thracian
pattern. Philip as well, after the failure of his diplomatic efforts,
did not reject such considerations. The victory allowed the possibility of a more rigorous course of action, of lending the idea of
partnership a more concrete form through a rudimentary organizational structure and an explicit common aim. The Greek defeat,
after all, gave grounds for hope that it might enable moderate
forces in the cities to take the helm. Within the framework of a

general peace treaty it would be possible to support these forces more than before. However, the creation of a general organization to rule Greece, as in Thessaly, was not considered. The southern Greeks were still not important enough to the Macedonians to justify such an effort. Now as ever the aim was that the Greek cities should be solely responsible for their own affairs, but that the Macedonian interest should receive more consideration and respect than in the past. This objective would most readily be reached if common interests could be found and promoted, if active cooperation could be achieved and if a state of mutual dependence could be evolved. Experience since 346 showed that such wishes would not be fulfilled on their own without Macedonian help. And even then, in the light of the irrational success of Demosthenes and his followers, scepticism was justified as to whether it would prove feasible to exclude so effectively those committed to torpedoing all attempts at cooperation that a voluntary rapprochement could take place.

It was important above all to assist supporters and win new friends. Again Philip concentrated mainly on Athens. As the most highly populous Greek state, the most important trading centre of the Aegean and still theoretically the largest naval power, Athens remained, even after Chaironeia, the target of Macedonian diplomatic efforts. There was no getting past Athens: there the attempt had to be made to support friends and help people such as Aeschines, Phokion and Demades gain influence. This goal could not be achieved by setting hard conditions but perhaps by acts of generosity that could be presented as gestures of conciliation. Philip was not, however, prepared to tolerate a continuation of the Athenian confederacy nor, it seems, the possessions on the Chersonnese, which in any case could not be held should Macedonia seriously want to take them.[25] But Athens received, at the cost of the Boiotians, the frontier town of Oropos with its important sanctuary of the hero Amphiaraios; it was allowed to retain the islands of Imbros, Lemnos, Skyros and Samos; in addition, those Athenians taken prisoner were returned without payment of the usual ransom. And that was all.[26] Philip's friends were able to profit. It was largely because of Demades that such an advantageous treaty had been negotiated, but the extremists were not punished other than by having to witness the failure of

their policies. Demosthenes was even elected to deliver the funeral oration for the fallen (whom he should have had on his
conscience), and political refugees from other states were given
asylum.[27] The defeat was generally considered to be an honourable one, but those responsible, the warmongers, for the time
being played no important, active role in the political arena. The
people now listened to the moderate realists, to men such as Ly-
kurgos, Demades and Phokion, who did not necessarily care for
Macedonia, but considered Athenian interests to be best guaranteed through cautious cooperation. With this attitude Philip
had to be content; he could hardly expect to meet with enthusiasm in Athens and did not personally visit the city.

Enthusiasm did not await him in Thebes either, although the
possibilities of effective interference there were greater than in
Athens. Thebes was the capital city of the Boiotian League, which
was ruled "democratically," that is, through a popular assembly.
Because the meetings of this assembly took place in Thebes, it
was in practice the population of Thebes itself that exercised decisive influence within the league. In the course of achieving this
position of preeminence in Boiotia the Thebans had razed or severely treated three cities—Plataiai, Thespiai and Orchomenos—
and had thus intimidated the others. The Thebans were by no
means loved in Boiotia—still less since the catastrophe at Chaironeia—so that a hard line taken with Thebes was wholly com-
patible with an attempt to win friends and acquire influence in
Boiotia. Three measures much reduced the Theban freedom of
political manoeuvre. First, Plataiai, Thespiai and Orchomenos
were to be rebuilt with Macedonian support. Second, the men of
means in the other Boiotian cities were to be given more opportunities to exert influence in the league by transferring the general
meetings of the assembly to the village sanctuary of Onchestos,
setting up a council with three hundred members, which consisted at least in part of returned exiles, and fining or exiling leading Thebans. Finally, a Macedonian garrison occupied the Theban acropolis, the Kadmeia.[28] Thus an expansion of direct
Macedonian involvement took place in Boiotia. Macedonia was
the protecting power of the reorganized league against the claims
of Thebes, just as it had been previously in Thessaly against the
claims of Pherai.

The third of the three former great powers of Greece, Sparta, had not participated in the disaster of Chaironeia. Nevertheless, already in the 340s some Peloponnesian politicians, at least in Arkadia and Messene, had built up hopes that Macedonia would take over the role in the Peloponnese of protector against Sparta. In the first phase of development of his policies towards the southern Greeks Philip had, in fact, given them diplomatic support. Now his friends there urged him to march with an army into the Peloponnese so that they could finally realize their territorial claims against Sparta. Without undervaluing the importance of the major powers, Philip was aware that he could gain much influence in the smaller states, which might serve to neutralize the effectiveness of the great powers. He therefore followed the request of the small states and detached a number of disputed territories from Spartan control.[29]

The core of Macedonian policy thus remained, even after Chaironeia, the preferment of political friends, a policy well in accord with the personality of a king who also in his private life laid great value on his friendships. However, the limit to his interest is clear. From the conquered territories in the north, including Thessaly, he had regularly taken a wife from the local aristocracy to strengthen the bond to Macedonia, but he entered into no such alliance with a woman from any of the states of southern Greece. He had no ambition there for direct, personal rule. Nevertheless, his experiences with the cities of Thessaly had taught him how advantageous a state organization operating above city level could be. First he had let himself be appointed archon; then came the revival of the tetrarchies, whose leaders he himself designated virtually as his deputies. It was also advantageous to be able to deploy Thessalian troops, and even beyond the area of purely military cooperation the common campaigns and shared victories strengthened the bonds between the two states.

No such organization existed in the other parts of Greece. Regional leagues, such as in Boiotia, in the Peloponnese and in the Aegean did indeed exist, but they were not much more than organizations for implementing Theban, Spartan or Athenian rule. No external power could build on them. Ever since the so-called King's Peace almost fifty years before, the Greeks had played about with the concept of a common peace (*koine eirene*). A characteristic of the peace treaty of 387/86 was that the king of Persia was its guarantor, although in practice he delegated the interpretation and implementation of the terms of the peace outside Asia Minor to Sparta.[30] The paradox, which ever since then many Greeks had been unable to accept, was that whereas on the one hand the "freedom and autonomy" of the Greek cities had been agreed, on the other hand the Greek cities of Asia Minor were recognized as belonging to the Persian king.

Although the interpretation of the autonomy clause was disputed, a guarantee clause that all participants could or should take action against infringers of the treaty was considered essential in all peace settlements ending subsequent wars in which more than two states were substantially involved. Philip had already met this flexible, readily expandable concept of a common peace during his negotiations with Athens in 346, when some Athenians wanted to incorporate such a special escape clause for the Phokians—one that would allow, within a period of three months, any state to join in the peace. Although he rejected this clause because his friends in Thessaly would never have accepted such a sellout of Amphiktyonic interests, he later toyed with the idea again during the negotiations for an improvement to the treaty, but this time the Athenians were reluctant.

The concept had now become very attractive to Philip, and because of the victory at Chaironeia it could now be implemented. Just such a common peace, to which every state was bound, might provide precisely that favourable foundation he sought for a future relationship between Macedonia and the southern Greeks. The guarantee clause usual in such treaties was exactly what Philip needed to justify in advance possible interventions in the interests of the peace or of his naturally peace-loving friends in the cities. In addition, the function of the guarantor could be expanded in the manner of the Thessalian League. Artaxerxes in 387/86 had exercised his guarantor function only by issuing threats and had delegated its practical implementation to Sparta. Nevertheless, the formal recognition of Macedonia as guarantor power would in principle be nothing new. The innovation was that Philip aspired to a formal framework for a relationship that had previously not been expressed in legally binding form.

A further consideration had much more import for the future than the creation of the Common Peace with Philip as *hegemon*, or leader, which was agreed at Korinth in 337 and so gave rise to the modern name Korinthian League. The selection of the active title hegemon shows the direction of Philip's long-term thinking. Although his main aim was the development of common Greek objectives, his experience with Thebes and Athens since 346 had taught him that a passive aim such as merely the keeping of the peace, however important it might be, was not likely in the long term to be sufficient to banish all causes of discontent. Only one active, common objective sprang to mind that offered such hopes—a war of revenge against the Persians, who still counted the Greek states of Asia Minor as part of their empire. Philip does not appear to have held any long-cherished plans for an involvement in Asia Minor. As in mainland Greece, local rulers and others in Asia Minor had had contact with him from time to time—Hermeias of Atarneus, the friend of Aristotle, for instance, or Pixodaros, the satrap of the Persian province Karia, who had even aspired to a marriage alliance. However, the Persians seem to have taken no action against Philip until the siege of Perinthos, a time when Demosthenes also was tempted to try to obtain money from Persia for use against Philip, just as in the 390s Athens had accepted Persian assistance against Sparta.[31]

By contrast, Athenian intellectuals, above all the rhetoric teacher Isokrates, had for more than half a century argued in favour of a campaign against the Persians. Isokrates felt strongly that this was the only way to unite the Greeks, and a predecessor of Philip as Thessalian archon, the *tagos* Jason of Pherai, seems to have toyed with the idea of taking up arms against the Persians.[32] Isokrates had indeed sent Philip a pamphlet in 346, the *Philippos*, in which he outlined his pet project, but at that time he aroused no concrete interest. Macedonian interest in the plan seems first to have been awakened during the war against Athens and Thebes, perhaps because of the contacts made with the Persians by the Athenian opponents of Macedonia. Not until after Chaironeia, in conjunction with the Common Peace, does an advance into Asia Minor seem to have become a fixed project. The reasons for this must have been far more numerous and varied than we can establish today. It does, however, seem probable that Philip would never have planned an Asia Minor campaign if the war against Athens and Thebes had not taken place. The resulting search for an active common aim for the Greek participants in the

Common Peace, which would help to accustom them to the idea of a partnership with the Macedonian great power, such as the Thessalians had already experienced, and ameliorate the pangs of defeat, was probably the decisive factor. The campaign was therefore to be basically a concrete expression of renunciation of the recent past, when the opponents of Macedonia had made a pact with their old enemy. To Philip's friends in the cities this undertaking would be reputable and would potentially bring renown. Enough booty would certainly be made to more than cover the costs of the campaign to Macedonia, and Philip must also have been stimulated by the idea of presenting himself as the avenger of the destroyed Greek temples, as hegemon of a Greek crusade and defender of the Common Peace, also in Asia Minor. Perhaps in this way he might be able to persuade the Greeks finally to accept Macedonia as their leader and as promoter of their interests.

It is idle to speculate whether the undertaking would have met with success had Philip not fallen victim in 336 to the personally motivated assassination attempt of Pausanias. Until then he had only set up the administrative apparatus to carry the organization for the "aggressive Common Peace."[33] A council, the Synedrion, had been established in which all participants in the peace—apparently all the Greek states except Sparta—were represented. Apart from the initial constituent meeting in Korinth, which was perhaps followed by a second to endorse the Persian campaign, the council was only reconvened at the time of the Panhellenic Games, as it had no other functions. The active guaranteeing of the peace was in practice the duty of the hegemon or his regional deputies, "those appointed for the common security," whose function resembled that of the Thessalian tetrarchs. As far as the exact conditions are known, the Greek states committed themselves to guaranteeing independence, external and internal, and freedom from tribute payment for all participating states and the inviolability of shipping and harbours. Changes of property rights and of the constitution and internal political structures of member states were forbidden under the threat of intervention by the league authorities. The same conditions were explicitly applied to Macedonia, which may not have been a formal member of the treaty organization. The hegemon was to organize any joint operations of the treaty members, including the campaign against Persia.[34]

As the creator of this organization—whoever may have advised him; with friends owing a debt of loyalty to him personally in power in the individual cities; and with a joint campaign, effective as propaganda, being planned—it is possible that Philip would have been able to convince many Greeks that Macedonian power constituted in itself a negligible threat to the Greek interests and way of life. There would certainly always be some people, the *laudatores temporis acti*, who would refuse to recognize the new power. But the prospects were perhaps not unfavourable that a certain consensus might be found that could provide a basis for long-term friendly coexistence.

The death of Philip before the joint campaign had even begun, when only a Macedonian vanguard had been dispatched and before the newly organized peace had had time to prove its value, had a catastrophic effect on the relationship with the Greeks. Philip, who had demonstrated a certain sensitivity and tact in his dealings with them, was replaced by his action-thirsty son Alexander, who from the beginning was much less ready to respect Greek sensibilities. Barely twenty years old, he was by nature impatient, and moreover his first priority was to set himself over the Macedonian aristocracy. It can easily be imagined that many Macedonians privately took the view that Philip had displayed far too much patience with the Greeks. From the beginning, therefore, a much harsher attitude towards them seemed for several reasons to be appropriate, and the leading Greek states did nothing to make milder treatment seem desirable—quite the contrary. Barely two years had passed between Chaironeia and Philip's death. The southern Greeks were certainly not the only ones to underestimate Alexander and ascribe too much significance to Philip's person, highly important though it had been, so that their lack of awareness of the solidity of the state structure he had set up led them astray. Their reaction only strengthened the position of the hawks in Pella. In Athens Demosthenes soon regained influence. He persuaded the Athenians to hold a festival thanking the gods for the death of Philip and decorate his murderer, Pausanias, with a wreath of honour.[35] The Thebans started making efforts to dislodge the Macedonian garrison from the Kadmeia, an undertaking that, if successful, would have meant renewing the war that had just come to an end. In Thebes as well as Athens the extremists had immediately come into power again; the time had simply been too short to create a pro-Macedonian consensus. The wounds of the recent past were still tender, and previous hopes were reawakened. In other states too the friends of Macedonia experienced difficulties from their internal opponents.[36]

But not for long. Already in 336 Alexander marched south. He had himself recognized in Thessaly as Philip's successor in the archonship; at Thermopylae the Amphiktyons recognized him as the legitimate successor to Philip in the Amphiktyonic Council; and in Korinth the hastily summoned delegates confirmed his hegemony in respect to the Common Peace and the Persian campaign. Along the way he had intimidated the Thebans and received envoys from Athens, who apologized for their embarrassingly late congratulations on his succession. He treated everyone with friendliness but also with the self-confident decisiveness his loyal Macedonian army made possible. He immediately gave the impression of someone not to fool with.[37]

The following summer he confirmed this impression in the most ruthless fashion. An unconfirmed rumour that Alexander was dead led the Thebans, now additionally goaded on by their exiles and Athenian extremists, to try to realize their project of the previous year of driving the Macedonian garrison out of the Kadmeia. It turned out to be not so easy to do, and while the siege of the citadel was still in progress, the Macedonian army under the leadership of an alive and extremely indignant Alexander appeared at the gates of Thebes. Whereas Philip might still have seen in Thebes the noble, venerable and onetime leading city of Greece in which he had spent three years of his youth and still have been prepared to negotiate, Alexander allowed no doubts of the fact that he was not prepared to tolerate such fickle friends. After savage fighting, in which the Macedonians were supported above all by the Phokians and the old Boiotian enemies of Thebes—Plataiai, Thespiai and Orchomenos, which Philip had recently restored—the total destruction of the ancient city followed. Those of the population who had not fallen or been able to escape were sold in the slave markets.[38] Athens also was made to feel the altered attitude of the Macedonians, and it was only

through exerting his personal influence to the maximum that Demades succeeded in persuading Alexander to drop his demand
that some politicians, named by him as his opponents, should be
extradited.[39]

The destruction of Thebes is evidence of more than a mere
alteration in the climate of the relationship between Macedonia
and the southern Greeks. It divulges an entirely different policy
and attitude towards the Greeks that basically ascribed to them a
much greater significance for Macedonia than had been the case
under Philip. An increase in importance implied a tendency at
least towards more control. In comparison, the destruction of cities by Philip occurred only in territories where he wished to exercise direct rule, at Methone and on the Chalkidike. Whereas
Philip put the Greeks under pressure but still, even after Chaironeia, sought to establish partnerlike relationships, a wish that
contributed to the shaping of the Common Peace, Alexander's
tendency to treat the southern Greeks as subjects, who had to
give way to Macedonian interests as represented by him, is immediately apparent. A certain accommodation to the other regions
dominated by Macedonia, where in the last resort no inhibitions
were felt about using force, is clearly recognizable. The blow
against Thebes was an awful example to the other states. If necessary, Macedonia was now ready to use force, even in southern
Greece, to assert rapidly what it saw as its own interests. Given
this attitude, the apparatus of the Common Peace could of course
readily be used as an instrument of power. Alexander seems to
have interpreted his position as hegemon in just this way when
he encouraged the local enemies of Thebes fighting on his side
to vote for the destruction of the city within the context of the
Common Peace.[40]

When Alexander set out in 334 on his Asia Minor campaign
against the Persians, the changing status of the Greeks towards
becoming Macedonian subjects, indications of which were already
discernible, became more evident. Without any consultations
troops and ships were levied under the regulations of the Common Peace and put under the command of Macedonian officers.
The home command, which was entrusted to Philip's old com-
rade Antipatros, illustrates this attitude even more clearly. Antipatros was made responsible for all Macedonian and Greek affairs

in Europe:[41] Alexander had appointed his own officer, without in any way consulting the Synedrion, to be a sort of deputy to him with responsibility also for the affairs of the Common Peace. Alexander thus utilized the apparatus of the Common Peace in just the same way as he deployed his internal power apparatus in Macedonia. Hence it is not surprising that opponents of Macedonia in Athens should now describe him as a tyrant.[42] Alexander's autocratic treatment of the peace organization prevented the evolution of any consensus and merely fed the suspicions of his opponents and seemed to justify retrospectively the policies of Demosthenes and his supporters since 346. This development emerges clearly from Demosthenes' success in 330 in the trial against Ktesiphon, who in 336 had proposed awarding a wreath of honour to Demosthenes.[43]

In practice, however, the Greeks were divided among themselves. Thebes no longer existed, and Sparta had kept clear of the Chaironeia campaign. Now, when in the absence of Alexander and the bulk of his army in Asia Minor the Spartan king Agis saw the possibility of joining with the Persians to offer more effective resistance, the Athenians were not prepared to cooperate. The opposition was thus split and ineffective, and in 331 Agis' rebellion was quashed by Antipatros in a major battle at Megalopolis in the Peloponnese.[44] The third of the traditional Greek great powers had now finally been eliminated as a potential opponent. The result was undoubtedly an even greater hardening of the attitude of the Macedonians, who were increasingly less able to view the Greeks as suitable partners. They had convinced themselves in two major clashes of arms that it was possible to operate without partnership, if they only acted decisively. The form taken by the Greek resistance, coupled with the nature of the absent king, loyally served by his officer Antipatros, led rapidly to the establishment of formal Macedonian dominion in southern Greece. In 331, however, things had not yet gone so far. For this further development an even greater catastrophe was needed.

Paradoxically the absence of Alexander had the effect of promoting his rule in Greece. The king himself, being far away, was not confronted with the aggravating and trivial complexities of affairs in southern Greece and tended anyway to favour simple solutions—like the severing of the Gordian knot—that in politics were easier to meet from a distance. By contrast, even the friends of Macedonia had much less access to the king now than in Philip's time, and it was Antipatros who decided most important matters, only leaving the decision to Alexander personally in particularly awkward affairs—for example, after the battle of Megalopolis, when the Synedrion of the Common Peace failed to reach a decision. Antipatros took fifty hostages, and the ultimate decision, unknown to us, was left to Alexander.[45] This practice led inevitably to an increasing estrangement between the Greeks and Alexander that could not be alleviated by spectacular, individual actions, such as the dispatch of three hundred suits of Persian armour to Athens as an offering to Athena after the battle of the Granikos in 334, or his promise to return to Athens the statues of the Athenian tyrant slayers that the Persians had carried off to Susa in 480.[46]

More significant for shaping Alexander's relationship with Athens was his refusal until 331 to free Athenian mercenaries who had fought for the Persians in the battle of the Granikos and then been taken prisoner, a refusal which he then rescinded in view of events in the Peloponnese.[47] On the death of Dareios in 330, the crusade against the Persians was formally ended and the contingents from the Greek states demobilized.[48] Up to that point the Greeks had formally participated in Alexander's Persian campaign just as Philip had planned, except that they were completely without influence on decision making. But in practice, despite all the military successes, the shared experiences did not lead to a rapprochement between Macedonia and the Greeks. Alexander had never seriously aspired to one, and the level of Macedonian participation had always been too great. Alexander's intention was now to continue his campaign without the Greeks, apart from volunteers serving as mercenaries. This decision shows clearly that now that the declared aim, conceived by Philip as a means of effecting his Greek policy, had been achieved, further adventures in Asia were much more important to Alexander than his relationship to his home country or a genuine reconciliation with the Greek states.

After the demobilization of the Greek contingents, and as a result of military operations that led Alexander ever farther away from Europe, the relationship between Macedonia and the southern Greeks emerged increasingly as one of subjugation. In a situation where not the king himself but his deputy was the usual contact person for the Greeks, nothing could be achieved by talks and negotiations since Antipatros did not have the necessary authority. His strength lay in his being only the king's deputy, and so always having available the comfortable possibility of relegating awkward decisions to the absent sovereign, and otherwise carrying out his duties without interference. The system functioned well as long as the king was practically inaccessible in eastern Iran and in India. Problems simply accumulated. But Alexander's return to the Near East in 325/24 meant that final decisions began once more to be taken and royal initiatives to be developed.

The years spent by Alexander in Asia had by no means increased his sensibility in regard to the Greeks. From the beginning he had preferred to order rather than negotiate, and this character trait had been exacerbated during his many years as commander in chief of the army and through his dealings with local populations themselves more accustomed to taking orders than negotiating. The Greeks, but not only they, soon came to feel the effects of this development. One of the gravest problems in the world of the Greek states, particularly in the fourth century B.C., was that of refugees who for some reason had been driven out of, or forced to flee from, their home cities.[49] Macedonian policies in Greece had contributed to this misery, but the causes lay much deeper and were rooted in the nature of the city-states, where the high emotions inevitable in a time of crisis could not be satisfactorily absorbed within their small confines. This inability to control and absorb emotion led in foreign affairs to the mistreatment and sacking of other cities and internally to the persecution of opponents, irrespective of whether a city was formally organized as a democracy. In every case the result was a stream of refugees. Some people found emergency quarters in neighbouring cities, and many men took advantage of the multifarious wars to make their way as mercenaries. Refugees were everywhere, but their fates were individual, differing from person to person and from city to city and only capable of improvement in the context of each person's own homeland, his or her own city. The small city-states were incapable of solving the problem because they could not comprehend it in its generality. For example, refugees from Tegea had nothing to do with Athens, as long as they did not seek asylum there; even then it was the individual applicant for asylum who was regarded as relevant, not the entire body of refugees from the place in question.

Alexander stood outside this particularist tradition and was in any case not inclined to view the Greeks in the traditional, differentiated fashion. Because the organizational structure of the Common Peace encouraged just such a global view, he was able to recognize the problem as being fairly general. He must have been helped to this insight by his dealings with Greek mercenaries, who fought both for and against him, and by his talks with Greek courtiers, who always sought to gain particular advantages for their own states from the king. It was probably the problem of the mercenaries—many of whom had fought under Dareios and under Agis, many of whom indeed were still in Asia and made up an unpredictable mass of desperate men—that was the trigger.[50]

Alexander's response was as typical as it was catastrophic for his relationship to the Greek states. Relying on his own position of absolute power, he ordered the return of all Greek exiles apart from those under a curse, such as murderers, and announced this decree at the Olympic Games of August 324. The threat was made openly that noncompliance would be met with force by Antipatros.[51] Never before had the Greek states been treated in this wholesale fashion; never before had there been such interference in the most sensitive internal affairs of any one of them, except following a defeat in war; and now it was happening to all at once. With this decree Alexander treated every single Greek state as though it had just been defeated. However, as became apparent, this act of authority, of mastery by force, reflected not the actual ascendancy achieved but only the king's claim to dominate the Greeks in the same way and from the same place, Susa, from which the Great King of Persia had for long years held sway over the Greeks of Asia Minor.

It was the big test. No longer was it a case of a couple of states driven by the fantasies of doom-happy politicians; now almost all Greek states had been directly challenged, despite the diversity of their respective situations. The gravity of the threat, becoming ever more blatant since the death of Philip, that the southern

Greeks might be reduced to a Macedonian province with a common administration was now plain to all. But because of the heterogeneity of the small Greek states, reactions varied in accordance with the degree to which each state was affected and its general situation at the time. Some appear to have complied rapidly and to have undertaken administrative measures to restore their exiles.[52] Others, including the Athenians and the Aitolian League, relied on gaining time by negotiation. Both states had grave, concrete problems. Since 365/64 the Athenians had occupied the island of Samos with their own settlers after banishing the inhabitants. The Aitolians had proceeded similarly at Oiniadai. Should these long-term possessions now be relinquished to Macedonian force, just because some people had gained access to the king's ear while he was concerned about the reserves of unemployed mercenaries?[53]

In case negotiations should break down, it was decided to establish contact with the mercenaries, who were assembling in particular around Tainaron in the southern Peloponnese. The Athenian Leosthenes, who had assisted disbanded mercenaries with transport from Asia, offered to do it. He was one of the highest state officials (*strategos*) for 324/23, and during the year, while Athenian negotiators held fruitless talks with Alexander in Babylon, he maintained contact with Tainaron, with the support of the Athenian council.[54]

Many aspects of the events of spring 323 are obscure, but the Athenians certainly reacted promptly when news reached Greece that Alexander had died in Babylon on 10 June. Mercenaries were employed, contacts taken up with the Aitolians and other central Greek states, and swift preparations made for armed resistance to the currently leaderless power of Macedonia. Not all states participated. The Boiotians remained conspicuously loyal to Macedonia, but most of the Thessalians—no longer, since Alexander's death, bound to Macedonia by his archonship—joined the cause, as with a few exceptions did the states of central Greece. From the Peloponnese Argos, Sikyon, Elis and Messene joined the insurgents.[55] When one compares the meagre response to the calls to arms of Demosthenes and later Agis, which led to the major defeats of Chaironeia and Megalopolis, with the grand alliance of Leosthenes, it is evident how many more states now found the domineering attitude of the Macedonians and their king unacceptable, even dangerous, and how many more people now shared the opinion that Macedonia under the leadership of Alexander and Antipatros had destroyed, or threatened to destroy, the essential nature of the Greek community structure. The people in whose name Alexander had opened his campaign now felt themselves browbeaten and menaced. The fact that it was above all the Thessalians who formed the loyal core of the resistance army symbolizes the extent to which Alexander had neglected the system of personal relationships and interdependencies so carefully fostered by Philip (even though pressure had sometimes been necessary). The system finally broke down completely as a direct result of the lack of personal attention.

The events of the war need not be related here in detail. At first the allies under Leosthenes had their successes. They were able to surround Antipatros, who at first had not been able to react with full force because of the uncertainties about the royal succession, and keep him shut up in Lamia for the winter of 323/ 22; they also managed to wipe out reinforcements and kill their commander, Leonnatos; but finally, around August 322, after Leosthenes had been killed, the united Greek forces had to admit defeat. Antipatros had obtained further reinforcements from Krateros, and the two generals united to win the decisive land battle near Krannon in Thessaly while the Athenian fleet was being defeated by the Macedonian admiral Kleitos.[56]

This time all combatants knew what they had been fighting for. This time the issue had indeed been a final attempt to save the old system of free states from Macedonian domination, whereas the Macedonians were concerned to break the last significant resistance to Macedonian rule over the Greeks of the south. Philip had wished to operate through a loose association based on personal relationships and without obvious coercion. This arrangement was not something that everyone could manage. Alexander might have acquired the skill eventually, but he was too young and disappeared too quickly to distant parts. Only a patient king, always present and always ready and willing to keep up his contacts, could have managed Philip's system; the aging Antipatros was certainly not capable of doing it, even supposing he had wanted to. Following Krannon, in sharp contrast to what had happened after Chaironeia, a Macedonian garrison occupied the fort of Munichia controlling the Piraeus; the Athenian democratic system was abolished, and active participation in affairs of state was limited to a wealthy middle class; lands in Thrace were offered to other Athenians. Other states suffered similar measures, and only the Aitolians in their mountains remained unsubdued.[57] Macedonian supremacy had been achieved.

6. PHILIP'S CONTRIBUTION TO
MACEDONIAN HISTORY

No Philip, no Alexander. This truism does not do justice to the specific contribution of Philip himself, and a short summary assessing his pioneering achievements therefore seems appropriate. It would be facile to assert that his innovations lay mainly in the military field, in the creation of an instrument later superbly exploited by Alexander, though indeed this achievement should by no means be minimized. He turned the Macedonian army into a practically unbeatable fighting machine. Reequipment of the army with sarissas and narrower shields provided, when necessary, at state expense; regular exercises; effective organization and deployment of cavalry; use of money reserves to engage mercenaries; the commissioning and employment of allies with particular military skills, slingers, archers and so on; the development of siege machinery and catapults—all these measures figure among his military achievements.

But that is only one aspect of his legacy. The search for reasons for this development reveals immediately the inadequacies of the previous state system, not only in military affairs. The impulse to military improvement came from the desperate security situation that existed after the death of Perdikkas, a situation that threatened the very existence of the state. Philip's strength lay not merely in his recognizing military necessities but also in his concept of the Macedonian state. The army was only a part of the whole.

With a goodly portion of luck he mastered the emergency situation of 359 and then set himself a task, the fulfilment of which in the end provided the basic preconditions for Alexander's campaign in Asia. This project was simple in its conception—in a way

self-evident, though admittedly never systematically pursued—
but its existence is often overlooked because of the fixation on
Athens of most of the sources. It was to guarantee the security
of all frontier areas by establishing in each case the power of the
central state government up to, and even beyond, the actual borders. It entailed not only the military destruction of enemy or
menacing powers and peoples outside the frontiers; much more
importantly it also demanded the winning of consent for the central government within the state, above all in Upper Macedonia,
and the creation of an organizational structure for institutional-
izing this consent. In all these efforts personal relationships
played a large part. No less than seven wives are attested for
Philip, and six of them were not Macedonians but came from
peoples or states directly adjoining the frontiers; each of these
marriages sealed the accomplishment of a diplomatic aim. Personal relationships of other kinds were also carefully nurtured;
the appointment of young men to be pages at the court attached
not only the youths themselves, but also their families, to the
king. The grant of lands in the newly conquered territories, especially around Amphipolis and on the Chalkidike, bound the
deserving recipients to the court; the continuous contact between
king and officers during the regular campaigns, the jointly experienced hardships and the hard-won victories all gradually and
inevitably contributed to consolidating the internal structures of
the kingdom. Their solidity is demonstrated by the ease with
which Alexander took over the succession, in spite of his seeing
danger lurking in every corner. Macedonia did not disintegrate.

Priorities in foreign policy were closely allied to the internal
consolidation of the state. The systematic destruction of the
power of those opponents who in the past had continually threatened Macedonia—Illyria, Paionia, Thrace and the Chalkidike—is
unmistakable. The removal of foreign bases from the Macedonian
coast at Pydna and Methone and the friendship with the Thessalian League, which culminated in Philip's appointment to the
Thessalian archonship, belong in the same context.

Macedonia had also become wealthier. Exactly how wealthy is
difficult to estimate. Regular supplies of precious metals were won
from the various mines in the kingdom, particularly in the neighbourhood of Philippoi, and they made possible the plentiful mint-

ing of coin; the taxes previously paid in Thrace to the local kings must now have been paid to Macedonia; customs duties and trading profits from Pydna and Amphipolis, as well as from Abdera, Maroneia and Ainos, must at least in part have benefitted the Macedonian state; and this must have been true also for Thessaly. Revenues from agriculture must have increased, as the altered and extended frontiers favoured its development. In addition came the single indemnity payments from defeated enemies, such as the twenty thousand Skythian mares, as well as booty, the importance of which should not be underestimated. All these factors gave the state an economic foundation that even without the Asian campaign would have promoted its further expansion.

Here lay the historical significance of Philip II for Macedonia— in the systematic improvement of the security of the state firmly rooted in the monarchy. In Philip's Macedonia the central monarchy was the source of all security, all wealth and all justice. The state was bound together by loyalty to the king. Because of his policy of giving priority to the frontier areas, Philip succeeded not only in defeating his external enemies but also in achieving, once and for all, recognition of the central monarchy in the border areas of Upper Macedonia and in eradicating effectively the regional separatist tendencies that had created problems for many of his predecessors. A crucial factor in this accomplishment was the army organization, the provincial regiments of Upper Macedonia being regularly employed for Pan-Macedonian purposes so that the local barons also became high-ranking officers in the royal army and hence could make a perceptible contribution to the successes of the army as a whole.

By contrast, policies towards Greece initially took second place. The first struggle with Athens arose out of a dispute about territories Philip claimed for Macedonia, not from any wish to destroy Athens. This is apparent from the Peace of Philokrates, which in practice envisaged a geographical separation of spheres of territorial interest and cooperation in areas of common interest, for example in the eradication of piracy. Philip would also probably never have taken an army into central Greece had there been no Sacred War in which the Thessalians were particularly concerned. The fact that here also an organization evolved that could be viewed as an instrument of power, and was used as such by his successor, was the consequence of the way events developed, not of initial intention. In the end, however, it was Philip who, through the particular form into which he moulded the Common Peace, created the conditions for the domineering treatment of the southern Greeks by Alexander and his successors that led to the irrevocable destruction of the partnership he had hoped to establish.

III

The Asian Dimension

1. INTRODUCTION

A detailed history of Alexander's campaigns cannot be undertaken within the framework of a general history of Macedonia. This is not the place for an appraisal of his role in world history or an assessment of his achievements as a whole. The topics selected are restricted to the concerns of the Macedonians and the state of Macedonia. The picture of Alexander that emerges from attempting to portray him using solely the yardstick of the interests of the Macedonians is very different from the usual one; many would doubtless describe it as unjust; it is at any rate incomplete and unfavourable. Nevertheless, it is perhaps refreshing to try for once to reach a judgement of Alexander based on how well he met the interests of those who made it possible for him to become such a significant figure in world history—the Macedonian barons and farmers—and to investigate how his people and his land reacted to the world power so suddenly thrust on them.

The domestic concerns of the Macedonian state and people provided no occasion for an advance into Asia or for the declaration of a war to the end against the Persian king, no reason for the young king to spend twelve years of hard military endeavour in penetrating to the farthest frontiers of the Persian empire and beyond, only to die in Babylon in 323 B.C. without ever having returned to Macedonia.[1] The prime motives for the Asian enterprise were certainly supplied by Philip in his efforts to consolidate Macedonian influence in Europe, particularly among the Greeks. To this end the vision of the Macedonians' liberation of the Greeks of Asia Minor from Persian control was born and the old slogan of the fifth century B.C. revived and adapted to the changed circumstances of the fourth.

However, it was Alexander who extended this concept to include the destruction of the Persian empire and the takeover by
the Macedonians.[2] The real motives are difficult to establish, lying
mainly in the personality of the king and the momentum of military victory. But even though no essential Macedonian interests
motivated the Asian campaign, it was the Macedonians themselves, whether as active participants or main sufferers, who were
directly affected by it both as individuals and as a state. There
could not fail to be consequences for Macedonia in the fact that
the Macedonian king and army destroyed the Persian empire; that
Alexander, who instead of staying at home to govern his people
crossed into Asia in 334 with a mainly Macedonian army and
never returned, still tried to govern Macedonia from wherever he
was and continually demanded further support and reinforcements. Some of the consequences of this attempt have already
been treated in connection with the Greeks of the homeland. But
also among the Macedonians themselves critical tensions were
generated by the massive expedition. These tensions finally affected all Macedonians, whether or not they took part in the campaigns, when Alexander died on 10 June 323, far away from Macedonia in Babylon, without having designated his successor.
Now, if not before, the devastating consequences to the state of
Macedonia of the royal adventures in Asia were clear to everyone.

2. THE OLD GUARD

The Asian campaign had been conceived by Philip with the support of his most trusted advisers. In the year of his death Attalos
and Parmenio, operating perhaps with a fleet, were active as an
advance guard on the coast of Asia Minor. They were welcomed
in Ephesos and, farther to the north on Lesbos, were able to gain
influence in Eresos;[3] but in 335 they had to fight battles on the
mainland at Gryneion and Pitane, and it appears that by the end
of the year they only held Abydos in firm control.[4] Perhaps on
account of these not very encouraging preliminaries Parmenio in
particular, but also Antipatros, foresaw perils for Macedonia in
the immediate continuance of Philip's plans and urged Alexander
not to embroil himself in the Asian venture until he had produced
a son.[5]

As is well known, the king paid no heed, and the royal rejection of Parmenio's advice came to be one of the secondary themes of history writing about Alexander (in later sources groundless rhetorical embroidery cannot be ruled out).[6] It can, however, be easily imagined that Philip's old counsellor, like Antipatros, was troubled by Alexander's neglect of what he and Philip had built together. Neither the Greeks nor the Macedonians were enthusiastic about Alexander's seemingly aimless advance against the Persians. This coolness became particularly evident in 331 when the Persian king Dareios offered to abandon to Alexander all claims to territories west of the Euphrates. Parmenio considered that this offer must surely satisfy the Macedonians, but Alexander rejected it with scorn: "Were I Parmenio, I would accept."[7] Neither the liberation of the Greeks nor the control of Asia Minor was now the ambition of Alexander but the destruction of the whole Persian empire, which Parmenio was unable to see as being in the interests of the Macedonian people. However, as loyal subject and, at first, indispensible military commander, he played out his allotted role in the battle of Gaugamela, only to be left behind some months later in Ekbatana at the same time as it was decided to disband the contingents levied from the Greek allies.[8]

This break, now formalized, with the successful Macedonian tradition of the previous generation and—in the opinion not only of Parmenio—with the interests of the Macedonians caused a tense situation. Alexander attempted to alleviate it in typically direct fashion by leaving behind his previous deputy, Parmenio, the embodiment of Philip's Macedonia, in the base at Ekbatana. For as long as Dareios was still alive, Alexander appears to have had no serious problems with the army, but these certainly arose after his death. Accounts survive of an arduous but ultimately successful attempt by Alexander to persuade the army to advance farther with him, and it is also reported that it had become the king's custom to wear parts of the Persian royal dress.[9] A court conspiracy against Alexander was discovered in Drangiana, in which Philotas, the son of Parmenio and commander of the companion cavalry, was suspected of complicity. A form of open hearing was held before the army; the charges against Philotas, not in any case a very popular man, could not be clearly disproved, and he was executed. Immediately afterwards Alexander ordered the death of Parmenio, whose loyalty no one had ever questioned. It seems that the king still saw the family of Parmenio as being a source of potential resistance to his plans to subject the entire Persian empire. This intention no longer had anything to do with the interests of the Macedonian state as defined by Philip. Those who were suspected of still wishing to pursue immediate Macedonian interests, who were not able to accept unreservedly the king's intentions and could not wholeheartedly support the venture, had to give way to others, even when this could only be accomplished by murder.[10]

The murder of Parmenio is symptomatic of the growing gulf between the king's interests and those of his country and people. But as long as the mass of the army continued to be ready to cooperate, to march with him and perhaps also be killed, it could be maintained that the army favoured the king's plans. As long as Alexander could count on the loyalty of his army in critical situations, he could permit himself deeds of brutality such as the murder of Parmenio and put the personal loyalty of his officers to the test by making the soldiery into a decisive political counterweight. The situation was not without danger. The soldiers, at least the older ones, also felt personal loyalty to their officers. Moreover, after the murder of Parmenio supporting measures had to be adopted, and a weeding-out operation took place among the soldiers as well. Dissidents were banded together in a disciplinary unit ("the undisciplined") so as not to "infect" the others, and some months later, before crossing the Oxos, Alexander discharged nine hundred long-serving Macedonian soldiers as well as the remainder of the Thessalian cavalry, which had served under Parmenio and now showed no spirit for further fighting.[11] The elimination of traditionalist forces in the army itself thus went hand in hand with the removal of traditionalists among the officer corps.

At the same time Alexander made moves to allow the whole army (not just the Macedonians), on whose loyalty he was ultimately dependent, a carefully directed say in decision making at critical moments and so induce a feeling of joint moral responsibility. The relevance of this development for the Macedonian state is that the practice evolved slowly almost into a kind of constitutional function once the army arrogated for itself the right to share in decision making, not only on issues of loyalty, where it followed the king always, but also on general military issues or the question of the succession after the king's death in Babylon.[12] Alexander also set out to reform the army so that he would not be permanently dependent on reinforcements sent from Europe. Sometime after these events, probably in 327, he mustered a troop of thirty thousand young Persians and had them trained in the Macedonian manner so that they could later be incorporated into the army.[13]

The traditional structure of the Macedonian state was called into question by these developments. Until now the king had ruled in consultation with, and with the cooperation of, his lords and barons, each of whom mobilized or controlled his own followers. All important decisions were made by him personally, but always with the support and advice of the most influential barons. That the king should occasionally consider it expedient, even necessary, to address himself directly to the soldiers against the opinion of an influential group of barons and in order to pressure others shattered the traditional framework of government by consent. This development can only be explained as resulting from the tensions produced by the controversial continuation of the campaign against the Persian empire and the determination of the king to do things that, in the opinion of traditionalist circles, did not lie within his competence. To be able to advance farther, he had to create a level of personal dependence on himself over and above what had become traditional, both in degree and in form, which would then permit him to neglect his main duties as Argead king in Macedonia and impress his will on the participants in the campaign.

Because of his personal popularity with the army, Alexander was indeed usually able to persuade it to do what he wanted. This was not easy, as old ties of loyalty could not be severed at one stroke. But he found a sufficient number of ambitious young men among the officers, such as Perdikkas, Hephaistion or Ptolemaios, who saw good career prospects in close cooperation with Alexander, who did not necessarily see their future as being merely that of loyal subjects in the Macedonian homeland and who were prepared to give Alexander their full support and go through everything at his side. And there were still men like Krateros and Polyperchon among the older officers, who considered themselves bound in loyalty to the king by virtue of his office in the Macedonian state regardless of what he did. Plutarch tells an anecdote in which Hephaistion is characterized as a friend of Alexander, whereas Krateros is called a friend of the king. The distinction is apt, and as long as Alexander could muster an adequate number of men of each kind among his officers—even when, as in the above case, they could not stand one another—he could survive well enough.[14]

The rejuvenating process among the officers and army was basically nothing new. The dropout rate particularly among officers was high on such a long and wide-reaching campaign, and new and competent replacements for them had to be promoted from the ranks of those present. That promotions were made rather on personal than on institutional criteria can be explained on grounds of military expediency, but a new tendency in the appointments is still apparent. It no longer seems to have been the old type of baron, those who together with their followers had been the traditional backbone of the army, who now attained high rank in the army and court but instead men who advanced from a combination of military ability displayed in the current campaign and personal friendship and service to Alexander. Thus the top levels of army and court not only became younger; a certain social change also took place.

Nonetheless, Alexander increasingly treated the army as a whole as an institution separate from the corps of officers. He cultivated a personal relationship with the soldiers beyond the normal one of a royal army commander in chief. It can have been no novelty when, after the death of Dareios and the consequent high enthusiasm in the army for returning home, Alexander personally countered this wish and attempted to persuade the soldiers directly of the need to continue the campaign.[15] No king, no commander, could have neglected this duty. But the Philotas crisis created a different and novel situation. Whatever the details may have been, there was certainly a grave crisis of confidence within the army leadership.[16] Alexander could not ascertain exactly how far latent discontent had spread among his officers (one conspirator was Demetrios, a member of the bodyguard) and became so uneasy that he preferred first to test his credibility and standing with the army before making an example of Philotas and Parmenio. He called the army together and presented them with his version of the situation before allowing Philotas to speak, a procedure that brought him precisely the outburst of angry feeling he had hoped for. After thus securing the support of the army in advance, he held all further deliberations in the matter according to tradition in the closest circle of friends and officers. The outcome, however, had already been decided in principle. Philotas, and therefore also Parmenio, could now be removed in whatever fashion he chose and without any great immediate political consequences.

Two years later in Marakanda (Samarkand) after Alexander, drunk, had murdered Kleitos with his own hands, he staged a similar performance, but this time it was not so easy. Kleitos was, like Parmenio, one of the old guard—his sister Lanike had even been Alexander's nurse—and he still provided a link to the Macedonia of Philip. The reasons for the murder, apart from the drunken condition of both men, lay in Kleitos' dislike of the increasingly oriental character of Alexander and the court. The cause of the alienation, however, is not so important to us here. Rather it is significant that after Alexander had hid himself away in his tent, when it was generally feared that he wanted to starve himself to death, a meeting of influential Macedonians—exactly who took part is not known, but it was certainly more than just a group of officers—declared the death of Kleitos retrospectively to be legal in spite of everything and asserted that he should not even be buried unless Alexander personally ordered the funeral.[17] The result was similar to that produced by the army hearing during the Philotas crisis. Alexander was covered, this time retroactively, by the consent wrung from the broad mass of those present in an affair that gravely jeopardized his relationship with his officers. A joint responsibility had been created, which the facts of the case should have made impossible.

How many other, less critical affairs of this kind took place we cannot know, as the sources give accounts only of outstanding events. The social cohesiveness of those who accompanied Alexander from the west doubtless increased steadily as a result of the hardships undergone together in distant parts and through Alexander's deliberate activities to this end. That this carefully promoted solidarity could indeed have an adverse side for the king became critically apparent in India in 326. When the army, despite the steady monsoon, had reached the Hyphasis (Beas) and Alexander had begun preparations for crossing the river and apparently continuing the campaign ever farther to the east, the lack of spirit and the unwillingness of the majority of the army became so clear that, as after the death of Dareios, Alexander again spoke to them to fire their enthusiasm before ordering the advance. This time, however, his lust for conquest failed to inspire the masses, and the solidarity that in the past he had been able to use for his own purposes was now directed against him. Their spokesman was Koinos, the *taxis* commander from Elimiotis and son-in-law of Parmenio, who despite his relationship had been one of the king's main supporters against Philotas; like Krateros, he was a man of unquestioned loyalty to the king and much respected by the soldiers. But Alexander, did not just give up after the speeches. Once again he withdrew to his tent in the hope that, as after the death of Kleitos, he would be able to provoke a counterreaction, but this time he did not succeed. He was now forced to accept that Koinos was indeed expressing the deeply held wish of the tired army and that no amount of persuasion would make it advance farther to the east. Nevertheless, he ordered sacrifices to be made for an advance, but only to save face. Fortunately the omens could be interpreted as unfavourable, and the enterprise was abandoned. A mutiny had not occurred; it was the gods who prevented the crossing of the Hyphasis. But the king and all concerned were well aware that he had suffered a defeat and that mass opinion, articulated by Koinos in an extreme situation, had prevailed against the king.[18]

There are no accounts of further political activity among the soldiers during the rigours of the return march. Not until they had arrived in the Tigris town of Opis did the Macedonians express the wish to be demobilized. The occasion was provided by the planned discharge of a group of ten thousand veterans and by discontent over the inclusion of Iranians in the army. Alexander acted decisively and forced a return to discipline. But even the extravagant joint festival for all the peoples represented in the army, held shortly afterwards, could not disguise the fact that a conflict of interests had arisen between the Macedonian soldiers and their king. The Macedonians retained their original, simple ambition for riches and power, whereas Alexander was constrained to pay attention as well to the demands of his Asian subjects, at least those of the Persian upper classes, without whom he could not possibly rule in Asia. The soldiers seemed to be ready to pursue their aims by force if necessary.[19]

The term *empire of Alexander* is used by modern historians for the short-lived state created by Alexander. It rightly draws attention to the fact that this construction of Alexander's was very different from the Macedonian state created by Philip. We have already seen examples of how Alexander eliminated those who did not accept his aims, of how he appointed to leading positions in the army and court those who owed everything to him and would have been nothing without him, and of how he replaced dissident elements in the army. The tendency characterizing these changes led to other consequences as well.

Since the main criterion for public service and honour was personal loyalty to Alexander, there was no compelling reason why only Macedonians should enjoy the king's favour. From the beginning, as in Philip's time, there had been Greeks in service at the court, and not only engaged in cultural activities like the historian Kallisthenes and various poets. Higher posts were occupied mainly by people from the cities of northern Greece that Philip had bound closely to Macedonia, for example from the Chalkidike (like Kallisthenes), Amphipolis (like Nearchos, Erigyios and Laomedon), Kardia (like Eumenes) or Thessaly (like Medeios of Larissa); but people from other areas were also sometimes appointed (like Chares of Mytilene), who particularly recommended themselves because of special personal abilities or favours to Alexander. Less prominent people received minor court appointments or lower administrative posts, as garrison commanders, tax collectors, administrators of small provinces, commanders of mercenary units and so on.[20] These assimilated Greeks posed no serious competition to the Macedonian nobles, just as the levied Greek contingents or mercenary units were not in competition with the Macedonian soldiery. Within the framework of the state structure created by Philip it was indeed a further development, but a natural and European one.

The case was different with the orientals. Here too the development promoted by Alexander ran on the two planes of the court and the army. Already in Babylon in 331 Alexander had given an indication that he wanted to win over the Iranian nobles to his side when he confirmed the Persian satrap of Babylon, Mazaios, in office. This was only the first of a large number of such confirmations or appointments designed to reconcile the influential classes in Iran to Alexander's rule so that they might be prepared to recognize him as successor to the Achaimenids.[21] Therein Alexander was going far beyond the traditional activity of a Macedonian king. It was one thing to conquer Asia Minor, "liberate" the Greeks living there and even destroy the rule of the Achaimenids; but it was quite another to want to take over as ruler without apparently seeking to make any significant changes. To what end had the Macedonians struggled? Why was Alexander king of Macedonia, when his people were used only to satisfy his own personal ambitions for power and in the end had to share the power they had won with the conquered? It is hardly surprising that from this time on tensions arose, and a gulf developed between the traditionalists and their king. Alexander was claiming for himself two virtually irreconcilable functions: to satisfy many Macedonians and Greeks, he had to be a traditional Macedonian king, whereas to satisfy the expectations he had aroused in the orientals, he had to be the successor to the kingdom of the Achaimenids. Only the strong military discipline demanded by the continuous campaign prevented worse conflicts than those that occurred. Many Macedonians disapproved of the increasing orientalism and pomp of the court, the departure from the relatively simple procedures that had traditionally characterized the relationships between king, barons and commoners in Macedonia. This factor played a large part in the murder of Kleitos and the dispute arising from the introduction of prostration before the king (*proskynesis*), which the Greek Kallisthenes refused to perform, as well as in a large number of other conflicts and irritations the details of which are unknown to us.

In the army also innovations were introduced that caused tensions. In principle it was nothing new that non-Macedonian units should fight. From the beginning not only Greeks but also Paionians, Illyrians, Agrianians and Thracians (and perhaps Triballians) had taken part.[22] But these were all familiar Balkan peoples, who fought in their own units and according to their own traditions. In 327, however, Alexander ordered that young Persians should be trained in the Macedonian fashion (the so-called *epigonoi*) so that they could fight in the phalanx alongside Macedonians. Already local units of orientals, both cavalry and infantry, had been deployed.[23] According to a speech the historian Curtius attributes to Alexander on the occasion of the disagreement at the Hyphasis—although he probably invented the details himself—Alexander threatened to advance further with "Skythians and Baktrians";[24] but even this late rhetorical exaggeration allows some insight into the extent to which Iranian elements in particular were incorporated into, or attached to, Alexander's army. According to Arrian one of the most important motives of the Macedonians at Opis was precisely that the privileged position in the army that they felt their king owed them was being reduced by levelling operations in favour of the Iranians.[25]

Alexander was indeed clearly aiming at something of the kind. Enough concessions were made to the Iranians, as two examples are sufficient to demonstrate. In Susa in 324 Alexander staged his famous mass wedding, at which each of his closest officers and friends received a bride from the highest ranks of the Iranian nobility. In practice it was not much more than a symbolic gesture; few of the marriages seem to have survived the king's death in the following year. But the direction of the king's wishes is clear: he was no longer just king of Macedonia, and a unique deracinated ruling caste of mixed origins was to be bred to take over the functions of government in that unique political construction known as the empire of Alexander.[26]

The second example shows this trend even more plainly. After the dispute with the Macedonian soldiers in Opis had been settled, Alexander held a large feast, to which nine thousand representatives of the different peoples serving in the army were invited. In Arrian's account, which is probably correct in its general outline, Alexander asked the gods for "many blessings, but especially solidarity [*homonoia*] and community of interest [*koinonia*] in the kingdom [or, in ruling] between the Macedonians and Persians."[27] By this he meant that there should no longer be even nominally an empire of the Macedonians alone but a joint empire of the Macedonians and Persians; the king was no longer content, even in respect to the Macedonians, to be merely king of Macedonia. It seems clear that Alexander's intention was to integrate Macedonia into his evolving multiracial empire, in which the sole common uniting element would be the king himself. In the central areas of the empire the Macedonians should then no longer be seen as conquerors but as partners. To free the future still more from the burden of Macedonian tradition, two of the remaining traditionalists among the high-ranking officers were sent home with the ten thousand discharged veterans. Krateros, of all people, whose loyalty to the institution of the Macedonian monarchy had been praised by Alexander himself, and Polyperchon, around sixty years old, were to have their influence restricted to Macedonia. This step also indicates that institutional loyalty of the old kind was no longer sufficient and that in future only loyalty to the person of the king would count.

Alexander's sudden death on 10 June 323 frustrated all these dreams. Although the men of the hour were his high officers, who until now had served him loyally, it soon became clear that none of these determined careerists actually shared the fantastic dreams of grandeur of their dead king. That does not, however, mean that they were in harmonious agreement to write off Asia as just an episode and take up again the limited lives of rich Balkan barons. Not for this had Perdikkas, Ptolemaios and their companions marched to India and back; not for this had they repeatedly put their lives at risk, ridden out Alexander's storms of anger and tolerated and cooperated without protest in his symbolic steps towards creating an unrealistic, polymorphic empire. In the eleven years of the campaign far too many people had invested far too much of their strength to be prepared to relinquish straight away all that had been conquered. The Macedonians never considered doing so. The clock could not be put back for this generation, and in the end even the Macedonian traditionalists had to come to terms with the conquest of Asia.

3. THE RETURN HOME

When Alexander III died, Macedonia was in serious trouble, and the king himself was responsible for it. He had never regarded his country as much more than a source of tireless and almost indomitable warriors—Antipatros was to have brought reinforcements again in 324[1]—and his hereditary monarchy gave him the institutionalized right of command over the army and a claim on the loyalty of the barons that he exploited to the full. Possible contenders for the throne, as well as dissidents and traditionalists among the officers and soldiers, had been systematically eliminated one after the other or at least rendered harmless. At the finish in Babylon only "his" men were left, men whose personal loyalty was unquestionable because without the king they had little backing in the army and in the country and so were completely dependent on him. Moreover, the thirty-three-year-old king had left behind no recognized son, though his Iranian wife Roxane was pregnant, and one could hope for the birth of a boy. Alexander had taken all possible advantage from the institution of the monarchy but had much weakened it by the increasingly personalized structure of the court and the officer corps. His evasive answer to the question of who should inherit his empire, "the best" or "the strongest" (the sources vary),[2] reveals this emphasis on personality; institutions and traditions were no longer respected, and the personal qualities of the individual were decisive. For his country and people, this attitude manifested disastrous irresponsibility and entailed practically a challenge to civil war. But the welfare of his country and people had never especially troubled Alexander.

The state of the nation was critical as never before. Tradition demanded that on the death of the king his successor from the family of the Argeadai should be agreed on and confirmed in office by the currently most influential representatives of the Macedonian aristocracy.[3] But what should happen now? Not only was there no undisputed successor, but two of the most important barons were absent—Antipatros and Krateros, the very two who on account of their age and traditional attitudes would in the long term have had the greatest influence among the Macedonians in the army and in the country. But with the army in Babylon needing a new commander in chief immediately, there was no practical possibility of arriving at the customary consensus among the Macedonian nobles. The highest-ranking officers in Babylon were forced to take immediate action, even at the risk of provoking a conflict with Antipatros and Krateros.

Shortly before his death Alexander had handed over his ring
to Perdikkas, son of Orontes, member of the ruling family of the
Upper Macedonian region Orestis, and in this way had singled
him out before the others as a kind of chancellor.[4] This distinction,
though, was not sufficient to secure for Perdikkas the recognition
of his fellow top officers for a permanent office, and he knew it.
Roxane's pregnancy could not simply be ignored, and because
the army was in Babylon, the officers' decision had an immediate
existential significance for it that it would not have had in the
normal course of events in Macedonia itself; hence interest ran
very high in the camp as well. Had the officers been able to agree
among themselves, even without Antipatros and Krateros, it is
probable that no immediate problem would have arisen. But Alexander's appointments policy had produced a situation in which
none of those present possessed such a position of preeminence
that he was the natural candidate for the guardianship of Roxane
and therefore, in the case of a daughter's being born, for the
succession. The officers were divided among themselves; opinions were voiced against the ambitiousness of Perdikkas, against
the child of an Iranian, even should it turn out to be a son, and
against the insecurity inherent in waiting for the birth.[5]

Since no united front could be presented by the officers in such
a vital question of state interest, the solution, already well tried
by Alexander in political crises, lay to hand: to persuade the army
to take sides and force a decision by the use of violence or the
threat of it. The first to try it was Meleagros, one of the commanders of an infantry *taxis*. He urged the soldiers to take over
the royal treasury, but in the middle of the turmoil someone put
forward the name of Arrhidaios. Arrhidaios, son of Philip II and
Philinna of Larissa, was indeed present in the camp, but he was
considered to be feebleminded, a judgement that had thus far
kept him alive. He was a little older than Alexander, who had
taken him along on campaign without ever regarding him as a
rival. Even during the current crisis he had behaved so incon-
spicuously that none of Alexander's chief officers, preoccupied
with his unborn child, had given a thought to this actual offspring
of the great Philip. But if an unborn child could be considered as
the nominal successor, then a feebleminded man in his mid-thirties was at least as suitable. Many Macedonian soldiers suddenly

thought this way, soldiers who wished to put an end to the insecurity and were anyway suspicious of Alexander's Iranian wife. Meleagros saw his opportunity: Arrhidaios was sent for and proclaimed king under his father's name of Philip by the large gathering of soldiers that had in the meantime assembled.

It was a manifest attempt to take Alexander's intimate friends by surprise using Alexander's own methods, and it rapidly produced the united front that had thus far been missing. The officers decided in favour of Roxane's child, to keep it at least for themselves, and determined that Perdikkas should take over as regent jointly with Leonnatos. They claimed the consent of Antipatros and Krateros, and therefore the control of Macedonia itself, by investing them jointly with responsibility for European affairs. They even swore an oath of loyalty to a son of Alexander, should one be born. The show of unity, however, came too late. Meleagros had known how to persuade the phalanx soldiers to declare their loyalty to the new Philip, but the cavalry followed the noble Perdikkans. The dispute immediately threatened to escalate into severe violence but was calmed by negotiations. The Perdikkans then managed to restore discipline in the army and get rid of Meleagros. But this action alone could no longer solve the problem. The soldiers had proclaimed Arrhidaios king, although they really had no right of decision. Much as the officers may have wished to eliminate Arrhidaios, the critical situation made such a drastic solution impossible. It was also impossible just to ignore him. The officers had indeed initially, in their obsession with Alexander, forgotten about him entirely, but the trouble in the ranks showed how much the soldiers still remembered Philip and how fervently they viewed Arrhidaios as being the only possible candidate.[6] Politically the Perdikkans had no alternative. To save the situation, the Officers' Council changed its tune and recognized Arrhidaios as king.[7]

The question of who should actually rule still remained to be answered. If absolutely necessary, Arrhidaios could perform the purely formal functions of a head of state, but no one was prepared to trust him with anything more. To avert the threatening chaos, Perdikkas now managed to assert himself so far that he obtained the overall command of the royal army. In practice this meant that as long as the army remained on active service, he also held the central power in the state. However, his fellow officers demanded a very high price. The provinces or satrapies of Alexander's empire were to be distributed, with the most attractive of them going to Alexander's favourite officers. Everyone who laid a claim was to be satisfied if possible, and so Egypt was assigned to Ptolemaios, Thrace to Lysimachos, Hellespontine Phrygia to Leonnatos, and other regions to other officers in accordance with their wishes and political strength.[8] Formally these regions were to remain provinces of the empire, ruled centrally by King Philip Arrhidaios, but the centrifugal tendency was clearly apparent in the very desire for distribution. Local regional rulers were, after all, no innovation for the Macedonians; their state had evolved from a number of such regional baronies. It could hardly be expected that the go-getting generation that had conquered Asia with Alexander would not take the opportunity offered of establishing traditional regional power bases. The advocates of the unity of the empire (mainly those who had not been appointed to a regional governorship) had little realistic hope of investing their formal central power with effective control over the whole empire. But they still had to learn that their aspirations were hopeless.

Two crucial problems remained even after the satrapies had been distributed. No one in Babylon can have believed that Antipatros could be removed from the homeland merely by a decision of the Officers' Council, nor that his removal could make Krateros agree to Perdikkas taking over the command of the royal army instead of himself. The rather naive hope of solving both these problems at one blow was manifest in the decision to entrust the two veterans with responsibility for all of Europe apart from Thrace. But even should one of them eliminate the other, the fundamental problem remained—that the man in control of the Macedonian homeland and the greater part of the empire built up by Philip was not the man who exercised control over the king, the son of Philip, and held the command over the royal army. The Macedonians in the army, who wished to return home with their king, would not be prepared to accept this discrepancy permanently. The Macedonian state remained in jeopardy.

The situation did not change when a few months later Roxane gave birth to a son, who was named Alexander. The officers had already recognized him as king before his birth, and Perdikkas, learning the political requirements of the situation from Meleagros, considered that the army should at all events do so as well. In this way the grotesque constitutional situation came about that Macedonia possessed two kings, both equally incompetent.[9] Moreover, the split in power between home government and kings remained unhealed. Perdikkas soon attempted to alleviate the situation by offering to marry Antipatros' daughter Nikaia. Antipatros, who immediately after Alexander's death had become embroiled in the Lamian War, did not at first react to this offer. He desperately needed assistance, which Perdikkas from Mesopotamia could not supply swiftly enough, and therefore turned to Leonnatos in Hellespontine Phrygia and to Krateros, who was still in Kilikia with his ten thousand veterans. Although Leonnatos was killed shortly afterwards by the Greeks in spring 322, the cooperation of Krateros and his army in summer 322 was decisive for the successful outcome of the war. After its conclusion Krateros married Phila, Antipatros' eldest daughter, in winter 322/ 21, and the two generals agreed to win for Krateros a territory in Asia for him to rule.[10] In spring 321 Nikaia was finally brought to Sardis. Antipatros, however, was not the only person seeking to influence events by dynastic policies. Alexander's mother, Olympias, hoped to win over Perdikkas by sending her widowed daughter, Alexander's full sister Kleopatra, into the marriage stakes to reestablish her own influence in Macedonia against that of Antipatros. But in view of the critical importance of his relationship with Antipatros and Krateros, Perdikkas preferred to marry Nikaia, who at present could damage him more than Olympias could help him.[11] Nevertheless, Kleopatra journeyed to Sardis and became an uncomfortable *intriguante.*

Another attempt posed a much greater threat to Perdikkas. Kynnane, daughter of Philip II and the Illyrian Audata, had married during Philip's lifetime his nephew Amyntas and borne him a daughter, Adea. Adea was as yet unmarried, as was Kynnane's half-brother, the new king Philip Arrhidaios. Kynnane hastened to the court with the fixed intention of marrying the two off to one another. Perdikkas, himself not an Argead, recognized the danger in this competition from the royal women and reacted brutally—but not brutally enough to be effective—by ordering the murder of Kynnane but not of Adea. Incensed soldiers reacted with such violence that Perdikkas was forced to allow the marriage between Adea and the king after all. To emphasize more strongly the relationship to her grandfather, the new queen, confidently and with an eye for its effect on the Macedonians, took the name of Eurydike, after Philip's mother, her own great-grandmother.[12]

Two further events of 321 contributed to Perdikkas' final downfall. In Babylon he had had to agree that Alexander, in accordance with his expressed wish, should be buried in Egypt in the Ammon oasis Siwah, not in the traditional burial place of the Macedonian kings at Aigai in Macedonia. He had won time by ordering the building of an extremely opulent funeral carriage for the long journey; but the work was finally completed after about two years, and Arrhidaios, the officer in charge of the operation, led the funeral procession on its way from Babylon. Perdikkas, however, realized that he could not afford to relinquish Alexander's corpse, with all its potential propaganda advantages, to Ptolemaios, who now controlled Egypt. Instead he wanted at all costs to retain the body himself and so perhaps use the funeral procession of Alexander to stage the triumphal return of the kings and the royal army to Macedonia. In this way he might perhaps even gain the upper hand over Antipatros. The order was therefore given to halt the funeral procession. Ptolemaios, however, had made contact with Arrhidaios at an early stage and sent troops to escort the hearse to Egypt. These were strong enough to withstand the units of the royal army that attempted to carry out Perdikkas' orders to take possession of the body. Thus Alexander did indeed find his first burial place in Egypt, though not in remote Siwah but in the old capital of the Pharaohs at Memphis.[13]

Perdikkas' opponents mustered their forces. Antigonos, satrap of Greater Phrygia since 333, felt himself threatened by Perdikkas and in 321 fled to Macedonia. He brought the news to Antipatros and Krateros that Perdikkas intended to divorce his new bride, Nikaia, straight away and marry Kleopatra instead. Antipatros, who was keen to prevent Perdikkas from staging a triumphal homecoming of Alexander's remains to Macedonia, had been cultivating friendly contacts with Ptolemaios for some time. When it became apparent in 321 that Perdikkas planned first to take action against Ptolemaios, Krateros and Antipatros made an alliance with him specifically for the fight against Perdikkas, which Antipatros was able to seal with the hand of another of his daughters, Eurydike. They agreed that Antipatros was to have control (*hegemonia*) in Europe (apparently coupled with the guardianship of the two kings), Krateros control in Asia and, it seems, Ptolemaios in Egypt.[14]

A direct military conflict with Perdikkas did not occur. A group of his officers, perhaps bribed by Ptolemaios, took advantage of grave discontent in the army following a disaster on the Nile, in which some two thousand men were drowned, to assassinate him. Ptolemaios had no desire to assume personal responsibility for the invading army and arranged instead for joint temporary leadership under Peithon, one of Perdikkas' murderers, and the same Arrhidaios who had brought him Alexander's body. Their immediate task was to lead the army and the kings out of Egypt. In this way Ptolemaios achieved his own aim of retaining Alexander's body and his control over Egypt while at the same time remaining true to his partners in the coalition.[15]

Events did not run as smoothly for Antipatros and Krateros as they had for Ptolemaios in Egypt. Shortly after they crossed into Asia Minor, Krateros fell in battle against Eumenes of Kardia, Perdikkas' Greek commander in the area. Although Antipatros subsequently managed to advance as far as Syria without further major difficulties, Krateros' death meant the loss of a cornerstone of their future policy. Antipatros himself had neither the desire nor the intention of assuming direct responsibility for the Asian part of Alexander's empire. When he met up with the royal army in Triparadeisos, he found it depressed and mutinous and urgently sought someone to replace Krateros. His own position was relatively strong since even the royal army recognized him, during a riotous assembly, as regent of the kings; in accordance with ancient Macedonian custom he also had himself recognized by the officers.[16] Nevertheless, despite his personal repugnance towards the Asian empire, he could not simply abandon the claims of his royal protégés for formal control of Asia. Eumenes and other members of Perdikkas' faction were still marching around Asia Minor with their armies and posed a definite threat to the peace of Macedonia. A replacement for Krateros therefore had to be found, and Antipatros settled on Antigonos, whose reliability, at least as an opponent of Perdikkas' faction, could not be doubted.

The royal commission to Antigonos was not, however, as extensive as that which had been projected for Krateros; it was restricted to the continuation of the war against Eumenes and the Perdikkans.[17] Safety measures were also built in. Antipatros' son Kassandros was appointed to serve Antigonos as *chiliarchos*, a form of deputy. His newly widowed sister, Phila, who had just borne Krateros a son, was once more available for a political marriage. Antigonos, now more than sixty years old, was not drawn to her himself, but he persuaded his sixteen-year-old son Demetrios to marry her despite the fifteen-year disparity in their ages. The negotiations in Triparadeisos concluded with a new arrangement of the satrapies of the empire that took account of events since their distribution in Babylon. "Antipatros advanced with the kings and his own army towards Macedonia with the intention of restoring the kings to their fatherland": with these words Diodoros describes the end of this miserable episode in the history of the Macedonian state. The adventure in Asia was now over for the royal house of Macedonia. The court was reunited with the homeland.[18]

4. THE END OF THE ARGEADAI

From the point of view of the administrator of Philip's legacy, Asia was not only irrelevant: it also posed a potential threat to Macedonia. The clear priorities set for the Asian campaign by Alexander had so stretched the military strength of Macedonia, carefully built up by Philip, that Antipatros had found it impossible to control properly all parts of his European area of responsibility. With the help of Krateros he had managed to defeat the Greeks in the Lamian War, but only at tremendous cost. The fragile, but cheap, consent to Macedonian rule in Greece was gone; garrisons now had to be maintained and, because of the changes they had made in the internal affairs of many cities, a watchful eye kept open. The Aitolians had even been able to withstand the Macedonian army successfully. Thrace was also largely out of control, apart from the coastal towns. The Officers' Council in

Babylon had created a special administrative district under Lysimachos for this area, a decision based on Philip's system and
confirmed by Antipatros at Triparadeisos. Not even in the west
were things what they used to be. Since the death of Kleopatra's
husband, Alexandros of Epeiros, Olympias, Alexander's power-
hungry mother, had gained in influence, and she would never be
content until she was reestablished with dignity and honour in
Pella. For this reason her personal enemy, Antipatros, had to regard Epeiros also as a security threat to Macedonia.

In Europe, therefore, there was more than enough to be done,
and Antipatros was not the only Macedonian who perceived this.
When, almost eighty years old, he died within a year of his return
from Syria, it was not his forty-year-old son Kassandros who became his successor but the aging Polyperchon. Antipatros' own
opinion is said to have been decisive in this succession.[1] Scru-
pulous care was thus taken to avoid giving the impression that a
form of hereditary succession was being introduced into the regency. Polyperchon, who had been closely associated with Krateros and had returned with him from Babylon, had just recently
acted as Antipatros' deputy during his absence in Asia. During
that time he had successfully countered an Aitolian attack on
Thessaly and a Thessalian insurrection connected with it.[2] However, his traditionalist patterns of thought and his limited military
and political abilities—under Alexander Polyperchon had not
risen above his initial rank of *taxis* leader[3]—would hardly be an
adequate substitute for the uniquely high esteem in which
Antipatros had been held. It was to Antipatros that all had ultimately deferred at Triparadeisos. Polyperchon, by contrast, even
equipped with the institutional authority the regency for the kings
brought him, possessed neither the necessary broad basis of good
will in the country nor sufficient political acumen to resolve the
problems facing Macedonia.

Polyperchon committed the decisive mistake that sealed the
fate of the house of the Argeadai right at the outset. Kassandros,
who had probably returned to Macedonia because of his father's
illness, was appointed *chiliarchos* to Polyperchon. Polyperchon,
however, naively trustful as he was, failed to see in him a possible
rival and initially allowed him a free hand. Kassandros exploited
this freedom to foster his contacts with his father's troops and

garrison commanders—he even sent his own man Nikanor to Athens to command the garrison at Munichia—as well as with his brother-in-law Ptolemaios and with Antigonos, to whom he soon deserted.[4] Polyperchon, whose greatest political advantages were the trust of the Macedonian aristocracy and his recommendation by Antipatros, had by this political gaucherie dealt into Kassandros' hands the political legacy of Antipatros outside Macedonia. Relying on the respect due his office, he appears to have expected Kassandros to show the same honour to the kings and those representing them that his own strong sense of tradition dictated to him. He completely failed to perceive the generational change that had taken place and, above all, the effect that the events in Babylon would have had on those, like Kassandros, who had witnessed the political wheeling and dealing for power that had led to the "kings" being proclaimed at all and the lack of respect towards Macedonian tradition that had ruled there— those who had perceived and experienced that egoistic ambition for personal power with which the protagonists had haggled and negotiated. To have failed to recognize that Kassandros also belonged to this group was merely further evidence of the catastrophic political naivety that characterized the official dealings of Polyperchon and branded him as utterly unsuitable to be regent.

Where Polyperchon really should have seized the initiative, Kassandros had forestalled him. Polyperchon was only able to react—at first not really in the interests of the Macedonian state but simply to strengthen his own position against Kassandros. Furthermore, although his only strength lay in taking over the political legacy of Antipatros, he felt himself compelled by Kassandros to go in new directions. Already in autumn 319 he attempted to win popularity among the Greeks by issuing a decree ordering the dissolution of the oligarchies introduced by Antipatros after the Lamian War in many places, including Athens, and the restoration of those exiled by them.[5] It was a feeble attempt to put into political practice something of the spirit of the partnership policies he had experienced with Philip. He had, however, taken no account of the fact that the Macedonian relationship to the Greeks had altered since 336 and that Antipatros had not introduced the oligarchies after the Lamian War merely because their members were more readily subservient to him but because the regimes that they replaced had proved unreliable in their attitude towards Macedonian supremacy. Through his dissolution of the oligarchies Polyperchon thus effected the removal from power of the very people who wished to keep their states loyal to Macedonia or who at least were prepared in their own interests to suffer Macedonian rule; and the exiles whose restoration he ordered were opponents of Macedonia who would not feel any less intensely hostile to it just because Polyperchon had exercised royal clemency and decreed their return. They were utterly unsuitable allies for an internal Macedonian dispute.

In spring 318 Polyperchon took yet another step away from the political legacy of Antipatros. Olympias, the old queen and personal enemy of Antipatros, was invited to return to Macedonia. She was offered an honourable position at the court as the person responsible for her young grandson Alexander IV. In this way Polyperchon certainly solved the immediate problem of Epeiros, but at the cost of losing the support of those influential friends of Antipatros who had helped to put him into office.[6] His third innovation fared no better: in Asia too he was forced to bet on the wrong horse. According to the system worked out by Antipatros, Antigonos, as governor of Asia apart from those areas controlled by Ptolemaios, was the nominal representative of the kings in the war against Eumenes and the Perdikkans. Polyperchon neglected to win him over to his side straightaway, and by the time Kassandros had taken refuge with him, it was too late. The only possibility open to him was thus to join with Antigonos' opponents, in particular with Perdikkas' ex-officer Eumenes, who in 320 had defeated and killed Krateros and caused Antipatros severe difficulties. Thus yet again Antipatros' successor failed to continue Antipatros' policies, as was urgently necessary in the state interest, but instead from purely personal motives of power politics allied himself to the enemies of his predecessor. Asia was certainly only a minor theatre in the struggle for supremacy in Macedonia. But Polyperchon, like Antipatros before him, could not merely abandon formal claims made by the central government. His support for Eumenes arose from this principle and was confined to formal letters, demands and decrees. It was important to Polyperchon to keep Antigonos occupied in Asia for as long as he himself had trouble with Kassandros. He could not, of course, know whether Antigonos also harboured the desire to rule in his home country, but the immediate struggle against Kassandros for the effective control of Macedonia had to take precedence over all other considerations.[7]

Whereas Eumenes in Asia enjoyed the sudden legitimizing of his authority and already in summer 318 undertook the representation of the kings, Polyperchon was faced with major problems in Europe. The oligarchies introduced by Antipatros after 322 in the Greek cities had not the slightest intention of dissolving themselves merely at royal behest. In Athens the presence of a Macedonian army under Polyperchon's son Alexandros was needed to get the revolution under way. Events probably took a similar course in other places and gave Polyperchon good reason to set out personally for the south in spring 317, accompanied by King Philip Arrhidaios. Even Olympias showed no enthusiasm for Polyperchon and delayed in following his invitation. She sought advice from Eumenes, whom she probably knew from Philip's time, and it was not until autumn 317 that she finally returned to Pella.[8]

By then, however, it was too late to take effective countermeasures against Kassandros. He had already arrived in Piraeus in spring 317 with a fleet given to him by Antigonos and was able to establish himself securely there. Polyperchon undertook a desperate attempt to win popularity for himself among the Greeks by enforcing his decree in the Peloponnese, where he ordered the deaths of previous adherents of Antipatros, and thus potential supporters of Kassandros, but thereby so appalled the basically pro-Macedonian city of Megalopolis that it successfully offered bitter resistance. In the meantime a royal Macedonian fleet had been destroyed on the Bosporos by Antigonos' ships under the command of Kassandros' officer Nikanor, and at court Queen Eurydike, who viewed with loathing the thought of Olympias' returning at Polyperchon's instigation, tried to raise a rebellion by proclaiming that King Philip had dismissed Polyperchon from his post. Polyperchon felt obliged to hasten back to Macedonia and thus abandoned most of the southern Greek cities to Kassandros.[9]

The urgent necessity of Polyperchon's presence in Macedonia arose from the division of "the kings." While Polyperchon had been taking drastic action in the Peloponnese against potential supporters of Kassandros, Eurydike had been doing all she could at home to weaken his position among the magnates in Macedonia. To this end she made common cause with the adherents of Antipatros, who like herself must have feared for their position should Olympias return to Pella. She had also contacted Kassandros and appealed to him to come to Macedonia.[10] She believed, certainly rightly, that Olympias' return would mean giving precedence to Alexander's son over Philip Arrhidaios and therefore to Olympias over Eurydike. Roxane, as an Iranian, played only a walk-on role in this female battle. Such practical political considerations were foreign to Polyperchon. He desired Olympias' return because he wished to bring all members of the royal family under his own protective control. His already weak position could not be maintained unless he had the exclusive right to act in the name of the monarchy. However, Olympias' long delay and Polyperchon's long absence and increasingly negative image allowed Eurydike the time she needed to exploit the political semi-vacuum to establish her own position. She had turned to good account the conflict of interests between the two incompetent kings and their female relatives and had won supporters for her cause. She had even been able to get an army together so that Polyperchon was forced to escort Olympias with his own army from Epeiros over the Pindos to Macedonia. In the event, however, Eurydike's soldiers were not prepared to fight against the old queen Olympias and Polyperchon, and Philip and Eurydike were taken prisoner.[11]

This event marked the beginning of the tragic last phase of the house of the Argeadai. The root of the problem clearly lay in the grotesque compromise reached in Babylon, which itself had merely resulted from Alexander's neglect of the welfare of his country. Olympias' return had disastrous consequences. Polyperchon, who until now had tried to rule with the traditional consent of the barons, found no means of restraining Olympias in the eruption of her pent-up anger. It was her word that counted after her return to Macedonia. Her driving motive was revenge, and the achievement of a basis of consensus on which government could function was no consideration for the embittered wife, mother and grandmother of Macedonian kings. She had Philip and Eurydike tortured before ordering Philip's murder and driving Eurydike to take her own life. Nikanor, a brother of Kassandros who had come into her power, was also murdered on her orders, and the grave of a second brother, Iolaos, was desecrated. A bloodbath was carried out at her behest among Macedonians held to be supporters of Kassandros, and more than one hundred victims are reported.[12]

By these brutal means Olympias set out uncompromisingly to achieve constitutional clarity. She insisted that only one person, her grandson, should rule in Macedonia. Rivals, real or imaginary, were ruthlessly eradicated. Thus Kassandros, without having done anything himself, had thrust on him the role of avenger of the royal couple, for which he could rely on the support not only of those who hated Olympias and her methods but also of the Macedonian traditionalists, who in any case did not consider the son of the Iranian a person fit to rule in Macedonia. The atrocities perpetrated, and the incompetence shown, by his opponents lent Kassandros, whose formal position was that of a rebel, an undeserved appearance of legitimacy for his aims, in addition to personal sympathy, and he well understood how to turn it to advantage.

Already in autumn 317 he had made a successful military reconnaissance expedition to Macedonia, but he spent the winter in the Peloponnese.[13] As soon as news of the events in Macedonia reached him, he hastened there with his army. It was now clear who his main opponent was—no longer the aging Polyperchon, who was held in check in Perrhaibia by one of his officers,[14] but Olympias, who had barricaded herself into the fortress of Pydna. With her were all remaining members of the court, including Alexander and Roxane as well as another daughter of Philip II, Thessalonike. There they sat together in deceptive safety, which turned out to be a trap when Kassandros managed to surround them with his besieging army and cut off promised help from Epeiros. Polyperchon once more proved his incompetence by failing to prevent his soldiers from deserting to Kassandros.

With this action the fate of Olympias was sealed. The siege, however, lasted for a whole year, during which time practically all remaining resistance to Kassandros disintegrated. After taking Pydna, Kassandros staged a form of trial against Olympias. Without being given the chance to speak, she was condemned by a mass assembly of his supporters and subsequently put to death.[15] It was spring 315, and the civil war was over. The young Alexander IV and his mother had survived the siege, but after all the atrocities committed by his grandmother in his name and the lost civil war, it seemed only a matter of time till he too would be eliminated. To avoid provoking those Macedonians still true to the Argeadai, Kassandros at first let him live, but not in Pella and without royal honours. He was taken with Roxane to the fortress of Amphipolis, where under strong guard they led secluded lives. Five years later the time was ripe. In 310 it was possible to get rid of Alexander and Roxane quietly without disturbing the political equilibrium of Macedonia.[16] The male line of the house of the Argeadai was then extinct.

IV

The Age of the Successors

1. KASSANDROS

When Kassandros came to power in Macedonia in 315 B.C., he could hope for a broad basis of support. The adherents of Antipatros appear to have followed his son. The dilettante fashion in which Polyperchon had run the state, combined with Olympias' atrocities, conveyed the firm impression that there was no real alternative to Kassandros. After a centuries-long monarchist tradition it is inconceivable that anyone should have thought of leaving the state without a king.[1] Kassandros did not yet name himself *basileus*, but until Alexander had come into close contact with the different customs of the Persian empire, none of the Argead kings had set much value on the title. There could, however, be no doubt of the fact that Kassandros, son of Antipatros, firmly held the reins of power in Macedonia.

As the loyal son of a father imbued with the ideas of Philip, Kassandros appears to have given clear priority to the European legacy of Macedonia—ensuring the security of the frontiers, consolidating internally and maintaining Macedonia's dominant ruling position in Greece. Naturally the practical handling of these problems was not dissociated from the personal status of the ruler himself; as always in the Macedonian monarchy the institutionalized personal leadership of the ruler involved a close interweaving of state and personal interests, which only diverged significantly from one another when the ruler could no longer carry the leading barons with him, as had threatened with Alexander and had just happened with Polyperchon. Because of this interlacing of interests inherent in its political system, Macedonia was faced with a specific immediate problem arising from the splitting of Alexander's empire and the elimination of the Argeadai, in addition to the traditional problems of the country. In spite of his success against Polyperchon and Olympias and his acceptance by leading circles in Macedonia, Kassandros had rivals and was not the only person to aspire to rule in Macedonia.

Antigonos, his own earlier well-wisher and ally of his father in the fight against Perdikkas, in the years up to 315 elaborated with increasing success out of his royal commission of 320 to combat the Perdikkans, an exclusive personal claim for the political legacy of Alexander; his ambition was to gain "the whole thing," as our ultimate source, his court follower Hieronymos of Kardia, described the empire of Alexander. It soon became apparent that the Macedonian Antigonos coveted not the riches of Asia but the succession to the Argeadai in Macedonia as the central jewel in his crown. Without Macedonia "the whole thing" lacked its essential kernel.[2] His ambition amounted to a declaration of war on the three Macedonians who had already established large regional power bases or still sought to do so—Kassandros, Lysimachos in Thrace and Ptolemaios in Egypt—and this threat largely determined the foreign policy of Macedonia for the next forty years. It inevitably exerted its influence on the practical handling of the standing problems of the state and of Macedonian possessions in Europe by Kassandros and his successors.

After winning the civil war Kassandros does not appear to have had any major internal problems. The legitimacy of a regime had never had mystical dimensions in Macedonia, for it had always depended on the readiness of leading aristocratic circles to mobilize their followers in the interests of the house of the Argeadai. The succession had always been a question of power, as shown, for instance, by the events of the 390s or the number of rivals who hopefully took up the struggle for power when Philip succeeded in 359. The reason the Argeadai had, until the death of Olympias, always provided the monarch was that in the last resort each successful member of that family had been able to win over the most powerful magnates in the land at the critical time. Legitimacy was thus largely the product of personal recognition—for whatever reason it was granted—and the translation of that recognition into a significant following.

Tradition must of course have played a part, at least among the common people, as finally became clear in Babylon even to the self-confident corps of officers. However, Kassandros found himself in a favourable position. The murder of Philip Arrhidaios had disposed of the problem of one of the kings, and the atrocities perpetrated by Olympias and the lost civil war in practice disqualified Alexander IV. Kassandros arrived on the scene as the bringer of peace and active helper of those who had supported his father, and he quickly found ways of endearing himself to the sensibilities of the common people. It must have been for this reason that Kassandros cultivated the memory of Philip II, his father's friend.[3] It is indeed often maintained, in line with the accusations of his opponents, that Kassandros deliberately fanned an ideological hatred of Alexander III and his family. This accusation, however, cannot be proved; earlier he had even aspired to the hand of Alexander's sister Kleopatra, and he appears to have buried the young Alexander IV after his murder in 310 with full honours, as is strongly indicated by the child's grave discovered at Verghina.[4] In 315 it was therefore probably not ideology and hatred that made the practical elimination of the young Alexander from Macedonian politics seem desirable and feasible but the civil war and Olympias' atrocities.

One of Kassandros' first acts after the end of the civil war was to order the burial with pomp and ceremony of the murdered Philip Arrhidaios in the burial place of the Macedonian kings at Aigai. The body of his wife, Philip II's granddaughter Eurydike, was buried with him; her mother, Philip's daughter Kynnane, who had been murdered by Perdikkas, was also interred at Aigai. The grave of the royal couple is probably one of the richly appointed tombs found at Aigai. With this act Kassandros clearly sought the support of those Macedonians who had helped proclaim Arrhidaios in Babylon and in the meantime had returned home, as well as those in the country who had at the time regarded his appointment as correct.[5]

Traditionalist circles must also have shown satisfaction at Kassandros' marriage in 315 with Philip II's daughter Thessalonike. Thessalonike, in her mid-thirties and still unmarried, had fallen into Kassandros' hands when he took Pydna. Kassandros could hope to have children by her, and they would make his alliance with the Argeadai apparent to all.[6] Kassandros continued the tradition of Philip in another matter as well. Since Philip's death no city had been founded in Europe by the Macedonians; all those founded by Alexander lay in Asia. Kassandros now founded no less than three new Macedonian cities: Kassandreia in the Chalkidike to replace Potidaia, which was settled by refugees from Potidaia and Olynthos; Uranopolis in the neighbourhood of Akanthos, founded under obscure mystical portents by Kassandros' eccentric brother Alexarchos; and the dazzlingly successful new city of Thessalonike, formed by amalgamating a number of small settlements on the Thermaic gulf.[7] The promotion of these cities reveals a policy of consolidating the settlement structure of this region of Macedonia, to which a policy of land grants, such as had been followed by Philip and Alexander, also made its contribution. A fortuitously discovered document from Kassandreia provides evidence of Kassandros' activity. It shows him confirming Perdikkas, son of Koinos, as the possessor of three pieces of land.[8]

The legitimation of Kassandros as ruler of Macedonia was based on his practical monopoly of power and his acknowledgement by the magnates of the country. He did not at first take the title of *basileus*. Only after the death of Alexander IV in 310 and the assumption of the title by Antigonos and his son Demetrios in 306 does Kassandros appear to have cautiously followed their example. According to Plutarch, he never used the title in diplomatic dealings, which implies that he also did not recognize the titles of the other successors.[9] But three pieces of evidence, all from within Macedonia, show the extent to which he did in fact use the title. This evidence appears on small bronze coins intended only for internal circulation, on the land grant from Kassandreia already mentioned, and on a dedication at the national sanctuary at Dion. None of this evidence can be dated exactly, but it is probable that it all comes from the last years of Kassandros' rule, between 306 and 297, when on specific formal occasions he allowed himself to be influenced by his rivals' assumption of the title.[10]

One of the most important and successful enterprises of the Macedonian central government since the time of Philip II had been the securing of the frontiers. Alexander's absence and the civil war following his death had jeopardized the system established by Philip. Thrace and Epeiros especially gave Kassandros cause for concern. The first moves towards reestablishing Mace-

donian rule in Thrace were made in the officers' compromise in
Babylon when Lysimachos received the province, a decision endorsed by Antipatros at Triparadeisos. The civil war following
Antipatros' death can hardly have failed to worry Lysimachos,
but he does not appear to have participated in it. That he so
quickly afterwards cooperated with Kassandros against Antigonos
suggests, however, that they had reached an agreement earlier.
Here again the "legal position" was of no further significance—
just as the majority of Macedonians in Macedonia recognized
Kassandros because of his actual power monopoly and not on
account of any legal rights, so Lysimachos was able to rule in
what used to be the kingdom of the Odrysians because of the
actual power he wielded and his recognition by Kassandros,
though his taking an Odrysian wife probably helped him as well.[11]
But he also had to fight. The revolt of the Odrysian Seuthes and
the refusal of many cities to acknowledge his regime caused him
problems for many years.[12] Macedonia itself, however, was not
directly affected by all this. Kassandros was indeed constrained
to give up Philip's province of Thrace, whose Macedonian frontier
lay along the Nestos, and recognize Lysimachos as ruler there,
but in return he obtained recognition of his own position in Macedonia, a safe frontier with Thrace and a strong ally in combating
Antigonos' claims. In connection with events of 302 Diodoros
comments that it was always Kassandros' custom to turn to Lysimachos in times of crisis.[13] The solution to the problem of Thrace
was, since the political circumstances had altered, different from
that at the time of Philip, but it was effective. Kassandros had no
problems with Thrace.

The same applied to the Paionians of the central Axios valley.
A Paionian contingent had indeed taken part in Alexander's campaign, but nothing is known of the attitude of the Paionians after
his death. Kassandros appears to have been able to establish good
relations with them, as his assistance for the Paionian king Au-
doleon when he was under threat from the Illyrian Autariatai in
310 shows. He was also able to win over the Autariatai themselves
by offering them settlement land in the area of Orbelos, between
the Strymon and the Nestos.[14]

Ever since Philip's marriage to Olympias, the cornerstone of
Macedonian policies in the west had been the close relationship

between the Macedonians and the royal house of the Molossians in Epeiros. But after Olympias had lost the civil war, Kassandros had to ally himself with her opponents in Epeiros to maintain Philip's well-tried policies. For other reasons too he could not afford to neglect this frontier region: his rival Polyperchon, who had supported Olympias' party in Epeiros, himself came from Upper Macedonian Tymphaia.[15] The Molossian king Aiakides was a son of Olympias' sister Troas and had come to power in Epeiros some time after her brother Alexandros' death in 331. Olympias had intended to continue the connection between the two royal houses into the next generation; Aiakides' daughter Deidameia was already betrothed to the child Alexander IV and had been present during the siege of Pydna. But Aiakides' failure against Kassandros provoked a resistance movement against him at home in Epeiros; he was deposed, and his opponents appealed to Kassandros, who dispatched his general Lykiskos there as military governor (*epimeletes kai strategos*). Aiakides had no choice in the meantime but to stay with Polyperchon and bide his time.[16]

His hopes were nourished by the Epeirots' southerly neighbours, the Aitolians. Unconquered in the Lamian War, they remained implacable in their opposition to whoever ruled in Macedonia and allied themselves now to Polyperchon. After Kassandros had opened the war in the west in 313 and had even come to an agreement with Glaukias, the ruler of the Illyrian Taulantians, who had taken Aiakides' two-year-old son Pyrrhos to live with him in 316,[17] Aiakides gathered an army in Aitolia and challenged Kassandros' brother Philippos. After two battles Aiakides was dead, and fifty of his followers had been taken prisoner.[18] Those who had wanted the return of Aiakides transferred their backing, after his death, to his elder brother Alketas, who, however, had the reputation of being violent and unpredictable and for this reason had even been rejected by his own father. Alketas was as little able as Aiakides to win against the Macedonians, but after his defeat Kassandros employed him as client ruler. For Kassandros, this appointment must have gone against the grain, but it was a real attempt to win for himself what remained of those political forces in Epeiros that had once favoured the Macedonian connection at the time of Philip and Alexander and finally bring peace to the country again.[19]

After a few years, in about 306, Alketas' brutalities provoked his murder just as Kassandros was fully occupied with the situation arising from Demetrios' invasion of Greece. He made no move to interfere when Glaukias presented Pyrrhos, now twelve years old, to the Epeirots as their ruler. Who in practice held power in Epeiros until Pyrrhos was banished again in 302 is not clear, but it is perhaps possible to determine the main influences. Pyrrhos' sister Deidameia was married in about 303 to Kassandros' main opponent Demetrios, to whom Pyrrhos went after his banishment. It therefore seems possible that already in 306 Glaukias had been stimulated to action by Demetrios. Kassandros appears to have tolerated Pyrrhos initially, but the long arm of the king of Macedonia was probably instrumental in having Pyrrhos replaced in 302 by Neoptolemos, grandson of Kassandros' friend Alketas and son of Alexandros.[20] Once again Kassandros did not aspire to direct control but attempted, as far as possible, to cooperate with the local power structure. His policy towards Epeiros was no different in principle from that of Philip and Alexander but had been adapted to the changed political circumstances.

Macedonia under Kassandros also had to get along with the Greeks of the south. Antipatros, particularly after the Lamian War, had introduced authoritarian ruling methods in Greece, and Kassandros was not the man to alter a well-functioning system without good reason, especially as Polyperchon had failed miserably in his attempts to change its principles. The Thessalian League seems to have been dissolved by Antipatros at the end of the Lamian War. Nevertheless, Kassandros appears to have had no problems there. He was able to pen up Polyperchon in Azoros in 316 and conduct armies through Thessaly in 315 and 313; in 309 he had Thessalian cavalry at his disposal, and when Demetrios set out to attack Kassandros in 302, he began not in Macedonia but in Thessaly, where he garnered some successes in cities garrisoned by Kassandros. Diodoros reports that after Demetrios' sudden withdrawal to Asia Minor in the same year, Kassandros "retook" the Thessalian cities, a statement implying previous possession. Thessaly was thus just as much under close Macedonian control under Kassandros as it had been under Philip. Kassandros' marriage to the half-Thessalian Thessalonike may have helped make his rule there palatable,[21] but his garrisons were probably in the end the decisive factor.

The situation in central and southern Greece was much more complicated since political developments in Asia, above all Antigonos' efforts to rule Alexander's empire, played an important formative role. Here more than elsewhere Kassandros was forced to take others into account and react to the actions and intentions of those who threatened his own position in Macedonia; here the personal position of the ruler influenced important considerations of state. The situation facing Kassandros in central and southern Greece was at first the one he had inherited from his father and, because of the Lamian War, was based on occupation troops and oligarchies. Best known to us is the situation in Athens, where the democracy had been abolished and a garrison force installed in Munichia, but, mutatis mutandis, such events had been repeated in many smaller communities. Kassandros' task was therefore to win over the Macedonian garrisons and the local oligarchies, a task made easy at the outset by the dilettante fashion in which Polyperchon had supported the democratic politicians. Thus his victorious campaign against Olympias and Polyperchon in 316 could set out from a relatively stable base in Athens and some of the Peloponnesian cities. Afterwards he saw no reason to change his Greek policies, particularly when Polyperchon escaped to the south, where, for lack of an alternative, he continued his hitherto-fruitless struggles against the occupation troops. Even had Kassandros considered making changes, he was committed from the beginning to the authoritarian policies of his father.

Kassandros' situation also had its disadvantages. Occupied Athens formed the centre of his position, and he appointed the Athenian Demetrios of Phaleron, a philosopher trained in the Aristotelian school, as governor, or *epimeletes*, there in 317.[22] But although Polyperchon was not at first able to take advantage of the suppression of democratic political forces, even Kassandros could only change immediate constitutional practice and could not make the Athenians forget their almost two-hundred-year-old democratic tradition. Thus even his stronghold, Athens, offered a potential opportunity for an opponent, should he be in a position to seize it.

Kassandros' authoritarian reputation among the Greeks was somewhat improved by his refounding of Thebes in 315. Super-ficially his motive seems to have been to present himself as right-ing the infamies of Alexander, but more important must really have been the creation of a home for the now-dispersed popu-lation of Thebes. The new foundation was certainly a contribution to solving the troublesome refugee problem, just as in the north the ex-inhabitants of Olynthos and Potidaia found new homes in Kassandreia. The high esteem accorded to Kassandros by the Greeks for this project is emphasized by Diodoros and confirmed by a preserved list of benefactors. Great sympathy and generosity for the undertaking were shown in particular by the Athenians, who had sheltered Theban refugees. While their enthusiasm was probably basically genuine and spontaneous, its direction and in-tensity were doubtless steered by the regime of Demetrios of Pha-leron. Plutarch describes how the Athenians decorated themselves with wreaths to celebrate the rebuilding of Thebes, an action that at any rate must have resulted from official action by Demetrios.[23]

Polyperchon could not compete with such effective publicity and had to confine himself to maintaining his positions in the Peloponnese, above all in Korinth. However, even there Kassan-dros already in 315 could take Argos, Messene and Hermione.[24] Without outside help Polyperchon and his son Alexandros would certainly have been ousted from all their positions one after the other. But at the end of 315 a new development made itself felt, one that was to put Kassandros' successes in question and involve Greece in a military struggle, the aim of which was ultimately power in Macedonia itself. The disruptive element was Antigo-nos. By 315 he controlled all the Asiatic area of Alexander's empire apart from Egypt and Phoenikia, and he was preparing an attack on Phoenikia. Seleukos, satrap in Babylon since 320, had recently fled before Antigonos to Ptolemaios in Egypt and had argued con-vincingly that Antigonos aimed to control "the whole thing," in Asia and in Europe. This can scarcely have been an utterly false interpretation of the situation, and negotiations with Kassandros and Lysimachos led to joint action by the so-called Separatists. The demands they delivered to Antigonos in spring 314 dem-onstrate that they did not want to wait for Antigonos' attack but fight, should it come to it, outside their own territories. Ptolemaios laid claim to Syria, Seleukos to Babylonia, and Lysimachos to the adjacent region of Asia Minor, the old satrapy of Hellespontine Phrygia. Only Kassandros had no obvious demands to make, but Kappadokia and Lykia were claimed in his name. The booty taken by Antigonos from Eumenes was to be shared among them all. As was to be expected, Antigonos refused, and Kassandros sent troops under Asklepiodoros to Amisos on the Black Sea coast of Kappadokia to begin a siege. However, this was no more than an attempt to divide Antigonos' forces.[25]

Antigonos continued to view Phoenikia as his first priority but sent his nephew Polemaios to Kappadokia and Bithynia to counter the diversionary actions in Asia Minor, which Kassandros, perhaps along with Lysimachos, had begun there. The main danger to Kassandros, however, lay rather in Antigonos' initiatives in Greece. One of the Greek members of Antigonos' court, Aristodemos of Miletos, was sent to the Peloponnese with a mercenary army to support Polyperchon and Alexandros and win them as allies for Antigonos. The pair of them were delighted to get this unexpected help, and Polyperchon let Aristodemos appoint him as Antigonos' military deputy, with the title *strategos*, for the Peloponnese while Alexandros journeyed to Antigonos to discuss the development of a common strategy. This objective was realized, however, more in the form of a propaganda statement than in military force. Quite in the style of Alexander Antigonos presented a detailed indictment of Kassandros to an assembly of his troops and other supporters besieging Tyros. Its eclectic accumulation of political items from Macedonian and Greek affairs and from his own and Polyperchon's policies is remarkably unsystematic. Kassandros is condemned for the murder of Olympias and for his rough treatment of the young king Alexander and Roxane, for his marriage to Thessalonike ("by force"), for his open ambition to secure the kingdom of Macedonia for himself, for the foundation of Kassandreia, which incorporated the "very hostile Olynthians," and for the rebuilding of Thebes, which had been "destroyed by the Macedonians." He demanded that where still possible Kassandros revoke these actions and that he obey Antigonos ("the legally appointed general who had taken control of the kingdom"). As icing on the political cake, Antigonos presented the demand that all Greeks should be free, autonomous and with-

out occupation troops. His listeners, all supporters completely dependent on him who would have applauded whatever he said,
were dutifully outraged about Kassandros and endorsed the col-
ourful programme.[26]

This policy was aimed above all at the soldiers in Tyros, particularly those who had now been away from their homes for
many years. Antigonos would never have got anywhere with such
unrealistic and unattractive demands among the Macedonians at
home, who had experienced Olympias' barbarity and the incompetence of Polyperchon. In the light of recent experiences no enthusiasm—certainly no spontaneous insurrection—could be expected from the Greeks, either, for such a "freedom" imposed
from outside. Ever since 319 they had continually heard similar
platitudes from Polyperchon, who in the meantime held his cities
in the Peloponnese by means of garrisons.[27] Freedom of self-determination in the traditional sense, not merely the freedom to
do what the ruler demanded, was hardly to be expected from the
unilateral decree of a Macedonian. There were Greek cities in Asia
Minor as well where Antigonos ruled at least in part through occupation troops. Should the programme conceived against Kassandros be applied to his own practice, he could find himself in
difficulties. Ptolemaios, who in 314 cannot have wished anything
to the disadvantage of his ally Kassandros, promptly published
his own demand with the same contents[28] and dispatched Seleukos with a fleet into Greek waters to force through this programme
in the cities held by Antigonos. Antigonos pretended to hold lib-
eral views in this respect, but his basic cynical pragmatism was
undeniable.

Military power, not grand statements, was what counted; and
since Antigonos sent no troops to Greece in 313, Kassandros even
succeeded in winning over Alexandros by conferring on him the
same title, *strategos* of the Peloponnese, that his father had received from Antigonos.[29] Neither the murder of Alexandros nor
Aristodemos' winning over the Aitolians for Antigonos made any
significant impact on the stability of the political constellation as
a whole. By autumn Kassandros could risk sending troops to
Karia to assist Asandros, the local governor who was friendly to
the coalition, and he also dispatched an Athenian fleet to Lemnos.
Neither operation met with much success.[30]

In 312 Antigonos finally took the offensive. He sent assistance to Seuthes, Lysimachos' main opponent in Thrace, and at last sent some of his own troops to Greece under the command of Telesphoros and his nephew Polemaios. The enlightened pragmatism of the Tyros manifesto had challenged the great weakness of Kassandros' authoritarian system, namely, that its acceptance in the cities did not stretch beyond small groups held together by a common interest; even his sympathizers found burdensome the necessity of tolerating and feeding occupation troops on a permanent basis. But it was only in 312, when Antigonos himself started making military investments, that some areas, until then held by Kassandros, began to waver. The Boiotian League, some members of which were annoyed by the loss of lands the refounding of Thebes had cost them (although they had formally assented), had come increasingly under Aitolian influence and now joined Antigonos. Polemaios received assistance there and managed for a time to "liberate" Boiotia, including Thebes (from where Kassandros' garrison was expelled), Euboia and Phokis. Even some Athenians were impressed by these successes and forced Demetrios of Phaleron to open talks. However, the movement rapidly dissipated; Telesphoros declared himself independent of Antigonos and even plundered the temple precinct at Olympia, so that Polemaios, to prevent further damage, had to rush to the Peloponnese to deal with him.[31]

Events in Syria were more important. A severe defeat near Gaza, which Ptolemaios and Seleukos inflicted on Antigonos' son Demetrios, afforded Seleukos the opportunity to return to Babylon and reestablish his rule there. Antigonos saw his position in the east threatened and opened peace negotiations with the coalition. The result amounted to mutual recognition of the status quo. The formal framework of the agreement, a concession to Antigonos, was shaped by the Argead monarchy. They agreed that the division of power now arranged should continue until Alexander IV came of age; Kassandros should rule in Europe with the title of *strategos*, Lysimachos in Thrace, Ptolemaios in Egypt and Kyrene, and Antigonos in Asia. And in another concession to Antigonos' programme they stipulated that the Greeks should be autonomous. Seleukos was naturally not mentioned because the reason for the agreement was that Antigonos wanted to have his hands free for the conflict with him. Polyperchon, though, was to be taken into account in some way.[32]

The peace treaty spelled out the death sentence for the twelve-year-old Alexander IV and Roxane. Kassandros especially was forced into action, and a few months after the agreement he ordered their discreet murder. According to Diodoros, who relates the opinion of Antigonos' adherent Hieronymos of Kardia, Kassandros, Lysimachos, Ptolemaios and Antigonos were now safe from any threats the "king" might pose. By "threats" he must certainly have meant imponderable risks that might arise from arousing feeling in favour of the Argeadai, for instance by Polyperchon. Kassandros must have been the one who profited most from the new situation. Antigonos now retained in Europe only those places in the Peloponnese taken by his nephew Polemaios, who in his disappointment then let himself be won over by Kassandros.[33]

The only remaining danger to Kassandros was Polyperchon, who still had not given up his dreams of revenge and taking power again. While the "great men" had been neglecting him, he had prepared a coup. Alexander the Great had fathered a son, Herakles, with the Persian Barsine. Herakles was never acknowledged by Alexander and grew up in seclusion in Pergamon, until now as much forgotten by the successors as he had been by his own father. But now that Alexander IV no longer lived, Herakles, now seventeen years old, had rarity value. Polyperchon sent for him and with Aitolian assistance prepared a military escort that was first to bring him through Aitolia into Polyperchon's home district of Tymphaia. Had he succeeded in finding loyal supporters there, the situation could have become dangerous for Kassandros. But Kassandros in the meantime knew his Polyperchon: the latter's typically subordinate nature valued only personal possessions and honours. Kassandros offered to restore to him his confiscated lands in Macedonia, give him an honourable position in the country and appoint him *strategos* of the Peloponnese, with an army provided by Kassandros, if he would in return eliminate Herakles. Consequently Herakles was murdered. Kassandros had finally taken control of Polyperchon.[34]

Ptolemaios' attempt to win over Kleopatra, Alexander's sister, who had been living at Sardis since 322, had a similar outcome. His interest in Kleopatra resulted from his position in Egypt, where he had had Alexander's body interred in the city named after him and where a personal alliance with Kleopatra would have emphasized his monopoly of Alexander's relics and also improved his public image. Kleopatra herself was willing enough to go to him, but the commander of Antigonos' garrison in Sardis prevented her departure and then, on the orders of his employer, had her murdered.[35]

These events give an idea of how fragile the peace of 311 in fact was. Through his own interventions in the Peloponnese, where in 308 he had taken and occupied Sikyon and Korinth, Ptolemaios had so challenged the position of his coalition partner Kassandros that it became necessary to forge a new agreement, by which each was to retain what he possessed.[36] However, the result demonstrated the basic strength of Kassandros' position in Greece. Ptolemaios had conducted his campaign under the banner that Antigonos had not respected the autonomy of the Greeks, but the lack of enthusiasm for this new "liberator" makes clear that the Greeks were not to be won over by a badly prepared and dilettante "liberation" campaign.[37] Kassandros' position in Macedonia had also been strengthened by the eradication of Alexander's family, and he must have been satisfied that Antigonos' challenge had been shifted from Macedonia to Greece and to the question of whether the Greeks should be autonomous; that question was much less important to the Macedonians than the extremely thorny problem of Kassandros' legitimacy as ruler, which had been the main point of Antigonos' indictment at Tyros in 314. For him, as for Philip before him, Greece, and especially the Peloponnese, was only a fringe theatre, though in principle he certainly would have preferred to control the Akrokorinth and the traffic across the isthmus himself; but he must have been content to see his opponents engaged there in an unproductive struggle with his *strategos* Polyperchon. The Greeks and not the Macedonians then had to bear the brunt of these struggles for power, which masqueraded as fights for freedom. As long as central Greece, above all Thessaly, was not threatened, Kassandros was free to observe the course of events and join in as and when he felt like it.

However, in 307 the old danger reemerged in a new guise. By 308 Seleukos had won his struggle against Antigonos in Mesopotamia and Iran, whereupon Antigonos revived his old plans.

Syria and western Asia Minor had remained in his possession, and he now took aim at Europe and Egypt. Had he concentrated on Macedonia, he would probably have had a good chance of success. The danger to Kassandros and Lysimachos would at any rate have been one to be taken very seriously. But Antigonos, despite his seventy-six years, was not single-minded enough in his assault on Macedonia, and dangerous though his advance into Europe was, he was distracted into expensive and time-consuming minor operations and so allowed his opponents time to unite to counter the danger. The decisive battle in 301, in which Antigonos fell, thus did not take place in Europe, as was certainly possible, but at Ipsos in Phrygia, in the heart of his own old satrapy; the participants were not only the otherwise-isolated Macedonians from Europe but also Seleukos, who had hurried from the east with a large army. The place and the manner in which Antigonos met his final defeat were the clear consequences of his lack of persistence and single-mindedness.

The defeat had been preceded by successes that gave Kassandros good grounds to tremble. In 307 Antigonos sent his son Demetrios to Greece with a large fleet "to liberate all the cities throughout Greece, but first of all Athens, which was garrisoned by Kassandros."[38] He succeeded in ousting the Macedonian garrison, which had occupied Munichia since 322, and replacing Kassandros' oligarchic regime under Demetrios of Phaleron with a reconstituted democracy. He was also able to dislodge Kassandros' garrison from Megara. It could have been a splendid start to the assault on Kassandros, but Demetrios was apparently content with his initial rapid successes. He let himself be feted by his admirers among the democrats, whom he had restored to power, and they did him proud with honours, granting him even those usually reserved for the gods. The result was that Demetrios felt so happy in the company of these liberated hypocrites that he spent the whole winter in Athens, to the disgust of the mass of the Athenians.[39]

It was his father, though, who was responsible for his making no further progress in the following year. Demetrios was ordered to Kypros to combat Ptolemaios' fleet. He dutifully withdrew from Greece and won such a great victory near Salamis on Kypros that he and his father marked the occasion by taking the title of *ba-*

sileus. Subsequently Demetrios had to support his father with his fleet in an assault on Egypt, but the action had to be abandoned around November 306 before they had even established a firm base of operations. Even in 305 Demetrios did not return to Greece but busied himself with the island of Rhodes, which had aligned itself with Ptolemaios. Because the island republic had used its freedom to join Ptolemaios, it came under attack from Demetrios, who in this way made clear that he acknowledged the much-sung freedom of the Greek states only insofar as the liberated states supported him. While the liberator of Athens was laying siege to Rhodes, the Rhodians were kept supplied with grain consignments not only from Ptolemaios but also from the garrison experts Kassandros and Lysimachos. This resupply enabled the Rhodians to hold out until the following year when, in view of Demetrios' still meagre prospects of success, the siege was broken off.

It was therefore already summer 304 when Demetrios returned to Greece. He landed near Aulis in Boiotia because Kassandros was besieging Athens, and he immediately took Chalkis. He also won back the Boiotian League and concluded a friendship treaty with Aitolia, whereupon Kassandros retired from Athens, and a large group of about six thousand Macedonians deserted to Demetrios. Those in power in Athens again gave Demetrios an extravagant welcome and even allocated him quarters in the rear section (*opisthodomos*) of the Parthenon, where he spent the winter satisfying his lust for pleasure at Athenian expense. He then spent the year 303 on the Peloponnese, where he fought against Kassandros' *strategoi* Polyperchon and Prepelaos, and was able to take important cities, such as Korinth and Sikyon, as well as a number of smaller towns. Probably during the following winter (303/02), which he again spent in Athens, he organized the participation of his Greek cities in the war against Kassandros along the formal lines of the Korinthian League, founded by Philip II.[40]

This time Demetrios gave the clear impression that Antigonos had set his order of priorities in Greece with a definite target. Kassandros proposed negotiations during the winter, but Antigonos rejected his offer out of hand and demanded unconditional surrender.[41] Kassandros' position suddenly seemed precarious. The bastions in Greece, Athens, Chalkis, Korinth and the Boiotian

League, which until now had defended his position, had all fallen; in eastern Greece he retained only Thessaly, to which Demetrios in 302 extended his systematic operations. Lysimachos was also worried, and it was easy to convince him that, as in 314, the enemy should as far as possible be encountered in Asia rather than in Europe. Kassandros himself had to remain in Europe because of the immediate danger posed by Demetrios; but he sent troops under Prepelaos to Lysimachos, who straightaway set out for Asia and, with Antigonos away in Syria, was able to obtain easy victories in Phrygia, Aiolis and Ionia as far south as Ephesos.[42]

In the meantime Demetrios continued with his Greek plans. His large army (he is reported to have fielded fifty-six thousand men against Kassandros' twenty-nine thousand) was able to establish itself on the Thessalian coast despite the resistance led by Kassandros personally.[43] He ejected Kassandros' garrisons from a number of cities, including Larissa Kremaste and Pherai. However, in spite of the extraordinarily favourable situation, no decisive engagement took place. The blame for Demetrios' failure rested yet again with Antigonos, who promptly revised his order of priorities when he learned that Seleukos had returned from eastern Iran and, like Ptolemaios, had joined the cause of the Europeans. Seleukos came to the support of his allies in Asia Minor with an army that included the corps of elephants he had recently acquired from the Indian king Sandrakottos (Chandragupta). At this Demetrios was immediately ordered to Asia Minor. He was forced to break off his promising campaign in Thessaly "because the king considered it necessary to obey his father."[44] All that could be salvaged there was an emergency agreement with Kassandros that dutifully included the freedom of the Greek cities.

Virtually at the last moment Kassandros had been saved by the actions of his coalition partners in Asia Minor, although the final outcome was still in the balance, and victory for Antigonos would have resulted in the prompt return of Demetrios to Thessaly. For this reason Kassandros dispatched a further twelve thousand infantry and five hundred cavalry to Asia Minor under his brother Pleistarchos while he personally concerned himself with Thessaly. He was not present in the following year, 301, when

the coalition army under Lysimachos and Seleukos defeated Antigonos and Demetrios at Ipsos, though Pleistarchos deputized
for him and his troops were engaged.[45] Kassandros remained in
Europe and prepared countermeasures against a possible unfavourable outcome of the battle. His priorities had not altered since
the time of his father. Kassandros was a European at heart and
stood for the traditional European interests of the Macedonian
state.

2. AFTER IPSOS

Even after the victorious battle of Ipsos Kassandros remained true
to his European principles. Although the empire of Antigonos was
now up for distribution, Kassandros laid no claim to territory in
Asia; his coalition partners were left to divide it among themselves. Lysimachos took possession of Asia Minor as far as the
Tauros, and Seleukos obtained the remainder apart from Kilikia,
claimed by Pleistarchos, and such regions as Ptolemaios occupied.[1]

The exact state of affairs in Europe after Ipsos is obscure, but
Kassandros does not appear to have made any great efforts to
restore his garrisons. Athens declared its neutrality, sent Demetrios' wife Deidameia to Megara and released his ships. In summer 299 the Athenians honoured an envoy who had conducted
negotiations with Kassandros, probably in connection with their
claimed neutrality. The Athenian friends of Demetrios were no
longer heard, and moderate democrats, not in principle antago-
nistic to Kassandros, gained significantly in influence. In the Peloponnese Korinth remained in the hands of Demetrios because
of his garrison there, but no further information is available. Kassandros appears to have been more active in central Greece. Elateia in Phokis, held during the war for Demetrios by the Athenian
Olympiodoros, was Macedonian again by 297. In the west Kassandros attempted without success to gain Kerkyra.[2]

It is unclear whether this lack of reported events reflects in fact
less active policies towards the Greeks or merely the paucity of
sources. At any rate, until the death of the not-yet-sixty-year-old
Kassandros in May 297 the most important factor in Macedonia
would seem to have been the illness of the king. But only with

the sudden death of the eldest of Kassandros' sons by Thessalonike—named Philippos according to Kassandros' political programme—just four months after the death of his father did the full extent of the loss suffered by the Macedonians become clear. Neither of the younger sons, Antipatros (who cannot have been more than sixteen) nor the even younger Alexandros, was considered old enough to reign without a regent. A regency for Antipatros would in principle have been no great disaster; everything depended on the acceptability and competence of the regent. However, Thessalonike wilfully constructed a unique scheme to promote the interests of Alexandros, and no one was able to withstand her. Her plan was for the two youths to reign jointly, but with separate regional responsibility, under the regency of their mother. This impossible model must have been inspired by the grotesque compromise in Babylon. It was not long before Antipatros murdered his mother, who had always favoured Alexandros, and set out to wage war on his brother. Each now looked for help where he could find it. This feud immediately endangered the position that Kassandros had so carefully built up for his family because it was not in fact completely self-evident, despite their descent along the maternal line from the great Philip II, that Kassandros' offspring were entitled to inherit his position. The descendants of Antipatros were by no means so firmly established as the Argeadai, in spite of the ease with which Philippos had assumed power and the strong position of Thessalonike. Much was at risk: Macedonia itself had experienced under Kassandros nineteen peaceful years, during which no military conflict had taken place on Macedonian soil. If neither of the two youths thought he could win without help from outside, then the precious stability of the country was at an end.[3]

In the meantime Demetrios and Pyrrhos had returned to Greece. Even after the defeat at Ipsos Demetrios, with his unvanquished fleet and volatile temperament, presented a danger to the stability of the new balance of power. Seleukos and Ptolemaios therefore tried to neutralize him through marriage alliances; his daughter Stratonike was married to Seleukos himself, and Demetrios was to receive Ptolemais, a daughter of Ptolemaios. Lysimachos also linked himself to Ptolemaios through Arsinoe, and Demetrios' friend Pyrrhos, whose recently deceased sister Deidameia had married Demetrios in about 303, received in 298 the hand of Antigone, a stepdaughter of Ptolemaios.[4] Were these conciliation attempts to succeed, it could only be at the cost of Kassandros. Indications of what might happen were apparent even before his death; Pleistarchos could not maintain his position in Kilikia against Demetrios and was given no help by Seleukos and very little by Lysimachos.[5] He soon emerged in Karia, where, probably with the agreement of Lysimachos, he managed to take control of a district south of the Maiander around Herakleia-by-Latmos, which he renamed Pleistarcheia. Here he ruled for some years, but played no known role again in Macedonia.[6]

The unexpected death of Kassandros and the resultant uncertain situation offered an opportunity that could not be passed up. First Ptolemaios organized Pyrrhos' return to Epeiros, where he soon took control. Shortly afterwards, in 295, Demetrios also returned to Greece. According to Plutarch, it was events in Athens, where a certain Lachares had set himself up as tyrant, that motivated Demetrios to go back to Greece; but the confusion surrounding the Macedonian crown must have been the decisive factor. In spring 294 he retook Athens, but only after a long siege. This time his troops occupied not only Munichia but also Mouseion Hill in the heart of the city. No attempt was made to pretend that freedom had been restored. Demetrios personally appointed the leading archon, Olympiodoros, who, contrary to tradition, held office for two consecutive years. The will of Demetrios was the decisive factor in all affairs, and the freedom slogans of his father were no longer heard.[7]

In 294, just as before, Athens was for Demetrios basically nothing more than a comfortable base for further operations; his target in Europe remained Macedonia, even though, as before, he first advanced into the Peloponnese. That he achieved his aim so suddenly and easily must have come even to him as a surprise. In that same year, 294, the crisis between the two sons of Kassandros reached its climax. Alexandros sought help desperately and appealed both to his new neighbour Pyrrhos and to Demetrios, whereas Antipatros, who in the meantime had married a daughter of Lysimachos, turned to his father-in-law. But Lysimachos perhaps owing to problems of his own with the Transdanubian Getai, gave him no assistance, and before Demetrios had responded to

Alexandros' plea, Pyrrhos had long been active. At the price of making over to Pyrrhos the Macedonian districts of Týmphaia and Parauaia bordering on Epeiros as well as the western possessions Ambrakia, Akarnania and Amphilochia, Antipatros was chased out of Macedonia and Alexandros secured in power over the whole country. It would seem that Pyrrhos simultaneously extended his power to include Thessaly, though perhaps at first only some border areas to the south of Tymphaia were taken.[8]

When Demetrios arrived in the area Alexandros, thanks to the intervention of Pyrrhos, was already established. They met at Dion in Pieria, where the embarrassed young king had to explain to his invited, but no longer welcome, helper that his assistance was no longer required. The consequences could not in the long term remain in doubt. The relationship was one of mutual distrust, but Demetrios still managed to tempt Alexandros and his escort away from Macedonian soil to Larissa. There the naive young man, isolated and surrounded by Demetrios' army, was murdered. According to the biassed account of Hieronymos, which Plutarch used as his source, Alexandros himself had planned to assassinate Demetrios, who just got in first. On the following day a rump Crown Council, consisting of members of Alexandros' escort, was convened. Intimidated by Demetrios' army, the members gave their consent and acknowledged Demetrios as king of the Macedonians, and he was also accepted by an assembly of the otherwise-leaderless army. Lysimachos was not currently in a position to offer Antipatros assistance and, as the price of peace, relinquished to Demetrios the claims of his son-in-law.[9]

3. KING DEMETRIOS

Demetrios had not lived in Macedonia since his early childhood. Shortly after his birth in about 335 his father had been made Alexander's satrap in Phrygia, and the small child grew up in Phrygian Kelainai. Ever since, Demetrios had led an unsettled life in the shadow of his father, and, apart from the short period after 307 spent in Greece, always in Asia. He had taken over from his father the project of winning Macedonia and pursued it determinedly. Antigonos appears to have regarded Macedonia as the final conquest, as the jewel that should complete his crown of conquest. It was a project in no way based on strategic thinking, and even less on economic considerations, but which can only be explained by his own Macedonian origins and patriotic feelings. For Demetrios, however, the situation in 294 was different from that of 307 and was much more similar to that of Kassandros in 318. When he advanced into Macedonia from Greece, which was still only partly under his control, he possessed only his fleet and a few military bases, and he took advantage of the confusion of civil war to put himself into power.

If Demetrios wanted to establish himself there, as Kassandros had done, he would also, particularly as a newcomer, have to attend to the traditional requirements of the Macedonian state. Demetrios had no close Macedonian friends in Macedonia. The magnates who under severe pressure had accepted him in Larissa and escorted him to Macedonia acted only out of self-protection, no doubt the motive of many who hoped at least for a stabilizing of conditions after the civil war. Only his first wife, Antipatros' daughter Phila, and their joint son, Antigonos, linked him to the tradition of Antipatros and could perhaps mobilize some supporters. Demetrios' strength therefore certainly did not lie in political support but in the army that he had brought with him. Difficulties were implicit in this situation. The whole of Demetrios' military high command had naturally accompanied him to Macedonia, and its members would expect to take over positions of political leadership, inevitably at the expense of those who currently constituted the ruling elite.

It seems that Demetrios at first turned his attention to the traditional foreign-policy needs of the state. He made peace with Lysimachos in Thrace and succeeded in asserting Macedonian interests again in Thessaly, where he crowned his activities by founding the harbour city of Demetrias on the Gulf of Pagasai.[1] The signals were clear: just as Kassandros had linked the Chalkidike more closely to Macedonia by the city bearing his name, so Demetrias should strengthen Thessaly's bond and simultaneously provide a home base for the fleet. He also tried to extend Macedonian influence in central Greece. Athens and large parts of the Peloponnese were already occupied, and now, though not without certain difficulties, Macedonian interests prevailed in

Boiotia as well.[2] He took over Macedonian state policies institutionalized under Kassandros, thereby contradicting his previous
personal alliances, such as hostility towards the Aitolians or towards Pyrrhos in Epeiros. As king in Macedonia he had to pursue
the current interests of the state, not just his personal inclinations.

This initial attitude might have brought Demetrios success had
he been content merely to continue the well-tried policies of Kassandros and thus endear himself to the Macedonians as their
ruler. It rapidly became clear, however, that unlike his father Demetrios regarded Macedonia not as the summit of his ambitions
but only as the starting point for the reconquest of Alexander's
empire, as the base for a new version of Alexander's expedition.
A first indication of this aim was given in 292 when news arrived
that Lysimachos was being held prisoner by the Getian chief
Dromichaites, and Demetrios promptly started preparations to
take Thrace. He was forced to abandon the undertaking when
Lysimachos was unexpectedly set free.[3] The incident nevertheless
made it plain that unlike Kassandros he placed little value on
peaceful coexistence with Lysimachos. Far more important to him
was the building up of a large fleet, and it became his passion.
He frequently visited ship-building yards in the whole of Greece—
in Piraeus, Korinth, Chalkis and Pella itself, where altogether five
hundred ships, some of very elaborate and expensive design, had
been commissioned. He also collected an enormous army.[4]

The prospect of having to take part in, or at least help finance,
yet another royal Asian adventure did not fill the Macedonians
with the slightest enthusiasm. The traditionalists would have
obeyed their king in spite of misgivings had he otherwise conducted himself as behoved a traditional Macedonian king. However, the years spent by Demetrios in Asia and his unbridled character had in no way trained him for this task. The Macedonians
were simply not accustomed to great luxury, even though there
are indications that the upper classes had adjusted their tastes to
fit Macedonia's rise in the world; some extravagant tombs and the
peristyle houses in Pella may well date from this period. But the
ostentatious personal luxury surrounding oriental kings and lords
remained—especially under Antipatros and his son—foreign to
the Macedonians. Demetrios delighted in displaying himself in
extravagant purple robes and in hats and shoes embroidered in

gold thread, and he ordered many more to be made. As the vestments of an oriental-style ruler these were unwelcome external symbols of an opulent life-style alien to the Macedonians.[5]

It was particularly his manner of dealing with ordinary people that demonstrated how unsuitable Demetrios was for the office of king of Macedonia. The people expected that their king be readily available to them and that they should be able to petition him and tell him of their problems directly and without fuss. Perhaps it did not bother them that an Athenian deputation once had to wait for two years before being granted an audience; but when the king treated the Macedonians themselves in such a summary and careless fashion, he was felt to be the wrong man for the job. Plutarch tells two anecdotes relating to this matter. Once Demetrios collected a number of written petitions and put them all inside his robe. The people were happy until they noticed that he had surreptitiously thrown them all over a bridge into the Axios. The second anecdote tells how an old woman once demanded of Demetrios that he hear her petition; on his replying that he had no time, she screamed at him, "Then don't be king."[6]

Of course anecdotes reflect only a limited aspect of historical reality, but it can still scarcely be doubted that the reason for Demetrios' undoing was his failure to win over the Macedonians. Plutarch wrote that Demetrios led his people so frequently on campaigns because when he left them at home they only created disturbances;[7] that is, under his rule they were unable or unwilling to live peacefully. Their military capability, however, was also limited, as is clearly demonstrated by the manner in which Demetrios finally lost control of Macedonia. Pyrrhos had already in 295 been granted two districts of Macedonia, Tymphaia and Parauaia, by Alexandros and seems to have made himself somewhat popular there. He also gained in popular esteem through his victory over Demetrios' general Pantauchos in Aitolia and his honourable treatment of the five thousand prisoners taken. On one occasion when Demetrios was ill, Pyrrhos advanced as far as Edessa without encountering any resistance, and it was only there that Demetrios succeeded in repulsing the attack.[8]

Not only the Macedonians, however, but above all Lysimachos, Seleukos and Ptolemaios were affected by Demetrios' plans for reconquest. Despite their differing interests they managed to band together to form a coalition, and Pyrrhos also promised his cooperation. In 288 Ptolemaios sent a fleet to the Aegean while Lysimachos marched into Macedonia from Thrace and Pyrrhos from Upper Macedonia. Demetrios did not think that his troops would be able to withstand Lysimachos' Macedonians, and so first he set out to deal with Pyrrhos, who had already penetrated as far as Beroia. The invasions had taken place while Demetrios was occupied in southern Greece with the preparations for his Asian campaign. The Macedonians had therefore from the beginning nothing good to say for a king who allowed their land to be laid waste from two different directions simultaneously—an experience they had never once had under Kassandros—and the soldiers began to desert to Pyrrhos. The remaining troops also made it clear that they did not want to fight against Pyrrhos. According to Plutarch's account, Demetrios was advised to withdraw and save himself "because the Macedonians refused to fight a war so that he could live in luxury."[9]

The ignominious defeat at Beroia marked the end of Demetrios' reign in Macedonia. He did not possess the decorum of his wife Phila, who refused to leave her home country for a precarious future and took poison in Kassandreia, where the couple first fled. He travelled to the Peloponnese, where he still controlled Korinth, but in spring 287 was taken by surprise by the insurrection that broke out in Athens in spite of his garrisons, and he had to suffer Ptolemaios' negotiator, Sostratos, forcing a peace treaty on him that included guarantees for the freedom of Athens. He then sailed for Asia Minor. This is not the place for a detailed description of his desperate attempt to reconquer the Asian empire of his father, nor of his death as an alcoholic under the honourable "protection" of his son-in-law Seleukos in about 283. After his loss of Macedonia and on leaving Greece, he had indeed presented for a short period all the dangers of someone run amok, but his political significance was gone.[10]

4. INTERREGNUM

The history of the following decades can be written only in outline. With the banishment of Demetrios the usual form of the state was suspended. Pyrrhos and Lysimachos divided the country between them. The dubious principle of division, perhaps along the Axios, had already been put into practice by Kassandros' sons, but there was a massive difference between power being exercised from within the country and its being exercised externally, from Epeiros and Thrace. Both Pyrrhos and Lysimachos were counted among the ranks of Macedonian kings by later chronographers, and we know that Pyrrhos was recognized as king at least by Demetrios' Macedonians. However, it is clear that despite this momentary preference for their new ruler, the Macedonians in practice had to suffer a division of their country and tolerate foreign rule. The Macedonian Lysimachos continued to keep Lysimacheia in Thrace as his seat of government even after he reunited the country in 284 by expelling Pyrrhos. Macedonia was important enough to him to fight for, but he appears to have regarded it only as an additional part of his empire, a sort of new province and not even the most important one.[1]

Political structures are hard to make out during these years. While Demetrios remained in Greece, Pyrrhos continued the fight against him. He occupied Thessaly, was appealed to by the Athenians and visited the city;[2] but he was unable to take the bases still occupied by Demetrios, namely the Piraeus, some forts in Attika, and the three bastions of Demetrias, Chalkis and Korinth. These remained occupied by Demetrios' son Antigonos after his own withdrawal to Asia. It is not really possible to ascertain whether Pyrrhos was following any long-term policy that stretched beyond the current war against Demetrios; but if he was, there is no indication of any divergence from the policies of Antipatros and Kassandros, which under quite different circumstances aimed at bringing the whole southern Balkan peninsula under Macedonian control or influence. For such policies he would doubtless have been able to gain the consent of the most influential political voices in Macedonia.

When Lysimachos then set out to win for himself Pyrrhos' share of Macedonia and Paionia, he persuaded the magnates by arguing that Pyrrhos was not Macedonian.[3] But considering the large army he had brought with him, any argument would have carried the day. The foreign policy he then pursued (nothing is known of his internal policies) bore little resemblance to that practised since the time of Philip. In the Balkans Lysimachos took

Thessaly, with the exception of Demetrias, but his interest in direct rule ceased at its southern frontier. He took pains to establish good relationships but appears to have displayed no interest in extending his rule over the Greeks; there is no evidence of any occupation ordered by him of a southern Greek city. He displayed the same carefree attitude in allowing Pyrrhos to continue to rule in Epeiros and western Greece after his withdrawal from Macedonia.[4]

These significant curtailments in the policies of the previous fifty years can be explained by the particular structure of Lysimachos' empire. Its heart was for him not Macedonia but Thrace. With Kassandros' agreement he had until 301 built up an empire there, few details of which are known, combining Thracian and Greek elements. Already in 314 he had registered interest in the adjoining districts of Asia Minor. He accordingly built his new capital of Lysimacheia, which replaced Kardia, at one of the points where Europe and Asia are closest, and so after Ipsos he made good his claim against his coalition partners to Asia Minor up to the Tauros.[5] When he then expelled Pyrrhos from Macedonia and became sole ruler there, Macedonia itself had only the status of a peripheral province—however proud and imbued with tradition—in an already functioning state. Macedonia's new role was a modest one; it was no longer a centre of power and a base for further conquests, as in the times of Antipatros and Kassandros, but merely an extra piece of territory that rounded off a state already founded elsewhere by a Macedonian, according to his own concepts and opportunities. The empire of Lysimachos was just as much a personal creation as Alexander's empire. But Lysimachos' plans had two points in common with the policies of Philip II, in contrast to those of his successors: the North Aegean region was given the highest priority, and direct Macedonian interests ceased at the southern frontier of Thessaly.

This model did not endure either. Lysimachos was already seventy-seven years old when his army drove Pyrrhos out of Macedonia. Though he did indeed have a son, Agathokles, whose mother Nikaia was a daughter of Antipatros, within the royal household severe disagreements arose with his third wife Arsinoe over the question of the succession, in the course of which, in 283, Agathokles was murdered. When two years later Lysimachos fell on the battlefield of Korupedion in Lydia in a struggle against

Seleukos, who was only some three years younger, there was no one left with sufficient authority to defend the European rump of his kingdom against the claims of the victor Seleukos. After a first reorganization of Asia Minor Seleukos carried his campaign against the empire of Lysimachos into Europe in autumn 281. It seemed that in the end it would be this old campaigner against Antigonos, who had contributed so much in Asia to the failure of the latter's exclusive claims to rule, who would himself be the one to unite the most important Asian and European parts of Alexander's empire.[6]

However, the resistance, at least of the younger generation, was not yet broken, even though no experienced army could be fielded. Shortly after Seleukos had crossed the Dardanelles and set foot on European soil, he was stabbed to death near Lysimacheia by a treacherous assassin who had observed the efficacy of such primitive methods while residing at the court of Lysimachos. The perpetrator, Ptolemaios, known as Keraunos ("Thunderbolt"), was a fruit of the marriage policies of the old Antipatros, whose daughter Eurydike had been given to Ptolemaios I and bore him a number of children, including Keraunos. Because his father favoured his son by Berenike, the later Ptolemaios II Philadelphos, Keraunos had no prospects if he stayed in Egypt, so probably during the 280s he left to join his sister Lysandra, the wife of Lysimachos' son Agathokles, in Lysimacheia. Subsequently (sometime before 283) he went to Seleukos, who offered him help with the Egyptian succession, and he was joined there by Lysandra, who sought refuge with Seleukos after the murder of her husband. This last circumstance gave Seleukos a political excuse for attacking Lysimachos' empire.

Nothing came of the help Seleukos had promised to Keraunos in Egypt. Ptolemaios I died in summer 282, and the well-prepared succession proceeded smoothly. Keraunos then accompanied Seleukos in the war against Lysimachos. As grandson of Antipatros he may well have played with the idea of ruling in Macedonia, should Seleukos be victorious, and perhaps it was his disappointment at Seleukos' intention of reigning in Europe himself that motivated him to the murder.[7]

However that may have been, the clear intention of the murder was to prevent Seleukos from setting himself up as ruler in Europe. During his short period of rule (the sources deem it one

year and five months) Keraunos does not seem to have laid any
claim to Asia Minor. He was given a friendly welcome in Lysimacheia, where he was known, and thereupon bound a diadem
round his head and presented himself to Seleukos' now-leaderless
troops as king. In this endeavour also he prevailed, but the gulf
between what he claimed and reality was very large. Lysimachos
had left no generally acknowledged successor. After the death of
Agathokles, who had been given such a marked amount of responsibility by his father that he could have taken over the succession unchallenged, there was simply nobody who enjoyed sufficient recognition in both Thrace and Macedonia to be able to
establish himself without difficulty. Since the death of Alexander
III short-term considerations had increasingly decided the succession in Macedonia. Just how fragile was a state form that depended on nothing more than the personality of the ruler became
clear after the death of Kassandros, when, in spite of all his attempts to follow traditionalist policies, the traditional consensus
among the country's nobility demonstrably fell apart. The current
power of the court to assert its will—even in putting through
impractical solutions to crucial state problems contrary to established custom, such as the division of the country between Thessalonike's two young sons—was relatively strong merely because
of the ineffectiveness and fragmentation of the regional political
forces. This situation also made it easy for Demetrios to assert
himself against Kassandros' sons, but only for as long as he had
a personally loyal army behind him. The monarchy as an institution had been so weakened by the extermination of the dynasty
and the shattering of the loyalties bound up with it that momentary advantages and purely military power had become the decisive factors in obtaining and retaining control of the land. The
end of Demetrios demonstrates these factors plainly; as soon as
his army was demoralized he had no more support in the country.
Pyrrhos, who was reputed to be the better soldier, was then able
to step into his place despite his purely Epeirot origins. Even
Lysimachos had in the end only been able to assert his position
in Macedonia by force.

After the death of Seleukos at least three people contended for
power over Macedonia: Ptolemaios Keraunos, who had assumed

the royal symbol of the diadem in Lysimacheia; Demetrios' son Antigonos ("Gonatas"), who held on in his father's Greek strongholds and had already taken the title of *basileus* as an easy way of staking his claim; and the eldest son of Lysimachos by Arsinoe, the perhaps-seventeen-year-old Ptolemaios, who had gone to Kassandreia with his mother after Korupedion and agitated there for his claim to the throne. There is a dearth of reliable details concerning what then followed. The sources tell of a sea battle between Keraunos and Gonatas; an arranged peace between Keraunos and Antiochos; a war between Keraunos and Ptolemaios, son of Lysimachos, who was helped by the Illyrian chieftain Monounios; an agreement between Keraunos and Pyrrhos, who was just on his way to Italy; and the marriage between Keraunos and Arsinoe, which culminated in the murder of her other two sons and her own exile. All this occurred roughly between September 281 and February 279.[8]

It is impossible to arrange these events—described in the sources only briefly and usually without causal connections being given—in reliable chronological order. All that can be concluded is that among those who considered they had a claim to rule in Macedonia Keraunos was at first the most successful. We can only speculate as to why it should have been so; a possible explanation is that in this period, when claims to power could only obtain recognition through strength of arms, Keraunos was able to take command of Seleukos' invasion army and of contingents in Thrace loyal to Lysimachos and that by winning over Arsinoe for himself, he robbed his main rival, her son Ptolemaios, of his most important supporter.

Ptolemaios Keraunos, assisted by his brother Meleagros, made a good start but was then overtaken by unforeseeable events. Celtic raiding parties from the central Danube region invaded the northern neighbours of Macedonia in unprecedented numbers during winter 280/79, and Keraunos proudly rejected an offer by the Celtic chieftain Bolgios to spare his lands in return for protection money, just as he also rejected an offer by the Dardanian ruler to supply him with soldiers for the fight against Bolgios. In about February 279 it came to a battle. Keraunos appears to have been taken by surprise, was not able to withstand the Celts and, together with a large number of his soldiers, fell in the struggle.[9] Macedonia was now delivered practically defenceless into the hands of the Celts. Neither Keraunos' brother Meleagros, who took over the leadership for two months, nor his replacement, Kassandros' nephew Antipatros "Etesias," son of Philippos, who himself only managed to hold out for about six weeks, was able to offer the Celts effective resistance, in spite of their impressive ancestry.[10]

In this emergency Sosthenes, one of the surviving officers and perhaps one of Lysimachos' former commanders in Asia Minor, was promoted to the leadership. How he came to be appointed is obscure: the sole source tells of despairing popular consent, and although the army hailed him as *basileus*, he refused to take the title. The royal title, granted by the army alone and without the agreement of the magnates, would certainly have been of no use to Sosthenes. With the state disintegrating, it was far more important to possess the practical loyalty of those capable of bearing arms than to lay formal claims—in any case not immediately realizable—that might provoke damaging objections from other political groupings. This had also initially been Kassandros' policy. However, Sosthenes was included in later lists of rulers and credited with a reign of two years.[11]

Sosthenes was at least able to repel Bolgios, and when a fresh Celtic raiding party under Brennos and Akichorios arrived in Macedonia in the autumn, they deemed it more profitable to proceed relatively quickly farther south. This decision may well have been influenced by the measures taken by Sosthenes, just as in the spring the Celts, having been defeated by the Greeks in the south, showed no disposition to linger on their march back through Macedonia. However, Sosthenes then died, and his death marked the beginning of such a chaotic period in Macedonian history that the extremely sparse sources tell of a period of anarchy without leadership. Three names are indeed mentioned: Antipatros, probably "Etesias," the nephew of Kassandros; Ptolemaios, probably the eldest son of Lysimachos and Arsinoe; and the otherwise-unknown Arrhidaios; but it is simultaneously related that none of them was able to assert himself.[12] Further information is available only from Kassandreia, where a certain Apollodoros took control of the city and ruled it as tyrant. His brief local success may serve to illustrate the total collapse of the central power in the state. The cities now had to rely on themselves and, at least in Kassandreia, had problems in coping with their sudden independence.[13]

V

The Antigonids

1. CONSOLIDATION

The evacuation of the three fortresses described later by Philip V as the "fetters of Greece" played a major role in negotiations during the second war of the Macedonians against Rome (200–197 B.C.). By this phrase he meant Akrokorinth, Chalkis and Demetrias, which not only were almost impregnable strongholds but also had come to stand as symbols for Macedonian domination.[1] After the withdrawal of Demetrios Poliorketes from Europe in 287, these "fetters," together with the Piraeus, formed the main substance of Antigonid possessions in Europe and stood under the control of Antigonos, son of Demetrios.[2] They therefore were the base from which the kingdom of Macedonia could be regained, and Antigonos finally succeeded in this aim by 276, after the chaotic years of the Celtic onslaughts.

Polybios, the main source for the war with Rome, gives reasons why the Romans, even after their annihilating military victory in 197, did not choose to abolish the Antigonid monarchy, as the Aitolians expected. Among these was the consideration that one of the historical functions of Macedonia had always been the protection of the southern Greeks from the menace of the non-Greek barbarians from the northern Balkans.[3] The Aitolians were not convinced then by this argument and would have been even less so during the years following 279, when the Macedonians so signally failed to fulfil this protective function that the Aitolians themselves were forced to undertake the defence of central Greece against the Celts. Nevertheless, the judgement of the Roman general T. Quinctius Flamininus in 197 was essentially right. The Celtic incursions into southern Greece in 279 had been made possible only by Macedonian weakness; and after the consolidation of the state by Philip V's grandfather Antigonos Gonatas Macedonian protection soon functioned effectively once more. The Romans laid value on retaining this positive attribute of the Macedonian state, and its negative side, the "fetters" that bound Greece under Macedonian domination, were to be relinquished. Until then the Greeks had had to pay for their protection with their acceptance of Antigonid supremacy.

The epoch of Macedonian history that begins in about 277/76 with the recognition of Antigonos Gonatas as king of Macedonia is one of the worst-documented periods of Macedonian and Greek history. The source material is simply not sufficient to allow a continuous history of events to be written, but it is perhaps possible to recognize some of the basic political principles and tendencies in state policies during these years.[4]

Little can be said for this period about the traditional internal problems confronting any Macedonian king. Absolutely nothing is known as to how Antigonos was able to assert himself in the country, from which circles he received his support or how he came at all to Pella. The flight of Arsinoe to Egypt in 279 and the disappearance of her son Ptolemaios, son of Lysimachos, from the vicinity of Macedonia doubtless relieved the political tension.[5] A breathing space was also won by the treaty Antigonos concluded with Antiochos I and his marriage to Antiochos' daughter Phila around 277/76, events that must have been precipitated by Antigonos' victory over a Celtic army near Lysimacheia.[6] It is not known whether Antigonos formally abandoned his claim to Thrace in this treaty, but he seems to have made no attempt to reestablish the European empire of Lysimachos. The Macedonian frontier probably lay again along the Nestos as at the time of Kassandros. At the latest in the 240s, and possibly even earlier, Ainos, perhaps Maroneia and probably Samothrake even became Ptolemaic without the Macedonian king taking any countermeasures;[7] and if even these important coastal towns were non-Macedonian, then the people of Thrace, insofar as they had survived the Celtic storms, probably also were left to themselves. But in the Axios valley the foundation of the Macedonian city of Antigoneia must have restored the Paionians, who seem to have enjoyed a certain independence under Lysimachos but had suffered badly under the Celts, squarely to the Macedonian fold.[8]

It must be assumed that Macedonia itself was first conquered militarily. Following the deaths of Ptolemaios Keraunos and Sosthenes it cannot have been excessively difficult for Antigonos, through his mother a grandson of the great Antipatros and supported by the rump of Demetrios' fleet, to gain control of the country. Indications of battles are to be found in the sources only for Kassandreia, where a long siege was needed to expel the tyrant Apollodoros.[9] A threat from Pyrrhos in the west did not arise before 274. When he then attacked Macedonia on his return from Italy, he was able to advance even as far as Aigai without meeting significant resistance. However, by then Antigonos was strong enough in the coastal areas to maintain his position there. Pyrrhos was not prepared to take the risks necessary for breaking the resistance, and he withdrew.[10]

The Macedonian army, worn out by the dynastic troubles and powerless against the Celts, needed time if it were to be brought into good order again. Since Antigonos' widely scattered bases in the south could only be coordinated by means of a fleet, he had brought one with him from Greece; the army he attempted to augment in the short term by recruiting Celtic mercenaries. This force was not sufficient to repel Pyrrhos in 274, but a few years later Antigonos' son Demetrios was able to claim military victory over Pyrrhos' successor, Alexander II.[11] Antigonos himself was also able to sustain and win a long war against a Greek alliance enjoying Ptolemaic support (Chremonidean War, ca. 268/67–262/61) without his personal position in Macedonia being challenged—proof of a certain degree of consolidation in military matters.

The emphasis in other areas as well must have been firmly on consolidation. The foundation of three cities can possibly be ascribed to this Antigonos—Antigoneia in the Axios valley, Antigoneia on the Chalkidike and Demetrias in Macedonia—but we know nothing of any of these places apart from their names.[12] During the last decade of his rule, perhaps even earlier, he allowed some of the cities in the country a measure of controlled civic independence. Around 242 four Macedonian cities, Kassandreia, Amphipolis, Philippoi and Pella, undertook to respect the sacred institutions on Kos in response to a Koan request and bound themselves to recognize the temple of Asklepios—or both it and the festival, the Asklepieia—as "sacred and immune" (*asy-los*).[13] In whatever manner political life in the cities may have been organized, this circumstance alone makes plain that externally these cities could certainly be regarded as city-states (*poleis*), even though each civic decree states specifically that it could only be passed because the contents conformed to the intentions of King Antigonos. A similar situation is evident from letters of the crown prince Demetrios in 248/47. Demetrios instructed the official Harpalos to oversee the repayment of monies that had been diverted for town purposes from the income of the temple of Herakles at Beroia.[14] This incident again seems to show a certain measure of local autonomy, though here too under royal supervision. The functioning both of these city constitutions and of royal supervision can be regarded as proof that a consolidation of the Macedonian state had indeed taken place.

Antigonos would seem to have cultivated Macedonian traditions and thus deliberately recalled the era of the Argead monarchy. The evidence is again difficult to interpret, but he appears to have busied himself with Aigai, the old capital and burial place of the Argead kings. Pyrrhos may well have supplied the immediate motive for this activity when he advanced to Aigai in 274 and allowed his Celtic mercenaries to plunder at will the tombs of the kings.[15] Not all were pillaged, and in particular the lavishly furnished "royal tombs" remained unviolated. The archaeologists excavating Aigai discovered fragments of broken tombstones among the rubble used as filling material for the large burial mound. The explanation that the use of this broken material occurred in the course of official clearance work following Pyrrhos' raid is very plausible. If so, the only person who could have commissioned the construction of this monument—the largest tumulus there had ever been in Greece, simultaneously a memorial to its builder and a monument to his traditional Macedonian values—was Antigonos himself.[16] However, the tumulus, which has since been removed by the excavators, was only the start. The palace at Verghina also dates, according to one opinion of the excavating archaeologists, from the early third century B.C.[17] This information leads to the conclusion that this imposing edifice was erected also as part of the cultivation of the old Macedonian royal tradition, as would certainly have befitted the founder of a new dynasty. The building of the palace and the great tumulus can then be considered to have been a deliberate attempt on the part of Antigonos Gonatas to ingratiate himself as ruler to traditional Macedonian aristocratic circles.

The extended periods spent by Antigonos in Macedonia during his long rule (till 240/39) also made possible the renaissance of cultivated courtly society. Antigonos' own taste must have been influenced by his years in Greece as his father's governor in Athens and Korinth. Despite the weakness of the sources, the names of some writers, poets and philosophers who were at least occasionally present in Pella are known. The historian Hieronymos of Kardia and the poet Aratos of Soloi, author of the *Phainomena*, are the most famous of these, but the tragedian Alexandros the Aitolian, the epic writer Antagoros, from Rhodes, and Persaios and Philonides, both pupils of Zenon, also resided at least for periods of time in Pella. Zenon himself is reported to have declined a royal invitation.[18]

It cannot, however, be assumed that Antigonos' occasional patronage of these and probably other Greek writers and intellectuals had much influence on his policies towards Greece. Even in the case of Athens sober pragmatism appears to have decided his policy. The four great strongholds had provided the power base for his reconquest of Macedonia. From Demetrias he was able to control the Thessalian hinterland; Chalkis allowed him to control the sea routes round Euboia and influence affairs in central Greece; the Piraeus enabled him to maintain a pressure on Athens that was always considered a burden by Athenian politicians—a measure of its effectiveness—and Akrokorinth ensured the possibility of exerting influence on the states of the Peloponnese. But the defensive function of these strongholds was just as important to Antigonos as their offensive function; as long as he held them, no one else could. The recent history of Macedonia underlined just how crucial this aspect was, as from Athens and Korinth both Kassandros and Demetrios and then Antigonos himself had set out on their successful attempts to establish their claims to Macedonia. The strongholds therefore were of practical strategic significance for the internal security of Macedonia, and their function in maintaining domination over the Greeks was only secondary. Recognition of this fact led in 272 to military intervention in the

Peloponnese, where Pyrrhos had advanced after his rapid conquest of western Macedonia. To obtain a toehold in the Peloponnese, he first attempted to bring the exiled Spartan Kleonymos back to Sparta. The real intention behind this move is uncertain, but given Antigonos' still rather unsure position, this attack, which may well have been directed ultimately against Korinth, spelled danger. After all, Pyrrhos himself had once been king of Macedonia and on his return from Italy he had gone there immediately so that his interest in it would seem to have been still active. It must have been for this reason that he cultivated his old relationship to Antigonos' opponent Ptolemaios II and received at least passive assistance from the Aitolian League. Antigonos hurried to the south with an army to render support to his half-brother Krateros, his deputy in Greece. However, all the excitement came to nothing. Pyrrhos was defeated at Sparta and then encountered the army of Antigonos shortly afterwards while attempting to take Argos. In the event, though, it was not the Macedonians who put an end to Pyrrhos' disturbing activities but the dexterity of an old Argive woman, who struck him dead with a roof tile during street fighting.[19]

This trivial accident granted Antigonos a certain breathing space, particularly on his western frontier. But even though his position in the north was immediately improved, his southern strongholds, above all Korinth and the Piraeus, remained threatened by those who suffered under them. Already at the time of Philip II Macedonian influence in the Peloponnese had been strengthened at the expense of Sparta, and it was no coincidence that Korinth, Megalopolis and Argos, all opponents of Spartan dominance in the Peloponnese, were still considered as bastions of the Macedonian interest. The threat of Spartan domination had not been a real one since the defeat of Agis III by Antipatros simply because Sparta had been too weak. But by now it had recovered some strength. The Peloponnese had not suffered under the Celtic raids, and none of the Peloponnesian states had even taken part in the resistance. Since 309 Sparta had been ruled by Areus, an experienced and ambitious king, who in 280 had already attempted at the head of a grand Peloponnesian alliance to wage war against the Aitolians on account of Delphi.[20] At that time his allies had left him in the lurch, but he did not give up.

He perceived the new shifts in power, and a few years later—
after Sparta's success against Pyrrhos, in which his had been the
decisive contribution—he organized an even-larger alliance for
the purpose of attacking Antigonos' Greek possessions. The alliance comprised Elis, the Achaians, Tegea, Mantineia, Orchomenos, Phigaleia and Kaphiai—all Peloponnesian states—some
Kretan cities, Athens and Ptolemaios Philadelphos.[21] The proclaimed aim of the alliance to fight against "those who are attempting to abolish the laws and the ancestral constitutions in
each state" leaves no doubt that those meant were Antigonos and
his adherents in the Greek states. The participants in the war
certainly all had different aims. That of Athens was clearly to
regain free disposal of the Piraeus and other forts in Attika still
in the hands of Antigonos; Areus and the Spartans fought for
more freedom of action in the Peloponnese, above all against Antigonos' possession Korinth; and the remaining Peloponnesian
states participated mainly because most of them were already under Spartan influence again but also because of their fear of Macedonian incursions such as had occurred in the time of Kassandros or Demetrios.

It is more difficult to assess Ptolemaios' motives, although the
Ptolemaic contribution of fleet and financing was the prime factor
in the resistance movement and can be held responsible for the
war's continuing until 261.[22] Pausanias draws attention to the ineffectiveness of the conduct of the war by Ptolemaios, whose
general Patroklos exercised the local command,[23] and thus gives
ground for the assumption that Ptolemaios did not wish to bring
down Antigonos but only to weaken him, thereby reducing his
ability to hamper Ptolemaic interests in the Aegean with his fleet.
This particular Ptolemaios cannot have forgotten that Demetrios,
Antigonos' volatile father, had with a similar fleet disputed the
ownership of Kypros and other important territories with his own
father. Ptolemaic activity in the Aegean appears to have been basically a reaction to this old threat, although it had in the meantime developed a momentum of its own. The league of islanders,
or Nesiotic League, originally founded by Antigonos and Demetrios, was now under Ptolemaic leadership[24]; Ptolemaios also
occupied some bases on the mainland, and at least since 294 regular active cooperation had taken place with Athens against De-

metrios. It is uncertain how old the friendship with Sparta was, but common interests must have been its basis. Thus for Ptolemaios the expulsion of Antigonos from the territories of his friends must have been a reason, if not the primary one, to join the alliance and fight, at least as long as those directly concerned were prepared to fight for themselves.

It is impossible to reconstruct in detail the events of the war. The Peloponnesian commitment was rapidly broken when Areus himself fell in a skirmish near Korinth, perhaps in 265.[25] Patroklos' subsequent attempts to keep Athens supplied by means of the Ptolemaic fleet were in the end not adequate to break the pressure of the siege by Antigonos, who all the time remained in possession of the Piraeus and Salamis.[26] In 261 Athens was compelled to capitulate, its will to resist broken. Antigonos had indeed proved equal to the challenge of the allies.

Before the Chremonidean War Athens had been treated relatively gently by Antigonos. Although his garrisons occupied the Piraeus, Salamis and probably some other inland fortresses, he refrained from building up the Piraeus to be the centre of Macedonian power in Greece, for which its geographical position well suited it. He had, however, already experienced how easily the Athenians could be provoked and had made Korinth, a city without democratic traditions, the seat of government of his half-brother Krateros when he himself set out to reconquer Macedonia. In making this decision, he was following the example, already emulated by his father Demetrios, of Philip II, who, however, had had no practicable alternative. Krateros took up residence in Korinth as protector of Macedonian interests in Greece. Korinth became a completely Macedonian possession; even the key to the town gates was in Macedonian hands.[27] The Macedonians maintained occasional garrisons in some other places on the Peloponnese or gave their support to tyrants. Polybios writes that Antigonos installed more tyrants in Greek cities than any other king had done.[28] In comparison the Athenians had been treated extremely well.

That the proud democrats of Athens were not willing to acknowledge this relatively favourable treatment and instead waged war over the Piraeus in alliance with the Peloponnesian states and Ptolemaios spelled the end of this rather milder policy. After winning the war, the Macedonian attitude inevitably hardened. A Macedonian garrison was once more set up on Mouseion Hill in the centre of the city, and Macedonia occupied all the forts in the countryside—at Panakton, Phyle and Eleusis as well as Rhamnous and Sunion, like Munichia and Salamis already. The garrisons were kept supplied by Athens. Antigonos appointed as head of the city administration one Demetrios, a man he could rely on, who seems to have been a descendant of Demetrios of Phaleron; he perhaps conferred on him the traditional title of *thesmothetes* (maker of rules of behaviour). One single official, instead of the previous commission, was appointed under him with responsibility for state finances. The office of commander in chief of the army in the field (the hoplite general) was abolished, and the king also exerted influence on the appointment of the other top administrators, the *strategoi*.[29]

That Antigonos was determined to retain his Greek strongholds is demonstrated clearly by the Chremonidean War and the tenacity with which he fought it. But this policy was not, even after the Chremonidean War, aimed at any significant direct territorial expansion of Macedonian power. As long as the Macedonian fleet, which had just proved its strength against Ptolemaios, was strong enough to guarantee the sea connections, it was not particularly important to control the lands lying between them. Antigonos could therefore at first observe with relative calm how the Aitolian League gradually extended its influence to include the Ainianians and Dolopians, Doris, Lokris, parts of Phokis and Phthiotic Achaia in central Greece. The league had not participated in the Chremonidean War and had taken advantage of it to extend its sphere of influence. Antigonos undertook no countermeasures apart from ordering the boycott of the meetings of the Delphic Amphiktyony, now dominated by the Aitolians, by most of the representatives from his territories.[30] In the northern Peloponnese as well Macedonia was in principle interested only in the main places; apart from Korinth the attempt was made to retain the loyalty of cities such as Argos, Megalopolis, Sikyon, Elis and Troizen, but elsewhere those friendly to Macedonia received occasional support, though not if they were politically weak. Thus from 280 on it was already possible for the small cities of Achaia gradually to join together in a league at the expense of the tyrants supported by Krateros without provoking any appreciable reaction from the Macedonians, even, as far as is known, when the Achaians participated in Areus' Peloponnesian alliance.[31] Achaia, in spite of its proximity, was apparently not important enough to pose a threat to Macedonian rule in Korinth. Antigonos seems to have considered it more expedient to observe and tolerate the secessionist movement, insofar as it did not take on any strong anti-Macedonian character, than to provoke an even more active resistance movement through overhasty intervention.

The Chremonidean War and the Second Syrian War between Ptolemaios and Antiochos II that followed shortly after it seem to have created for the Macedonian king greater freedom of manoeuvre in the Aegean for his fleet. It is unclear whether Antigonos directly participated in the Syrian War or merely took the opportunity offered to weaken Ptolemaios on his own account; but a sea battle near Kos, perhaps in 254, was decided in favour of Antigonos without bringing him any significant territorial gain and apparently without his seeking any.[32] The battle is only explicable within the context of a general policy of weakening the Ptolemaic position in the Aegean. The marriage alliance sometime in the 250s between Antigonos' son Demetrios and Stratonike, sister of Antiochos II, is also in line with such a policy without its necessarily implying the active participation of Antigonos in the Second Syrian War.[33] It is perhaps possible also to set into this context the withdrawal of the garrison from Mouseion Hill in Athens and the renunciation in about 255 of further formal active influence on the Athenian constitution (officially described as "restoration of liberty") to remove a bone of contention and deny Ptolemaios an excuse for intervention in Athens. During the following years some Athenians in the royal service are known to have been entrusted with duties in Attika. The most famous of these was Herakleitos of Athmonon, who even commanded the troops in Munichia in the early 240s, but Athenians also served in the inland forts.[34] Antigonos must have been fairly confident of his position if he felt that by these means he could reduce the occasions for friction and make the Macedonian presence less evident.

In the Peloponnese, by contrast, a clear weakening of the Macedonian position during the 250s can be discerned. The death in that period of Krateros, whose relationship to his brother is described by Plutarch as exemplary and who for twenty years had taken care of Macedonian relations with the cities of the northern Peloponnese, was probably the beginning of this process. His son Alexandros, who followed him in office, was endowed neither with the reputation of his father nor, as became apparent, with his loyalty to Antigonos. Towards the end of the 250s Argos, Megalopolis and Sikyon, governed until then by tyrants friendly to Macedonia, drifted out of the sphere of direct Macedonian influence.[35] The insurrection of Alexandros himself, which followed around 250, can perhaps be interpreted as his taking refuge in attack. As he continued to control Euboia, though Athens remained in Antigonos' hands, he now seemed to present precisely that phenomenon against which Antigonos had deemed it necessary to retain the strongholds all those years[36]—a potential rival to his own position in Macedonia and one starting from the same base he had used himself.

If Alexandros intended to challenge the aged Antigonos and his son Demetrios, his designated successor in Macedonia, external help was essential for success, and the only practical possibility lay in Ptolemaic support, such as had been given to Aratos of Sikyon for his anti-Macedonian stand with the Achaian League. However, if this were the case, Antigonos' victory over the Ptolemaic fleet near the island of Andros off the Euboian coast must have drowned his hopes.[37] When Alexandros died in 244, the allegation that Antigonos had poisoned him was almost inevitable.[38] Shortly afterwards Antigonos again won control of the Akrokorinth by successfully pressing the suit of his son Demetrios on Alexandros' widow Nikaia, who now governed in his stead, and then occupying the Akrokorinth with his own troops during the nuptial celebrations. This time Persaios, a pupil of Zenon and an old confidant of the king, was appointed as commander; but his philosophical training did nothing to help him when in 243/42 Aratos, at that time *strategos* of the Achaian League, mounted a successful night attack on the city and its citadel. Korinth promptly joined the Achaian League,[39] thereby bringing down one of the pillars of Antigonos' defence system. Macedonian self-confidence was doubtless severely shaken, but this latest loss was not nearly as dangerous as the recent occupation by the renegade Macedonian Alexandros. Even Antigonos cannot have imagined that the Achaians posed a serious threat to him in Macedonia. A traditional defensive strongpoint had been lost, and shortly afterwards Megara, Troizen and Epidauros also joined the Achaian League;[40] but their admission was of no great immediate significance for Macedonia itself. Antigonos did indeed conclude an agreement with the Aitolians with the declared intention of dividing the territories of the Achaian League between them;[41] but when the Aitolians again made peace with Achaia shortly afterwards, active hostilities ceased without the Akrokorinth having been regained. Such resignation seems to reflect the behaviour of a tired old man, and this impression may well be right. However, the old man found it relatively easier to come to terms with his loss because he had not principally utilized the Greek strongholds as active instruments of power but had held them within the framework of a broadly based security system.

Antigonos died soon afterwards, in 240/39. His son Demetrios, who must certainly have been increasingly active in state affairs in the past years and had already held a commanding office in the army during the Chremonidean War, succeeded to the throne.[42] There was no reason for the succession not to have been carefully prepared, and no difficulties are known. Demetrios does not appear to have developed any new political initiatives during the ten years of his reign but merely to have reacted to events. On the Peloponnese the Achaians, under the leadership of the versatile Aratos, who was financially supported by Ptolemaios III, allied themselves to the Aitolians and conducted a war of liberation against the remaining areas under Macedonian influence in the south, the so-called Demetrian War. Little is known of the course of events, but Demetrios seems to have been provoked into trying to boost the image of the Macedonians in the south. Argos and some other smaller places on the Peloponnese remained loyal to Macedonia and the winning over of Boiotia relaxed Achaian pressure on Athens. However, a further erosion of the Macedonian position on the Peloponnese occurred in 235 when Lydiadas, the tyrant of Megalopolis, incorporated his city into the Achaian League.[43] Demetrios appears not to have taken any action in response, nor in the matter of Korinth. Had he lived longer, the whole of the Peloponnese would probably have drifted out of the Macedonian sphere of influence. But essential Macedonian interests would only then have been affected if a serious threat to Macedonia itself had arisen there, and even Korinth seems not to have merited any great effort as long as it was only the Achaians who held it.

The north, though, was considered important as ever. The Epeirot king Alexandros II died at around the same time as Antigonos. He left two young sons, whose mother, Olympias, ruled the country on their behalf. Under threat from the Aitolians, who coveted the northern part of Akarnania, won by Alexandros for Epeiros, Olympias offered Demetrios the traditional association between the two royal houses: her daughter Phthia was to go to Pella as Demetrios' bride. It seems that Stratonike had already returned from Pella to her brother Antiochos some time before 246, and Demetrios had in the meantime taken up an alliance with Chryseis, whose origins are unknown but who bore him a son, Philippos, probably in 238. This relationship, however, was not considered a hindrance to the politically advantageous marriage to Phthia, who now came to Pella as queen,[44] just as the marriage of Demetrios I to Phila and Philip II's marriage to Olympias had not inhibited the further marriages of those rulers. But the new alliance was neither dynastically nor politically fertile. Phthia produced no rival to the son of Chryseis, who herself returned to a position of honour on Phthia's death (perhaps as soon as 235/ 34);[45] nor did the connection lead to the Macedonian engagement in the west that Olympias must have hoped for. Alexandros' two sons died in rapid succession, and shortly afterwards their mother died as well. Only a girl, Deidameia, remained of the royal house of the Aiakidai, and when she was murdered in 233, a politically incalculable federal republic was established in Epeiros without Demetrios doing anything at all to prevent it.[46] He also undertook nothing personally against the Aitolians. When they attacked the Akarnanian city of Medeion in about 233, he promised the Illyrian chief Agron a money payment and so persuaded him to go to the aid of the Akarnanians, but he did not involve himself.[47] However, shortly before his death in 229 he again became active enough to lose an important battle against the Dardanians, who for reasons unknown to us marched into Paionia and advanced at least as far as Bylazora (Titov Veles).[48]

Demetrios II was probably the most inactive Macedonian king ever, if the little that we know of him gives a correct impression. Historians have often wondered whether the reason for the dearth of recorded activity perhaps lies in a preoccupation with the northern frontier that has found no echo in the fragmentary sources. It is, though, more probable that the long years of co-operation with his venerable father had set the pattern for his behaviour during his own reign. Demetrios savoured the consolidation of Macedonia achieved by his father and preferred peace to more active pursuit of traditional territorial interests. Whether this attitude was the result of a positive decision or should be ascribed merely to sloth cannot be ascertained from the sources.

2. A NEW BEGINNING

The unexpected death of Demetrios II precipitated a grave crisis in Macedonia. His only son, Philippos, was only eight years old, and his mother Chryseis neither commanded the respect of an Olympias or a Thessalonike nor had the inclination to claim the regency for herself. During the reign of Demetrios the Greeks had gained the impression that the Macedonian commitment had become so weak that there was little danger in attacking Macedonian possessions, and even the friends of Macedonia had in the end sought to save their position with other policies. Unfortunately it is impossible, as it is so often, to establish the exact chronology, and the assumption of a chain of cause and effects entails risks and uncertainties. It is not known when direct Aitolian influence extended into Thessaly (apart from Magnesia); it could have happened either gradually during the last years of Demetrios' reign or in a sudden surge as a result of his death. There is, however, evidence that the Thessalians again sent delegates (*hieromnemones*) to the meetings of the Delphic Amphiktyony, now under the control of the Aitolians, as they had not done under Macedonian rule; and Justin recounts that one of the first duties of the new Macedonian ruler Antigonos Doson was to combat the rebellious Thessalians.[1]

The loss of Thessaly and the renewal of political uncertainty in the Axios valley were a blow to the foundations of what Philip II had established as the core of Macedonia's security system. But the loss of influence did not end there. The Boiotian League now found itself split: one party was inclined to offer resistance to its powerful neighbour Aitolia, which was only possible with Macedonian support, and the other party would have preferred to come to an arrangement with the Aitolians. During Demetrios' war against the Aitolians and the Achaians the Boiotians had remained loyal, but shortly after his death a reversal took place despite the Macedonian occupation troops in Chalkis.[2] Even graver was the loss of the Piraeus, probably shortly after the death of Demetrios. Already under Gonatas there is evidence of Athenians in the royal service both as officers and as men in the country forts of Attika, and even a commander of the Piraeus in the early 240s, Herakleitos of Athmonon, was an Athenian. It seems that another Athenian, Diogenes, now commanded the Piraeus garrison, but on the death of Demetrios he did not wait for the threatening dynastic chaos nor an attempt by the Athenians to depose him but negotiated directly with Athenian leaders and demanded 150 talents for the surrender of the Piraeus. The sum was high but, in view of the risk taken by Diogenes, who also had to pay his mercenaries out of it, not unreasonable. The Athenians scraped the money together, and in this way, for the first time since 294, Munichia was freed from Macedonian occupation.[3] Now that Diogenes, in the citadel of Macedonian influence, had chosen to negotiate with his subjugated countrymen rather than await the reestablishment of Macedonian supremacy, the few remaining tyrants in the Peloponnese must rapidly have abandoned their hopes of further support from Pella. Aristomachos incorporated Argos into the Achaian League (229/28), as Lydiadas had already done with Megalopolis, and his example was followed at least by Xenon of Hermione and Kleonymos of Phlious.[4]

The new ruler of Macedonia, initially appointed by the leading aristocrats as regent for the young Philip, was the son of a half-brother of Gonatas and also bore the name of Antigonos. He is known to posterity under his nickname, Doson, "the man who will give." As regent he married Chryseis, the mother of Philip; and after a time, "when they had experienced his moderate character and recognized that it was beneficial for the country, they granted him the title of king." How long this process took is not known. It could have been either months or years, but the situation must have been clarified before about 226.[5] In the short term, however, much more important than the formal position of the ruler was the fact that he enjoyed the trust of the leading nobles and was himself both active and circumspect. The first problem to be settled was posed by the Dardanians, and then came the rebellious Thessalians. In each area an acceptable solution was arrived at through concessions: the Dardanians retained the Paionian capital of Bylazora, and in Thessaly the old league of the Thessalians seems to have been revived, though with limited competence.[6] Details are unknown, but Antigonos was certainly in a position after two or three years to take up activities outside Macedonia and Thessaly again, which must presuppose a state of peace in the central regions of the kingdom. In Macedonia itself Doson was soon sufficiently in command of the situation to assert himself against some unruly elements.[7] The dynastic problem was elegantly solved by his adopting the boy Philip at the time of his marriage to Chryseis;[8] it had thus already been clarified when Antigonos was proclaimed king. Even were Chryseis to have sons by Antigonos, Philip was recognized from the outset as the eldest and as heir to the throne. The nobles must have been satisfied with this solution they had found to the crisis of 229.

Although the sources give an inadequate picture of the situation in Macedonia itself and in the frontier areas, they let us see the first steps towards a new policy towards Greece. After 228 only Demetrias and Chalkis remained as Macedonian possessions. Antigonos does not appear at first to have reacted at all to the liberation of Athens and the secession of Macedonian friends in the Peloponnese to the Achaian League. The loss of prestige and practical influence during the last years, coupled with the massive expansion of the Achaian and, above all, Aitolian leagues, appears to have led to a rethinking of Macedonia's relationship to the southern Greeks and a new definition of state priorities, which had neither been necessary nor had happened since the time of Philip II. The result seems to have been a return to the principles of that period: in the last resort everything beyond Thessaly could be abandoned, but Thessaly itself was worth fighting for, as were the Axios valley and Paionia in the north. Beyond this area of vital interest Chalkis remained under Macedonian control, but only because it was already there; otherwise opportunities to exert influence were to be sought only with the greatest circumspection and only with the concurrence and active cooperation of Greek allies.

The first episode appears to have little to do with this policy and is indeed very obscure. Perhaps in January 227 Doson sailed with a fleet to Karia in southwest Asia Minor. The only literary source refers to a conquest, but that remark is perhaps a misunderstanding.[9] Documents from Labraunda from the time of his successor credit Doson only with the role of an arbitrator, and it is easily possible that his military escort, the size of which is unknown, was present only to lend his judgements the necessary weight. A possible explanation is that he had been summoned, perhaps through Rhodes as intermediary, by Mylasa (or even Iasos, where Philip exerted influence in about 220) to arbitrate in certain matters the city disputed with the local dynast, Olympichos of Alinda.

The reason for this choice could have been precisely that he had no traditional political interests to pursue in Karia, as was certainly not the case with other powers that came into question, such as the Attalids of Pergamon, the Ptolemies, the Seleukids or even the Rhodians. Why Doson should have accepted such an invitation remains a puzzle; but whatever the reason was, his brief activities in Karia demonstrated that Macedonian assistance and cooperation did not necessarily have to culminate in domination, even though the Macedonian military commitment had been large enough to impress Olympichos and curb him. Macedonian influence there was maintained during the first years of the reign of Philip V, when in 220 Philip was also requested by Mylasa and Iasos to regulate local affairs, again in connection with their relationship to Olympichos. But to speak of an area of effective Macedonian dominance in Karia would be to strain the statements in the sources unduly.[10]

In this light Doson's activities in Karia provide the first example for the new cautious approach in the Macedonian relationship to the Greeks. The second example had far-reaching consequences.

The withdrawal of the Macedonians from the Peloponnese had occurred simultaneously with renewed ambitions for power on the part of Sparta. King Agis IV and, after his death, King Kleomenes III attempted first to reform Sparta internally and then to reestablish its old dominant position in the Peloponnese. This ambition inevitably gave rise to tensions followed by war with the Achaian League, which, through the incorporation during the previous decade of large parts of Arkadia (including Megalopolis) and Argos, had had to assume the traditional strategic problems of the new members and the associated political attitudes. In the fourth century B.C. the Arkadians had been able to fight successfully for their independence from Sparta with Boiotian help, and the city of Megalopolis, a euphoric new foundation of that time, symbolized the freedom just wrested from Sparta—a freedom, however, that from the time of Philip II had been maintained in the last resort only through repeated support of the Macedonian kings. Thus through the incorporation of Arkadia and the membership of Argos, which was for several reasons both anti-Spartan and pro-Macedonian, a deeply rooted disposition in favour of Macedonia was introduced into the league, in flat contradiction of the current anti-Macedonian policies of the league under Aratos of Sikyon.

These inherent tensions were brought to a peak when in 227 Lydiadas, who had previously been tyrant of Megalopolis, died in battle against Kleomenes, and Megalopolis itself was seriously threatened by Sparta. As a result semiprivate exploratory talks were held in Pella by leading Megalopolitans.[11] However, in view of current political attitudes in Achaia it did not make sense for Antigonos to consider intervention in the Peloponnese, even when the Aitolians gave assistance to Kleomenes. The Peloponnese had always interested Macedonia only in connection with the possession of Korinth; accordingly the loss of Korinth and the resulting waning of Macedonian interest in the Peloponnese damaged Megalopolis above all. In central Greece the Aitolians were the main enemies of Macedonia, for obvious immediate reasons, since they had just conquered parts of Thessaly. But even if they allied themselves to Kleomenes, the Peloponnese must have remained for the Aitolians, as for the Macedonians, only a minor theatre compared with central and western Greece. These indeed offered Antigonos more attractive opportunities for curbing the Aitolians, with which Megalopolis could not compete. In any event, already before 224 Doson had again entered into treaty agreements in the west with Epeiros and the independent part of Akarnania and in central Greece with Boiotia, Phokis and the Lokrians from Opous.[12] Although it is most probable that the initiative in each case had been taken by these small, weak states on the Aitolian borders (just as by the Megalopolitans), it was still absolutely in the Macedonian interest to support them against Aitolia. In no instance, then or later, was a permanent Macedonian presence installed.

That the course of events in the Peloponnese developed more tempestuously than in central Greece, so that an actual state of war with direct Macedonian participation rapidly came about, resulted not from a change in priorities but from the opportunity that suddenly arose of regaining the Akrokorinth and winning over the Achaian League with the general consent of the Achaians themselves. Thus was formed an actively pro-Macedonian power block in the Peloponnese, and the Aitolians were surrounded on all sides with Macedonian allies. The investment in the Peloponnese was also made more attractive by a change in the patronage extended by Ptolemaios III. After years in which he had supported Aratos and the Achaian League he suddenly transferred his patronage to their enemy Kleomenes. Ptolemaios regarded Aitolia in a markedly friendly light as well, and Athens was granted Ptolemaic aid as soon as it became clear that it opposed Aratos' wish to incorporate it in the Achaian League.[13] Exactly what Ptolemaios' intentions were could not be ascertained at the time, and now there is even less chance of doing so. However, his abandoned clients could be nurtured and deployed in the interests of a new patron.

As Kleomenes' successes continued and the Achaian League suffered ever larger territorial losses, Aratos in his extremity finally managed to swallow his pride and, in 225, continue on his own account the talks with Antigonos opened by the Megalopolitans two years before. But the Macedonian point of view remained the same. The price of a Macedonian commitment was the return of Korinth; only afterwards would Macedonia and Achaia have a common interest in combatting Kleomenes. It was only with great reluctance that the Achaians were prepared to agree to a renewal of the old Macedonian presence; but since the league could not reckon with any other assistance against Kleomenes, who in the meantime had taken Argos and Korinth and had started to lay siege to Sikyon, in winter 225/24 they were finally ready to accept Antigonos' demand. The immanent conflict between an emergent power-hungry Sparta and the Peloponnesians affected thereby had again, as in the fourth century B.C., worked to the advantage of Macedonia. Of interest here is the verdict of Polybios, himself an Achaian from Megalopolis. Just as he continued to justify the Peloponnesian sympathizers of Philip II against the old accusations of Demosthenes and present Philip himself as the friend and saviour of the Peloponnesian cities, so his verdict on Doson is also extremely favourable.[14] Macedonian power in the Peloponnese thus again under similar conditions played a similar role and was once more judged positively by Polybios. The liberation propaganda of Aratos, which had provided the camouflaging banner for the Achaian expansion of the 240s and 230s, and even at that time—in view of the lethargic attitudes of kings Antigonos and Demetrios—had rung artificial and had by no means convinced all his hearers, was now completely out of place.

Antigonos' first appearance in 224 scared Kleomenes away immediately. He instantly relinquished Korinth, and he could not hold Argos; and when Antigonos stormed into Arkadia, he chased the Spartans out of two Megalopolitan forts. In the autumn he took part in an assembly of the Achaian League, where he discussed the further course of the war and had himself recognized by the Achaians as commander in chief of the allied forces.[15]

Then in spring 223 Antigonos led a campaign through Arkadia, where he won over a number of cities that had, whether willingly or unwillingly, joined the Spartans, reincorporating them into the Achaian League. Macedonian garrisons moved into Orchomenos and Heraia; and Mantineia, after severe reprisals against the population, was refounded by the grateful Achaians under Aratos and given a new name, Antigoneia. Even then Kleomenes was unprepared to make peace, as is shown by his successful attack on Megalopolis in late autumn.[16] In 222 Antigonos called on his allies for support, and for the first time we have evidence of a new organization, the Hellenic League. It is improbable that the separate treaties concluded with the states of central and western Greece had provided from the start for participation in a war in the Peloponnese, as neither Macedonian nor allied interests were at the time directly involved there. The Hellenic League first became necessary when Antigonos wished to have the forces of his allies at his disposal for purposes not foreseen in the separate treaties. A commitment of this kind can first be found in the sources in 222, and the conclusion may be drawn that the league was created during the previous winter.[17]

The aims and purposes of the new league, in which the federations of the Epeirots, Akarnanians, Phokians, Boiotians and Achaians as well as the newly formed Thessalian League formally participated, are not known to us, but the central provision was probably for mutual assistance in case of threat.[18] The interests of the Achaian members must then have provided the occasion for rallying the forces of the league in 222. But even though Antigonos had skilfully created this instrument ostensibly in the Achaian interest, it must have been fairly clear to everyone that this unlikely association could only have been brought together through the authority and prestige of the Macedonian king. However vague the formal provisions of the treaty may have been, the prominent position of the Macedonian king within the new league granted openings that could lead to its use as an instrument of domination. The incorporation of the Thessalians, who despite their own new formal league organization belonged to the area of direct Macedonian rule, throws a harsh light on the inequality of the members and unmasks the league as a Macedonian creation.

The immediate aim, however, was magnificently achieved. A large allied army under the personal leadership of Antigonos—according to Polybios he led altogether twenty-eight thousand infantry and twelve hundred cavalry—encountered the twenty thousand men mustered by Kleomenes at Sellasia on the northern frontier of Lakonia in the summer of 222. Kleomenes' army suffered an annihilating defeat, and even the city of Sparta was then peaceably taken by Antigonos while Kleomenes fled to Egypt.[19] With this victory Antigonos had absolved his duty to the Achaian

League, paying the price for Korinth in full. Sparta was now a somewhat embarrassing irrelevancy, and Antigonos tried as far as possible not to get involved in the political whirlpool created by the social reforms of Kleomenes. Especially among Kleomenes' opponents he sought to create goodwill, but goodwill associated with peace and order so that the newly installed Macedonian presence in Korinth and influence in Achaia should not lead to an expensive permanent commitment in the southern Peloponnese. He relied on a policy of pragmatic leniency. One disputed territory, the Denthalietis, was granted to Messenia, and Sparta seems to have joined the Hellenic League; but otherwise exiles were permitted to return, the office of *ephoros*, which Kleomenes had abolished, was restored, and an attempt was made to smooth out the social upheavals of Kleomenes' time. Antigonos initially left a governor behind in Sparta, the Boiotian Brachyllas, but his presence was not intended to indicate any long-term Macedonian responsibility. Sparta was to be left to rule itself in peace.[20] Although Sparta was not a central object of Macedonian interest in the Peloponnese, if a basically well-disposed attitude could be created there, as in other places outside the immediate region of the isthmus, it would of course serve admirably the general aims of Antigonos' policy. That Antigonos achieved initial successes is clearly demonstrated by cult festivals founded for him (*Antigoneia*), by some general statements of Polybios and Plutarch and by inscriptions in his honour from Epidauros, from Geronthrai in Lakonia and from Arkadian Mantineia, which after its sacking during the Macedonian conquest had even been refounded as Antigoneia.[21]

Antigonos did not manage to conclude matters in the Peloponnese. When he was forced to return to Macedonia shortly after Sellasia, he left temporary garrisons behind in Heraia, Orchomenos and Korinth. Some Illyrians had taken advantage of the absence of the royal army to undertake a plundering expedition into Macedonia. Doson commissioned his trusted friend Taurion to represent Macedonian interests in the Peloponnese and hastened north.[22] He was able to win a battle against the Illyrians but died some months later. He suffered from tuberculosis and had also burst a blood vessel in the battle, from which he never recovered. However, he had been able to set Macedonia's relationship to the Greeks on a new course and establish a basic climate of goodwill towards Macedonia in large parts of the Peloponnese as well as among other neighbours of the Aitolian League. This goodwill created the necessary preconditions for future political cooperation and found formal expression in the organization of the Hellenic League.[23]

Doson had not developed this new policy alone. Friends and officers had contributed to it and helped in its execution. In an attempt to guarantee the continuity of his policies he wrote in his last months a political testament, in which he not only delivered a sort of account of his years of rule but also left instructions for the future. Of paramount importance was the maintenance of continuity in the officeholders so that Philip, his designated successor, who was still only seventeen years old, should not through youthful exuberance put at risk all that had been achieved. Already before his death he had made plain to Philip the great importance he attached to personal acquaintance with the leading Greek political leaders. He dispatched him to the Peloponnese, where he got to know among others Aratos in Achaia and created a basis of trust on which Doson's policies could be continued.[24] By means of his testament Doson attempted to endow his ministers with sufficient prestige for them to continue to influence Greek policy under Philip. Apelles was appointed as a kind of prime minister (*en tois epitropois*), Megaleas as state secretary (*epi tou grammateiou*), Taurion as deputy in the Peloponnese, Leontios as general of the peltasts and Alexandros as court chamberlain.[25] Philip therefore initially retained the services of these men, allowed himself to be integrated into their plans and, according to Polybios' account, earned for this behaviour the appelation "darling of Hellas."[26]

But the priorities for Philip V, as for every Macedonian king, lay in the north. About this there could be no conflict of opinion; in this respect Philip was an out-and-out traditionalist. The current menace was again the Dardanians. Justin describes the situation around this period: "The Dardanians and all the other neighbouring peoples, who nourished an almost incurable hatred for the kings of the Macedonians, challenged Philip continually because they despised his youth." Polybios mentions more explicitly military actions in winter 220/19, summer 219 and spring

217. In his last campaign Philip even succeeded in regaining Bylazora, which the Dardanians had captured from the Paionians in
about 230, and with this achievement peace returned for some
years.[27]

In those areas where Doson's achievement was new and out
of the ordinary and where a return to the policies of Gonatas
would rapidly have destroyed the subtle relations based on partnership Doson had established, continuity can be readily discerned. Doson's provisions for the succession functioned effectively at first, though not entirely without problems. But even in
Karia, from where we have the earliest state documents of Philip's
reign, the relationship Doson initiated in 227 to Olympichos of
Alinda and to Mylasa was upheld by Philip. We can be fairly certain that the two extant letters in Philip's name, from 220, were
formulated by the same chancellor, Apelles or perhaps Megaleas,
who had earlier written those of Doson.

Through the association of Doson's treaty partners in the Hellenic League the Aitolians had been completely surrounded, and
through the expansion of Macedonian influence in the Peloponnese the only Aitolian allies there, Messenia and Elis, had
been put under such great pressure that Messenia at least toyed
with the idea of joining the league, although probably not until
after its old enemy Sparta had become a member.[28] Had that happened, Aitolian influence would have been confined to Elis. The
Aitolian leaders made a serious miscalculation, however, when
they decided to intervene in Messenia. The Messenians appealed
for help to Achaia, as did the Achaians soon afterwards to the
members of the league; and because fear of the Aitolians was the
sole uniting element of the league, it was not difficult to persuade
Philip and his advisers to intervene militarily, in the spirit of Doson's policies. In summer 220 war was declared on the Aitolian
League at an assembly of delegates to the Hellenic League meeting at Korinth. The members also engaged to liberate those cities
and territories captured by the Aitolians since the death of Demetrios and fight for the freedom of the Amphiktyonic Council to
administer the affairs of Delphi without Aitolian interference. It
was above all the interests of the league members from central
and western Greece that found expression in this undertaking.
Under Doson they had participated in the war against Kleo-

menes, although it had hardly concerned them directly, and now they hoped they themselves would benefit from the league's activities.[29]

The aims set for this war accorded with Macedonian state interests, even though the immediate cause had arisen in the Peloponnese, and hence reflected Doson's initial objectives for the league. Under Doson Macedonian influence had been strengthened, especially in the west, through treaties and the Hellenic League. Now the aim was to gain concrete advantages that would not only weaken the Aitolians but also strengthen Macedonia's friends in Epeiros and Akarnania. For this reason Macedonian activity in 219 was confined to this region, the current importance of which can be measured by the fact that neither an attack on Thessaly by the Aitolian general Skopas, nor his sacking of the Macedonian national sanctuary at Dion in Pieria, nor the collapse of the new administration in Sparta could divert Philip from his purpose. He broke off his campaign there and hastened to the north only when rumours reached him of Dardanian military movement; but when they turned out to be false, he spent the rest of the summer at Larissa while his soldiers brought in the harvest at home. After Skopas' attack there must have been plenty to do in Thessaly. Not until winter 219/18 did the Macedonian army arrive in the Peloponnese and there, in an unusual winter campaign, largely make good the Achaian losses of the previous year.[30]

The priorities set by Philip during these first years of his reign did not diverge from Doson's. The king's youthful vigour seems to have been guided into the projected courses by Apelles and the court. But during the war of 219/18 tensions arose, which at first had no significant bearing on state policies. Our source, Polybios, represents strongly the Achaian point of view, particularly that of Aratos; but because Aratos was heavily involved, there having been much friction between him and Apelles, Polybios' tendency is certainly misleading but not easy to appraise exactly. As the tensions increased, they affected more and more people during the following year and led to grave differences of opinion both within the Crown Council and between Philip and individual members of it. The situation at court was complicated still further by Philip's granting asylum to Demetrios of Pharos, who had been expelled from his Illyrian lands by a Roman expeditionary force in 219, during the so-called Second Illyrian War. Demetrios had fought with Doson at Sellasia in 222 and was employed by Taurion in 220 for operations in the Peloponnese, so that at the time of his exile he was certainly regarded as a friend and ally of the Macedonians.[31] However, the permanent presence at court of such a high-ranking refugee created a new situation there, and although the hostile tone of Polybios' report makes it impossible to assess Demetrios' real importance, it is clear that he gave strategic and tactical advice that made sense to Philip and Taurion but was viewed with suspicion by Apelles.

The point of dispute about which tensions finally crystallized was the employment of a fleet. It could not be denied that operations in Akarnania and Epeiros especially could be carried out more easily and efficiently with the aid of one.[32] No Macedonian fleet had operated in the west since the time of Demetrios Poliorketes, but Taurion had already attempted to deploy Demetrios' Illyrian fleet in the Peloponnese. Taurion's purpose in favouring the deployment of a fleet was to increase the effectiveness of Macedonian pressure on the Aitolians. But should Demetrios gain even more influence over Philip, he might eventually be able to persuade him to operate in Illyria itself. Macedonian state interests could gradually become identical with Demetrios' own interests, and the traditionalists baulked at such a possibility. Personal motives of Apelles, who felt himself pushed to one side, doubtless also played a part, and these are stressed by Polybios.[33] State interests, however, must have been decisive. A serious Macedonian engagement in Illyria would be unique in the history of Macedonia; Illyria would become an entirely new sphere of interest that could in no way be as useful to Macedonia as, for example, the reconquest of Thrace. The presence of Demetrios therefore produced a new political dimension, the magnitude of which could not even approximately be gauged. Those who foresaw how the future might develop—above all Apelles, it seems—rejected the risks uncompromisingly; others, such as Taurion, saw the fleet as lending the Macedonians that mobility that had been lacking thus far in their struggle against the Aitolians, and they supported the new development—and survived.

The crisis reached its brutal climax in 218. The main event of the year was a successful attack on the sanctuary of the Aitolian League at Thermon in retaliation for Aitolian attacks on Dion and

Dodona, during which members of the league demolished or carried away large votive offerings and other valuable objects. While this campaign was going on, the main opponents of the new activism, Apelles, Megaleas and Leontios, found themselves increasingly entangled in political and personal difficulties. With the loyal support of Alexandros and Taurion Philip took advantage of these difficulties to isolate them and then either murder them or drive them to suicide. Polybios' account of this sombre episode is so obscured by the subsequent official presentation of the events as a plot directed against Philip, and by Aratos' egocentric emphasis on his own influence with the king, that the real reasons can scarcely be identified. Demetrios of Pharos, even if at first he only gained influence as a protégé of Taurion, seems to have made a significant, perhaps even decisive, contribution. The young king must surely have felt himself circumscribed by the counsellors Doson had bequeathed him; and the lively personal loyalty displayed by the crack regiment of the peltasts towards their general, Leontios, which spelled danger for Philip, showed that his feelings were well founded. In the end it may well have been the excessively patronizing pressure on the king by the old counsellors, who themselves had massively contributed to Doson's successes and enjoyed great prestige and authority in the country and the army, that furnished the real reason for their downfall.[34]

By eradicating the Apelles clique, Philip achieved more for himself than just the opportunity for untrammelled development. Differences of opinion about Macedonian policy had been partly responsible for the crisis. As long as the "western policy" was pursued in traditional fashion from the land, Macedonian interest remained limited to Epeiros and Akarnania, and the ultimate aim of the war remained the limitation of the Aitolian League's possibilities of expansion. This aim had been the starting point for Doson's Greek policy, and the basic principles were still the determining factors in 218. The Hellenic League was simply an alliance of the opponents of Aitolia. It was natural and had to be accepted that Aratos, as representative of league member Achaia, should seek to further his own local interests, and the leading politicians of the other member states can certainly have acted no differently. In contrast to this attitude stood the personal interests of Demetrios, who sought his own return to Illyria, which was not a league matter, nor could it in any way be regarded by traditionalists as lying in the Macedonian interest. The fleet indeed enabled a more efficient conduct of the war against Aitolia, but at the same time it made feasible rash adventures in other regions. The consequences could not be foreseen.

It soon became apparent that Philip in the meantime regarded Doson's political precepts as too arduous and lacking in imagination. In 217 he left the southern Greeks on their own and was busy in the north and with the Illyrians. He regained Bylazora from the Dardanians and then paid a lot of attention to Thessaly, where he captured Phthiotic Thebes from the Aitolians and renamed it Philippoi; in about September he wrote to Larissa that the city should accept new citizens to compensate for the lives lost in the war. He also prepared a campaign against the Illyrian baron Skerdilaidas, who seems to have established himself over the Ardiaioi after Demetrios' banishment.[35]

In late summer he opened negotiations with the Aitolians, which led to the conclusion of a peace, the Peace of Naupaktos, based on the respective possessions at that time. Since Polybios, whose interpretation was strongly influenced by subsequent events, the assumption tends to be made that the main motive for Philip's peace with the Aitolians was the news of the massive defeat of the Romans by Hannibal at Lake Trasimene and his hope of being able to participate advantageously in those momentous events. It is more likely that his motives were more modest. The most that could be concluded from the current plight of the Romans was that they would be unlikely to wish to undertake countermeasures in Illyria should Philip, at the urging of Demetrios, proceed against Skerdilaidas, who had just made provocative raids into Pelagonia, and then establish Demetrios in Illyria again. That Philip did indeed harbour intentions in Illyria that had nothing to do with the Aitolians can be clearly deduced from his instruction, at the suggestion of Demetrios of Pharos, that during the winter a fleet of one hundred light ships of Illyrian pattern (*lemboi*) be built. These small ships were completely unsuitable for any sort of engagement in Italy but ideal for swift commando raids in Illyrian coastal waters. Philip's building a fleet had nothing to do with Rome or Hannibal, but there could be no room for doubt that the cautious era of consolidation of Doson and his advisers was over. A new activism governed Macedonian policies, which at once led in a new direction.[36]

3. THE NEW ACTIVISM

Since the reign of Philip II the two cornerstones of the Macedonian solution to the Illyrian problem had been the maintenance of close relationships to the Paionians of the Axios valley in the north and to Epeiros in the west. If in addition friendly relations could be established with some or any of the Illyrian clans, as had recently happened with the Ardiaioi, they strengthened the Macedonian position further. But apart from occasional raids nothing is known of any Macedonian operation intended to obtain the kind of direct influence in Illyria that was aimed for in Paionia and Epeiros.

During the last few years, however, the situation in the west had altered in important respects. First, during the 230s under Agron the Ardiaioi had expanded their area of interests towards the south, and at least some of them carried out occasional raids on the coast of Epeiros.[1] Second, Epeiros itself, which previously under the monarchy had been in general strong enough to match the Illyrians militarily, had become so feeble since the setting up of the republic that it was no longer effective as a buffer zone. One of the main reasons why this weakness persisted was the hostility of the Aitolians in the south, and this hostility in turn exacerbated the fact that Epeirot inadequacy had made Macedonia itself more vulnerable. A main aim of the war recently waged by the allies of the Hellenic League, the so-called Social War, had indeed been to strengthen the position of Macedonian allies in the west. A third factor was more difficult to assess accurately in 217. In 229 a Roman army had been sent to Illyria to combat the Illyrians, at that time led by Teuta, and secure free passage unendangered by Illyrian piracy through the Straits of Otranto for travellers from Italy. Teuta quickly accepted Roman terms guaranteeing the independence of various cities and clans, including Epidamnos, Apollonia and Kerkyra as well as the Atintanes and the Parthinoi, and limiting the activities of the Ardiaioi to the region north of Lissos (Lezha). The communities thus protected counted as friends (*amici*) of Rome; in particular Demetrios of Pharos received Roman encouragement. Demetrios gradually extended his sphere of influence over the kingdom of the Ardiaioi and acted as regent for Prince Pinnes so that in practice his position was that of their new ruler. He continued to cultivate the good relations Agron had enjoyed with Macedonia, and on this account he took refuge there when in 219 the Romans decided that he now posed the same threat to the security of the Straits of Otranto as Teuta had in 229 and overthrew him.[2]

Thus far Macedonia does not appear to have had any contact with Rome. The simple granting of asylum to Demetrios, although he was persona non grata in Rome, was not in itself a hostile act. However, as soon as Philip came under Demetrios' influence and considered solving Macedonia's Illyrian problems by restoring to Illyria a Demetrios who would then remain dependent on him, the chance of a conflict of interests with Rome immediately arose. The development of Macedonian naval policy, also influenced by Demetrios, indicates that Philip was in the last resort prepared to take this risk. The new solution was hazardous for various reasons, and even without the Roman dimension it is legitimate to ask if the gains could ever have justified the risks. However, the operation seemed attractive at the time, even though Demetrios must in principle have known that the danger of renewed Roman involvement had to be taken seriously. He probably heard that in 217 the Senate had asked Pinnes about overdue reparation payments, and Philip was even alleged to have been requested to extradite Demetrios;[3] but the Roman disaster at Lake Trasimene must have seemed to have obviated this danger. That Philip was indeed aware of the Roman danger but did not initially take it seriously because of Trasimene emerges from the events of 216. The new *lemboi* were operating in the region around Apollonia that Philip wanted to take when the alarm was sounded by Skerdilaidas. Roman ships then crossed the Adriatic, and this act alone was sufficient to make Philip abandon his plans immediately; there was no conflict—Philip simply gave up and sailed back home with his new fleet.[4]

However, the annihilating defeat of the Roman army by Hannibal at Cannae in 216 opened up new prospects for Macedonia. An ultimate victory by the Carthaginians was at the time considered a possibility not only in Italy. In Macedonia the question arose of what would happen in Illyria should Hannibal gain the upper hand in Italy. The new neighbour would then be not Rome but a southern Italy under Carthaginian protection. To establish contact in advance, a Macedonian envoy, the Athenian Xenophanes, travelled to Hannibal in 215 and negotiated a treaty of alliance. The formal aim was indeed cooperation, but the real intention of the treaty was plainly to realize the new Macedonian claim to Illyria. Within the framework of a general state of friendship it was agreed that Carthage and Macedonia should be allies in the war against Rome "until the Gods accord us the victory"; Philip would give assistance "when necessary and as from time to time agreed on." Philip had now ranked himself firmly among the opponents of Rome. But he must have felt sure that he was coming to terms with the future great power and that by doing so he was protecting at little cost his Illyrian claims. This conviction is clear in the single concrete clause of the treaty: after their defeat the Romans were to be forced not to make war against Philip; they were no longer to be allowed to "rule" (a word that gives us Demetrios' interpretation of the independence guaranteed by Rome for its friends in Illyria) over Kerkyra, Apollonia, Epidamnos, Pharos, Dimallon, the Parthinoi and the Atintanes; and the friends and relatives of Demetrios of Pharos who had been interned in Italy since 219 were to be surrendered to him.[5]

This unequivocal and quite gratuitous partisanship for Carthage, through which Philip publicly embraced Demetrios' enmity with Rome, was an overprecipitate act that had appalling long-term consequences. Certainly it was an attempt to protect the effectiveness of the new Macedonian policies in Illyria even after the apparently imminent conclusion of the war in Italy. The treaty perhaps in the long term would not have caused so much damage had not its contents, through a stupid coincidence, immediately become known to the Romans: Xenophanes' ship was captured off the coast of Calabria, and three high-ranking Carthaginians and the draft of the treaty were found on board. As it then gradually became evident that the victor of Trasimene and Cannae could win battles but not the war, the Macedonian catastrophe was foreseeable. Philip had irresponsibly ranged his state on the side of the loser in one of the greatest conflicts the Mediterranean region had ever known, purely for the sake of a new policy towards Illyria that had been developed by Demetrios in his own interest.

Some years passed before the full consequences were apparent. At first the Senate rightly did not take seriously the threat contained in the treaty. Fifty ships were held in readiness, and their commander, M. Valerius Laevinus, was ordered to cross the Adriatic "to Macedonia," as his potential field of action was officially called, should suspicions against Philip harden, to prevent Philip from joining with Hannibal. When in 214 Philip took the pro-Roman city of Orikos with 120 *lemboi*, the citizens immediately sent for Laevinus, who drove out Philip's garrison; some time later, when the Macedonians attacked Apollonia, they were driven back so fiercely that Philip saw an overland retreat as the only possibility of saving himself and his army. He ordered the firing of his entire new fleet at the mouth of the Aoos because it seemed impossible to save it. This activity ensured that the Roman fleet remained stationed in Illyrian waters but also meant that the naval phase of Philip's Illyrian policy was at an end.[6]

The death of Demetrios, probably in autumn 214,[7] robbed the new Macedonian policy in Illyria that had been tailored for him personally of its prime mover and its raison d'être. However, Skerdilaidas still remained dangerous, and the aims and purpose of the Roman fleet were not clear. The underlying aim of Macedonian policy in Illyria, the security of Macedonia, now had to be pursued without Demetrios and the fleet. During the next two years Philip operated in the mountains to the west with the object of winning territories and peoples from his opponents. From the Roman *amici* the Atintanes, the Parthinoi and the fortress of Dimallon were taken, and from Skerdilaidas his fortress at Lissos; Philip also seems to have made Macedonian influence felt in the Dassaretis. Hence although the Romans continued to hold the important harbours of Orikos, Apollonia and Epidamnos, Philip controlled almost the whole hinterland as well as Lissos.[8]

In fact the war could really have ended at that point. Lacking a fleet and with no Adriatic harbour apart from Lissos, Philip posed no danger to Italy, and the Romans, limited as they were to the harbour towns, posed no threat to Macedonia. But Philip's ominous treaty with Hannibal still remained valid, itself the reason for the Roman presence in the first place. Because of it Macedonia continued to be considered as an enemy of Rome that despite limited resources must still be combatted. Laevinus was therefore acting according to the logic of this policy when he concluded an alliance with Macedonia's old enemies the Aitolians in the hope of tempting them into a new war against Macedonia. The conditions of the treaty were trimmed to fit the Aitolians: in the north as far as Kerkyra any conquered land would belong to the Aitolians, and the Romans would receive only a proportion of the transportable booty related to the circumstances of the conquest. Akarnania would be the main target of their common effort. Other friends of Aitolia were expected to participate in the struggle: Sparta and Elis in the Peloponnese, Skerdilaidas and his son Pleuratos in Illyria and a newcomer on the Balkan scene, Attalos of Pergamon, were specifically mentioned.[9]

The composition of the alliance made it inevitable that the First Macedonian War would take place in precisely those regions that had also suffered during the Social War from 220 to 217. The Romans welcomed anything that damaged Philip and his allies and kept them away from the Straits of Otranto; they gladly agreed to operations taking place in Akarnania, Phokis, Lokris and Thessaly as well as on the Peloponnese but themselves sent in only twenty-five quinqueremes. In 211 Philip still found it possible to lay waste the Illyrian hinterland of Apollonia and Orikos and attack the Dardanians and the Maidoi on the middle reaches of the Strymon.[10] Later, however, he was forced to neglect the north in order to prevent the loss of the Macedonian position in central and southern Greece that had been reestablished by Doson. Apart from autumn 209, when he had to counter Illyrian attacks on Lychnidos and a Dardanian advance into Orestis, and another short period in 208, he was until 206 fully occupied with the war in the south.[11]

The depressing details of this war, which led repeatedly to sackings and atrocities but brought significant strategic advantages to no one except the Romans, who at that time merely wanted to damage Philip and keep him occupied, need not be related in detail here. It is sufficient to note that almost all the places gained by the Aitolians in 211 and 210 were later recaptured by Philip, with the exception of Aigina, which Attalos bought from them. Even Akarnania, the main declared target of the Aitolians, was not taken. As a result the Aitolians concluded a peace treaty in 206, although it was bound to bring them trouble with the Romans because the treaty of 212/11 did not allow one partner to make peace without the other, and Rome itself was not yet prepared to make peace with Philip. However, a year later, after a new Roman commander had conducted operations in the region behind Epidamnos and Apollonia, winning back the Parthinoi and Dimallon and taking two forts, Bargullon and Eugenion, the war parties met for negotiations in the Epeirot city of Phoinike.

The Romans wanted, at least for the time being, to end the war in the Balkans because they were preparing for the invasion of Africa, and Philip had nothing to lose by making peace. The Parthinoi and Dimallon were, after all, only of strategic significance to Macedonia when an enemy fleet was stationed at Epidamnos or Apollonia; and as compensation for these losses Philip was allowed to retain the Atintanians. It is unlikely that he continued to hold Lissos, as the city played no part in the negotiations. Also written into the treaty by Philip as signatories (*adscripti*) were his relative Prusias, king of Bithynia (who had not, however, as far as is known, taken part in the war), and the most important members of the Hellenic League—the Achaians, Boiotians, Thessalians, Akarnanians and Epeirots. Along the coast the harbour cities of Orikos, Apollonia and Epidamnos as well as the island of Kerkyra remained free Roman friends, as did the Parthinoi and the inhabitants of the three strongholds. Skerdilaidas' son and successor, Pleuratos, was certain to keep a careful watch on his southerly neighbour from his residence in Skodra.[12] But Philip must have been relieved that the Illyrian adventure embarked on more than ten years earlier had apparently reached such a happy end. A conflict in principle between him and Rome seemed to exist no longer. Macedonia had no real need to control the Illyrian coast, and Roman interests seemed to continue confined to that area. The Hellenic League was also preserved, in spite of some tensions. In Achaia, for instance, as it became clear that the king could not protect every place with his personal presence, the Macedonian garrisons in Orchomenos, Heraia, Triphylia and Alipheira came to be considered (by their hosts) to have more than a protective function.

The peace of Phoinike consolidated the Macedonian frontier regions bordering on Illyria. As the peace also appeared to serve the Roman interest, a further conflict with Rome was not anticipated. Philip may have continued to cultivate some contacts with Illyrian clans, which may have given rise to complaints in Rome, but he does seem in the following years to have concerned himself primarily with the east. Once again the sources are extremely deficient—both fragmentary and hostile—and much remains vague. But what seems to emerge from them is the first systematic attempt since the time of Ptolemaios Keraunos to bring some of the previous Macedonian territories in Thrace under Macedonian control again. Philip had already in 209 defeated the Maidoi on the central Strymon, and by 202 he had advanced as far as the Sea of Marmara, supported by a larger, newly built Aegean fleet. He operated also on the Asiatic side of the sea in support of his relative Prusias and took Chalkedon, Kios and Myrleia. In Europe by this time he must also have taken at least Lysimacheia and Perinthos as well as Thasos. The selection of these cities seems to have been at least partly decided by the fact that they were allies of the Aitolians. However, when the Aitolians complained about Philip in Rome in 202, they were merely reminded of their own treaty infringement in 206.[13]

It was not only the Aitolians who were perturbed by Philip's activities. No one knew exactly what he intended, perhaps not even Philip himself. His operations in Thrace were in the tradition of Philip II or Lysimachos, and the great fleet that he deployed in them called to mind Demetrios Poliorketes, his great-grandfather. Both Attalos of Pergamon and Rhodes felt their security threatened. Attalos, himself an ambitious expansionist and hostile neighbour of Prusias, had participated in the war against Philip as soon as the Aitolians offered him the opportunity. Since 210 he possessed the island of Aigina, and he doubtless cherished further hopes and ambitions. Rhodes, a state whose citizens conducted extensive trade with the Black Sea regions, saw its commerce endangered by Philip's activities around the Sea of Marmara; and the brutal destruction of the city of Kios so distressed the Rhodians and damaged their interests that they were prepared to go to war.[14] This readiness was reinforced by the suspicion that Philip supported the Kretan pirates, against whom

Rhodes was fighting at that time. At any rate, confidential agents of Philip were busy in Krete, where Philip, like many of his predecessors, kept up his influence because of the possibility of recruiting mercenaries. (In 220, when war broke out on the island, he had even dispatched league troops there to help his friends, and on this account had been accorded the honorary title of president [*prostates*] of the Kretan League.)[15]

The states of Asia Minor were also perturbed by the restoration of the Seleukid empire by Antiochos III. It had been largely at the cost of the Seleukids that Attalos had been able to expand his own kingdom in Asia Minor so far. Antiochos' return from Iran in about 206/5, after reestablishing his empire in inner Asia, and his renewed attention to Asia Minor inevitably occurred at the cost of the Pergamenes. Zeuxis, the Seleukid governor of Asia Minor, had been residing since about 213 in Sardis, always on the lookout for opportunities to extend the influence of his master; and the king himself was in Ionia in either 204 or 203, where we have evidence for his visiting Teos, which accorded him lavish honours.[16]

The activities of Philip and Antiochos in the years following 202 gave Polybios reason to suspect a robber treaty between the two kings directed against Ptolemaios V, who was still a minor. Antiochos did indeed in 202 take advantage of the weakness of the young king to seize from him Koile-Syria, which had been disputed for a century;[17] and Zeuxis did nothing to prevent Philip from taking Samos and Miletos from Ptolemaios in 201 and Ainos and Maroneia in 200. Philip seems also to have reckoned on receiving actual assistance from Zeuxis in operations against Pergamon and Rhodes in 201. Hence there does seem to have been some sort of agreement, though not necessarily with the aim of dividing the whole Ptolemaic empire between them, as Polybios thought.[18] The powers that felt themselves most affected were undoubtedly Rhodes and Pergamon. When Philip attempted to conquer Chios in 201, he was countered by the united fleet of Rhodes and Pergamon, and his own fleet was so severely damaged that it neither wanted nor was able to continue the fight. He then proceeded to plunder his way with a land army through Pergamene territory, penetrating as far as the suburbs of the city of Pergamon in his fury over Attalos' intervention. In the same year—whether earlier or later is not known—his fleet fought against the Rhodians alone at Lade, this time successfully. However, when he advanced into northern Karia, the reunited fleet of the Pergamenes and Rhodians was able to keep the Macedonians bottled up in the Bay of Bargylia for the whole winter of 201/200.[19]

What motives can Philip have had for doing all this? What did he seek to gain for Macedonia in Asia Minor, in particular in Karia? How are these events to be interpreted in their total political context? Macedonia had had interests in Thrace since the time of Philip II, and it is easy to appreciate the desire to revive them. Philip's great-grandfather Demetrios Poliorketes had once held great power in the Aegean, so that here there was a family tradition that Philip could continue and that sufficiently explains his interest in Lemnos, Samos, Chios and other islands, where he was reestablishing Macedonian influence.[20] But his operations in Karia do not fit into this pattern, and no entirely satisfactory explanation can be given for them. Philip's active interest in northern Karia is, however, only documented within the context of the war with Rhodes,[21] and it is tempting to explain it mainly as a tactical attempt to damage the Rhodians within their own sphere of power. For this end it would be possible to revive the old friendships in northern Karia first entered into by Doson. To proceed against Rhodes, Philip needed a land base in the immediate neighbourhood: Iasos, Bargylia and Euromos (renamed Philippoi before Philip finally evacuated Karia in 196),[22] together with Pedasa and Stratonikeia, finally provided the necessary Macedonian outposts. It was from this area that he attacked Knidos in 201, and he also took Prinassos and the tiny island of Nisyros from the Rhodians and perhaps other cities and strong points in their possession on the mainland (the Peraia).[23]

Just what Philip's intentions were in Karia may be unclear, but what he had certainly not intended to do was spend the whole winter of 201/200 there. The length of his enforced stay and the necessity of quartering and provisioning his men through the winter gave rise to friction even with friendly states. The region around Euromos, Iasos and Bargylia could not provision the Macedonians out of its own spare capacity, and because the enemy fleet prevented supplies being brought in by sea, Philip was forced to take unpopular measures. There are reports of attacks made on Mylasa, Alabanda and Magnesia-on-the-Maiander, carried out solely to obtain food supplies. Zeuxis, who appears to have promised help, in the event did hardly anything,[24] though Philip does not seem to have taken any action against cities bound to Antiochos. Not until spring 200 was Philip able to break out of Bargylia. He left some soldiers there to protect the small cities of the region that had come out on his side—whether voluntarily or under pressure from possible Rhodian reprisals—and continue to keep the Rhodians busy in Karia and thus hinder their ability to interfere in the North Aegean. However, it is clear that in 200 it was not Karia and the war against Rhodes that had priority but Thrace; had it not been for Rhodian alarm over Philip's activities in the Marmara region in 202, there would probably have been no Macedonian attack on Karia.

In 200 operations in Thrace were more systematic. Maroneia and Ainos were taken, as well as the inland Thracian cities of Kypsela, Doriskos and Serrhaion. On the Chersonnesos every large community and a number of smaller ones followed the example of Lysimacheia; Eleious, Alopekonnesos, Kallipolis, Madytos and Sestos are specifically mentioned. Philip crossed the Dardanelles from Sestos and began to besiege Abydos. The aim was clearly to gain control of the two most important ferry harbours on the narrowest section of the Dardanelles.[25] The doggedness with which Philip pursued his Thracian plans during 200 shows that he was following a definite immediate aim, which for the moment was not the reconquest of the large Thracian possessions of Lysimachos or Philip II, the inland parts of which remained largely out of his control. His priorities were the harbour towns and the east-west lines of communication, and he was primarily following a policy of advanced defence. The chief potential threat to the region was posed by the aging but still-rapacious Attalos of Pergamon.

In 200 Attalos must have appeared even more dangerous because in autumn 201 he joined together with Rhodes in appealing to the Senate in Rome. The Senate was immediately ready to listen to those of its members who considered that the time was ripe to settle accounts with Philip now that the final battle against Hannibal had been won in 202. Already at the end of the winter a group of three legates travelled to Greece to work up enthusiasm for a war against Philip. One of them, P. Sempronius Tuditanus, had even negotiated the Peace of Phoinike.[26] At the consular elections an old commander of the First Macedonian War, P. Sulpicius Galba, was elected and assigned Macedonia as his province. The Popular Assembly, which was formally responsible for declaring war (*comitia centuriata*) did initially offer resistance and rejected the consul's first proposition, but after negotiations with the leaders of opinion the declaration of war "against Philip and the Macedonians under his rule" was made in early summer 200. Galba promptly levied his legions and assembled his equipment, and shortly after Philip had finally managed to take Abydos, he received the news that the consul had landed near Apollonia.[27]

No negotiations took place. The Roman legates twice delivered demands to Philip that he not make war against the Greeks and that he bring his dispute with Attalos over the depredations of 201 to arbitration. The first time was at Athens in the spring, and the message was sent via his general Nikanor; the second time was in late summer at Abydos, to Philip personally; and their demands were made known everywhere they went in Greece. Nevertheless, war preparations continued in Italy regardless of the possibility of concessions by Philip. One function of the legates was indeed to deliver the ultimatum, but their main task was to arouse anti-Macedonian sentiment in Greece. It was not particularly easy for them. Because Philip's current war, conducted at times with extreme brutality, had taken place outside the central area of the Greek motherland, most of the Balkan Greeks felt no enthusiasm for a new conflict on their own doorstep, neither for nor against Macedonian rule, and only Attalos and the Rhodians were strongly in favour. Now as ever many Peloponnesians felt that sufferance of the Macedonian garrisons was a reasonable price to pay for their relative safety from Sparta and Elis. The Achaians did not consider themselves as being "fought down" by Philip, and although the legates spent some time there and endeavoured to channel any anti-Macedonian sentiment in a pro-Roman direction, nothing much could be accomplished along these lines in 200. The situation was the same in Epeiros, where the militarily weak federation was not able to commit itself to a position in principle for or against Rome or Philip, though it had mediated in the Peace of Phoinike. The legates also visited Amynandros, ruler of mountainous Athamania in the middle of the Pindos range, though he was not bound in any way to Macedonia, and paid a visit to the Aitolian League, where the relationship to Rome had remained clouded since 206 despite the league's traditional enmity towards Macedonia.[28]

Only in Athens did the Romans receive a cordial welcome, arriving there in April 200 together with Attalos and some Rhodian representatives. The reason for this friendly reception was not, however, any sympathy in principle but a particular immediate development. Two young men from Akarnania had participated in the Eleusinian Mysteries of September 201, although they had not been initiated according to the required ritual. The Athenians allowed their fury at this sacrilege to boil over and punished the two young men with death. In response Akarnanian bands of troops made their way to Attika with the support and consent of Macedonia and laid waste rural areas. As Macedonians from Chalkis and Korinth also took part, the Athenians decided to retaliate by destroying all monuments to Macedonian kings, including even erasing mere references to them in inscriptions, and by dissolving the two tribes named after Macedonian kings, Antigonis and Demetrias.[29] With this unreasonably sharp reaction to a relatively trivial incident the basic neutrality displayed by the Athenians towards Macedonia since 229 was broken. During the winter the Athenian Kephisodoros set out in search of allies and was naturally granted a sympathetic ear by Rhodes and Attalos as well as by Ptolemaios, the Kretans and the Aitolians. However, because only Attalos and the Rhodians, whom Philip was fighting anyway, took positive action, he also travelled to Rome, though whether before or after the visit of the legates to Athens is unclear.[30] During their sojourn and under pressure from the Rhodians and Attalos the Athenians declared war against Macedonia. This act cannot have been as desperate and foolhardy as it appears: because the Athenians' only real hope of success lay in assistance from Rome, it must be considered certain that the legates had told the Athenians that Roman troops would be dispatched against Philip.[31] Thus events in Athens offer further proof that the legates had no intention of negotiating with Philip.

Perhaps it cannot be conclusively explained why the Romans suddenly took so much interest in Balkan and Greek affairs that they considered it necessary to force an end completely to Macedonian rule outside Macedonia itself and were prepared to tolerate four years of war to do so. It cannot have been due only to the appeal of the Rhodians and Attalos in autumn 201, which can at most have been the event that sparked things off. Philip's activities in the Aegean and Thrace can therefore only have served as an excuse and were not the real reason for the renewal of the Roman war against Macedonia, because Roman interests, insofar as they can at all be determined for the Balkans, were not affected. Neither are Illyrian affairs sufficient to explain the drastic Roman aims, although since the Peace of Phoinike Romans had several times been sent there to protect Roman allies against unspecified threats.[32] Roman control of the harbour cities was, however, in no way threatened. The fact is that although after the war Philip was made to relinquish all his new possessions, the Roman priority was clearly the destruction of the traditional Macedonian position among the Greeks of the southern Balkans. Right from the beginning, from the first propaganda mission in spring 200, the Romans sought to divide Greek aims and interests from those of Macedonia to produce a fissure in the historically developed structure of Macedonian supremacy and create a somewhat artificial conflict between the interests of the Greeks and those of Philip.[33] By the end of the four-year war this breaking up of power was complete.[34] It had hardly anything to do with the immediate complaints of 201/200, but the Senate was absolutely determined to enforce it.

The only sufficient reason for this determination by the Senate can be found in a connection with the war against Hannibal. In 202 Hannibal lost his last battle against Rome at Zama, and the peace treaty that followed restricted Carthage to what was claimed to be its traditional sphere of influence in North Africa.[35] Macedonia then remained the only power that had collaborated with Hannibal and had not yet been punished. Instead Philip had expanded his sphere of influence and thereby angered friends of Rome. Several members of the Senate had been commanders in the earlier war against Philip and had certainly understood it as part of the war against Hannibal, even though they had been unable at the time to achieve any spectacular successes because of the limited nature of their commission. These men in particular, but certainly others also, must have taken the view that the earlier war against Philip should now be continued so as to dismantle Macedonian rule over its neighbours, on the lines of the peace treaty with Carthage. Roman desire for revenge and private hopes of famous victories were probably the decisive reasons for the outbreak of the war.

These considerations did not initially have anything to do with the development of long-term policies towards the Greek states, which resulted more from the outcome of the war and the way it was conducted. From the beginning Roman tactics were aimed at separating from Macedonia those Greeks who tolerated or even supported Macedonian rule. The long-term consequences—the establishment of new chains of interdependent relationships—were certainly not thought through in advance. All that was planned was the destruction of the ties to Macedonia. With the exception of those few states already at war with Philip, the Greek states were not impressed by the programmatic polemic of the Roman legates. Only reluctantly and under the influence of the first victories, or even under direct military pressure from the legions, did they one after another join the side of the Romans after the latter had made it clear that they were not prepared to tolerate neutrality.[36] After the first direct attack from the Illyrian bases had failed because of supply problems, T. Quinctius Flamininus in spring 197 advanced on Thessaly from the south, just as earlier Macedonian conquerors of Macedonia—Kassandros, Demetrios or Antigonos Gonatas—had done before him. Already during negotiations a year previously he had announced Roman intentions of also "liberating" Thessaly.

To defend the land that since the time of Philip II had constituted a crucial part of the Macedonian system, Philip V was prepared to take on the main armies of the Romans and their allies. The result, however, was not long in doubt. Philip's phalanx was annihilated by Flamininus' army at Kynoskephalai.[37] That June day of 197 was one of the most significant single days in the history of Macedonia. But it would be a mistake to believe that a Macedonian victory in the battle of Kynoskephalai would in the long term have made any appreciable difference to the outcome of the war. The Roman Senate had determined to bring down Macedonia as it had brought down Carthage, and its military strength was many times greater than that of Philip. When the political will was there, as it certainly was, military power in plenty was there to back it.

It is well known that the Romans had no preconceived ideas of how to handle Greek affairs outside Macedonia and that T. Quinctius Flamininus only gradually developed his policies for the "liberation" of the Greeks and had to realize them against opposition in the Senate based either on principle or on tactical considerations. There seems, though, to have been no difference of opinion among Romans about dismantling Macedonian power and limiting their enemy's territory to an area that could be recognized as "traditional." This aim, laid down at the beginning, was achieved. For Macedonia, it entailed giving up all possessions south of the Olympus range; particularly painful was the loss of Thessaly and the three traditional strongholds of Demetrias, Chalkis and Korinth. In the east it lost all possessions beyond the Nestos—that is, Thrace up to the Sea of Marmara—as well as all holdings in the Aegean and Asia Minor; the crest of the Pindos range was made the western frontier in principle, but Orestis became independent, and Lychnidos was granted to the Illyrian Pleuratos. The Macedonian fleet was limited to five small ships and an ancient naval monument; Philip had to pay by installments an indemnity of one thousand talents towards the costs of the war and hand over his second son Demetrios as hostage.[38] Macedonia therefore remained as a bulwark against the barbarians of the northern Balkans—the explanation given by Flamininus to the Aitolians for Rome's allowing the continued existence of the state of Macedonia[39]—but within frontiers that had not existed since the middle of the fourth century B.C. The external spheres of dominion and influence that had turned Macedonia into a great power had been abolished, and the Romans took care that they were never reestablished.[40]

4. IN THE SHADOW OF ROME

Thirty years after Flamininus had outlined the future function of Macedonia to the Aitolians, the state of Macedonia had been broken by Rome, the military strength of the country destroyed, the monarchy abolished and the last king, Perseus, banished to Italy. A Roman province of Macedonia was not immediately established, but the state of Macedonia as the Greek world had known it since the sixth century B.C. no longer existed. This section will explain how it happened.

External events prevented the development of a "normal" post-war relationship between Rome and Macedonia immediately after 196. Concurrently with the Roman war against Macedonia the Seleukid Antiochos III had been systematically extending his influence in Asia Minor. No one in Europe knew exactly what he intended. However, that he did not in principle exclude Europe from his ambitions and perhaps had his eye on the long-lost legacy of Lysimachos became plain in 196 when he crossed the Dardanelles and took Lysimacheia. This unanticipated insecurity was one factor that determined the Roman treatment of Macedonia after the war; another was the grave discontent of the Aitolians with the Romans because the Roman conception of the "liberation" of the Greeks allowed no extension of Aitolian influence to the territories evacuated by Macedonia.[1] Under these circumstances Philip had already in 196 received the advice that as an earnest of his future reliability in respect to Rome, he would do well to open negotiations for an alliance.[2]

It is unlikely that an alliance was in fact made. Nevertheless, as relations between Rome and the Aitolians and Rome and Antiochos steadily deteriorated, Philip undertook nothing that would make the Romans suspect his reliability. When Flamininus fought against Nabis of Sparta in 195, he was accompanied to the Peloponnese by fifteen hundred Macedonians.[3] Philip rejected out of hand overtures and offers made by the Aitolians and later by Antiochos himself. A strengthening of their position in Greece was certainly not in his interest.[4] When it became plain in 192 that the Romans would not be able to settle with the Aitolians without a war, Flamininus, now returned to Greece as legate, was not prepared, when he visited Demetrias, publicly to dispute the suggestion that the city might under certain circumstances be returned to Philip;[5] during the first active phase of the war in 191 the Roman praetor M. Baebius Tamphilus came to an agreement with the Macedonian king. Since the Aitolians had in the meantime, with the support of Antiochos, reoccupied large areas of Thessaly and central Greece, Philip's treaty with Baebius provided that as recompense for military assistance he should be permitted to retain such places in Thessaly as he might capture.[6] Philip was now considered to be both useful and reliable, and the agreement was respected by Baebius' successors.

In this fashion Demetrias and Magnesia, parts of Perrhaibia, certain places in western Thessaly, including Dolopia, and some communities in the Phthiotis came under Macedonian rule before peace was made with the Aitolians in 188.[7] This position was a long way from the traditional dominant role in Thessaly that Macedonia had played since the time of Philip II. Nonetheless, the independent Thessalian League, the state form selected and organized by Rome for liberated Thessaly in 195, gained in self-confidence from year to year, did not allow itself to be intimidated by Philip and in 188 was not prepared to consent to the quite modest gain in Macedonian power in its territory. The contradiction between the loudly proclaimed freedom for the Thessalians of 196 and current Roman toleration of territorial gains by Philip in Thessaly, even when the emergency created by the war was resolved, produced tensions that resulted in the Thessalians appealing to Rome.

In 186/85 envoys from Thessaly, Perrhaibia and Athamania travelled to Rome to lay their complaints against Philip. The Senate took the view that it was not competent to decide about the accusations in detail and instead appointed a commission of three legates, including M. Baebius Tamphilus, who had made the agreement with Philip in 192, to travel to Greece and examine matters on the spot. In spring 185 the legates invited all concerned to a hearing at Tempe. Each detailed his complaint, and in each case the commission decided against Philip. The principle of the peace treaty of 196 was reendorsed; all Macedonian occupation troops were to be withdrawn from the disputed cities, Philip's territory was to terminate at the traditional frontiers, and local territorial disputes were to be resolved according to a defined procedure.[8] The Thessalians had clearly not expected the Romans to treat Macedonia with such all-embracing cynicism: neither Demetrias and Magnesia nor Dolopia and the cities occupied by Philip in the Phthiotis appear to have been cited in their complaint. Had the Thessalians included them, the decision would certainly have gone in their favour, but as it was, these areas remained "traditionally" Macedonian.

This procedure exemplifies the Roman attitude towards Macedonia after 196, when it was confined to those territories defined as traditional—in practice those territories not claimed by any other state friendly to Rome. For the sole purpose of obtaining Philip's help against Antiochos he had been allowed to reoccupy some regions and cities in Thessaly. Had those affected been content with this situation after 188, the Romans would certainly not themselves have taken any initiative to revoke the agreement with Macedonia. However, now that angry resentments had been provoked, the interests of a defeated ex-enemy had to give way to those of Rome's protégés. This second decision had nothing to do with legality or justice, and Philip was forced to swallow it as he had had to swallow the first ten years before.

"In doubt against Macedonia" was also the Roman motto in dealing with the problem of Ainos and Maroneia. Shortly after 196 the two cities had been captured by Antiochos III. After his defeat it was unclear what would happen to them. Eumenes, who had been granted the Chersonnesos—including Lysimacheia, just evacuated by Antiochos—would have liked to have Ainos and Maroneia too, but Philip, whose coastal frontier stretched as far as Abdera, wanted the cities back. In 188, to avoid giving way to either Eumenes or Philip in this frontier area, the two cities were granted to neither and left independent. But in 187 or 186, at the request of sympathizers, Philip put garrisons in both cities, whereupon Eumenes and local opponents of Philip's faction appealed to Rome. The decision was delegated by the Senate to the same commission that was to regulate matters in Thessaly, and in a second hearing in Thessalonike the parties to this affair were heard. This time the three legates were impressed by Philip's indignation and employed different tactics from those they had used in Thessaly; Philip's garrisons would have to be withdrawn, but the question of principle was referred back to the Senate. The Senate, however, merely endorsed the independence of the two cities and dispatched a new commission to oversee it. Before the commission could arrive, Thracians perpetrated a massacre at Maroneia, in which it was alleged that the remaining opponents of Macedonia were the victims. Philip denied responsibility for these brutalities but was pressured to evacuate the cities, which he did, but not until 183.[9] The basic principle of Rome's treatment of

Macedonia is again clear: no matter what the grounds for conflict might be, it was always Macedonia that should go away empty-handed.

In 197 Flamininus had justified Rome's treatment of Macedonia with the argument that Macedonia fulfilled an important function as a bulwark against the non-Greek peoples of the north. This argument seemed also to prevail in Rome, which had good reason to be chary of the Celtic tribes from the Alpine and Transalpine regions. Thus it was only the Greeks who were "liberated," and it was only in connection with Greek cities and states that the Romans continued to intervene in Macedonian affairs after 196. In fulfilment of Macedonia's function as a bulwark Philip was able to develop active policies in the non-Greek north during these years. The general advantages of such policies should have become obvious even to the Aitolians when immediately after Kynoskephalai Philip had been forced to counter a Dardanian invasion. Bato, the Dardanian ruler, had offered Rome his assistance in 200, an offer that was immediately accepted and resulted in the Dardanians attacking simultaneously from the north when Sulpicius Galba advanced on Upper Macedonia in 199. They did not, however, take part in the battle of Kynoskephalai, nor do they appear to figure in the peace treaty. Philip was nonetheless compelled to muster his remaining force of sixty-five hundred men from the cities of Macedonia in 197 to defeat them in a battle near Stoboi when they were plundering in the region.[10]

During the following years Philip was also regularly active in Thrace. When the Scipio brothers wanted to lead the Roman army overland to Asia Minor in 190, Philip was able to guarantee them safe passage and adequate provisions. His influence on the Thracians was so well known that when in 188 Cn. Manlius Vulso set out, without first informing Philip, to take the same route back from Asia and was set on by bands of Thracians, it was Philip who came under suspicion of having organized the ambush. In just the same way he was suspected of responsibility for the already-mentioned massacre by Thracians in Maroneia.[11] Philip was thus credited with great influence in Thrace, far beyond the actual eastern frontier of Macedonia. When Q. Fabius Labeo fixed the territories for independent Ainos and Maroneia in 189, he chose to define the east-west road as the limit to the sphere of Macedonian influence.[12] Hence one must conclude that the Romans were prepared to tolerate further activity by Philip in the non-Greek areas of Thrace. Only the Greek cities and the Chersonnesos, now granted to Eumenes, were denied him. In this region therefore, probably because of Macedonia's function as a bulwark, the "traditional" frontiers were not enforced.

There are, then, in Thrace indications of a resurgence of the Macedonian state and a renewed consolidation in the only direction left open by Rome, albeit the direction of the main thrust of state expansion under Philip II. For 184 a war is reported on the Marmara coast against the Odrysian baron Amadokos, which also involved Byzantion. Philip subsequently gave a daughter in marriage to the Thracian king Teres, and there are even reports of Thracian settlements on Macedonian soil, perhaps between the Strymon and the Nestos, as part of a general policy of controlled population increase. In 183 Philip operated with his army in the central Hebros valley. He once more fought the Odrysians and occupied Philippopolis while operating against the Bessoi; on his way back through Paionia, he fought against the Dentheletoi and founded a new city, Perseis, in the neighbourhood of Stoboi. In 181 he again fought the Maedoi and the Dentheletoi.[13] The system behind his policy in Thrace thus seems fairly clear: failing more attractive possibilities, the conquest of the economic centre of Thrace, the onetime target of Philip II, had again become the top priority of Macedonian policy. Already in 183 one of Philip V's officers, Onomastos, is mentioned as being responsible for administering the Thracian region.[14] Philip also wanted to settle accounts with the recalcitrant Dardanians. He proposed to the German tribe of the Bastarnae, which at the time occupied an area near the Danube delta, that they take up arms against the Dardanians and, having driven them out, settle down on their lands. This connection was also sealed with a personal tie when the crown prince Perseus received a Bastarnian princess as bride.[15]

Just as in the times of Philip II and Lysimachos, the Greek sources only mention Philip V's Thracian operations in passing and, through failure to understand them, from a false viewpoint: their interpretation is made to accord with the personal range of interests of the writer. Because the Romans irrevocably destroyed the Macedonian state in 168 for motives that were later considered even in Rome to be not strictly honourable, the myth of Macedonian preparations for war and of a Roman preventative strike was promulgated. However, since it was clear right up to the outbreak of war that the current ruler, Perseus, was planning nothing of the kind, the blame for the idea had to be thrown onto his long-dead father Philip, regardless of the contradictions inherent in this theory. Perseus was represented as merely carrying out what Philip had planned. Such was the interpretation given in Rome to Polybios, for example, and which he made his own. A myth was also developed that the Bastarnai planned to make their way over the mountains and the Adriatic to Italy after driving out the Dardanians, and similar wild speculations were vented about Philip's contacts with the Skordiskoi, a tribe settled in the neighbourhood of Belgrade.[16]

In point of fact Philip, like Perseus after him, displayed not the slightest desire to wage another war against Rome. The theory that he had ever had intentions on Italy was merely a result of the comprehensive, hostile Roman interpretation of his treaty with Hannibal, which even at the time had had little to do with real plans. All indications suggest that the expansion into Thrace was nothing more than an attempt to consolidate the state within the bounds and possibilities left open to it and specifically endorsed by Flamininus. Philip indeed accepted only with gritted teeth and under occasional protest the Roman decisions against him in Thessaly and concerning Ainos and Maroneia, but those areas were by now probably of secondary importance despite the humiliation and disappointment associated with them. The massive investment in the Thracian region shows that future consolidation of the state would take place in the north, in a region where Rome itself had thus far shown no active interest.

A realignment in state policy of such dimensions did not go undisputed, particularly as Philip also organized new settlements in the north, of which Perseis was only one, and in the south, where Thracians were granted land. A certain amount of force would seem to have been exercised in carrying out this settlement programme, which was probably inevitable but in practice led to general opposition even among the top ranks of the aristocracy. In 183/82, as in 218, a bloody purge took place, once again officially described as countermeasures against a conspiracy, and once again high-ranking personalities fell victim—Admetos, Pyr-rhichos and Samos, son of Chrysogonos, a childhood playmate of Philip's, are mentioned.[17] The available sources do not allow us to penetrate the mist created by official obfuscation and by the Roman interpretation that the whole thing was ultimately directed against Rome. Even more obscure are the origins of the deadly dispute between Philip's sons, Demetrios and Perseus, that heav-ily burdened Philip's private life in his last years. The tradition in the sources is again extremely unreliable because it is a later interpretation that sets out to find the motives for Perseus' war with Rome in the murky waters of these private relationships at the court. Demetrios was persona grata in Rome, where he was well known from the time he spent there as hostage after 196. During a visit to Rome in 183 he was even able to bring about a positive decision for Philip in connection with renewed demands from Thessaly, and Flamininus in particular showed favour to the young prince. On returning to Pella he seems to have played with the idea of setting out to replace his elder brother as heir to the throne, an ambition lent wings by his good contacts with the Sen-ate. The dispute continued until summer 180, repeatedly ex-pressed in mutual conflicts and provocations. Perseus, however, knew how to defend himself; he was intimately involved in Philip's northern policies and was eventually able to eliminate Demetrios. The precise reasons for this conflict are unclear, as they also were to contemporaries,[18] though this obscurity did not prevent a mass of spectacular and speculative explanation. The most likely is that private motives were the root of the trouble, motives not unconnected with Demetrios' ambition to replace his brother in the succession. Whether political differences, perhaps over the future relationship to Rome or to the Thracians, played any part must remain uncertain. As Demetrios' sole advantage over his brother was his good contacts with Rome (which does not imply that Perseus' relations there were bad), it is indeed likely that the self-seeking young man tried to get as much as possible out of them. It is, however, less likely that the Senate was willing to intervene so deeply in the internal affairs of Ma-cedonia as to declare its support for Demetrios, although indi-vidual senators may well have played with the idea.[19] At any rate, Perseus had no difficulties in taking over the succession when the sixty-year-old Philip died unexpectedly a year later, and his first embassy to Rome was given a friendly reception. The Senate made no problems about recognizing him as successor.[20]

Both the Roman and the Greek traditions veil the reign of Perseus in obscurity. Certain alterations to his father's policies, both internal and external, can, however, be identified. The Thracian policies were maintained. Their fundamental importance was already made plain in 179 or 178 when Abrupolis, the ruler of the Thracian Sapaioi, perhaps at the instigation of Eumenes of Pergamon, advanced as far as Amphipolis before Perseus could defeat him and drive him out. Although good relations existed with the Odrysian ruler Kotys, Kotys himself was not so secure that Eumenes' *strategos* Korrhagos could not spur on the minor ruler Autlesbis to attack him at a critical moment in 171.[21] Thus there was certainly a security problem in Thrace. Perseus also continued the policies of his father towards the Bastarnai and the Dardanians, and these even culminated in a complaint being laid in Rome by the Dardanians. The first attempt by the Bastarnai had taken place at about the time of Philip's death and for various reasons had failed; the impetus of the second attempt in 177/76 was accordingly weaker and Macedonian complicity ultimately so difficult to prove that a Roman investigating commission failed to find concrete support for the persistent Dardanian accusations.[22]

It may be that Perseus did not in fact accord the Bastarnai as much importance as Philip, who had considered them more acceptable neighbours than his old enemies the Dardanians. They were, however, very unpopular with the Greeks,[23] and Perseus took great pains to cultivate his contacts with the southern Greeks. Macedonia had in any case never been completely cut off because of its territorial gains in Thessaly after 192. In the first extant list of members of the Delphic Amphiktyonic Council after its reorganization in 188, dating from autumn 178, two representatives of Perseus are named. Unfortunately we have no way of knowing whether this was the first time that the Macedonian king had sent representatives to the meeting.[24] But whatever the case may have been, this step certainly demonstrates willingness once more to take part in the affairs of the south.

The tensions produced by Philip's internal policies had caused a large number of people to leave the country for either political or economic reasons. Many found refuge in Greece, partly per-

haps because of the opportunities for asylum offered by the sanctuaries. When Perseus sought to defuse these tensions from the
past by means of an amnesty, he took particular care to have his
decree published in the sanctuaries of Apollo at Delphi and Delos
and of Athena Itonia in Boiotia. His decree allowed runaway
debtors and political refugees to return to their homes and lands
in Macedonia without suffering reprisals. This comprehensive solution to the problem of the Macedonian refugees was, as Polybios
makes clear, also a contribution towards improving relations with
those Greek states and institutions that had given them shelter.
But those who had remained in Macedonia also benefitted from
the amnesty, because all public debtors and political prisoners
were freed.[25] It was a clear signal for a new beginning, an attempt
to ameliorate the consequences of the dismal last years of Philip's
reign.

If this activity displays a cautious new approach to the Greeks,
the great respect in which Perseus was held by contemporary
kings is indicated by two marriage alliances. In 177 Perseus married the daughter of Seleukos IV, and because their peace treaties
with Rome allowed neither the Macedonian nor the Syrian king
to cross the Aegean with the necessary naval pomp and security,
the Rhodians took responsibility for the transport arrangements
in return for generous supplies of ship-building timber. A little
later his sister Apame married Prusias II of Bithynia. It is unclear
who took the initiative for these alliances, but they demonstrate
a new opening of Macedonia to the larger Greek world and a
normalization of relationships.[26]

Other old problems were also taken in hand. At some time,
exactly when is not known, the Achaians had passed a law that
forbade Macedonians to set foot on Achaian soil. This law had in
the meantime become an embarrassment to the Achaians, not
least because Achaian slaves who had escaped to Macedonia could
not be recovered since the law made negotiations practically impossible. The current leader of the Achaians, Kallikrates, himself
strongly pro-Roman and aware of the fundamental severity of the
Roman attitude to Macedonia, considered that to repeal the law
in 174 would inevitably produce tensions with Rome. His opinion
just managed to prevail. However, the party in favour of repeal
was also strong, and the affair shows to what extent the antag-
onisms of the war years had been reduced even in Achaia and

how far relations might have been normalized had it not been for Kallikrates.[27] In central Greece Perseus risked much more activity than Philip had done since 196. When in 174 the Dolopians showed their resentment at Macedonian "protection," Perseus even moved against them with an army: immediately afterwards he visited Delphi, perhaps at the time of the Pythian Games, with a large military escort, which was promptly described by his enemies as an army. He even concluded a treaty of alliance with the Boiotians.[28]

What from one point of view could be regarded as a normalization, the natural cultivation of good relations between neighbours, could be seen by a less benevolent observer as a regaining of influence and a first step towards the renewed buildup of power. Such was the hostile opinion of Eumenes of Pergamon, Rome's great friend in Asia Minor, who was at the time in conflict with Perseus' brother-in-law Prusias and perhaps with his other brother-in-law, Teres, but certainly with Perseus himself on account of Ainos and Maroneia. When he visited Rome in spring 172 he gave full vent to his hatred in a speech before the Senate in which he presented Perseus' every action as being fundamentally directed against Rome.[29] We have no reason to assume that those senators conversant with Balkan affairs found Eumenes fully credible or that the Senate really felt there was reason to fear Macedonia. Perseus, like his father before him, had, in every situation where his attitude might be suspected, done all he could to mollify the Senate, and he continued to do so now. But Eumenes had chosen his time cleverly. The long Roman wars in Spain and Liguria that had rewarded the fortunate commanders with a large number of triumphs and other military honours were for the time being largely at an end. The great freedom enjoyed by those making war on a population considered to be less civilized had promoted the innate Roman brutality and ruthlessness, which could indeed be curbed but here had been allowed full rein. The years-long unrestricted habit of simply taking booty and slaves wherever the opportunity arose, and the constant pressure on the Senate to grant to the annual consuls provinces in which they also could gain the military honours necessary for an influential standing in the state, resulted already in the consuls for 172 demanding to be given Macedonia as their province. This happened shortly after Eumenes' visit, during which his contacts were obviously not limited to the one formal appearance before the Senate portrayed by Livy.[30] The Romans may have been ready to fight in Iberia without political preparations but still not in the Greek east, where, as in 200, political groundwork was considered essential. The consuls of 172 were therefore given work to do in Liguria instead, but it seems almost certain that the Senate, many of whose members had fought in Spain, had already made a decision in principle, even though the formal declaration of war did not follow until the beginning of the consul year 171. Several groups of legates were sent to the east in 172 to ensure that the Greeks could be relied on in the event of a war against Perseus.

Not one of these delegations, however, was instructed to visit Perseus, and no demands were delivered to Macedonia, neither at the time nor later. The whole proceeding was so single-minded, so extraordinarily brutal, that the conclusion must be drawn that the decision to destroy Macedonia had already been taken in principle in 172. Perseus' efforts to normalize relations with the Greek states may have supplied the Senate with an excuse or justification after Eumenes had expounded his own hostile interpretation of this development. But ultimately, because Perseus undertook nothing against Rome and continued to seek desperately a basis for negotiations even after the legions had already arrived, all such individual factors seem trivial in comparison to the brutal determination of the majority in the Roman Senate to destroy a state in which they saw the opportunity of making rich booty and at the same time, on the political plane, put an end to the vexations resulting from their previous mildness and consideration.[31]

The inimical Roman attitude meant that Rome did not take part seriously in negotiations before the war or even during it despite some Roman defeats in the field and the war's continuation until 168. Anyone attempting to mediate merely came under suspicion of favouring Perseus. Even Greek states loyal to Rome came to experience the brutality that had been practised in Spain, to such an extent that the Senate was forced to take unusual disciplinary measures against some of its own members since, at least while the war was still going on, they could not afford to alienate the Greek states excessively.[32] The decisive battle this time took place, just as the Romans wanted, in the central territory of lower Macedonia, near Pydna in Pieria. After the annihilation of his army (more than twenty thousand Macedonians are reported to have been killed) Perseus fled first to Amphipolis and then to Samothrake, where he was finally forced to recognize the hopelessness of his position and surrender himself to the victorious Roman commander, L. Aemilius Paullus.[33] A centuries-long tradition thereby came to its end.

5. AFTER THE STORM

The dismantling of the Macedonian state by the Roman Senate after the victory of L. Aemilius Paullus was thorough and comprehensive. The monarchy was abolished and its enormous riches transported to Italy, together with the king and all his functionaries, who were interned there; the political structure of the country, that unified Macedonian state which was perhaps the greatest achievement of Philip II, was totally demolished. Instead of the centralized state no less than four separate republics were founded, each forbidden to hold any official political or even social contact with the others—even marriages between inhabitants of different republics were forbidden. The economic strength of the country was suppressed; the gold and silver mines were closed; the felling and export of ship-building timber were forbidden; a tax equal to half of the previous royal tax was to be paid to Rome, an annual amount of one hundred talents; an army was allowed to be maintained only on the frontiers.[1]

These measures spelled the irrevocable end of Macedonia as a state. It is obvious that the Macedonians were no longer able to fulfil the historical function as bulwark against the non-Greek tribes that they had exercised under the monarchy. This artificially created weakness is illustrated by the following events. When in 150 a pretender, Andriskos, who claimed to be a son of Perseus, tried to revive the Macedonian monarchy, he did not come from the south with Greek support but from the east with support from Thrace; it was necessary in the end to call in a Roman army to defeat him since the republics, which by and large did not want to join him, had been denied effective defensive forces.[2]

A direct result of the dissolution of the Macedonian state was thus that Rome itself was ultimately forced to take over the external functions of the destroyed state to avoid chaos in the Balkans. In 167 it had attempted to avoid this consequence, but after the defeat of Andriskos the decision was made to set up a direct Roman administration in the Balkans. From 148, the date of the decisive battle of Q. Caecilius Metellus Macedonicus against Andriskos, a new calendar reckoning was introduced into Macedonia. The event was therefore indeed seen as marking the beginning of a new epoch. It is not clear from the sources whether a Roman official was sent to Macedonia every year.[3] It is clear, though, that from this time on all extraterritorial state activity known to us was Roman activity. Insofar as extraterritorial state activity was undertaken at all, it was exercised directly by Roman officials. The Macedonians had become subjects of Rome, and their further history was determined by the occupying power of Rome.[4]

VI

The Macedonian State

1. KING AND STATE

This last chapter attempts to treat systematically certain aspects of the structure of the Macedonian state over the entire period of the monarchy. Three broad areas will be considered: the monarchy and its function within the state, the general administrative system including that of the cities, and the military system. All these aspects were in practice interdependent, but the main feature characterizing the Macedonian state, the monarchy, dominated everything else. It will therefore be treated first.

The king stood at the centre of the Macedonian state system. When the Romans set out to demolish the Macedonian state after 168 B.C., their first step was to abolish the monarchy and destroy the royal administrative apparatus by deporting the king and his officials to Italian internment centres. The monarchic system, however, was so deeply rooted in the Macedonian way of life that the regional councils appointed by the Romans failed to find favour, and a string of pretenders to the throne, of whom Andriskos was only the most successful, was again and again able to win a certain measure of popular support and had to be suppressed by the legions.[1]

The Macedonians had never really had serious doubts about the monarchy as an institution, even during earlier crises. During the crisis over the succession that followed the death of Alexander III Kassandros was able to rely on the readiness of the Macedonians to uphold the monarchy and ultimately accept him as king; even during the chaotic years that preceded the recognition of Antigonos Gonatas as king, the monarchy as an institution never seems to have been called into question. Even those Macedonians who founded their own states after the death of Alexander I thought only in terms of transplanting the Macedonian institution of the monarchy and adapting it to suit the new situation. The most powerful dynasties were the Ptolemies in Egypt and the Seleukids in Asia, and the former at any rate claimed as their legitimation a fictional descent from the Macedonian Argeadai. Kassandros' position was easier, because through his marriage to Philip's daughter Thessalonike he could prove a direct connection with the Argeadai; but even the Antigonids went to great pains to demonstrate their commitment to the founding royal house and its traditions. Gonatas restored the old royal capital of Aigai and the royal tombs there, and his successors even purported to fit the Argeadai into their own family tree.[2]

The monarchy thus was deeply rooted in the Macedonian state and dominated all aspects of state affairs. Its supremacy was due to the close relationship between the king and the nobles together with their adherents, but what distinguished the Macedonian monarchy from others was that the king behaved in a way that kept him in close contact with his people. For this reason the external trappings of monarchy remained modest. As far as we know, there were no particular distinguishing features before Alexander the Great. It may be that the occasional wearing of purple robes had already become customary in court circles, but this privilege was never reserved exclusively for the king. After Alexander had adopted the Persian royal insignia of the diadem, a band of white cloth wound round the head, the custom appears to have been introduced into Macedonia as well. It is at any rate attested for the later Antigonids.[3] But even after Alexander royal pomp remained taboo in Macedonia; in particular the preference displayed by Demetrios Poliorketes for extravagant dress was regarded as strong proof of his fundamental unfitness to reign in Macedonia. A further grave shortcoming of Demetrios was his "oriental" remoteness from ordinary people because the cultivation of a good relationship with his subjects was considered the sine qua non of a good king. Philip II is said to have toured the whole country and talked with people personally at the beginning of his reign, and Polybios observed during the reign of Philip V that the Macedonians were accustomed to speak their minds openly and vigorously to their king.[4] There was no place in such a state for a king who held himself aloof from his people or had recourse to an ancestor cult, or even the worship of himself or his family, as the unifying state ideology, as did the Ptolemies or the Seleukids in their multiracial states encompassing several different traditions. There was no official royal cult in Macedonia.

Ready access to individual petitioners and respect for public opinion were the price the king was expected to pay for the absence of formal political representation of the people—the price of his absolute monarchy. Several modern historians have thought to see evidence for an assembly of those capable of bearing arms (army assembly), assumed to function in the same manner Homer's poetic imagination led him to describe for the Achaian army at Troy or the Popular Assembly on Ithaka. But the Achaian army at the gates of Troy in no way formed a state, and the tiny island state of Ithaka cannot be compared with Macedonia. Apart from abnormal periods of crisis there is no evidence that in Macedonia an assembly of soldiers during peacetime exerted any political influence on the state, and there is certainly no evidence of a constitutional right to do so. Apart from the king, power in the state lay in the hands of the aristocracy, whose most influential members usually had the deciding voice in the royal succession, though for as long as the Argeadai had male family members available it was always an adult son of the dead king who succeeded. Nonetheless, it seems that he still had to be accepted and acknowledged by the barons. After the murder of Philip II in 336, for example, it was the influential Antipatros and his son-in-law Alexandros of Lynkestis who immediately spoke out in favour of Alexander, and it was also the aristocratic clique composed of Antigonos, Ptolemaios, Lysimachos and Kassandros that in 311 regulated the affairs of the empire and of the minor Alexander IV to suit their own interests. Only a single time, at the crisis in Babylon in 323, did a riotously expressed army opinion play a part in deciding the succession, when the nobles present wished to deviate substantially from the traditional principles respected until then.[5]

It was therefore the king and his barons who conducted the affairs of the state, and this fundamental principle seems to have held equally true for Alexander I as for Philip V or Perseus. Speaking of political decision making, Demosthenes contrasts the sole, and therefore advantageously rapid, competence of Philip II to make a decision with the laborious, and correspondingly slow, process of establishing consensus opinion in democratic Athens.[6]

The king took both political and administrative decisions personally but in consultation with his closest advisers, initially known
as *hetairoi*, companions, and then later, when Alexander III had
debased the title by extending it to cover thousands of soldiers,
as *philoi*, friends.[7] These advisers were personally selected by the
king himself, though it was probably usual for a new king initially
to continue to listen to the advisers of his predecessor, as did
Alexander the Great and Philip V in the first years of their reigns.
Those magnates who had taken a decisive part in recognizing the
new king doubtless at the beginning exerted the greatest influence. The criteria for the selection of later advisers are largely
unknown, but a mixture of political and personal considerations
may be assumed.

Royal absolutism found expression in many different ways.
The royal name could be used when new cities were founded;
Philippoi and Philippopolis, for instance, are only the earliest
known examples of a Macedonian practice that was carried so far
under Alexander that it set a pattern for city names in the whole
eastern Mediterranean area. The king and the royal family both
represented and led the state; their position was a privileged one,
but they were at the same time servants of the state, employable
in state interests. The aging Antigonos Gonatas once described
the kingship in a weary hour as "honourable servitude."[8] The
importance of good personal relationships even beyond the frontiers of the state was recognized at an early stage when Alexander
I gave his sister Gygaia in marriage to the Persian noble Boubares.[9] This readiness to promote state interests, as well as personal ones, through intimate personal alliances continued right
until the end of the monarchy. Philip II is probably the best-
known instance—though in his case duty certainly combined with
inclination[10]—but the marriages of the young Perseus to the Bastarnian princess and that of his sister to the Thracian king Teres
in the last years of the monarchy had an identical function.[11] In
military matters the king was naturally commander in chief, an
office that entailed the personal participation of the king in battle,
as is continuously attested from Alexander I to Perseus.

State treaties were apparently concluded with the king personally and not with the people, and in 346 it was the king himself,
not the people nor the state, who received seats on the Amphik-

tyonic Council in Delphi. The state administration was always centralized, insofar as details are known. The kings sent, in their own names, letters that were in fact official documents addressed to their administrators in the cities and in the country. That these men were addressed by name and not by title implies that they were, at least nominally, personal servants of the king (*epistatai*).[12] There is no evidence as to what kind of people these administrators were or where they came from, but it may be assumed that they came from the same circles that provided the top ranks of army officers, from the wider circle of the *hetairoi*, or later the *philoi*, who might themselves also be recruited from the corps of pages (*basilikoi paides*) founded by Philip II.

Although it is possible to establish the fundamental characteristics of the Macedonian state, the workings of important sections of the state apparatus are hardly known. We know little more about the judicial system than that the king himself was the chief judge. It may be that some form of urban judicial system existed in the cities, but we must be cautious in drawing conclusions. Judges (*dikastai*) are only known from Thessalonike, but these may possibly have been royal judges, such as certainly existed under Philip II.[13] At any rate the idea of a "democratic" system of people's courts (the *dikastai* in Thessalonike were an administrative body) can be dismissed even for the cities. It is more likely that judicial competence should be ascribed to the *epistatai*, at least in those places where there was no special board of judges as in Thessalonike; but this ascription, alas, can only remain speculative.

Our knowledge of the economic system is similarly limited. The principal mines, those yielding gold and silver, seem to have been in royal possession, but it is not known whether the kings ran them themselves as state enterprises or, as was the case with at least one brickworks, followed the Athenian practice and leased them out to tenants. The point is hardly important since whatever the form of organization, it is clear that the major share of the profits flowed into the royal treasury. From the time of Alexander I coins were struck out of the metal to cover royal expenditures.[14] Another source of revenue was customs duties levied by the state on both imports and exports.[15] Macedonian timber (particularly for ship building) and pitch, and their export, also appear to have been largely under royal control, by which the monarchy demonstrated its dominant position as owner of these commodities. Because timber, like the gold and silver mines, was a main source of royal income, the Romans later ordered that the felling of trees for ship building and the working of the mines be stopped.[16] Thus royal monopoly can also be assumed for timber, as the abolition of the monarchy entailed the abolition of its main economic basis; but this is no more than a supposition. It is probable that the kings exported grain within the Aegean region. A certain Aristoboulos of Thessalonike is known to have spent several years in the commercial centre of Delos as authorized grain dealer (*sitones*) of Demetrios II, and since Macedonia was agriculturally self-supporting, his function must have been to sell grain, not to buy it. In that period Macedonia also controlled Thessaly, which in the second century B.C. still produced, at least in most years, a grain surplus. The Macedonian sovereign must have received a portion of the harvest.[17]

The Macedonians paid taxes, probably on their harvests, and the Romans demanded payment of half the amount previously paid to the king.[18] Perseus' income is reported to have been two hundred talents annually,[19] but we do not know what items are included in this calculation. If this figure only became public because Rome later received half of it, as seems probable from the context of Plutarch's account, then it can only have represented the revenues from the land tax and not total state income.

Just as politics and economic matters seem to have been largely shaped by the central government, so too the cultural life of Macedonia was mainly determined and paid for by the monarchy. We know of participation in the major international festival at Olympia by Alexander I, Archelaos (also at the Delphic Pythian festival) and particularly Philip II, whose coins commemorate his victories, even though the motive for their participation must to some extent have been to boost the king's personal prestige both at home and abroad. Archelaos even founded his own Macedonian festival at Dion in Pieria, probably on the pattern of the games in Olympia.[20]

Macedonian cultural life in any period must have largely reflected the personal tastes of the reigning monarch. Although Alexander I commissioned a eulogy from Pindar, the then-fashionable poet of the aristocracy, and Perdikkas is said to have invited the medical pioneer Hippokrates of Kos and the poet Melanippides to his court, it was apparently Archelaos who first enjoyed regular visits to his court from artists and intellectuals. Euripides, Agathon, Timotheus and Choirilos visited Pella during his reign; even Sokrates is reported to have received, but declined, an invitation.[21] Amyntas III is known only to have encouraged the doctor from Stageira, Nikomachos, to reside at his court, but his sons were more culturally interested: Perdikkas received Plato's pupil Euphraios, who apparently remained some time in Pella, and Philip II was sufficiently versatile and cultivated to be described in Athens as "thoroughly Greek."[22] His intellectual inclinations cannot have sprung from nowhere, and despite a report that his mother Eurydike first learned to read as an adult for the sake of her children,[23] her sons must have become acquainted at the court with cultivated intellectual pursuits. Philip engaged Aristoteles, the son of his father's personal doctor, to act as private tutor to his own son Alexander and conducted lively and informed discussions on intellectual matters with envoys from Greece. He also took great pleasure in theatre and music, even if his taste did not always satisfy that of the carping, derisive Demosthenes. Actors, poets, historians and philosophers were warmly received in Pella,[24] and Alexander, who had grown up under the tutelage of Aristoteles in this stimulating court ambience, was accompanied on his great campaign against Persia by many such people in his retinue.

This cultivation of general intellectual and cultural interests did not cease with the end of the Argead dynasty. Antigonos Gonatas, who had represented Demetrios for many years in the cities of central Greece, including Athens, developed close contacts to Menedemos of Eretria and to Zenon, the founder of the Stoic school of philosophy. His attempts to lure the latter to Pella were unsuccessful, but other literary figures visited the court.[25] Philip V was apparently partial to witty epigrams, but he also showed how much he honoured his namesake Philip II by having excerpts from the Philippika of Theopompos collected and copied.[26] The writing of history seems to have been a favourite pastime of the Macedonian upper class. Antipatros chronicled the Illyrian campaign of Perdikkas II; Marsyas of Pella and Marsyas of Philippoi both wrote histories of Macedonia; the Macedonian Krateros compiled a systematic collection of decrees of the Athenian Popular Assembly, probably as a member of Aristoteles' school; Nearchos, who had immigrated to Amphipolis, wrote a book describing his return from India; Aristoboulos composed his history of Alexander while living in Kassandreia; Hieronymos of Kardia wrote a history of Alexander's successors in Pella under Gonatas; and Ptolemaios I himself was the author of a famous history of Alexander. Unfortunately all these works are lost, apart from a few brief fragments, but it is clear that from the fourth century B.C. on, much literary activity took place among the members of the Macedonian court and aristocracy.[27]

An appreciation of good architecture and painting is also clear, though much remains obscure in detail. When Archelaos built his new palace in Pella at the end of the fifth century B.C., he engaged the famous painter Zeuxis as decorator. The quality of the gold and silver work found in fourth-century tombs is evidence of contact with the developments in Greek artistry in this field. The same influence is apparent in the wall paintings of the royal graves in Verghina and the other finds there, in the graves at Lefkadhia and in the mosaics and architecture of the imposing peristyle houses in Pella. The palace built by Gonatas at Verghina must also have been a magnificent example of contemporary architecture. All these things were certainly created for the wealthy elite of Macedonian society; unfortunately nothing can be established about the cultural level of the lower classes.[28]

The erection of temples and other edifices in the sanctuaries of the gods was one of the main public investments of any Greek state. It has not yet been possible to identify with certainty any such large building in Macedonia, apart from in the old Greek cities; but in view of the increased archaeological activity there it can only be a matter of time before the ruins of larger religious buildings come to light. Nonetheless, something can still be said about Macedonian cults. The religious system must have functioned conventionally in the cities. In Amphipolis the priest of Asklepios was the nominal head of state; hence there must have been a large temple of Asklepios. Kassandreia followed the Greek tradition in honouring Kassandros as city founder and, later for a period, Lysimachos, probably as the new founder; the annual priest of the founder was nominal head of state in the city.[29] It is logical to assume founder cults for Philippoi, Thessalonike and Demetrias as well. Zeus was worshipped especially in Dion, and Herakles the hunter, Kynagidas, at Beroia; the royal family at least once showed so much interest in this latter cult that the young Demetrios II intervened with the city administration on behalf of the priest of Herakles. It is not known whether the motive for this action lay in the particular identification of the kings with Herakles, who was widely worshipped under a range of different appellations and from whom they all, including the Antigonids, liked to claim descent. Athena Alkidemos, the "protectress of the people," was particularly honoured at Pella in times of crisis.[30] Thus, as far as the sparse source material allows a judgement, cult life in Macedonia appears to have been quite normal. Even when the Egyptian cults spread to Greece, the kingdom of Macedonia made no exception; in Thessalonike as early as 187 a temple to Sarapis had already existed for some time, and the king personally felt it necessary to keep it under fairly strict control.[31]

The Macedonians also maintained good relations with several non-Macedonian "international" cults and cult centres. For at least the period from Philip II to Perseus the sanctuary of the ecstatic cult of the Kabiroi on Samothrake received particular attention from the Macedonian royal house. Philip is supposed to have met Olympias for the first time there. Alexander IV and Philip Arrhidaios (or, more probably, Antipatros or Polyperchon in their name) made a large votive offering there and concerned themselves with temple property on the mainland; both Arsinoe in 280 and the defeated Perseus in 168 came there for refuge. The sanctuary of the Kabiroi on Lemnos also enjoyed special attention from Philip V.[32]

Records of contacts with Delphi and Olympia stretch over a period of many years. Alexander donated a statue of himself at Delphi after 479, and Archelaos took part in the Pythian Games. Philip II's championship of the cause of Delphic Apollo during the Sacred War even altered the constitution of the Amphiktyonic Council, as from then on representatives of the Macedonian king regularly took part in the council meetings until Aitolian rule put an end to this practice in the third century B.C. Later, however, probably after the reform of the Amphiktyony after 188, the Macedonian royal representatives again attended the meetings. At the time when Perseus was defeated at Pydna, a monument to him, still only half finished, was being erected at Delphi and was reputedly intended to carry a gilded statue of the king. In the event the victorious L. Aemilius Paullus commandeered it and completed it for himself.[33]

Good relations with Olympia were cultivated ever since Alexander I took part in the games. In addition to participation in the games by Archelaos and several times by Philip II, both Philip II and Philip V made large votive offerings there. After his victory at Chaironeia Philip II erected a round building, in a prominent position next to the prytaneion or tholos, later known as the Philippeion. It housed gold and ivory statues of Philip and Olympias, of his parents, Amyntas III and Eurydike, and of Alexander; it probably was completed by Alexander. Philip V donated a group of statues that portrayed the crowning of Philip and Doson by a personalized figure of Hellas.[34]

The Antigonids maintained close contacts with Delos, a connection probably dating from the time of the naval supremacy of Antigonos Monophthalmos and Demetrios Poliorketes, who founded the League of the Islanders, or Nesiotic League, with its headquarters on Delos. During the third century B.C. several Antigonid kings and queens donated smaller or larger monuments and buildings, dedicated votive offerings and founded festivals on the island of Apollo, evidence of their close tie to it.[35] This relationship was probably particularly cultivated because of the increasing importance of the island as a trading centre for Macedonia. In the first years of Philip V's reign there were, at least at times, so many Macedonians residing on Delos that they formed a small community or club (koinon) and once dedicated a statue of the king, perhaps at the time when he was building his large stoa there.[36]

Votive offerings in less well known temples were probably made as a direct contribution towards fostering good political relations. Alexander the Great's offering to Athena Lindia on Rhodes following the battle of Gaugamela can probably be explained in this way, as can that of Philip V in the same temple probably during his first war with Rome, when the Rhodians tried to negotiate a peace that seemed to be to his advantage.[37] In the same way the offerings made at Karian Panamara by Philip V are probably connected with his activities in Karia between 201 and 197.[38]

Thus it is clear that the Macedonian kings were well aware that generosity shown to the international sanctuaries of the Greek world was excellent for public relations. Contacts with the great traditional sanctuaries were cultivated, and when during the third century B.C. several states started campaigning for international recognition of their own sanctuaries, the Macedonians did not let themselves be left out; under Antigonos Gonatas, in about 242, they joined in recognizing the asylum of Kos and similarly accepted the claims made by Magnesia-on-the-Maiander for the cult of Artemis Leukophryene in 207. When Teos launched a similar campaign in 204, it also received support from Philip V.[39] International cult centres had always served the public image of those who maintained them. Viewed in this light, the Macedonian kings acted according to tradition and as normal members of the international Greek community.

The modern observer is so distant in time and therefore has such different moral and religious preconceptions that it is difficult to assess to what extent religious convictions played a role in this behaviour. The Macedonians did not act any differently from other of their contemporaries who had sufficient financial means. There was, however, certainly in Macedonia another side to religious experience. This side is perhaps most evident in Alexander the Great but is also shown by the importance of the ecstatic cult of the Kabiroi; it lay in a strong inclination to mysticism. With Alexander, because of the nature of the late accounts, some aspects of religious matters are emphasized in the sources, whereas others remain very obscure. Alexander's regular offering of sacrifices and his honouring of all kinds of gods, including foreign divinities, which culminated in his private audience with the priest of Ammon at the Egyptian oasis of Siwah, seem to indicate a genuine religious conviction, though it is difficult for us to comprehend it exactly; under the continual stresses of his long campaign it seems to have driven him to the paranoid belief that he was superhuman.

Although the other Macedonians in general give the impression of acting rationally, there is another example of this inclination to mysticism, this time not merely related to an individual. In Babylon in 323, after the riots provoked by the death of Alexander, a ritual cleansing of the army was carried out; a dog was hacked into two pieces and the whole army marched between them. A similar ritual is reported to have taken place a century and a half later under Perseus.[40]

Such primitive ritual cleansings are known from other parts of the Greek world. Several times they are recorded as official Macedonian state acts, and they clearly took place regularly. This fact demonstrates that the apparently rational Macedonians retained in certain matters their belief in the effectiveness of formal ritual ceremonies. This attitude is corroborated by the popularity of the cult of the Kabiroi and the visit of Amyntas, son of Perdikkas III, to the oracle of Trophonios in Lebadeia, where those seeking advice were dragged through a dark, narrow hole in a deep cave.[41] It is thus clear that mysticism and irrationality had a part to play in Macedonia until the end of the monarchy and later. But to what extent they influenced the running of the state cannot be ascertained.

2. ADMINISTRATION AND CITIES

When L. Aemilius Paullus took up residence in Amphipolis in 168/67 to supervise the reorganization of Macedonia, he required each city in the country to send ten representatives to Amphipolis. There they received first information about Roman intentions. The Macedonians were to remain independent, retain their own cities and territories, and be governed by annually elected officials.[1] Livy's account makes clear that the Romans formally recognized the existing legal organization of the cities. There is insufficient source material to define with any exactness the status of the cities within the kingdom of Macedonia. Some inscriptions do, however, reveal that certain cities possessed a limited local administration with their own laws and annually changing officials.

Nevertheless, it seems unlikely that during the period when the royal administration was able to assert itself throughout the country any city enjoyed real independence, apart from in strictly local affairs.[2] Philip II appears to have set this pattern. Amphipolis, which was incorporated into the Macedonian kingdom in 357, seems to have retained its "democratic" constitution, with a popular assembly, a city council (*boule*) and annually changing officials, but a garrison was also stationed there, and a royal commissioner (*epistates*) was appointed as general political supervisor.[3] It is interesting to note that the only other city for which a fully "democratic" constitution with a popular assembly as decision-making body is attested is Philippoi, the first new city to be founded by the young Philip, situated not far from Amphipolis.[4] Macedonia itself had no tradition of popular assemblies, and it is possible that Philip let himself be influenced by the example of nearby Amphipolis. If so, his example was apparently not emulated by Kassandros, who was otherwise a great admirer. There is no evidence of a popular assembly in Kassandreia, and though Thessalonike had an assembly (*ekklesia*), it seems to have had only a passive, listening function. In both these cities the surviving municipal decrees were voted on exclusively by the council; hence it cannot be assumed without further evidence that the single decree surviving from Pella and passed by "the city" had been voted by a popular assembly, not by the council.[5]

Although it is only possible in rare instances to establish the existence of a democratic, decision-making popular assembly, the position is different when it comes to the annually changing officials. There is ample evidence relating to these functionaries as well as to annually changing priests, each of whom, as nominal head of state, gave his name to his year. Philippoi, where the eponym was, as in Athens, simply known as archon, probably offers the earliest evidence, followed by Amphipolis, where the priest of Asklepios gave his name to the year. There is evidence for an eponymous priest in Kassandreia already under Kassandros and an eponymous official in Beroia under Demetrios Poliorketes, in Pella under Gonatas and in Thessalonike under Doson.[6] Since in each case the known date of the earliest available evidence is purely accidental, the system doubtless was much older, and with newly founded cities it must have been introduced from the beginning.

At least some cities had municipal revenues of their own, even if they were very limited, but it is unknown whether they came from local taxation or royal grants. A treasurer (*tamias*) is attested for Pella, Philippoi and Kassandreia, where the treasurer of 242/ 41 made funds available for entertaining the sacred emissaries (*theoroi*) from Kos; in Thessalonike there was a board of treasurers.[7] A municipal legal system also existed, though perhaps not in every city. Philippoi and Kassandreia had laws regulating the hospitality due foreign envoys—hence such visits must have been a regular event—and Kassandreia even had a board of keepers of the law (*nomophylakes*). Slaves were freed in Beroia and real estate sold in Amphipolis, apparently in accordance with a municipal legal system that was not necessarily the same everywhere.[8] Kassandreia and Philippoi, perhaps also Beroia, possessed one or more *strategoi*, who from their title must have been basically a defence board; but more precise evidence of their activities is available only from Philippoi, where the *strategoi* of the third century B.C. had command of some mercenaries in the town service. These are mentioned as having escorted the sacred emissaries from Kos to the harbour of Neapolis; they cannot have comprised more than a small troop deployed mainly for policing cities.[9] Directly following Kynoskephalai, however, when combatting the Dardanians, Philip V was able to recruit a new army of sixty-five hundred men "from the cities."[10] It therefore seems possible that in times of emergency the urban *strategoi* had considerable numbers of citizens at their disposal who could also be deployed in the national defence, not just a few mercenaries.

Some cities seem therefore to have enjoyed a certain degree of local autonomy. That it remained extremely limited is demonstrated by the fact that even in such a trivial matter as the recognition of the sacred immunity (*asylie*) of Kos, the four cities that recognized it justified their decision by, among other things, its conformity with the policy of the king.[11] Thus even with such a decision it must have been necessary first to clear its acceptability before it was formally taken. The king also kept a sharp eye on municipal finances. The crown prince Demetrios wrote in an instruction in 249/48 concerning the priests of Herakles at Beroia that certain temple revenues that had been diverted to municipal ends were to be restored to the god.[12] This evidence demonstrates direct royal intervention in city finances, in this case to the disadvantage of the city. The same picture emerges from the decree of Philip V in 187 concerning the finances of the Sarapis temple in Thessalonike. In this case the king not only forbade the use of temple revenues for illegitimate purposes; he also decreed that the temple treasury should only be opened in the presence of the *epistates* and the judges, who may also have been royal functionaries.[13] A letter written by Perseus found at Alkomenai, unfortunately only in a very fragmentary condition, also concerns religious finances.[14] Insofar as it is possible to draw a general picture from the contents of these documents, it is one of very strict control of municipal finances by royal officers.

Many such officials whose functions had to do with the cities are known, but all for the period after Philip II. The largest number comes from Amphipolis, where no less than five are known. They are all named in the protocol section, in the dating formula, of documents spanning the period from the fourth century till the second half of the third; one stands alone, the others are named together with the eponymous priest of Asklepios. The title of the royal official in Amphipolis was *epistates*, a perfectly normal title for a supervisory official appointed by the king. It seems that in Amphipolis he might hold office for longer than a year, the normal period for a municipal office, since the *epistates* Spargeus is mentioned twice in the second half of the third century B.C., each time with a different annual priest.[15] Just what duties were performed by the *epistates* in Amphipolis is, however, unknown, but he must have been responsible for coordination with the king and presumably for the censorship of municipal decisions and the superintending of finances, as well as perhaps being commander of the garrison. There was also an *epistates* in Thessalonike, who even had a deputy (*hypepistates*) and is named as joint proposer in the only well-preserved decree of the city council we have together with the judges (*dikastai*), who may also have been royal appointees.[16]

In the light of this evidence it is reasonable to suppose that Harpalos, to whom the crown prince Demetrios wrote concerning the revenues of Herakles in Beroia, was also an *epistates*. He was clearly responsible for this financial matter, just as the *epistates* of Thessalonike was responsible for the Sarapis monies there; hence he was responsible for an aspect of civic life that normally in an independent Greek city would have been regulated by city bodies or officials themselves. Both for Beroia and for Thessalonike, the conclusion can be drawn from the documents that the municipal organs or elected boards had dealt normally with religious revenues until the royal decree arrived and put an end to the claimed normality. It is unknown whether Harpalos was responsible for Beroia alone or whether Beroia was just a part of his official district.

In two other cases apparently not concerned with city affairs, the extent of the district involved is also unclear. In 181 the royal official Archippos received a letter from King Philip concerning a grant of land to some soldiers. The stone, found about twelve miles north of Kozane, did not originate in a community organized as a city-state; but Archippos had his office (*epistasion*) somewhere where the royal documents were published.[17] The *epistates* Archippos therefore not only must have administered the unknown community in which he had his *epistasion* but also was involved in the administration of what were clearly royal demesne lands. He obviously had duties to perform outside the immediate city area. The same must have applied to Plestis, who came from the market community of Gazoros near modern Serrhai and was there apparently in the royal service in the fifth and sixth years of the reign of an unnamed king, probably Philip V or Perseus.[18] His case demonstrates that patronal supervision need not always have been negative in its effects. The community, together with the neighbouring villages under his administration, praised Plestis for ensuring in an emergency that sufficient grain went to market at a fixed price and informed the king of his good services. However, the clumsy formulation of the inscription and its bad workmanship make it seem likely that Gazoros did not normally pass decrees nor publish them—was not in fact organized as a city-state, a conclusion that seems to be supported by the Thracian names mentioned. Here again we have a community organized along nonurban lines apparently administered by a royal functionary.

The activities of Plestis and Archippos, and also perhaps of Harpalos, allow some suppositions (though there is still great uncertainty) about the form of the general administration of Macedonia from the time of Philip II. The central royal administration was active everywhere. Polybios remarked in connection with difficulties in the provincial council of Third Macedonia (Makedonia Trite) around 163 that the Macedonians were simply not used to a democratic system.[19] The majority of them can have had no democratic experience at all; only for two cities in the country, Amphipolis and Philippoi, is there evidence of a normal popular assembly. In other cities there was a council (*boule*), which governed the town jointly with the royal supervisor and probably appointed, perhaps from its own ranks, the annual officials. Where there was no form of community structure in the Greek city-state tradition, as was the case in all areas away from the coast, the *epistates* in the market centres, villages and demesnes had a different function. Even in the second century B.C. a large part of Macedonia seems to have consisted of such areas. It is unknown whether these areas were organized into regular provinces, but that is perhaps unlikely. When under Philip II, Alexander III and later Philip V large regions of Thrace were governed by Macedonia, a *strategos* was appointed to be responsible (there was also a *strategos* for Paionia under Philip V).[20] However, for the central areas of Macedonia itself, there is no evidence of this practice. Perhaps it was possible to dispense with larger administrative units when, as in the case of Plestis, local figures of authority could regularly be employed as royal administrators, who then enjoyed direct access to the king. Moreover, the city *epistates* may conceivably also have occasionally, or even regularly, been citizens of their respective towns. If so, then both Kassandros in 318 and Gonatas in 259 were only conforming to Macedonian tradition when they appointed an Athenian as royal representative in Athens.

In comparison to cities enjoying traditional Greek self-determination, the cities of Macedonia were politically exceedingly weak and had no real function as cities within the kingdom; the greatest independence they were allowed was that of self-administration under royal supervision. An essential precondition for city autonomy was financial autonomy, and most Greek cities covered their current expenditure by levying indirect taxes, the most important being harbour dues, import and export duty and market dues. When Philip V embarked on the reform of the country's finances after 187, he raised, among other items, the harbour dues.[21] More than a century before, Kassandros had exempted Perdikkas, son of Koinos, from paying harbour dues in Kassandreia at the same time as he confirmed him in the ownership of his lands.[22] We can therefore conclude that in Macedonia harbour dues were a royal tax like the taxes on agriculture, but it is not known whether that was also the case with market dues.

The cities and communities were, however, allowed a certain freedom of action for their own self-defence. Even when the whole army was mustered before the battle of Kynoskephalai, at least sixty-five hundred men capable of bearing arms remained in the cities and could then be levied by the king in the subsequent emergency of the Dardanian raid. It is unknown whether these men were mercenaries from the garrisons or local militiamen or a mixture of both, but they were efficient enough to defeat the Dardanians. In general, then, it is clear that both the cities and the nonurban areas were closely integrated into the central royal administrative system.

Because few communities in the central areas of Macedonia were organized as traditional city-states and because of the particular historical development of the Macedonian state, conflicts between royal power and a free Greek state did not arise with the same intensity in Macedonia as they did, say, in Asia Minor under the Seleukids and Attalids. There Macedonian royal power had first been established with Alexander's campaign and had been achieved through conquest and, in part, long struggles for supremacy. Macedonia had to deal with such conditions only in the territories outside the traditional frontiers. When Thrace was governed from Pella, it had its own *strategos* or military governor, just as Paionia did under Philip V; he was responsible both for the collection of tribute payments and for levying troops.[23] In Thessaly Philip II and Alexander the Great were both archons of the Thessalian League and by virtue of their office had control of the league share of tax revenues and of the league army. Following the participation of many Thessalian cities in the Lamian War nothing more is heard of the league for another century; around 227 Antigonos Doson, probably in the wake of renewed discontent, seems to have revived it.[24] The suppression or abolition of the league after the Lamian War entailed a strengthening of direct Macedonian authority. Kassandros maintained several garrisons in Thessaly, and Demetrios even built on the Gulf of Pagasai the city bearing his name, Demetrias, later regarded as one of the key strongholds of Macedonian influence in Greece and described by Philip V as one of the "fetters of Greece."

However, even after the revival of the league the direct power exerted by the Macedonian rulers did not slacken. Under Antigonos Doson and Philip V the league participated formally in the wars against Kleomenes, the Aitolians and the Romans. The king seems to have intervened when, where, and as he wanted, even in vital internal affairs of individual cities, as Philip V's two letters to Larissa show.[25] In the first letter (217) the king urged the city to grant citizenship to noncitizens to increase the population and improve the economy. The city, which still had its own elected officials and an assembly that passed decrees, at first complied; but it soon changed its mind, and Philip had to write a second letter (214), in which he exhorted the authorities to comply with his wishes and cited to them the Romans' successful granting of citizenship to freedmen and their practice in founding colonies. Polybios wrote with reference to this period that "the Thessalians gave the impression that they lived according to their own laws and were very different from the Macedonians, but they really differed in no way; they were treated just like the Macedonians and did everything that royal officials instructed them to do."[26] The revival of the league had therefore not altered this fundamental relationship. Thessaly was still regarded as Macedonian territory and was often attacked and pillaged, in lieu of the much-less-accessible Macedonian homelands, by enemies of Macedonia, by Demetrios fighting against Kassandros, by the Aitolians and the Romans fighting against Gonatas or Philip V. The Macedonian rulers themselves, from Kassandros to Philip V, who suffered his final defeat near Kynoskephalai in Thessaly in 197, also preferred to fight in Thessaly rather than in Macedonia.

South of Thessaly Macedonian rule was of necessity less comprehensive. After the battle of Chaironeia only Korinth and perhaps some places in western Greece seem to have been garrisoned, but it is probable that the Macedonian "supervisors of the general security" of the Korinthian League were able to exert more than simply moral pressure. However, the basic principles laid down by Philip II for Macedonian policy in southern Greece were adhered to: Macedonian influence was to be established and maintained with the least possible use of force and, if at all possible, with the consent and cooperation of the local rulers. This aim could not always be realized. Occupation forces entered the Piraeus, Chalkis and many other places as a result of the Lamian War, and in 317 Kassandros (and later, around 260, Gonatas) appointed his own men to safeguard Macedonian interests in Athens itself and almost certainly in other places as well.[27] Only once does an attempt seem to have been made to introduce direct regional administration, when the historian Hieronymos of Kardia was appointed by Demetrios Poliorketes to govern Boiotia after 293,[28] but there is no evidence whatsoever of other such appointments. Chalkis and Korinth were built up as major fortresses, the strongholds of Macedonian influence. Polybios tells how they were regarded in 198 by hostile Greeks: "The Peloponnesians could not breathe freely as long as the royal garrison remained sitting firmly in Korinth, nor could the Lokrians and Boiotians and Phokians take courage while Philip held Chalkis and the rest of Euboia."[29]

The reminders given by the "fetters" were in fact usually sufficient to ensure that Macedonian influence remained paramount. These fortresses were reinforced, frequently under Kassandros and Philip V, by additional smaller garrisons; the Macedonians also cooperated with political forces friendly to them, such as the tyrants who were supported by Gonatas, or Aratos of Sikyon, who was courted in Achaia by Doson and Philip V. By these methods Macedonia was able to maintain at relatively low expense a dominant position among the Greeks generally sufficient to keep the influence of rival powers within acceptable limits. The system of Macedonian influence and power began to erode only when the Romans deployed enormous military strength in the Second Macedonian War and simultaneously set out systematically to woo adherents, even among the basically Macedonia-friendly states of Greece; after Kynoskephalai it was deliberately destroyed.

3. THE MILITARY

Every state must for its own survival look after the security of its members. It is therefore no coincidence that the gradual consolidation of the Macedonian state system went hand in hand with the development of an efficient military system. The relatively small state ruled by Alexander I, which offered no resistance to the Persians, seems to have largely relied on its cavalry, and because cavalry service was expensive, it is a plausible assumption that the Macedonian cavalry of this period was recruited from the richest section of the community, the aristocracy. At the time of Perdikkas II the cavalry still appears to have been the mainstay of the army; the foot soldiers raised for the campaign against the Lynkestian Arrhabaios made a miserable showing and disintegrated at the first sign of danger. These foot soldiers had almost certainly never been regularly trained and were probably no more than simple shepherds and farmers pressed into the service of their king. Archelaos, according to Thukydides' account, invested a lot in the infrastructure of the state and may well have even taken the first steps towards providing arms at public expense, which has the advantage that the arms are at least uniform. However, much of his achievement went for nothing during the chaotic years at the beginning of the fourth century B.C. when Macedonia was continually under threat from the Illyrians and Amyntas III could only keep them at bay by paying them tribute.[1]

When Philip II, after his brother's disaster, found himself having to confront the Illyrians right at the beginning of his reign, he copied the well-proven methods of the Greek city-states and introduced regular military exercises and uniform weapons. The enormous sixteen-foot sarissa, the great Macedonian thrusting spear, was now introduced and distributed at state expense so that the poorer farmers could now be properly trained.[2] The first victories of 359 and 358 encouraged an extension of these successful measures. It was therefore not until the time of Philip II that the Macedonians possessed a successful, battle-tested army.

All that had happened before were bravura, dilettante cavalry actions by the aristocracy and some discouraging attempts to mobilize the farmers as foot soldiers.

Despite the undoubted military successes of Philip II and his successors it is difficult to grasp the nature of the army organization. Even the simplest questions about the basic units, their size or their structure can in the end only be answered unsatisfactorily, and assertions about the social structure of the new army can be little more than speculative. An intensive study of the Macedonian army is therefore frustrating work. So much remains uncertain, even after the efforts of generations of scholars, that no more will be attempted here than to pose some basic questions and provide some hesitant, necessarily speculative answers.[3]

A significant factor in the defensive potential of any country is the number of men available for conscription. This figure cannot be accurately determined for Macedonia. An indication is given by the number of Macedonians who under certain circumstances—in battles, say—could be mustered, but in no single instance do the sources put it in relation to the potential army size; there is sometimes no distinction made between the Macedonian troops and their allies, and we have no way of checking the veracity of the figures reported. Modern historians attempt to reach figures from the source material on the basis of assumptions and combinations, some more convincing than others. One fact that does impress, however, is the frequency with which a number of between twenty thousand and thirty thousand men is cited in the sources, from Philip II right through to Perseus. A total of thirty thousand infantry and two thousand cavalry is given for the battle of Chaironeia in 338, although it is not known what proportion was Macedonian.[4] But when Alexander set out for Asia in 334, he took with him, according to the most reliable source, twelve thousand infantry and eighteen hundred cavalry from Macedonia, as part of a total force of thirty-two thousand infantry and fifty-one hundred cavalry, and left another twelve thousand infantry and fifteen hundred cavalry behind with Antipatros in Macedonia.[5] In 334, therefore, Macedonia had available a total of twenty-four thousand infantry and thirty-three hundred cavalry. Philip must then have had a similar number of Macedonian soldiers at his disposal four years earlier.

It is possible, however, that not all those capable of bearing arms were included in this figure, as a further three thousand infantry joined Alexander in Gordion in 333,[6] and two years later in Susa another six thousand infantry and five hundred cavalry arrived;[7] at the same time Antipatros is reported to have mobilized forty thousand men for the battle at Megalopolis, although many of them were allied soldiers loyal to Macedonia.[8] When Alexander sent ten thousand veterans home from Opis in 324, he expected Antipatros to replace them with an equal number of men;[9] but these never arrived. Instead soldiers moved in the opposite direction. In the battle of Krannon in 322 against the united Greek forces Antipatros and Krateros commanded more than forty thousand infantry and five thousand cavalry, of whom at least two-thirds were probably Macedonians.[10]

Until shortly before the battle of Ipsos in 301 the recorded figures for army strength cannot be properly related to the Macedonian state. Only after Kassandros had established his position are figures available, and once again they fall within the usual range. When Kassandros fought against Demetrios in Thessaly in 302, he fielded an army of twenty-nine thousand infantry and two thousand cavalry and had already dispatched some soldiers to Asia Minor under Prepelaos, though the majority of these may have been non-Macedonian. It is not known what proportion of his own thirty-one thousand troops were Macedonian; but since he needed to field his best against Demetrios, the majority were probably Macedonians.[11] For decades afterwards no usable figures are available, until the battle of Sellasia in 222, where Antigonos Doson provided thirteen thousand infantry and three hundred cavalry from a total force of twenty-eight thousand infantry and twelve hundred cavalry. However, it is clear that the whole concept of this campaign required no mass levy of Macedonians and that the Greek allies were expected to contribute their share. Two years earlier Doson alone had commanded an army of twenty thousand infantry and thirteen hundred cavalry.[12] The figures for Kynoskephalai in 197 likewise fall within the usual range. Philip V deployed eighteen thousand infantry and two thousand cavalry in the battle, had at the same time fifteen hundred Macedonians stationed in Korinth and a further five hundred in Asia and was able to muster an additional sixty-five hundred men from the Macedonian cities straight after the battle.[13] For Pydna, the last great battle in the history of Macedonia, in 168, no exact figures are recorded; but from the reported death toll of twenty thousand Macedonians and the figure of eleven thousand taken prisoner it seems that at least the usual number, perhaps more, had participated, particularly since for 171 Livy gives as a total forty-three thousand men, of whom half were Macedonian phalangists.[14]

These figures, unsystematic and capable of yielding differing interpretations, do not tell us much; but one conclusion can perhaps be drawn: for a period of more than 150 years after the Macedonian state had taken firm shape under Philip II, the kings and their deputies were regularly in a position to muster between twenty thousand and thirty thousand Macedonian troops. How many more could be mustered at times of extreme emergency, such as the Gallic invasion, what recruitment measures were necessary and which age groups of soldiers were levied in each case are all fundamental questions, none of which can be answered with any certainty.

The arms borne by at least the infantry seem to have remained much the same over the whole period. Philip II introduced the sarissa, and Philip V published an army regulation, a partly preserved copy of which was found at Amphipolis, laying down a fine of two oboloi for a soldier not carrying his sarissa in specified situations.[15] Unlike most Greek hoplites Philip II's phalangists wore no breastplates, and these are also duly omitted from the equipment listed in the army regulation from Amphipolis 150 years later. Only officers wore breastplates; the soldiers of Philip V were equipped with stomach band (*kotthybos*), helmet, greaves, a sword or dagger and a shield. The weapons thus remained basically unchanged, though whether the equipment was identical over the whole period is unknown; it would perhaps not be unreasonable to assume that innovations were made, at least in detail, in the light of experience.[16]

Another consistent characteristic of the Macedonian military was the incorporation of contingents of allies from the Balkans—Thracians, Illyrians and Paionians—and the employment of mercenaries. They may have been specialists, such as slingers, spear throwers, archers and so on or have been hired because of their particularly fearsome fighting techniques to augment the other

troops. At least from the time of Philip II until Perseus such sup-
plementary troops were almost always included in Macedonian
armies. Whether these non-Greek contingents were conscripted
into the army—as, for example, a condition of a treaty of alliance—or served as mercenaries is in most cases unclear; the
sources, even if they knew, do not always inform us.[17] Mercenaries
seem to have been preferred for garrison duties, and they were
often Greeks, particularly from Krete.[18] As a result Macedonian
contacts with Krete gradually became very close. Recruitment of
mercenaries there was provided for in interstate treaties. Fragments of three such documents under Demetrios II and Antigonos Doson have been found, in which either these matters were
regulated explicitly or such regulation may be restored with great
probability in the fragmentary text.[19] Philip V was even politically
active on the island and was elected as honorary protector (*prostates*) of the Kretan League.[20] Macedonia, however, was not the
only power to compete for the favour of the Kretan cities.

Non-Macedonians served in their own units and are generally
listed separately in the sources. But how were the Macedonians
themselves deployed? The lack of explicit description in the
sources makes it a disputed question, and only under Alexander
the Great can even the broad organizational structure be recognized. Regional regiments (*taxeis*), or at least regiments with regional names, served in Alexander's army, and there are records
of *taxeis* from Tymphaia, Orestis-Lynkestis and Elimiotis. The
same seems to have applied to the cavalry, where squadrons (*ilai*)
from Anthemous, Amphipolis, the otherwise-unknown Leugaia,
Bottiaia and Apollonia are attested, as well as the "cavalry from
Upper Macedonia." It is, however, doubtful whether the entire
Macedonian army was organized on regional lines, or whether
the regional *taxeis* from Upper Macedonia and the regional *ilai*
from Lower Macedonia were not each formed for particular reasons.[21] Alexander certainly recognized and respected regional loyalties, as is shown by his distributing the reinforcements that arrived at Susa in 331 among the units according to their region of
origin.[22] It is dubious whether the local regional principle, perhaps
in any case not universally employed, continued to be respected
in later reorganizations, above all when Iranians were incorporated into the phalanx units in and after 324.

Changes seem to have been made in the structure of the sub-units of the *taxeis* over the years. Under Alexander, and probably also under Philip II, the *taxeis* comprised about fifteen hundred men and had to be subdivided. Two such subunits are known under Alexander: the *dekas*, officered by a *dekadarchos*, which seems to have been expanded from its original ten men (under Philip II?) to be, under Alexander, a unit of sixteen men;[23] and the *lochos*, under a *lochagos*, comprising perhaps about 250 men (in theory probably 240, or 256 if the *dekades* were units of sixteen men).[24] By the time of Philip V the titles of the army units had changed, but it cannot be established whether these changes were also functional. The *taxeis* were now apparently called *strategiai* under a *strategos*, the *lochoi* had become *speirai* under a *speirarchos*, the *dekades* had become *lochoi*, and between the last two were units called *tetrarchiai* under a *tetrarchos*, which comprised four of the new-style *lochoi*.[25] If the *strategiai* also corresponded in size to the earlier *taxeis*—which is quite uncertain—then the changes had produced a typically hellenistic expansion in personnel, at least among the officers: instead of 103 officers for every *taxis* (one *taxiarchos*, six *lochagoi* and ninety-six *dekadarchoi*) there now were 127 in each *strategia* (one *strategos*, six *speirarchoi*, twenty-four *tetrarchoi* and ninety-six *lochagoi*). Parallel to the changes in the serving army, an expansion of the bureaucracy also seems to have taken place. We now have records of scribes and auxiliary workers, *hyperetai*, and, as though part of the natural order, several super-intendents of the auxiliaries, *archihyperetai*, who took over administrative duties doubtless formerly performed by the officers themselves, such as the collection of fines or the distribution of booty. There is no way of knowing what their numbers were relative to those of the army units.

Within the army there were always elite units of both infantry and cavalry that were particularly associated with the king personally. The cavalry, initially comprising the aristocracy, had always been closely tied to the king and probably originated in a guard of his closest companions, the *hetairoi*. In the course of time and as a result of continued state expansion, particularly under Philip II, the number of those who could afford to enter the king's service as cavalrymen increased, and the kings were not inclined to reject them. The name *hetairoi*, which had first applied only to the closest companions of the king and then been extended to cover an elite unit within the cavalry, was used by Alexander for the entire Macedonian cavalry; hence it was known under him as the Companion Cavalry. The cavalry remained socially loyal to its aristocratic origins, and in the crisis following the death of Alexander there was a real risk of civil war over the question of the succession between the exclusive, aristocratically minded cavalry and the mass of the phalanx soldiery. Under Alexander there was also, however, an elite cavalry unit (*ile*) under the direct command of the king, the *ile basilike*. Though other *ilai* may have been recruited regionally, this one was probably a selection of the best and must have fulfilled the function of the original *hetairoi* of the cavalry.

Macedonian infantry was always less effective and less respected than the cavalry, until its reorganization by Philip II. Only then was this farmers' militia capable of playing a serious role in the country's defence. The example of the cavalry organization seems to have shown the way here as well. Under Alexander the whole phalanx was known as the foot *hetairoi* (*pezhetairoi*), and Anaximenes of Lampsakos ascribed the giving of this name to an Alexander, who was probably Alexander the Great. Under Philip II this title seems to have still been reserved for an elite unit serving the king personally, like the *hetairoi* of the cavalry. This extension of a privileged title to the whole mass of the infantry made it essential to find a new title for the elite unit of the infantry, as for the cavalry—thus the origin of the *hypaspistai*, which under Alexander were the infantry equivalent of the *ile basilike* of the cavalry.[26]

This inflation of honours apparent in the title changes certainly had more to do with political considerations than military ones. Alexander wanted to honour the whole Macedonian army and thus bind it inexpensively to himself personally. Whether popular sentiment towards him was indeed affected we do not know, but the gulf between cavalry and infantry, originating as it did in social differences, was certainly not easy to bridge. In Babylon in 323 it was the foot soldiers who preferred Philip's son Arrhidaios to Alexander's unborn child, and at the Hyphasis and then again in Opis it was the infantry troops who developed their own concept in opposition to that of the king and partly had their own way.[27] It was their opinion in particular that Alexander courted in every crisis.

For the period following Alexander we are much worse informed. An elite unit of Macedonian troops, perhaps ex-*hypaspistai*, was known in the years immediately following Alexander's death as the silvershields (*argyraspides*),[28] and under Philip V and Perseus there was a unit of bronzeshields (*chalkaspides*);[29] but these titles were probably not functional, perhaps not even official. Two other developments in Macedonian army organization are evident after Alexander. One is the evolution of the *hypaspistai* from an elite unit to a form of military police or bodyguard under Philip V; the only thing the two functions had in common was the particular closeness to the king.[30] The other development, which happened at the latest under Doson, was the formation and training of a special unit of *peltastai* separate from the phalanx. This unit operated as a form of royal guard similar in function to the earlier *hypaspistai*.[31] It is not known whether, like the *peltastai* of the fourth century B.C., they were more lightly, or at least differently, armed than the phalangists, but their function had become so important that the post of *peltast*-general was one of the court appointments mentioned by Doson in his testament.[32] We can only speculate on the reasons for this development. With the elevation of the *hypaspistai* to being a small group of royal functionaries, the need for an elite unit in the army by no means ceased, and certain advantages might then have been seen in the king's elite troops not being integrated into the phalanx organization. If the *peltastai* also carried lighter arms, that fact might have facilitated their close association with the king.

Occupation troops played a relatively large role under the kings after Alexander, but apart from the fact that many of the soldiers in the garrisons were non-Macedonian mercenaries, little is known about them. An administrative document dating from the last years of the third century B.C. has survived from Chalkis, which throws light on some aspects of the administration of the stores in some of the garrison cities.[33] It may be assumed that a similar system operated at least in Korinth and Demetrias and probably also in Amphipolis and other places where large numbers of soldiers were stationed on a long-term basis. The garrison commander (*phrourarchos*) shared responsibility for the stores with a financial administrator (*oikonomos*), who had a staff of *cheiristai* working under him. The regulations from Chalkis concern the storing of grain, wine and wood; they specify for how long and under what conditions these commodities were to be stored and how long and when they should be exchanged for others and fix rules for access to the storerooms, stipulating even who should hold the keys to the different rooms. These regulations are an indication of the same sort of bureaucratic regimentation, of joint responsibility by several functionaries, that is familiar from, say, Egypt, where the information about such things is more nearly comprehensive. A similar regimentation in other affairs is also revealed by the army regulations from Amphipolis.

The tendency of other centralistic hellenistic states towards an increasingly bureaucratic administration seems therefore to have also extended to Macedonia and have affected even military affairs, although there is no more than rudimentary evidence, and then only for certain fields. Whether the civil administration was as carefully structured as the military seems doubtful, but perhaps new inscriptions will be found that shed more light on the matter.

Characteristic of the Macedonian army over the whole period of the monarchy is the large number of Macedonian citizens who served either in the phalanx or in the cavalry. After Philip II had introduced regular military exercises, the length of time served by the soldiers must inevitably have increased. Some form of payment other than the occasional division of spoils must then have been introduced. As a result of the revenues gained from the newly acquired territories, in particular from Mount Pangaion, the state could have afforded such payment relatively easily. The significantly increased coinage under Philip II and Alexander was probably produced largely for this purpose. Just what wage was paid to the individual Macedonian soldiers, whether they were paid more or less than the mercenaries who fought alongside them, is unknown. An inscription from the time of Alexander reveals that different ranks received different rates of pay,[34] but this practice is so universal that it could have been assumed even without evidence.

The great achievements of the Macedonian land forces under Philip II and his successors cannot have been due solely to organizational factors. The whole of Greek military history is char-

acterized by the relatively simple fact that except in special circumstances it was the most strongly motivated and best trained
army that won almost every battle. This principle had been demonstrated in the sixth and fifth centuries B.C. mainly by the Spartans and in the fourth century B.C. by the Thebans. The uniform
weaponry distributed by Philip II to the Macedonian soldiers may
have given them a slight advantage in battle over the hoplites
from the southern states of Greece. Philip also appears to have
assigned a much greater attacking role to his traditionally strong
and socially elite cavalry than was usual in Greece, and this factor
must have been equally significant. The really decisive factors,
though, were the motivation and training of his troops. A char-
ismatic king motivated by his constant presence and sympathy
and above all by the personal lead he gave in battles and other
military actions. Philip II and Alexander set examples unmatched
in the ancient world. Their successors, who inherited the tradition, did not always have the necessary personal gifts, but those
who were militarily most successful were demonstrative in taking
personal military leadership.

The crucial necessity of drilling troops must have become clear
to Philip at the latest during his time as a hostage in Thebes.
From the very beginning of his reign he held military exercises
for his Macedonian soldiers and was rewarded by speedy victories, which proved that he was working on the right lines. Subsequently, however, continual military action probably made exercising superfluous, except for new recruits, and the main
Macedonian troops became in practice almost professional soldiers. The tradition that evolved seems to have been maintained
right up to the end of the monarchy, and even in the other countries under Macedonian rule the tradition of Macedonian farmers
as professional soldiers was artificially fostered by founding new
agricultural settlements for soldiers and their families.[35]

The military strength of Macedonia lay indubitably in its land
army. An adequate navy was only rarely assembled and then for
a particular purpose. Philip II appears to have been the first Macedonian king to have had any sort of fleet, but it was not strong,
and we do not know where the ships came from. They may
merely have been collected ad hoc from the Greek coastal communities under his protection, as seems to have been Alexander's

practice.[36] The situation must have been much the same under their successors, but under Kassandros in 313 there is mention of thirty-six ships from Pydna, indicating that a small fleet was based in Macedonian home waters.[37] When Demetrios became king in 294 and began to build a new fleet, he also commissioned ships from the neighbourhood of Pella; hence competent and experienced ship builders must have been working there.[38] Gonatas maintained a small fleet from the beginning of his time as Demetrios' deputy in Greece because it was the only way to keep up contact with his scattered mainland possessions, particularly Demetrias, Chalkis, Piraeus and Korinth. The first evidence of an effective larger war fleet comes from the Chremonidean War, and that fleet was later able to win sea battles against Ptolemaic fleets, around 255 near Kos and perhaps in 245 near Andros, and exert Macedonian influence in the islands of the Kyklades.[39]

Doson also possessed a fleet and deployed it for his campaign in Karia, but Philip V had to commission new ships when he took over the Illyrian plans of Demetrios of Pharos. He was forced to burn these ships in 214 at the mouth of the Aoos,[40] and it was not until 205 that he attempted to assemble a fleet again. At the battle of Chios in 201 he was able to deploy about two hundred ships, some of which he had just captured from Ptolemaios at Samos, but there is no evidence of where he acquired the others, including 150 *lemboi*.[41] Even though the fleet was ineffective against the Romans, it remained significant enough until 197 for the Romans to include a clause in the peace treaty with Philip limiting the Macedonian fleet to six ships, five of them very small.[42] This clause spelled the end of the less-than-glorious history of the Macedonian navy, an end that could not be averted by the few *lemboi* hastily assembled by Perseus, perhaps from Illyria, when war once more broke out against the Romans in 171.[43]

EPILOGUE

The state of Macedonia was a pivotal point of the Balkan political system from the middle of the fourth century B.C. until the middle of the second. Because of their geographical position, environment and way of life the Macedonians always had far more in common with the other inhabitants of the North Aegean than with the Greeks of the southern city-states, despite speaking the same language. As soon as Philip II was in a position to do more than just defend and consolidate his frontiers, he made expansion towards the east his first priority for extending state influence. Had he not been caught up in the meshes of the political conflicts of the Greek states of the south, it is probable that a greater Macedonian empire would have evolved in the region between the river Danube and the Aegean.

Involvement in Greek affairs led to involvement in Persia. Alexander's campaign was of lasting significance for world history, opening the way for an enormous dissemination of the Greek way of life and language, a cultural expansion that formed an important precondition for the Roman and Byzantine empires in the east. For Macedonia itself the campaign turned into a catastrophe when the death of Alexander in Babylon sparked off a civil war that lasted for two generations and involved in its sufferings the Greeks of the Balkan region, who had no immediate interest in the conflict, and caused many to join the stream of emigrants to the newly conquered countries of the east. The power structures that evolved from the struggle became ever more brutal. That Philip V should describe the three great garrison cities of Demetrias, Chalkis and Korinth as the "fetters of Greece" illustrates his own subjective view of the relative power relationships of the time.

This development in Macedonia's relationship with the Greeks was a long way from the partnership originally envisaged by Philip II and was largely a consequence of Alexander's treatment of them, the uncertainties of his great expedition, and the subsequent bitter rivalry among the leaders of the Macedonian aristocracy for power and possessions. After two generations of fighting over the succession the original Macedonian homeland—the former kingdom of the Argeadai, where everything had started—was now only one of three separate Macedonian kingdoms and by no means the richest, largest or strongest. It was no longer fought over but had indeed been conquered. A new ruling dynasty replaced the chaos of the civil war; its first king, Gonatas, attempted to uphold the traditions of the old ruling house of the Argeadai, refurbish the state organization and withstand possible competition from the other two new Macedonian dynasties, the Ptolemies and the Seleukids. The Antigonids were successful enough up to about 220 to encourage their next-to-last representative, Philip V, to aim to make Macedonia the dominant power in the whole Aegean area, in conscious emulation of his great predecessor and namesake. But he failed to recognize that the Romans, at whose expense it was to happen, presented a political challenge very different from the decaying empire of the Achaimenids at the time of Philip II.

When the Romans dispossessed Macedonia of most of its foreign territories after 197, they justified their decision to let it continue to exist as a state with the argument that the Macedonians protected the Greeks from the raids of the Balkan tribes. Even if this argument was merely developed ad hoc to block Aitolian territorial claims, it presented an important pragmatic point of view that did full justice to the historical function of the Macedonian kingdom. After Rome took direct responsibility for security in the Balkans after 148, raids continued to take place that could have been repulsed at an early stage by a Macedonian state. The Romans themselves were now responsible for countering such raids, an arduous undertaking. The result, after long reluctance and many bitter experiences, was the expansion of the frontiers of the Roman empire to the banks of the Danube, a solution to the problem that was little different from the objective that Philip II had already set for Macedonia in the fourth century B.C.

List of Kings

This list merely gives a general chronological indication and does not pay attention to every uncertainty the sources leave. The first three Argeadai were probably mythical figures, and for kings before Amyntas I not even approximate dates can be suggested with any confidence. Only those persons who ruled as king in Macedonia proper are listed. The names of fathers of kings who themselves did not rule as kings are printed in italics.

Argeadai	Dates (B.C.)	Father
Karanos		
Koinos		
Tyrimmas		
Perdikkas I		
Argaios		Perdikkas I
Philip I		Argaios
Aeropos I		Philip I
Alketas		Aeropos I
Amyntas I	until ca. 497	Alketas
Alexander I ("the Philhellene")	ca. 497–ca. 454	Amyntas I
Perdikkas II	ca. 454–413	Alexander I
Archelaos	413–399	Perdikkas II
Orestes	399–396	Archelaos
Aeropos II	396–ca. 393	
Pausanias	ca. 393	Aeropos II
Amyntas II ("the Little")	ca. 393	Archelaos
Amyntas III	ca. 392–370	*Arrhidaios (son of Alexander I)*
Argaios	ca. 390	
Alexander II	370–368	Amyntas III

Argeadai	Dates (B.C.)	Father
Ptolemaios Olorites	ca. 368–ca. 365	*Amyntas (?)*
Perdikkas III	ca. 365–359	Amyntas III
Philip II	359–336	Amyntas III
Alexander III ("the Great")	336–323	Philip II
Philip III Arrhidaios	323–317	Philip II
Alexander IV	323–310	Alexander III

Antipatrids

Kassandros	315–297	*Antipatros*
with royal title	ca. 305–297	
Philip IV	297	Kassandros
Antipatros	297–294	Kassandros
Alexander V	297–294	Kassandros

Antigonids and others

Demetrios I ("the Besieger") ("Poliorketes")	294–288	*Antigonos ("Monophthalmos")*
Pyrrhos	288/87	*Aiakides (of Epeiros)*
Lysimachos	287–281	*Agathokles*
Ptolemaios ("Keraunos")	281–279	*Ptolemaios ("Soter" of Egypt)*

Anarchy	279–ca. 277	
Meleagros		*Ptolemaios ("Soter")*
Antipatros ("Etesias")		*Philippos (son of Antipatros)*
Sosthenes		
Ptolemaios		Lysimachos
Arrhidaios		

Argeadai	Dates (B.C.)	Father
Antigonos I ("Gonatas")	ca. 277–239	Demetrios I
Demetrios II	239–229	Antigonos I
Antigonos II ("Doson")	ca. 229–222	*Demetrios*
Philip V	222–179	Demetrios II
Perseus	179–168	Philip V

Genealogical Tables

These genealogical tables are intended merely to offer a general orientation concerning the family connections of the Macedonian rulers (whose names are printed in capital letters). To avoid unnecessary complexity, only those members of the families are included who are relevant as family links or are otherwise mentioned in the text of the book. The dates given are for the years of rule in Macedonia (Tables 1, 2, and 4) or Macedonia and Epeiros (Table 3), regardless of whether the royal title was adopted in Macedonia itself or elsewhere. Complete source references and discussion of details may be found in Beloch, *Griechische Geschichte*, vols. 3.2 and 4.2.

Genealogical Table 1
The Argeadai until Philip II

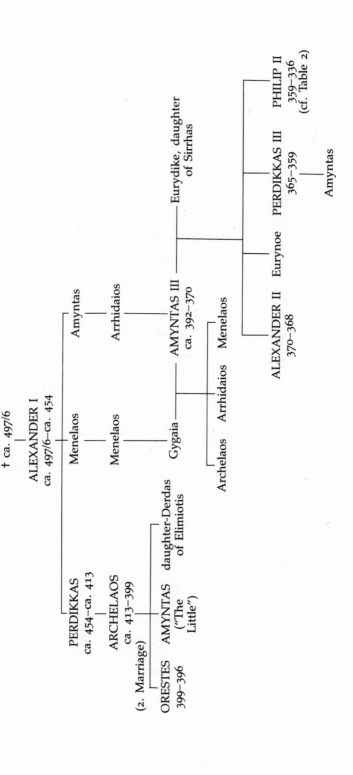

Genealogical Table 2
The Interlinking of the Macedonian Dynasties

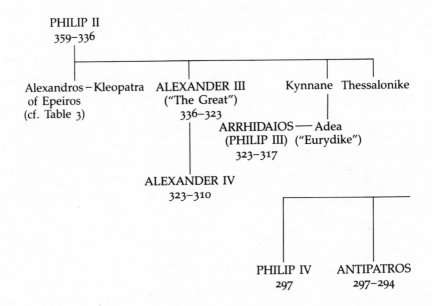

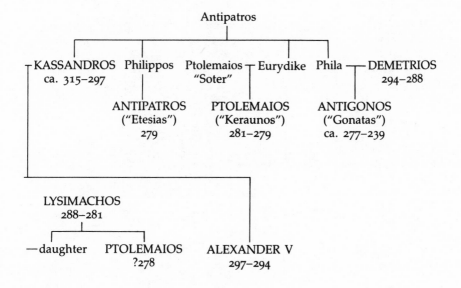

Antipatros

KASSANDROS   Philippos   Ptolemaios — Eurydike   Phila — DEMETRIOS
ca. 315–297   "Soter"   294–288

                          ANTIPATROS   PTOLEMAIOS   ANTIGONOS
                          ("Etesias")   ("Keraunos")   ("Gonatas")
                              279   281–279   ca. 277–239

LYSIMACHOS
288–281

—daughter   PTOLEMAIOS   ALEXANDER V
                  ?278   297–294

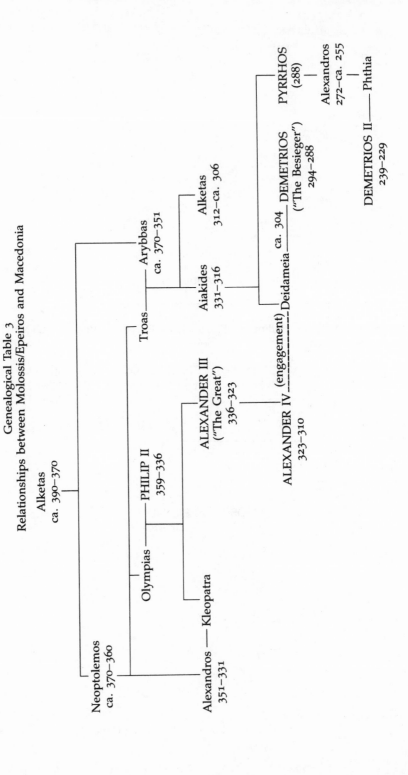

Genealogical Table 3
Relationships between Molossis/Epeiros and Macedonia

Alketas
ca. 390–370

Neoptolemos
ca. 370–360

Olympias —— PHILIP II
359–336

Troas —— Arybbas
ca. 370–351

Alexandros —— Kleopatra
351–331

ALEXANDER III
("The Great")
336–323

Aiakides
331–316

Alketas
312–ca. 306

ALEXANDER IV —— (engagement) —— Deidameia ——ca. 304—— DEMETRIOS —— PYRRHOS
323–310   ("The Besieger")   (288)
                                                              294–288

Alexandros
272–ca. 255

DEMETRIOS II —— Phthia
239–229

Genealogical Table 4
The Antigonids

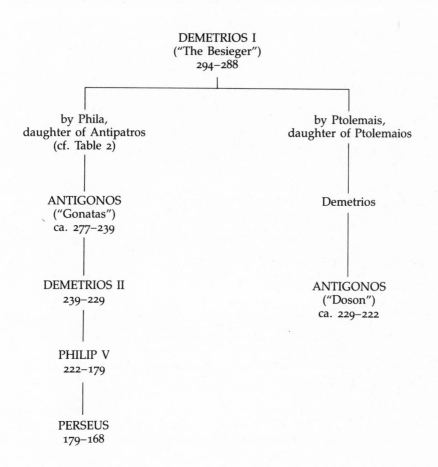

DEMETRIOS I
("The Besieger")
294–288

by Phila,
daughter of Antipatros
(cf. Table 2)

by Ptolemais,
daughter of Ptolemaios

ANTIGONOS
("Gonatas")
ca. 277–239

Demetrios

DEMETRIOS II
239–229

ANTIGONOS
("Doson")
ca. 229–222

PHILIP V
222–179

PERSEUS
179–168

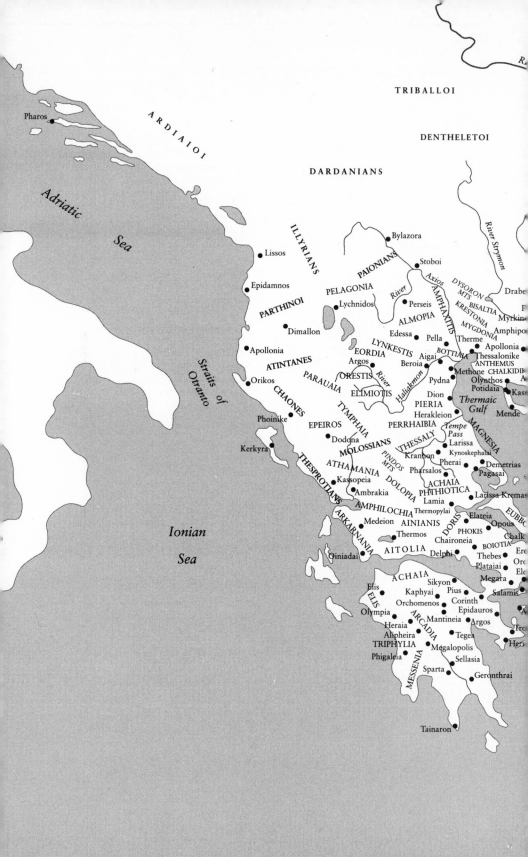

TRIBALLOI

DENTHELETOI

DARDANIANS

Adriatic

A R D I A I O I

Pharos

Sea

Lissos

Epidamnos

ILLYRIANS

Bylazora

PAIONIANS

Stoboi

PELAGONIA

PARTHINOI

Lychnidos

Perseis

River

Axios

DYSORON
MTS

Drabe

BISALTIA

AMPHAXITIS

KRESTONIA

Myrkin

River Strymon

ALMOPIA

MYGDONIA

Amphipo

Dimallon

Edessa

Pella

Apollonia

Apollonia

LYNKESTIS

EORDIA

Beroia

Aigai

BOTTIA

Therme

Thessalonike

ANTHEMUS

ATINTANES

Argos

ORESTIS

Pydna

Methone

CHALKIDIK

Olynthos

A

Orikos

PARAUAIA

ELIMIOTIS

Dion

PIERIA

Potidaia

Kass

Thermaic

Mende

CHAONES

Herakleion

Haliakmon River

Gulf

Phoinike

TYMPHAIA

PERRHAIBIA

MAGNESIA

EPEIROS

Dodona

Tempe
Pass

Kerkyra

MOLOSSIANS

Larissa

THESSALY

THESPROTIANS

ATHAMANIA

PINDOS
MTS

Krannon

Kynoskephalai

Demetrias

DOLOPIA

Pherai

Pagasai

Kassopeia

Pharsalos

ACHAIA

Ambrakia

PHTHIOTICA

Larissa Kremas

AMPHILOCHIA

Lamia

EUBB

Ionian

ARKARNANIA

Medeion

Thermopylai

Elateia

Opous

AINIANIS

DORIS

PHOKIS

Sea

Thermos

Chaironeia

BOIOTIA

Chalk

AITOLIA

Delphi

Thebes

Ere

Oiniadai

Plataiai

Orc

ACHAIA

Sikyon

Megara

Ele

Elis

Kaphyai

Pius

Salamis

ELIS

Orchomenos

Corinth

Olympia

Mantineia

Epidauros

Argos

fro

Heraia

ARCADIA

Tegea

Heri

Alipheira

TRIPHYLIA

Megalopolis

Phigaleia

Sellasia

MESSENIA

Sparta

Geronthrai

Tainaron

Danube

BASTARNAI

HAIMOS   MOUNTAINS

Black

Sea

Kabyle   Apollonia

River

Hebros

Philippopolis

THRACIANS

Selymbria   Byzantium   Hieron
Heraion Teichos   Chalkedon
Abdera   BITHYNIA
Doriskos   Perinthos
Maroneia   Kypsela   Ganos   Sea of
Thasos   Ainos   Hieron Oros   Marmara
SAMOTHRAKE   Kardia   Lysimacheia   Kios
CHERSONNESE   Myrleia
AIGOSPOTAMOI   Kallipolis
Alopekonnesos
IMBROS   Madytos   Sestos
LMNOS   Alopekonnesos   Abydos
Hellespont   R. Granikos

Aegean   HELLESPONTINE
Sea   PHRYGIA

Atarneus   AIOLIS
SKYROS   Eresos   LESBOS
Pergamon   R.
Mytilene   Kaikos
Pitane   LYDIA   R. Hermos
Gryneion
Sardis
CHIOS
athon
ANDROS   Teos   IONIA
Euromos   River   Maiander
SAMOS   Ephesos
Lade   Alinda   Alabanda
Miletos   Herakleia
DELOS   Iasos   Labraunda   KARIA
Bargylia   Mylasa   Stratonikeia
Pedasa
KOS   Knidos
NISYROS

RHODES

Kretan Sea

KRETE

Notes

Modern works referred to in the notes in abbreviated form may be traced via the list of abbreviations and the bibliography.

I. Macedonia in the Power Game

1. COUNTRY AND PEOPLE

1. Thukydides 2.100.
2. Arrian, *Anabasis* 7.9. Arrian lived in the second century A.D. but used contemporary sources no longer extant.
3. Herodotos 8.137–39.
4. Justin 7.1.
5. Demosthenes 19.308.
6. The social and political structure of the Macedonian state is much discussed. The view represented here is based on my study in *Chiron* 8, 1978. There are other views: Hammond and Griffith, *History*, 2,150, follow the older views of Hampl and Granier in assuming a more formal structure. On the early development of the state see Rosen, *Chiron* 8, 1978, 1f.; Borza, *Hesperia*, Supplement 19, 1982, 9f.; Zahrnt, *Chiron* 14, 1984, 325f. On other aspects of the state see below, chap. 6.1. Both Hammond and Rosen, for different reasons, have questioned the fact that the royal family was called Argeadai, but this name is confirmed by an unpublished inscription from Xanthos dating from the third century B.C. (cf. Robert, *Amyzon*, 1.162, n. 31). There the Ptolemies refer to their ancestors as Herakleidas Argeadas.
7. Thukydides 2.99.2f.
8. On the prehistory and historical geography of the Macedonian area see Hammond, *History*, vols. 1 and 2 (to be used with great care: cf. Zahrnt, *Gnomon* 55, 1983, 366f.). See also Geyer, *Makedonien*, 1–42.
9. *StV* 2,186. See below, pp. 15f.
10. The export of timber was frequently regulated by interstate treaty: see *StV* 2,186 (Perdikkas and Athens); *IG* 1³,117 = *ML* 91 (Archelaos and Athens); *StV* 2,231 (Amyntas III and the Chalkidians). See also below, chap. 6,1.
11. Strabo 14.28 = *FgrHist* 124 F 54 (Kallisthenes and Midas); Etymologicum Magnum s.v. Echeidoros (Echedoros); Herodotos 5.17 (Dysoron); Gaebler, *Antike Münzen Nordgriechenlands*, vol. 3, pt. 2, 148–53, with Tafel XXVIII (the coins). See also Hammond, *History*, 1,12f., 2,70f. (sources of metals).

2. BEFORE THE PELOPONNESIAN WAR

1. Herodotos 4.143f., 5.17f. On the Thracian satrapy see Castritius, *Chiron* 2, 1972, 1–16.
2. Herodotos 5.94.1.
3. Herodotos 5.22; Justin 7.2.14. This participation almost certainly took place before he became king (around 497/96). Doubted by Borza, *Hesperia*, Supplement 19, 1982, 9f.
4. Herodotos 8.136.1. On the *proxenia* see Marek, *Die Proxenie*, passim; Wallace, *Phoenix* 24, 1970, 199f.; Meiggs, *Timber*, 124.
5. Herodotos 6.44.1.
6. Herodotos 5.21.2. See Errington, *Macedonian Studies Edson*, 139f.
7. Herodotos 7.22.2, 25.
8. Herodotos 8.136, 140f.
9. Justin 7.4.1; Herodotos 5.17.
10. Herodotos 8.136.
11. Herodotos 8.121.2. Solinus 9.13 speaks of a statue in Olympia (he does not mention the one at Delphi), but he has probably simply mixed up the two places. There is no reason because of his mistake to assume two such statues (Geyer, *Makedonien*, 48; Hammond, *History*, 2,102), of which the contemporary Herodotos knew only one. Each ancient writer mentions only one statue. In the fourth century B.C. there was talk of ransom money for Persian captives, though it probably had no historical basis ([Demosthenes] 12.21). Herodotos knows nothing of such ransom.
12. Herodotos 5.17–21; see Errington, *Macedonian Studies Edson*, 139.
13. Herodotos 7.173.2 (Tempe); 8.136, 140 (winter 480/79); 8.34 (Boiotia); 9.45 (Plataiai).
14. The earliest datable mention of this soubriquet is from the second century A.D. (Dio Chrysostom 2.33). It probably has its origin in the activities of Alexandrian scholars, whose writings provide the basis for the scholia to Thukydides 1.57.2 and Demosthenes 3.35.7 as well as Harpokration s.v. Alexandros.
15. Herodotos 7.107.
16. Scholion to Aischines 2.31. Alexander's takeover of the lower Strymon valley, near the later town of Amphipolis, which is claimed for him in Philip's letter ([Demosthenes] 12.21), probably belongs to the 460s, if the information is correct. For another view see Hammond, *History*, 2,102.
17. On the development of the Delian League see Meiggs, *Athenian Empire*, passim; Schuller, *Herrschaft*, passim.
18. Thukydides 1.100.3. On Thasos see Meiggs, *Athenian Empire*, 83f.; Pouilloux, *Thasos*, vol. 1.
19. Plutarch, *Kimon* 14.

3. THE PERIOD OF THE PELOPONNESIAN WAR

1. E.g. Geyer, *Makedonien*, 51.
2. Thukydides 2.100.3 (Philippos); Plato, *Gorgias* 471a–b (Alketas); *IG*

1³.89 = *StV* 2,186 line 53 (Menelaos); Synkellos, p. 500, Dindorf (Amyntas).

3. The text of the treaty is in *IG* 1³,89 = *StV* 2,186. Scholars have different opinions about the date of the treaty. A date before 432 seems to be supported by Thukydides 1.57.2, where he speaks of Perdikkas' being an enemy of Athens in that year, whereas he had earlier been a friend and ally (cf. *ATL* 3,313); the treaty whose text we have would then have been the foundation document for this good relationship. It seems to me to fit very well into the 440s (see Kagan, *Outbreak*, 276), a time when Perdikkas was relatively weak and Athens relatively strong. Above all, the partially preserved clause (lines 23f.) guaranteeing the Athenians the export of oar timber fits into the earliest period of such a relationship; and the mention of a son of Philippos among those who take the oath (in 429 he lived in exile, after a rebellion by his father had failed, and in that year failed to get himself restored [Thukydides 2.95.3, 100.3]) speaks strongly against a later dating (this objection remains valid regardless of whether the name of Philippos is restored in the list of oath swearers). Other dates are around 423/22 (*StV* 2,186), apparently supported by Thukydides 4.132, where an agreement (*homologia*) between Perdikkas and Athens is mentioned; but against this date is the additional fact that Arrhabaios of Lynkestis, who just then was at war with Perdikkas, played a major role in the treaty. Hammond (*History*, 2,132f.) offers a highly subjective restoration of the text, which he then uses to support an improbable argument for a date around 415.

4. On the royal title see Errington, *JHS* 94, 1974, 22f.

5. Thukydides 1.56.

6. The membership of Argilos and Berge in the Athenian League is proved by the so-called Athenian tribute lists: *IG* 1³,259–90. There is a convenient table in Meiggs, *Athenian Empire*, 538f. Plutarch, *Perikles* 11.5 (Perikles' settlement in Bisaltia); *IG* 1³,46 = *ML* 49 (Brea); Thukydides 4.102; Diodoros 12.32.3; scholion to Aischines 2, 34 (Amphipolis).

7. Hammond, *History*, 2,119f.; see also Raymond, *Coinage*, 136f. The coins are published in Gaebler, vol. 3, pt. 2, 153–55, with Tafel XXVIII and XXIX. Whether this unusual coining activity of Perdikkas can be explained by the coining of a certain Mosses, who at some time around the middle of the century issued coins in this area (Gaebler, vol. 3, pt. 2, 145–46, with Tafel XXVII) is uncertain (this is Hammond's view, *History*, 2.119f.). Mosses' coins cannot be precisely dated, and he issued only relatively small values and not many of them (only four types, as opposed to the twelve types of Perdikkas, and all of them are merely drachma pieces).

8. The figures are from Meiggs, *Athenian Empire*, 538f.

9. Thukydides 1.57.4–5, 58.2. On the Chalkidian state see Zahrnt, *Olynth*, 49f. On the general course of the war see Kagan, *Archidamian War*, passim, where the extensive literature is listed. Every general history of Greece deals with the events of the war.

10. Thukydides 1.58f.

11. Thukydides 2.29.7.

12. Thukydides 2.29.

13. Thukydides 2.100–101.

14. *IG* 1³,61 = *ML* 65, lines 1–32.

15. Thukydides 2.80.7.
16. IG 1³,61 = ML 65, lines 32f.
17. F 63,8.
18. Thukydides 4.78–82.
19. Thukydides 4.124–28. On the topography see Hammond, *History*, 1,104–8.
20. Thukydides 4.132 (agreement with Athens); 5.6.2 (Kleon).
21. The text in Thukydides 5.18–20, with Gomme, *Commentary*, ad loc., who cites the older literature. A newer discussion is in Kagan, *Archidamian War*, 342f.; on Chalkidike see Zahrnt, *Olynth*, 66f.; see also Hammond, *History*, 2,131f.
22. Only in the assessment list of 422/21 are the names completely preserved (IG 1³,77 = ATL A 10 V, lines 21–26), but they can be restored with virtual certainty for 425/24 (IG 1³,71 = ATL A 9 IV, lines 108–13). Hammond's argument against it (*History*, 2,132 and n. 3), that Thukydides mentions no Athenian activity in this area in 425/24, is not decisive. The last preserved tribute list from the Thracian region is that of 429/28; the three cities could easily have been won for the Athenians in one of the following years. Moreover, Thukydides does not mention every little incident; even an important event like the capture of Methone is missing.
23. IG 1³,76 = StV 2,188.
24. IG 1³,370 = ML 77, lines 9, 26.
25. Thukydides 5.80.2–83.4.
26. Thukydides 6.7.3–4.
27. Thukydides 7.9.
28. Andokides 2.11.
29. Diodoros 13.49.
30. IG 1³,117 = ML 91.
31. IG 1³,89 = StV 2,186.
32. Plato, *Gorgias* 471a.
33. Plato, *Gorgias* 471b–c.
34. Thukydides 2.100.2; see above, p. 1.
35. Such as the so-called Markovo Kule on the Axios, which Hammond (*History*, 2,146–47) has mentioned in this context.
36. Ailian, *Varia Historia* 14.17.
37. Ailian, *Varia Historia* 2.21, 13.4 (Agathon and Euripides); Athenaios 8.345d (Choirilos); Plutarch, *Moralia* 177B (Timotheus); Suda, s.v. Euripides, Genos Euripidou; cf. Schmid and Stählin, *Griechische Literaturgeschichte* vol. 1, pt. 3, 325f. (Euripides).
38. Diodoros 17.16.3; Arrian, *Anabasis* 1.11.1 (Dion); Solinus 9.16 (p. 65 Mommsen) (Archelaos' victories).

4. On the Edge of the World

1. Aristotle, *Politics* 5,1311b.
2. The source is the much-discussed text, Ps.-Herodes, *Peri Politeias*, 19f.; cf. Meyer, *Theopomps Hellenika*, 201f.; Albini, *Erode Attico*, passim. The philologists seem unable to agree whether the text is a contemporary speech from the end of the fifth century B.C. or a rhetorical school exercise of the second century A.D. But even in the latter case the situation the

speech deals with need not be wholly invented but, like so many such pieces, may have been taken from an author whose work is lost to us, perhaps even of the fourth century B.C.

3. Aristotle, *Politics* 5,1311b. A "softer" tradition is preserved by Diodoros 14.37, according to which Krataios accidentally killed Archelaos in a hunting accident, but Aristotle is a more credible witness. The murderer's name is not always given in the same form: Krateros (Diodoros 14.37), Krateas (Plutarch, *Moralia* 764F [Amatorius]), Krateuas (Ailian, *Varia Historia* 8.9). Hammond, *History*, 2,167, prefers the much-later Ailian against the almost-contemporary Aristotle: he gives no reason.

4. Hammond, *History*, 2,167–68 and n. 1, regards these young men as royal pages and, despite the explicit statement of Arrian (*Anabasis* 4.13.1) that this institution was founded by Philip II, regards Archelaos as its founder. He produces no argument. Ailian, *Varia Historia* 8.9, fantasizes about a "three or four-day tyranny" for Krataios; but neither Aristotle nor Diodoros knows anything of such an event, and it is quite unbelievable.

5. Diodoros 14.37.6, 84.6. The chronology is rather uncertain: the best discussion remains that of Beloch, *Griechische Geschichte*, vol. 3, pt. 2, 55f.

6. The genealogy was established by Beloch, *Griechische Geschichte*, vol. 3, pt. 2, 62f., with wholly convincing arguments; there is no need to exchange it for the argument in Hammond, *History*, 2,168f. Hammond's attempt to establish Amyntas "the Little" as a son of Perdikkas' brother Menelaos is unconvincing. The Philip, son of Amyntas, in Ailian, *Varia Historia* 12.43, is clearly Philip II, son of Amyntas III. Ailian's comment that he was a grandson of Menelaos is simply wrong. (Whenever Ailian mentions a Philip, he always means Philip, son of Amyntas, except for once, when he clearly indicates the father of Antigonos Monophthalmos [12.43]). The same mistake is in Justin 7.4.3.

7. The coins are in Gaebler, vol. 3, pt. 2.

8. Aristotle, *Politics* 5,1311b 3–4 (Amyntas "the Little"); Diodoros 14.89.2 (Pausanias).

9. Xenophon, *Hellenika* 5.2.38f.; Aristotle, *Politics* 5,1311b 13.

10. Polyainos 2.1.17, 4.4.3.

11. Strabo 7.7.8 (C 326).

12. On Bardylis see Hammond, *BSA* 61, 1966, 239f.

13. Diodoros 14.92.3f.

14. Diodoros 16.2.2.

15. It has been occasionally maintained (most recently by Hammond, *History*, 2,174f.; cf. Geyer, *Makedonien*, 118) that Amyntas was driven out by the Illyrians twice and twice gave ground to Olynthos since Diodoros rather clumsily mentions these events again under 383/82 as the origin of the mistrust that at that time characterized the relationship between Amyntas and Olynthos (15.19.2). Ellis, *Makedonika* 9, 1969, 1–8, saw the correct solution: the same events are repeated in abbreviated form simply because the first mention lies more than forty chapters back.

Both the date and the circumstances of the usurpation of Argaios are disputed. To reconcile the two years that he is said to have ruled with the twenty-four years of Amyntas (Diodoros 14.92.3–4), he must have shared power for a time with Amyntas, that is, as his competitor. This could have happened in 393, where Diodoros puts it, and the context may have been his exile by the Illyrians: in that case a connection between Argaios and the Illyrians is probable (see also Hammond, *History*, 2,172). It could, however, have been in the 380s, where the late chronographic tradition puts it (see Beloch, *Griechische Geschichte*, vol. 3, pt. 2, 56f.), perhaps in the context of the dispute with Olynthos (see Ellis, *Makedonika* 9, 1969, 1–8); Geyer, *Makedonien*, 116f., though with differing dates). Hammond, *History*, 2,175–76, argues that Argaios was a further son of Archelaos and cites Theopompos (*FgrHist* 115 F 29) in support. This argument is not improbable and could help to explain why Argaios achieved the success he did.

16. Ps.-Herodes, *Peri Politeias* 19f. (Archelaos); Xenophon, *Hellenika* 2.3.4 (Lykophron in 404); Diodoros 14.82.5–6; Aristotle, *Historia Animalium* 9.31 (618b) (events of 395). On Thessaly see Sordi, *Lega tessala*, 138f.; Westlake, *Thessaly*, 47f.

17. Thukydides 1.58.2.

18. Text in *Syll.*³ 135 = *StV* 2,231. Important observations on the epigraphy of the treaty are in Zahrnt, *Olynth*, 122–24. The inscription is not dated but must be from this period.

19. According to Isokrates, *Archidamos* (VI) 46, the actual period of exile lasted only three months.

20. Aischines 2.28; cf. Geyer, *Makedonien*, 119.

21. Diodoros 15.19.2.

22. Xenophon, *Hellenika* 5.2.12–13 (speech of Kleigenes of Akanthos).

23. Diodoros 15.19.3.

24. Xenophon, *Hellenika* 5.2.11–24.

25. Xenophon, *Hellenika* 5.2.25–5.3.26 (events of war); cf. Zahrnt, *Olynth*, 91f.

26. Isokrates, *Panegyrikos*, 126.

27. On events in central Greece cf. Buckler, *Theban Hegemony*, 15–45; on the Second Athenian Confederacy see Cargill, *Second Athenian League*, with extensive bibliography. Accame, *Lega ateniese*, is still valuable.

28. *Syll.*³ 157 = Tod 2,129 = *StV* 2,246. The Macedonian witnesses are Amyntas and his eldest son by Eurydike, Alexandros (lines 20–21).

29. Aischines 2.32.

30. Diodoros 15.60.2. On Jason of Pherai see Sordi, *Lega tessala*, 156f.; Westlake, *Thessaly*, 67f.

31. *BSA* 17, 1910–11, 193f.; Hammond, *History*, 1,117f., 2,178 and n. 3, is correct to reject the view of Rosenberg, *Hermes* 51, 1916, 499f., who wished to conclude from Amyntas' decision that he exercised some kind of dominance (Oberherrschaft) in the area.

32. Cf. Buckler, *Theban Hegemony*, 46f.

II. The European Great Power

1. THE SUCCESSION IN THE ROYAL HOUSE
OF AMYNTAS

1. Diodoros 15.61.3–5.
2. Diodoros 15.67.4, 71.2; Plutarch, *Pelopidas* 26; Justin 7.5; Aischines

2.29 with the scholion ad loc.; Marsyas (*FgrHist* 136–37) F 3 (Alexander and Ptolemaios); Aischines 2.26–29 (Pausanias). The chronology is uncertain in detail: see Beloch, *Griechische Geschichte*, vol. 3, pt. 2, 61–62; 239f.; Buckler, *Theban Hegemony*, 245f. Hammond, *History*, 2,182, offers the unfounded speculation that Ptolemaios, who was son of an Amyntas, was son of Amyntas "the Little." The sources give no support, and Amyntas is one of the commonest Macedonian names (but see above, chap. 1.4 n. 9).

3. Diodoros 15.77.5; scholion to Aischines 2.29.

4. Demosthenes 2.14; Polyainos 3.10.14; see Diodoros 15.81.6.

5. Aischines 2.29–30 (Kallisthenes); Demosthenes 2.14; Deinarchos 1.14 (Methone and Pydna). The chronology is again very uncertain; but since in 361/60 the exiled Athenian politician Kallistratos went to Methone (Demosthenes 50.48), the city can only have been taken by Timotheus after that date.

6. When precisely the Orestians attached themselves to Molossis, and whether all of them or only a part of the region did so, is quite unclear. An undated inscription from Dodona from a rather later time (*SEG* 23,471; Cabanes, *L'Épire*, 536 no. 2) provides evidence of an Orestian as member of a college of officials. Hammond, *History*, 2,185, would like to date it to this time.

7. Frontinus, *Strategemata* 2.5.19.

8. Diodoros 16.2.4–5.

9. I leave aside here the question of whether Philip was not at first merely regent for his young nephew Amyntas, son of Perdikkas, as Justin says (7.5.9–10), and the newly developed thesis that there were about four years without a king, during which Philip was only regent. (Hatzopoulos in Adams and Borza, *Macedonian Heritage*, 21f.). I regard both theories as improbable. It is in any case certain that Philip immediately exercised power, and under the prevailing circumstances that fact should be sufficient to prove that he was king.

10. Diodoros 16.3.4.

11. Justin 8.3.10, cf. 7.4.5.

12. Diodoros 16.3.5–6, 4.1; Demosthenes 23.121; cf. *StV* 2,298; Griffith in Hammond, *History*, 2,211f.

13. Diodoros 16.3.1.

2. Security in the West

1. Diodoros 16.3.1; Polyainos 4.1.10.

2. Diodoros 16.4.

3. Diodoros 16.8.1.

4. Athenaios 13.557d = Satyros (*FHG* 3,161) F 5; cf. Tronson, *JHS* 104, 1984, 116f. Philip probably was already connected through marriage with the ruling family of Elimiotis, which had been a major support to his father, through Phila, sister of Derdas and Machetas (Satyros, [*FHG* 3.161] F 5).

5. Diodoros 16.22.3 with *IG* 2^2,127 = Tod 2,157; Plutarch, *Alexander* 3; Justin 12.16.6.

6. Isokrates, *Philippos* 21; cf. Demosthenes 1.13, 23.

7. Diodoros 16.69.7; see Pompeius Trogus, *Prologus* 8; Justin 8.6.3. The chronology and the extent of the campaign are very uncertain; cf. Griffith in Hammond, *History*, 2,469f. Philip may have also campaigned against Pleurias (Diodoros 16.93.6), but the reference could apply to the 340s.

8. Arrian, *Anabasis* 1.5–6, with Bosworth, *Commentary*, ad loc. (335); Diodoros 18.11.1 (323).

9. Demosthenes 4.48; Justin 8.3.7–8; cf. Polyainos 4.2.12. Extensive discussion in Hammond, *History*, 2,652f.

10. Diodoros 17.57.2; cf. Berve, *Alexanderreich*, 1,112f.; below, chap. 6,3.

11. Sources are in Berve, *Alexanderreich*, vol. 2, ad loc.

12. Arrian, *Anabasis* 4.13.1. Hammond, *History*, 2,168 n. 1, finds this institution already under Archelaos, but the sources do not support his view. Kienast, *Philipp II*, 264f., argued the view that it had been developed in imitation of the Persian institution, but this argument hardly convinces. Philip's aim to develop a sense of national identity through this institution is in any case clear.

13. On the sons of Aeropos see Berve, *Alexanderreich*, vol. 2, nos. 37 (Alexandros), 144 (Arrhabaios), 355 (Heromenes); see also Bosworth, *Commentary*, 159–60; on regionalism see Bosworth, *CQ* 21, 1971, 93f.; Fears, *Athenaeum* 53, 1975, 120f.

14. Justin 7.6.10–12; Plutarch, *Alexander* 2; Athenaios 13,557c–d (= Satyros F5). On Epeiros in general see Franke, *Altepeiros*; Hammond, *Epirus*, passim.

15. The main source is Justin 8.6; cf. Demosthenes 1.13; Pompeius Trogus, *Prologus* 8; Diodoros 16.72.1; [Demosthenes] 7.32. The chronology of these events is disputed. I follow the system I developed in *GRBS* 16, 1975, 41f.; for a different view see Griffith in Hammond, *History*, 2,504f.

16. Around 330 Kleopatra is mentioned as *thearodokos* (host to the ambassadors of a god) for Epeiros in a list from Argos (Charneux, *BCH* 90, 1966, 156–239 and 710–714, line 11 of the inscription). The Thesprotai and the towns of Kassopeia are not mentioned in the list, but the Chaones are (line 12). The Thesprotai seem therefore to have given up their independent state, though the list cannot support the argument that Epeiros must have been the official name of the new state. On this point see Cabanes in *La géographie administrative*, 19f., though Cabanes does not comment on the probable Macedonian influence.

17. Sources are in Berve, *Alexanderreich*, vol. 2, s.v. Alexandros (38), Kleopatra (433 and 434), Olympias (581), Antipatros (94).

3. THE EAST

1. On the Thracians in general see Wiesner, *Die Thraker*.

2. Diodoros 16.3.3.

3. Diodoros 16.8.2–3; Demosthenes 1.8; Tod 2,150 (exile of Stratokles and Philo). The inscription is unfortunately not precisely datable and is generally regarded as reflecting a result of Philip's conquest. But it is

possible that Stratokles had already been banned when, together with Hierokles, he tried to secure Athenian help.

4. [Demosthenes] 7.27; Theopompos (*FgrHist* 115) F 30A and B; Demosthenes 2.6 (negotiations); Diodoros 16.8.3 (Pydna). A detailed discussion by Griffith is in Hammond, *History*, 2,230f.

5. Demosthenes 2.6. (Athens); Robinson, *TAPhA* 69, 1938, 44 no. 2 = *StV* 2,307. The engraving of the stone was not completed; but the explanation of the first editor, that the treaty was not ratified, is impossible: nobody engraved unratified treaties in stone. Probably Philip's offer arrived while the stone was being worked on.

6. Diodoros 16.8.4–5.

7. Diodoros 16.3.7, 8.6–8. On the order of events see Griffith in Hammond, *History*, 2,246f., 358f. On Alexander see the inscription, *SEG* 34, 1984, 664.

8. *IG* 2²,127 = *Syll.*³196 = Tod 2,157; cf. Demosthenes 23.179f. From the Athenian side this alliance was merely an attempt to persuade others to fight their war for them. Grabos, and perhaps Lyppeios as well, was defeated by Parmenio (Diodoros 16.22.3).

9. Diodoros 16.31.6, 34.4–5. When precisely Methone fell is uncertain. An Athenian decree of about November 355 for Lachares of Apollonia, who had sent off some member of his family to Methone, means that the threat must be dated earlier (*IG* 2²,130). Demosthenes (4.35) asserted that Athenian help arrived too late. If therefore Lachares' relative was a member of the expedition that arrived too late, we must conclude that the siege was also over by the end of 355.

10. The region administered from Amphipolis, which might have been extended by Philip after his taking the city, seems to have received a number of well-placed settlers, who now came to Macedonia for the first time. Two happen to be known: Androtimos from Lato in Krete (father of Nearchos: Berve, *Alexanderreich*, vol. 2, no. 544) and Larichos from Mytilene (father of Erigyios and Laomedon: Berve, nos. 302 and 464). The fact that Alexander could raise a cavalry regiment (*ile*) from Amphipolis also suggests that not only ordinary farmers were settled there.

11. *IG* 2²,126 and add. 658 (*StV* 2,303; Tod 2,151) (Berisades et al.); *IG* 2²,127 (*Syll.*³ 196; Tod 2,157) (Ketriporis etc.). On the Athenian League see Cargill, *Second Athenian League.*

12. *IG* 2²,128 (*Syll.*³ 197; Tod 2,159; *StV* 2,312); Polyainos 4.2.22.

13. Demosthenes 23.183; Polyainos 4.2.22; cf. Diodoros 16.34.1.

14. Diodoros 16.34.3–4; cf. Demosthenes 23.103.

15. Scholion to Aischines 2.81; Demosthenes 3.4 (Heraion Teichos). Complete clarity about the situation in Thrace in 352/51 is impossible. In particular Amadokos' role remains obscure: it looks as if Philip fought against Kersebleptes to defeat Amadokos, but this impresssion is doubtless due to the miserable state of the sources. Theopompos (*FgrHist* 115) F 101 spoke of two Amadokoi, father and son, and said that the son joined Philip in fighting Kersebleptes. Griffith, in Hammond, *History*, 2,282–83, thinks it possible that the son had replaced the father, but the fragment of Theopompos does not say that the son was king. It may have been merely an attempt by Amadokos to appease Philip once he

had recognized his own weakness. After 351 we hear nothing more of either of them.

This campaign threw the Athenians into a panic (Demosthenes 3.4), but in fact Philip seems to have had no inclination to attack the Chersonnese or interfere with traffic through the Dardanelles. The Athenian panic, which expressed itself in an urgent desire to do something, slackened as soon as the false report reached Athens that Philip was dead (before anything had been done by the Athenians). But more important as proof that their mood was short-lived is the fact that the Athenians continued to do nothing even after they learned that the report was false.

16. Demosthenes 3.7, 23.108; cf. *StV* 2,317 (peace with Athens); Justin 8.3.10–11 (half-brothers), cf. Ellis, *Historia* 22, 1973, 350f.

17. Main source: Diodoros 16.52.9, 53.1–3. Also, from an Athenian point of view, Demosthenes' Olynthian speeches (nos. 1–3), which, however, as a result of Demosthenes' very personal view of Athens' real interests, merely obscure the Macedonian point of view. There is a large modern literature: perhaps the best account is by Cawkwell, *Philip*, 82f., and *CQ*, n.s., 12, 1962, 122f.; the most detailed is by Griffith in Hammond, *History*, 2,315f.

18. Aischines 2.82f., 3.73f.; Demosthenes 9.15.

19. Aischines 2.90, 92.

20. Diodoros 16.71.1–2; [Demosthenes] 12.8–10.

21. Sources are in Griffith in Hammond, *History*, 2,557f.

22. Diodoros 17.62.5.

23. Justin 9.2.1.

24. Cf. Griffith in Hammond, *History*, 2,364f., 379f.

25. Cf. below, chap. 2,5.

26. [Demosthenes] 12.2f.; Demosthenes 8, passim; 9.15.

27. Main source: Diodoros 16.74.2–76.4, 77.2; detailed discussion by Griffith in Hammond, *History*, 2,566f.

28. Theopompos (*FgrHist* 115) F 292; cf. Demosthenes 18.87–94; Plutarch, *Phokion* 14. On the attitude of the orators see Demosthenes 8, passim; 10.15–16.

29. See below, chap. 2,5.

30. Arrian, *Anabasis* 1.3.3.

31. Athenaios 13.557d = Satyros (*FHG* 3.161) F 5; Jordanes, *Getica* 10.65 (Kothelas and Meda); Justin 9.2.1–3.4 (Atheas and Triballoi). Cf. Papazoglu, *Central Balkan Tribes*, 18f.; Griffith in Hammond, *History*, 2,559f.

32. Arrian, *Anabasis* 1.1.5f., with Bosworth, *Commentary*, 53f. (autonomous Thracians); Theopompos (*FgrHist* 115) F 217; Polyainos 4.4.1 (Tetrachoritai).

33. Arrian, *Anabasis* 1.2–4, with Bosworth, *Commentary*, ad loc. (campaign); Diodoros 17.17.4 (participation in the Asian campaign). The number of Triballian soldiers is uncertain since they are only mentioned as part of a group of Thracians and Illyrians, whose number, itself disputed, is given as seven thousand. Cf. Berve, *Alexanderreich*, vol. 1, nos. 139, 178. For the Triballians in general see Papazoglu, *Central Balkan Tribes*, 9f.

34. Arrian, *Anabasis* 1.3.5–4.5.

35. Berve, *Alexanderreich*, vol. 2, no. 712 (Sitalkes); *IG* 2²,349 and add.

659 = Tod 2,193 (Rhebulas). Interpretations remain very speculative: cf. Tod's commentary, ad loc.; Berve, *Alexanderreich*, vol. 2, no. 686; Curtius 10.1.45, cf. Berve, *Alexanderreich*, vol. 2, no. 702 (Seuthes).

36. Sources in Berve, *Alexanderreich*, vol. 2, no. 37.

37. Diodoros 17.62.4–6; Curtius 9.3.21, cf. Berve, *Alexanderreich*, vol. 2, no. 499.

38. Curtius 10.1.44–45; Justin 12.1.4–5, 2.16–17, cf. Berve, *Alexanderreich*, vol. 2, no. 340 (Zopyrion).

4. THESSALY

1. On Thessaly in general see Sordi, *Lega tessala*; Westlake, *Thessaly*; Martin, *Sovereignty and Coinage*.

2. IG 2²,116 (= Syll³ 184 = Tod 2,147 = StV 2,293, all with commentaries); also Sordi, *Lega tessala*, 228.

3. Justin 7.6.8f.; Athenaios 13.557c. The content of Justin's account cannot be accurate; cf. Griffith in Hammond, *History*, 2,220f., esp. 226, who, building on Sordi's research (*Lega tessala*, 230f.), sorts out the complicated chronological problems as far as possible. I follow him in the main.

4. Diodoros 16.14.2.

5. Diodoros 16.23f. On the chronology see Hammond, *JHS* 57, 1937, 44f., whom I follow here. On the Amphiktyony see Roux, *L'Amphictionie*, passim.

6. Diodoros 16.35; Justin 8.2.1–7.

7. Diodoros 16.37.3, 38.1.

8. Cf. Sordi, *Lega tessala*, 246f.; Griffith in Hammond, *History*, 2,270f.

9. The older title, *Tagos*, which earlier archons of the league had used, was avoided by Philip, probably deliberately. On the whole question see Sordi, *Lega tessala*, 249f.; Griffith in Hammond, *History*, 2,220f.

10. This list of functions is constructed from the archon's actual activities. How far these "rights and duties" had in fact been formalized up to this time is very uncertain; cf. Sordi, *Lega tessala*, 334f.

11. Demosthenes 1.22.

12. Polyainos 4.2.19.

13. Athenaios 13.557c.

14. Diodoros 16.38.1.

15. Diodoros 16.37.3, 38.1–2; Justin 8.2.8f.; Demosthenes 4.17, 19.319.

16. Demosthenes 1.22, cf. 2.8–11.

17. Diodoros 16.52.9.

18. Main source: Diodoros 16.59–60; Aischines 2.132f. On Athens see Demosthenes 5, 19.73f. Cf. Roux, *L'Amphictionie*.

19. Theopompos (*FgrHist* 115) F 81; cf. Isokrates 5.21.

20. Demosthenes 19.36; [Demosthenes] 11.1; cf. Sordi, *Lega tessala*, 362f., 286f.

21. Demosthenes 18.48; Aristotle, *Politics* 1306a26; Polyainos 4.2.19; Theopompos, (*FgrHist* 115) F 81, reports in his usual insulting way that Agathokles had been a former serf (*penestes*). It is at least certain he did not belong to the ruling clan of the Aleuadai.

22. Diodoros 16.69.8; Isokrates, *Epist.* 2.20; [Demosthenes] 7.32, cf. 19.260, 320.

23. Theopompos (*FgrHist* 115) F 208; cf. Griffith in Hammond, *History*, 2,527f.

24. Demosthenes 18.295; *Syll*³ 274.

25. Aischines 3.107–29; Demosthenes 18.143–52; cf. below, chap. 2.6.

26. Plutarch, *Demosthenes* 18.2.

27. Diodoros 17.17.4.

28. Diodoros 17.4.1. Diodoros obviously had not understood his source properly. He speaks of the recognition of "the leadership of Greece," which the Thessalian League could not bestow; cf. Justin 11.3.2. Polyainos 4.3.23 has an undated story of Thessalian resistance to Alexander at Tempe. The incident cannot be satisfactorily fitted into 336, despite Westlake, *Thessaly*, 217–18, and Tarn, *Alexander*, 1,4; cf. Sordi, *Lega tessala*, 302 n. 2, who thinks of the Lamian War, but no Alexander was involved in it. Perhaps Polyainos names the wrong Alexander: Alexander II certainly had trouble with Thessalian resistance in 369, and it could well have produced the stratagem Polyainos relates.

29. A badly damaged inscription has often been interpreted in this sense: *IG* 2²,236; Heisserer, *Alexander*, 8f. (cf. *Syll*³ 260; Tod 2,177). But the significance of the numbers in the inscription seems to me still to be inadequately explained. On the Korinthian League see below, chap. 2.5.

30. Aischines 3.167.

31. Diodoros 18.11.1, 15.2. On details of this development see below, chap. 2.5.

32. Diodoros 18.15.4, 17.6–7.

33. Diodoros 18.38. See also below, chap. 2.5; cf. Sordi, *Lega tessala*, 306f.

5. The Southern Greek States

1. Xenophon, *Hellenika* 7.5.27.

2. Polybios 18.14.

3. Aischines 2.120.

4. On these events see above, chap. 2.4.

5. Cf. Demosthenes 4 (first Philippic) of 351.

6. Demosthenes 4.37 (Euboia).

7. Aischines 2.112.

8. Aischines 2.13.

9. Sources are in *StV* 2,329. Modern literature on the Peace of Philokrates is already immense, and the flood threatens never to stop: for representative modern treatments see the relevant chapters of Griffith in Hammond, *History*, 2,329f.; Cawkwell, *Philip*, 91f.; Ellis, *Philip II*, 90f.

10. Aischines 3.89–90.

11. Demosthenes 6.13. Despite Demosthenes' extreme choice of words—"Philip *ordered* the Spartans to leave Messene free" (emphasis added)—it is clear that only a diplomatic initiative can be meant.

12. Demosthenes 18.43, 48, 295; Polybios 18.14.

13. Nevertheless, the most detailed analysis is that of Griffith in Hammond, *History*, 2,450f.

14. Hegesippos' speech survives as [Demosthenes] 7. On details of these events see Griffith in Hammond, *History*, 2,489f.; Cawkwell, *CQ* 13, 1963, 120f., 200f.

15. Demosthenes' speech "On the Chersonnesos" (8) allows us to measure Athenian feelings about these events.

16. A version of this letter is preserved in the Demosthenic corpus as [Demosthenes] 12. Since Pohlenz's investigation (*Hermes* 64, 1929, 41f.) most historians agree that the version we have was written by Philip; cf. Griffith in Hammond, *History*, 2,714f.

17. [Demosthenes] 12.23.

18. Diodoros 16.74.4, 75.1–2. When Philip captured the Athenian corn fleet, Chares was away from his post for talks with the Persian satraps: Philochoros (*FgrHist* 328) F 162.

19. Philochoros (*FgrHist* 328) F 162; Theopompos (*FgrHist* 115) F 292.

20. Philochoros F 55.

21. Philochoros F 56.

22. Philochoros F 56; Plutarch, *Demosthenes* 18.3 (= Theopompos F 328).

23. There were voices raised against the war: in Athens Phokion (Plutarch, *Phokion* 16.1–2), in Thebes those politicians whom Demosthenes called paid agents of Philip (Demosthenes 18.175: this standard charge was thrown at all Demosthenes' opponents and in most cases seems to have the flavour merely of a not-too-coarse insult; despite the repeated charges Demosthenes never accused a political opponent of taking bribes before a court). However, they were not sufficiently influential.

24. The main source is Diodoros 16.84–86. There is a detailed discussion of the events by Griffith in Hammond, *History*, 2,596f.

25. Pausanias 1.25.3.

26. Pausanias 1.34.1 (Oropos); Aristotle, *Athenaion Politeia* 61.6, 62.2; Plutarch, *Alexander* 28.1; Diodoros 18.56.7 (the islands); Diodoros 16.87.3 (prisoners), cf. *StV* 3,402.

27. Plutarch, *Demosthenes* 21 (Demosthenes); *IG* 2²,237 (= *Syll*³ 259 = Tod 2,178) (Akarnanians).

28. Diodoros 17.13.5 (rebuilding the cities); Justin 9.4.7f., cf. Roesch, *Études Béotiennes*, 266f.; Gullath, *Boiotien*, 8f.; Griffith in Hammond, *History*, 2,610f. (new organization); Diodoros 16.87.3; Arrian, *Anabasis* 1.17.1 (garrison).

29. Sources and detailed discussion are in Roebuck, *CPh* 43, 1948, 73f., cf. Griffith in Hammond, *History*, 2,616f.

30. Sources in *StV* 2,242; on "common peace" see Ryder, *Koine Eirene*, passim.

31. The precise nature of the relationship with Hermeias is not clear: see Wormell, *Yale Classical Studies* 5, 1935, 57f.; Diodoros 16.74.2; Plutarch, *Alexander* 10.1 (Pixodaros); Diodoros 16.75.1–2 (Perinthos); Plutarch, *Demosthenes* 20.4–5 (Demosthenes). The origin of Philip's plans for a Persian expedition is disputed: see my discussion in *AJAH* 6, 1981, 69f.

32. Isokrates, *Philippos* (5),119–120. Isokrates' first known statement in this direction is the *Panegyrikos* (4) of 380.

33. Badian, *Ehrenberg Studies*, 62 n. 13.

34. Sources are in *StV* 3,403; the most recent discussion, including the older literature, is by Griffith in Hammond, *History*, 2,625f.

35. Plutarch, *Demosthenes* 22.
36. Diodoros 17.3.3–5.
37. Diodoros 17.4.
38. Arrian, *Anabasis* 1.7–9; Diodoros 17.8.3–14.
39. Arrian, *Anabasis* 1.10.4–6, with Bosworth, *Commentary*, 92f.
40. Arrian, *Anabasis* 1.9.9–10.
41. Arrian, *Anabasis* 1.11.3.
42. [Demosthenes] 17.19.
43. Plutarch, *Demosthenes* 24. Demosthenes' speech for the defence, the famous *De Corona* (18), is extant.
44. Diodoros 17.48.1; 62.6–63.4; Curtius 6.1, cf. Badian, *Hermes*, 95, 1967, 170f.
45. Diodoros 17.73.5; Curtius 6.1.19–21.
46. Arrian, *Anabasis* 1.16.7 (Granikos); 3.16.8, with Bosworth, *Commentary*, ad loc. (tyrant slayers).
47. Arrian, *Anabasis* 3.6.2.
48. Arrian, *Anabasis* 3.19.5, with Bosworth, *CQ* 26, 1976, 132f.; cf. Bosworth, *Commentary*, 335.
49. On the general problem see Seibert, *Politische Flüchtlinge*, passim.
50. Cf. Badian, *JHS* 81, 1961, 16f.; Jaschinski, *Alexander und Griechenland*, 62f.
51. Diodoros 18.8.2–4.
52. Documents from Tegea (*Syll*[3] 306 = Tod 2,202 = Heisserer no. 8) and Mytilene (*OGIS* 2 = Tod 2,201 = Heisserer no. 5) give us two examples.
53. On Samos see Errington, *Chiron* 5, 1975, 51f.; Habicht, *Chiron* 5, 1975, 45f.; Rosen, *Historia* 27, 1978, 20f. For a brief review see Seibert, *Diadochen*, 95.
54. Cf. Badian, *JHS* 81, 1961.
55. For members of the alliance see Diodoros 18.11.1–2.
56. The main source is Diodoros 18.11–13, 14.4–15.9, 16.4–17.5.
57. Diodoros 18.18.1–6; Plutarch, *Phokion* 26–28.

III. The Asian Dimension

1. Introduction

2. The Old Guard

1. Out of the flood of books on Alexander, I name here only a few general works. Seibert, *Alexander der Grosse*, offers a review of the literature until 1970; since then see Schachermeyr, *Alexander der Grosse*; Hamilton, *Alexander the Great*; Lane-Fox, *Alexander the Great*; Hammond, *Alexander the Great*.
2. Questioned by Fredericksmeyer in Adams and Borza, *Macedonian Heritage*, 85f.
3. The sources offer only fragmentary information, which is inadequate to reconstruct the campaign: Diodoros 16.91.2 (Parmenio and Attalos); Arrian, *Anabasis* 1.17.10f. (Ephesos); *IG* 12,2.526 in the most recent edition, Heisserer no. 2 (Eresos).

4. Diodoros 17.7.8. Apparently in 336 (Attalos, who was murdered shortly after Alexander's coming to rule [Diodoros 17.2.3–6] was still alive) there was a struggle with the Persian king's commander Memnon near Magnesia (Polyainos 5.44.4). Polyainos does not say which Magnesia it was, Magnesia-on-the-Maiander, near Ephesos, or Magnesia-by-Sipylos, north of Smyrna. But for an army operating out of Ephesos it seems most reasonable to conclude that it was Magnesia-on-the-Maiander. Most historians prefer Magnesia-by-Sipylos because they connect it with the campaign in Aiolis in 335 (e.g. Badian in *Ancient Society and Institutions*, 40–41).

5. Diodoros 17.16.2.

6. E.g. Arrian, *Anabasis* 1.13.2 (battle on the Granikos); 1.18.6–9 (Miletos); 2.25.2–3 (Euphrates); 3.10.1–2 (Gaugamela); 3.18.12 (Persepolis) in each case with Bosworth, *Commentary*, ad loc.

7. Arrian, *Anabasis* 2.25.2–3; Plutarch, *Alexander* 29.7–8; Curtius 4.11.1–22. On the date see Bosworth, *Commentary*, 227f.

8. Arrian, *Anabasis* 3.19.5–6. On Parmenio see Berve, *Alexanderreich*, vol. 2, no. 606.

9. Curtius 6.2.15f.; Plutarch, *Alexander* 47.1.

10. All the sources are in Berve, *Alexanderreich*, vol. 2, nos. 606, 802. Discussion is in Bosworth, *Commentary*, 359f.

11. Diodoros 17.80.4; Arrian, *Anabasis* 3.29.5; Curtius 7.5.27; cf. Arrian, *Anabasis* 5.27.5.

12. On details of this development see Errington, *Chiron* 8, 1978, esp. 105f.

13. Plutarch, *Alexander* 47.6; Curtius 8.51; Diodoros 17.108.1–3; cf. Arrian, *Anabasis* 7.6.1.

14. Plutarch, *Alexander* 47.5. For the sources see Berve, *Alexanderreich*, vol. 2, nos. 357 (Hephaistion), 446 (Krateros), 654 (Polyperchon), 668 (Ptolemaios).

15. Curtius 6.2.15f.; Diodoros 17.74.3; Plutarch, *Alexander* 47.

16. Arrian, *Anabasis* 3.26–27; Curtius 6.7.1–7.2.38; Plutarch, *Alexander* 48–49; Diodoros 17.74–80. The details are much discussed: see Bosworth, *Commentary*, 359f. On the interpretation given here see *Chiron* 8, 1978, 86f.

17. Curtius 8.1.20f.; Arrian, *Anabasis* 4.8.1f.; Plutarch, *Alexander* 50–51, cf. Hamilton, *Commentary*, 139f.; Errington, *Chiron* 8, 1978, 107–8.

18. Arrian, *Anabasis* 5.25–28; Curtius 9.2.12f. On Koinos see Berve, *Alexanderreich*, vol. 2, no. 439.

19. Arrian, *Anabasis* 7.8f.; Curtius 10.2.12f.

20. For a complete list of Greek participants in the campaign see Berve, *Alexanderreich*, vol. 2, 446.

21. Cf. the list in Berve, *Alexanderreich*, vol. 1, 276 and the individual articles in vol. 2.

22. Cf. Diodoros 17.17.4.

23. Sources in Berve, *Alexanderreich*, vol. 1, 150f.

24. Curtius 9.2.33.

25. Arrian, *Anabasis* 7.8.2.

26. Plutarch, *Alexander* 70.3; Arrian, *Anabasis* 7.4.4f.; cf. Diodoros 17.107.6; Curtius 10.3.11–12.

27. Arrian, *Anabasis* 7.11.9. On the widely differing modern interpre-

tations of these two events see Seibert, *Alexander der Grosse*, 186f. I owe
most to the interpretation of Badian, *Studies*, 201f.

3. The Return Home.

1. Arrian, *Anabasis* 7.12.4.
2. Diodoros 18.1.4; Curtius 10.5.5; Arrian, *Anabasis* 7.26.3.
3. For this principle see Errington, *Chiron* 8, 1978, esp. 99f.
4. Diodoros 17.117.3, 18.2.4; Curtius 10.5.4.
5. The main sources on events in Babylon are Curtius 10.5f.; Diodoros
18.2f.; Justin 13.1f.; and the fragments of Arrian's *History of the Successors*
(*FgrHist* 156). The basis of the present interpretation was argued in detail
in Errington, *JHS* 90, 1970. Seibert's detailed survey of the modern literature is now available (*Diadochen*) so that detailed references to the
modern literature are hardly necessary.
6. On Philip's reputation then and in the following years see Errington in Badian, *Alexandre le Grand*, 137f.
7. Curtius 10.10.1.
8. List of satrapies in Diodoros 18.3; Curtius 10.10.1–6; Arrian, *Successors* (*FgrHist* 156) F 1.5–8; Dexippos (*FgrHist* 100) F 8; cf. Justin 13.4.9–
25. Discussion of modern literature in Seibert, *Diadochen*, 89f.
9. Arrian, *Successors* 9. That the arrangement really functioned this
way was shown by Habicht, *Akten des VI. Int. Kongr.*, 367f.
10. Diodoros 18.18.7.
11. Arrian, *Successors* 21; Diodoros 18.23.1–3.
12. Arrian, *Successors* 22–23; Diodoros 19.52.5. On Kynnane see Berve,
Alexanderreich vol. 2, no. 456. On the marriages see Seibert, *Historische
Beiträge*, 11f.
13. Diodoros 18.26f.; Arrian, *Successors* 25, F 10.1. Aigai is only mentioned by Pausanias 1.6.3. For a rather different interpretation of these
events see Badian, *HSPh* 72, 1968, 185f.
14. Diodoros 18.23.3–4, 25.3–5; Arrian, *Successors* 20, 26. The date of
Eurydike's marriage is uncertain, but it fits beautifully into this political
context: Pausanias 1.6.8; Appian, *Syriake* 62; cf. Seibert, *Historische Beiträge*, 16f. That it had been agreed at the time that Antipatros should take
over direct responsibility for the kings seems to be indicated by Ptolemaios' reluctance to assume this function himself after the death of Perdikkas, even for only a short time (Diodoros 18.36.6–7).
15. Diodoros 18.33f.; Arrian, *Successors* F 9.28–30.
16. Diodoros 18.39.2; Arrian, *Successors* F 9.33.
17. Diodoros 18.39.7.
18. Plutarch, *Demetrios* 14 (Phila); Diodoros 18.39.7; Arrian, *Successors*
F 9.38 (Kassandros); Diodoros 18.39.5–6; Arrian, *Successors* F 9.34–38 (division of the satrapies).

4. The End of the Argeadai

1. Diodoros 18.48.4 writes as if Antipatros had formally made the appointment. But in fact it can have only taken place after his death and

certainly fell within the competence of the Crown Council. For the chronology of events after Antipatros' death see Errington, *Hermes* 105, 1977, 478f.

2. Diodoros 18.38.6.

3. On Polyperchon under Alexander see Berve, *Alexanderreich*, vol. 2, no. 654.

4. Diodoros 18.49.1–3, 54; Plutarch, *Phokion* 31.

5. Diodoros 18.55–57.1; cf. Plutarch, *Phokion* 32.

6. Diodoros 18.49.4, 57.2.

7. Diodoros 18.57.3–4, 58; Plutarch, *Eumenes* 13.1–2.

8. Diodoros 18.64f.; Plutarch, *Phokion* 32–33; see Errington, *Hermes* 1977, 487f. (Athens); Diodoros 18.58.3–4; Plutarch, *Eumenes* 13; Diodoros 19.11.2 (Olympias).

9. Diodoros 18.68f. (events in Greece); Justin 14.5.1–4; Diodoros 19.11.1 (Eurydike).

10. Diodoros 19.11.1.

11. Diodoros 19.11.2–3.

12. Diodoros 19.11.4–9.

13. Diodoros 18.75.2, cf. 19.35.7.

14. Diodoros 19.35.3.

15. Diodoros 19.35–36, 49–51.

16. Diodoros 19.52.4, 105.2.

IV. The Age of the Successors

1. KASSANDROS

1. Some kind of Crown Council exercising the functions of the king was apparently recommended by Ptolemaios in Babylon (Curtius 10.6.13f.), but the idea never crops up in Macedonia again. Cf. Mooren in *Egypt and the Hellenistic World*, 233f.

2. On Asia cf. Seibert, *Diadochen* and Will, *Histoire politique*; on Hieronymos cf. Hornblower, *Hieronymus of Cardia*.

3. Cf. Errington in Badian, *Alexandre le Grand*, 145f.

4. Diodoros 20.37.4. On the date see Seibert, *Historische Beiträge*, 21. In general see Goukowski, *Essai*, 1,105f. On the child's tomb see Andronikos, *Verghina*.

5. Diodoros 19.52.5. On the tombs ("Philip's tomb"), the discovery of which by Manolis Andronikos in 1977 caused such a stir, there is a large bibliography (for works up to 1982, see Green in Adams and Borza, *Macedonian Heritage*, 129f.; up to 1987 see Borza, *Phoenix* 41, 1987, 105f.) The chances that the large grave is that of Philip Arrhidaios and Eurydike seem to have been enhanced by the discovery of the boy's tomb, probably that of Alexander IV. An unprejudiced examination of the bones (Xirotiris and Langenscheidt, *Archaiologike Ephemeris* 1981, 142f.) produced no objection to this view. The investigations according to criminalistic methods of Prag, Musgrave and Neave (*JHS* 104, 1984), who already knew of the proposed identification of the skull in the large tomb as that of Philip II and also used alleged portraits, is doubtless a clever interdisciplinary jeu d'ésprit, but is hardly a serious contribution to historical investigation.

See also Rotroff, *Hesperia* 53, 1984, 342f., for the argument that some of the objects in the tomb (saltcellars) must be dated significantly later than 336. Fine colour photographs of the tombs are in Andronikos, *Verghina*, and Hatzopoulos and Loukopoulos, *Philip of Macedon*.

6. Diodoros 19.52.1.

7. Diodoros 19.52.2 (Kassandreia); Strabo 7 F21 (Thessalonike); Strabo 7 F55; Pliny *HN* 4.10.37 (Uranopolis).

8. *Syll³* 332.

9. Plutarch, *Demetrios* 18.

10. The coins are in Gaebler 3.2,176–7. *Syll³* 332 with Errington, *JHS* 94, 1974, 23f., cf. Goukowski, *Essai*, 1.201 (Kassandreia); Pandermalis, *Dion*, 10 (Dion).

11. Pausanias 1.10.4; Appian, *Syriake* 64.

12. Cf. Diodoros 19.73.1–2.

13. Diodoros 20.106.3.

14. Diodoros 20.19.1. On the Paionians see Merker, *Balkan Studies* 6, 1965, 35f.; on the Autariatai see Papazoglu, *Central Balkan Tribes*, 87f.

15. Diodoros 19.36.2, 52.6. On Polyperchon's place of birth the source is indeed late (Tzetzes, *Ad Lykoph.* 802) and not always reliable, but there is no good reason for doubt here.

16. Aiakides had married Phthia, a daughter of Menon of Pharsalos, the Thessalian freedom fighter from the Lamian War, and she had borne him Deidameia, Pyrrhos and Troas (Plutarch, *Pyrrhos* 4). The marriage was before the war. Plutarch, *Pyrrhos* 4.2 (betrothal of Deidameia with Alexander IV); Diodoros 19.35.5 (Deidameia in Pydna and Lykiskos). The most recent investigations of the Epeirot royal family are Kienast, *RE* s.v. Pyrrhos; Lévêque, *Pyrrhos*, 83f.; Hammond, *Epirus*. Still worth reading is Beloch, *Griechische Geschichte*, vol. 4, pt. 2, 143f. On Aiakides and Polyperchon see Diodoros 19.52.6.

17. Diodoros 19.35.2, 67.3f. On the chronology see Errington, *Hermes* 105, 1977, 478f.

18. Diodoros 19.78.1, 74.3–4.

19. Pausanias 1.11.5; Diodoros 19.89.2.

20. Pausanias 1.11.5; Plutarch, *Pyrrhos* 4. The chronology is uncertain, but the arguments of Lévêque, *Pyrrhos*, 102f., seem convincing.

21. After the Lamian War the next evidence for the league is under Antigonos Doson (see below, p. 177). In 322 Antipatros had demanded the capitulation of each city singly (Diodoros 18.17.7–8); and the late chronographic tradition represented by Eusebios records a separate list of Thessalian rulers beginning with Philip Arrhidaios. It seems most likely, therefore, that Kassandros ruled directly over the cities without the constitutional paraphernalia of the league. On the events see Diodoros 19.52.1 (Azoros and Polyperchon); 53.1, 63.3 (march with the army); 20.28.3 (cavalry); 20.110.2, 111.1 (Demetrios in Thessaly).

22. Diodoros 18.74.3, cf. Bayer, *Demetrios Phalereus*; on the question of whether the philosophically trained Demetrios also ruled according to philosophical principles see the negative answer of Gehrke, *Chiron* 8, 1978, 149f.

23. Diodoros 19.54.2, cf. Pausanias 9.7.1; Plutarch, *Moralia* 814B; Gullath, *Untersuchungen*, 86f. (rebuilding); *Syll³* 337, cf. Holleaux, *Études* 1,1f. (list of contributors).

24. Diodoros 19.54.3–4.

25. Diodoros 19.56–57.2. The chronology in uncertain; I follow here my reconstruction in *Hermes* 105, 1977, 478f. The significance of Kassandros' demand for the two separate and distant territories of Kappadokia and Lykia is unclear. A change of text (to Kilikia instead of Lykia, as Tarn, *CAH¹* 6, 484, or Lydia, as Aucello, *RFIC* 85, 1957, 382f.) would create a single geographical block for Kassandros, and one could explain Pleistarchos' demand for Kilikia in 301 by a family claim going back to 314. But Lykia is in the text, and as far as we know, Kassandros was active neither in Lykia, Lydia nor Kilikia, which would give reason for preferring one or the other over the transmitted text. For Droysen's suggestion—instead of *Kassandros* read *Asandros*, the satrap of Karia, palaeographically an easy correction to make—there is no good argument apart from the palaeographical. Kassandros was certainly active in Kappadokia (Diodoros 19.60.2), whereas Asandros was not one of the leading members of the coalition who could make such demands. On the problem see Seibert, *Diadochen*, 155f.

26. Diodoros 19.60.1 (Aristodemos); 61.1–5 (Tyros). Diodoros' account, which is favourable to Antigonos, doubtless comes from Hieronymos of Kardia, who must have been present.

27. E.g. Korinth (Diodoros 19.63.4); Messene (Diodoros 19.64.1).

28. Diodoros 19.62.1.

29. Diodoros 19.63.3, 64.3–4.

30. Diodoros 19.67.1–2 (murder of Alexandros); 66.2 (Aitolia); 68.2–4 (action in autumn).

31. Diodoros 19.73 (Lysimachos and Seuthes); 74–78 (Antigonos' successes); 87 (Telesphoros).

32. Diodoros 19.105.1; *OGIS* 5 = Welles, *RC*, no. 1; no. 6 (agreement); *OGIS* 5 lines 38f. (Polyperchon). There is an extensive literature on this agreement, which is systematically discussed by Seibert, *Diadochen*, 123f. Here only Kassandros is relevant. On the one hand Diodoros gives the impression that the time limit, until the coming of age of Alexander IV, applied only to Kassandros, but on the other hand he says that *all* were relieved when Kassandros had him eliminated (105.3–4), which can only mean that all were equally affected. The false impression can be explained either through Diodoros' having substantially abbreviated his source, Hieronymos of Kardia, or as a deliberate attempt by Antigonos' court historian, Hieronymos, to give a false impression. It cannot represent the facts.

33. Diodoros 19.105.3 (death of Alexander); 20.19.2 (Polemaios).

34. Diodoros 20.20, 28 (Herakles). Diodoros' text at 28.1 must be slightly adjusted (from the unknown "Stymphaia" to "Tymphaia"), but the change must be correct. In 303, when Polyperchon is mentioned by Diodoros for the last time (20.103.6–7), he was still loyal to Kassandros.

35. Diodoros 20.37.

36. Diodoros 20.37.2. On Ptolemaios in Greece see Seibert, *Ptolemaios*, 185f.

37. Diodoros 20.19.3; see Welles, *RC*, no. 1, for Antigonos' self-presentation.

38. Diodoros 20.45.1.

39. Diodoros 20.45–46; Plutarch, *Demetrios* 8f.

40. Diodoros 20.100.2–6; 102–103; Plutarch, *Demetrios* 23–26 (events); *IG* IV² pt. 1, 68 (= *StV* 3,446); Moretti, *ISE* 1,44 (league charter).
41. Diodoros 20.106.2.
42. Diodoros 20.106.3–109.7.
43. Diodoros 20.110.4.
44. Diodoros 20.110–111.2.
45. On the battle see Plutarch, *Demetrios* 28f.

2. AFTER IPSOS

1. On the distribution after Ipsos see Seibert, *Diadochen*, 155f. There is no good reason to return to the old theory of Wilamowitz (*Antigonos von Karystos*, 198) that Pleistarchos received a large kingdom in southern Asia Minor including both Karia and Kilikia. The literary sources mention only Kilikia (Plutarch, *Demetrios* 31.4–5), whereas not precisely datable documentary sources give evidence for his rule in Karia. Since Pleistarchos was driven out of Kilikia already in 299, Robert's solution (*Sinuri*, 55f., no. 44), that he ruled in Karia after this date, is convincing, even if the area he ruled—doubtless granted him by Lysimachos—was rather larger than Robert had reckoned. Evidence from Hyllarima (*Ist. Mitt. 25*, 1975, 339), Tralleis, Herakleia-by-Latmos and Euromos shows him ruling at all these places (Merkelbach, *ZPE* 16, 1975, 163f.; Amyzon, however, should be deleted). A Pleistarchos son of Pleistarchos from Olba is mentioned as *epimeletes* in an inscription, which on autopsy I would date to the early third century B.C., from Kanytelleis in Kilikia (Maier, *Griechische Mauerbauinschriften*, no. 78, however, dates the inscription to the late third century or second century). Did the son of Pleistarchos perhaps serve Seleukos after his father had been expelled from the area, or is it a different contemporary?
2. Plutarch, *Demetrios* 30f.(Athens and Demetrios); *IG* 2²,641, cf. Marmor Parium (*FgrHist* 239) B27 (Athens and Kassandros); Plutarch, *Demetrios* 31 (Korinth?); Pausanias 10.18.7, 34.2–3 (Olympiodoros); Porphyrios (*FgrHist* 260) F3.5 (death of Philip at Elateia in 297); Diodoros 21.2 (Kerkyra).
3. Justin 16.1.1–7; Diodoros 21.7.
4. Plutarch, *Demetrios* 31–32(Stratonike, Arsinoe, Ptolemais); Plutarch, *Pyrrhos* 4 (Antigone). On the marriages in detail see Seibert, *Historische Beiträge*, 30f., 48f., 74, 76.
5. Plutarch, *Demetrios* 31.4–32.3, 20 (Lysimachos at Soloi).
6. Cf. note 1.
7. Plutarch, *Pyrrhos* 5 (Pyrrhos); Plutarch, *Demetrios* 33–34 (Athens). On the chronology of events at Athens cf. Habicht, *Untersuchungen*, 1f.
8. Plutarch, *Demetrios* 35 (Demetrios in the Peloponnese), 36; *Pyrrhos* 6, cf. Justin 16.1.5–19 (Pyrrhos); cf. Diodoros 21.12 (Lysimachos and the Getai); Plutarch, *Pyrrhos* 7.2 (Thessaly).
9. Plutarch, *Demetrios* 36–37; Justin 16.1.8–19.

3. KING DEMETRIOS

1. Strabo 9.5.15 (C436); Plutarch, *Demetrios* 53.
2. Plutarch, *Demetrios* 39–40; Diodoros 21.14, cf. Gullath, *Untersuchungen*, 186f.
3. Plutarch, *Demetrios* 39.3, cf. Diodoros 21.12.
4. Plutarch, *Demetrios* 43. Plutarch gives the numbers as ninety-eight thousand infantry and twelve thousand cavalry, but they are doubtless exaggerated.
5. The large private tombs at Lefkadhia (Petsas, *Ho taphos ton Lefkadion*) and the richly appointed houses at Pella (Petsas, *Pella*) are doubtless only a few examples of the investment of private wealth dating from the late fourth and the third centuries B.C. Such finds, however, are fairly isolated—except for the "royal tombs" at Verghina. It would in any case be expected that if there was a more extravagant way of life anywhere in Macedonia, then it must have been in that area where the rich finds have been made, especially Pella, Aigai and the old Macedonian settlement area on the Bermios. It may not be legitimate to extrapolate a similar development for other areas, at least on a large scale. On Demetrios' personal extravagance see Plutarch, *Demetrios* 41.
6. Plutarch, *Demetrios* 42.
7. Plutarch, *Demetrios* 41.
8. Plutarch, *Demetrios* 41; *Pyrrhos* 7, cf. 8.1 (Pantauchos); Plutarch, *Demetrios* 43 (Edessa).
9. Plutarch, *Demetrios* 44; *Pyrrhos* 11.
10. Plutarch, *Demetrios* 45.1 (Kassandreia), 46.1–2; *SEG* 28, 1978, no. 60 (= Shear, *Kallias of Sphettos*) (Greece and Athens). On the chronology and the interpretation of the inscription see Shear, op. cit.; Habicht, *Untersuchungen*, 45f., whose results are incorporated here. Plutarch, *Demetrios* 46.3–52 (Demetrios' end).

4. INTERREGNUM

1. Plutarch, *Pyrrhos* 12.1 (division). The later ruler lists are in Eusebios, *Chronographia* (ed. Schöne), vol. 1; cf. Porphyrios (*FgrHist* 260) F3. 7f.; Plutarch, *Pyrrhos* 12.6–7; Justin 16.3.1; Pausanias 1.10.2 (expulsion of Pyrrhos).
2. Plutarch, *Pyrrhos* 12.4–5. Eusebios names Pyrrhos among the rulers of Thessaly, where he assigns him a reign of three years and four months (*Chron.* 1).
3. Plutarch, *Pyrrhos* 12.6. On Paionia see Polyainos 4.12.3; Merker, *Balkan Studies* 6, 1965, 48.
4. Friendly relations with Athens (cf. Habicht, *Untersuchungen*, 79f.), with Elateia in Phokis (*Syll³* 361), with Thebes (Robert, *OMS* 1,171f.) and with Oropos (*Syll³* 373), as well as with Aitolia, where a city was renamed Lysimacheia (cf. *RE* s.v. Lysimacheia) are explicitly known.
5. Pausanias 1.10.4; Appian, *Syriake* 64 (marriage); on the Thracian kingdom see Michailov, *Athenaeum* 39, 1961, 33f.; Danov, *ANRW* 2, 7, 21f.; Diodoros 20.29.1 (Lysimacheia).
6. Justin 17.1, cf. Pausanias 1.10.3–5; Memnon of Herakleia (*FgrHist*

434) F 1.5.6–7, cf. Heinen, *Untersuchungen,* 3f.; short mise-au-point in Seibert, *Diadochen,* 165f., 192.

7. Memnon of Herakleia F1.7–8.3; Justin 17.2.1–5. On Keraunos see Heinen, *Untersuchungen,* 3f. On the children of Eurydike see Beloch, *Griechische Geschichte,* vol. 4, pt. 2,178f.

8. Memnon of Herakleia F1.8.4–6 (sea battle); cf. Justin 24.1 (peace with Antiochos); Pompeius Trogus, Prologus 24 (Ptolemaios and Monounios); Justin 17.2.13–15, 24.1.8 (Pyrrhos); Justin 24.2.1–3.9 (Arsinoe). On the events and the chronology see Heinen, *Untersuchungen,* 54f.

9. Justin 24.4f.; Pausanias 10.19.5f. Cf. Heinen, *Untersuchungen,* 88f.; Nachtergael, *Galates,* 126f.

10. Porphyrios (*FgrHist* 260) F3.10. Antipatros received this nickname because his six weeks (forty days) in office are the traditional length of the summer winds (*etesiai*).

11. Justin 24.5.12f.; Porphyrios F3.10. Whether Sosthenes may be identified with Lysimachos' *strategos,* who is known from Priene (*OGIS* 12 = *Inschr. Priene* 14, line 12, where the name is restored) is very uncertain. If, however, he returned with Lysimachos to Macedonia, this fact could help to explain his support from the soldiers, many of whom doubtless had served Lysimachos, as well as give a reason why Justin, apparently contradicting himself, once calls him *unus ex principibus* and once *ignobilis* (24.5.12, 13). He certainly did not belong to any of the families that had thus far ruled in Macedonia.

12. Porphyrios F3.10–11.

13. Polyainos 4.18, 6.7.

V. The Antigonids

1. Consolidation

1. Polybios 18.11.4–13.

2. Antigonos counted the years of his reign from the death of his father, although he himself did not rule in Macedonia until 277/76. Cf. Chambers, *AJPh* 75, 1954, 385f.

3. Polybios 18.37, esp. 8–9.

4. The shortage of good sources has stimulated the imagination of many historians. Tarn, in *Antigonos Gonatas,* still widely regarded as a standard work, speculated so wildly that his book is one of the most unreliable in the whole of Greek history. It is not possible to remark ơn every unfounded statement here; see the carefully formulated chapters of Will, *Histoire Politique*[2], and the relevant chapters of Walbank in *CAH*[2] 7.1 and in Hammond, *History,* vol. 3.

5. Justin 24.3.10, cf. Longega, *Arsinoe II,* 69f.

6. Justin 25.1.1 (the peace); Vita Arati (Westermann, *Biogr. Graec.*) 53, 60 (marriage); Diogenes Laertius 2.141 (battle at Lysimacheia).

7. See Bagnall, *Administration,* 159f.; on Ainos see Buraselis, *Hellenistisches Makedonien,* 127f.

8. See Robert, *OMS* 2, 144–45.

9. Polyainos 4.6.18.

10. Plutarch, *Pyrrhos* 26.2–7, cf. Lévêque, *Pyrrhos,* 557f.

11. Justin 26.2.9–12.

12. Sources in Tscherikower, *Städtegründungen*, 2–3, but see Robert *OMS* 2, 144–45. Antigoneia in Chaonia (Tscherikower no. 15), attributed to Antigonos by many historians, was more probably founded by Pyrrhos and named after his wife, Antigone; so Hammond, *Epirus*, 278–79.

13. Texts and discussion in Herzog and Klaffenbach, *Asylieurkunden*; cf. Giovannini, *Archaia Makedonia* 2, 1977, 40f.; cf. below, chap. 6.2.

14. *SEG* 12, 311 (older text in *Syll³* 459).

15. Plutarch, *Pyrrhos* 26.6.

16. See e.g. the report of Manolis Andronikos in Hatzopoulos and Loukopoulos, eds., *Philip of Macedon* 188f. His opinion that the tumulus was built for Antigonos' own grave (204) was not confirmed by further excavation.

17. Andronikos, Makaronas, Moutsopoulos, and Bakalakis, *To Anaktoro tes Verghinas*; Andronikos, *Verghina*; but see also Andronikos, *Studies in Mediterranean Archaeology* 13.

18. The main sources are the anonymous *Lives* of Aratos of Soloi in *Biographoi* (Westermann), esp. 60; for Zeno, Persaios and Philonides see Diogenes Laertius 7.6–9 (but Persaios was not just a literary figure: in 243 he was commandant in Korinth; Plutarch, *Aratos* 23). There is no evidence in the sources for a visit by the wandering preacher Bion of Olbia (Borysthenes) in Pella, such as Tarn, *Antigonos Gonatas*, 233f., assumes ("the most important figure . . . from the point of view of philosophy"). A meeting in Athens and Bion's death in Chalkis are the only points of contact Diogenes Laertius 4.54 mentions. See also Kindstrand, *Bion of Borysthenes*, 14f., who follows Tarn.

19. Plutarch, *Pyrrhos* 26.8f.

20. Justin 24.1.1–7, but without a precise date.

21. *Syll³* 434–35; *StV* 3,476. The chronology and the significance of the various events connected with the Chremonidean War remain uncertain and are much discussed: see Heinen, *Untersuchungen*, 95f.; Habicht, *Untersuchungen*, 95f.; Walbank in Hammond, *History*, 3,276f.; Will, *Histoire politique*, 1²,219f.

22. There is an excellent discussion of Ptolemaic foreign policy in Will, *Histoire politique*, 1²,153f.

23. Pausanias 1.7.3.

24. Cf. Buraselis, *Hellenistisches Makedonien*, 60f. and 180f.

25. Trogus, Prologus 26; Plutarch, *Agis* 3.7.

26. On the Macedonian occupation of the Piraeus see Habicht, *Untersuchungen*, 95f.

27. Krateros, son of Phila and Alexander's marshall Krateros, is mentioned first in 281 (Epikuros, ed. Arrighetti, no. 42). His brotherly loyalty is praised by Plutarch (*De Am. Frat.* 15) as exemplary; on the keys of Korinth see Plutarch, *Aratos* 23.4.

28. Polybios 2.41.10.

29. Detailed discussion of this complex matter is in Habicht, *Studien*, 13f.

30. Cf. Flacelière, *Aitoliens*, 179f.

31. On this see Urban, *Wachstum*, 5f.

32. Plutarch, *Moralia* 545B; Athenaios 209e, cf. Buraselis, *Hellenistisches Makedonien*, 141f.

33. Justin 28.1.2; Josephos, *C. Apionem* 1.206, cf. Seibert, *Historische Beiträge*, 34f.

34. Pausanias 3.6.6; Eusebius, *Chron.* 2,120 (ed. Schöne) (Museion garrison); *Syll*³ 454 (Herakleitos of Athmonon); *SEG* 25, 155 (Athenians as garrison troops), cf. Habicht, *Studien*, 16f.

35. Plutarch, *Aratos* 2.4f. with Urban, *Wachstum*, 13f. (Argos and Sikyon); Polybios 10.22.2; Plutarch, *Philopoimen* 1.1–2 (Megalopolis).

36. On the chronology of Alexandros' revolt see Urban, *Wachstum*, 13f.; whether Alexandros took the title *basileus*, which seemed to be attested for him in an inscription from Eretria, is now made doubtful by a new reading by Dr. R. Billows. The dating phrase of the Suda *basileuontos Alexandrou* (s.v. Euphorion) is not sufficient in itself to prove the use of the title.

37. Cf. Buraselis, *Hellenistisches Makedonien*, 119f.; Walbank in Hammond, *History*, 3,587f.

38. Plutarch, *Aratos* 17.

39. Plutarch, *Aratos* 17–24.

40. Plutarch, *Aratos* 24.3.

41. Polybios 2.43.9, cf. 9.34.6.

42. Justin 26.2.9–11 (Chremonidean War); *SEG* 12, 311 (= *Syll*³ 459) (Demetrios' letters to Harpalos in 248/47). I believe I have disproved the common assertion that Demetrios ruled jointly with Antigonos and used the royal title in *Archaia Makedonia* 2, 1977, 115.

43. A discussion of these events is in Urban, *Wachstum*, 63f. A good general account is in Will, *Histoire politique*, 1², 343f.

44. Justin 28.1–4. Not all contradictions in Justin's account are explained by Cabanes, *L'Épire*, 93f., who, on the one hand, seems likely to be right when he places Stratonike's return to Antiochos before 246. On the other hand, Demetrios is called *regem*, which would only be correct after 239; but Chryseis must have been with Demetrios by 239 since Philip was born in 238 (this excludes Seibert's solution, *Historische Beiträge*, 38–39, putting the marriage with Chryseis after Phthia's death). The solution presented in the text tries to account both for the source problem and for Macedonian traditions about these things. Of the older literature see Dow and Edson, *HSPh* 28, 1937, 127f., who make it clear that Philip was certainly son of Chryseis. New doubts, also not convincing, are in Bohec, *REG* 94, 1981, 34f.

45. Cf. *IG* 2².1299, where her name is missing from a context where it might be expected in 234 (?): cf. Tarn, *CQ* 18, 17f.; Hoffmann, *RE* s.v. Phthia no. 8.

46. Justin 28.3.2–8; Polyainos 8.5.2. On the republic the best account is in Cabanes, *L'Épire*, 198f.

47. Polybios 2.2.5.

48. Trogus, Prologus 28; cf. Papazoglu, *Central Balkan Tribes*, 144f.

2. A NEW BEGINNING

1. Justin 28.3.14, cf. Flacelière, *Aitoliens*, 254f.

2. Polybios 20.5.7–11, cf. Flacelière, *Aitoliens*, 279f.

3. Plutarch, *Aratos* 34; Pausanias 2.8.6, cf. Habicht, *Studien*, 79f. Rob-

ert, *REG* 94, 1981, 359 n. 101, also concludes that Diogenes was an Athenian.

4. Polybios 2.44.6.

5. Plutarch, *Aemilius Paullus* 8. Detailed discussion is in Dow and Edson, *HSPh* 48, 1937, 127f., who plead for ca. 226, but their argumentation leaves great uncertainties.

6. Justin 28.3.14; cf. Frontinus, *Strategemata* 2.6.5; Fine, *TAPhA* 63, 1932, 126f. Bylazora became Macedonian again only in 217: Polybios 5.97.1. The Thessalians became members of the Hellenic League, for which the first evidence comes from 222 at Sellasia (*StV* 3,507); the inscription (Gallis, *AAA* 5, 1972, 277, cf. Robert, *BE* 1973, 240, with a new reading by Habicht) certainly belongs to the period before the refounding of the league by the Romans in 195 because of the dating by the secretary (*grammateus*) and because of the letter forms; therefore it proves the existence of the league in the late third century B.C. The Thessalians are also mentioned as *adscripti* to the Peace of Phoinike in 205 (Livy 29.12.14). It is therefore reasonable to conclude that it was Doson who refounded the league after 229.

7. Justin 28.3.11–16 (though the details are improbable).

8. Justin 29.1.2; Polybios 4.24.7, 87.6.

9. Trogus, Prologus 28. The text is corrupt, and because of the brevity of expression it seems possible the verb *subiecit*, which refers to Thessaly, was also (wrongly) applied to Karia. See also Polybios 20.5.11.

10. The documents: Crampa, *Labraunda*, vol. 3, pt. 1, nos. 4, 5, 6, 7 with pp. 123f. (Labraunda); *IBM* 3,441, cf. Holleaux, *Études* 4,146f.; Crampa, *Labraunda*, vol. 3, pt. 1, 93f. (Iasos). It is often stated on the authority of *Inschr. Priene* 37 lines 137 and 141 that Macedonian influence was also dominant in Priene. But Wilamowitz's objection (*SB Berlin* 1906, 41f., mentioned in *Inschr. Priene*, 309) to the restoration printed there, which implies removing Philip's name, seems decisive. The Antigonos mentioned on the stone is probably Monophthalmos. Recent accounts of the Karian expedition are by Will, *Histoire politique*, 1², 356f.; Walbank, *CAH²* 7, 1, 459f.; Walbank in Hammond, *History*, 3, 343f., cf. Robert, *Amyzon*, 147f.

11. Polybios 2.48f.; Plutarch, *Aratos* 38.11, cf. the detailed source criticism in Urban, *Wachstum*, 117f.

12. This relationship emerges from their participation in Doson's Hellenic League. Sources in *StV* 3,507; cf. Walbank, *Commentary* 1,256 *ad* Polybios 2.54.4.

13. Polybios 2.51.2, cf. Urban, *Wachstum*, 135f. (Achaia and Ptolemaios). The great monument to the Ptolemies at Thermon must belong to this period and provides evidence for Aitolian policy: *IG* 9.1².56 = *ISE* 2,86. Ptolemy III Euergetes even received a cult in Athens in 224/23; cf. Habicht, *Studien*, 105f.

14. Polybios 18.14 (Philip II), 2.70.7, 5.9.10, cf. 9.36.2–5 (Doson); cf. Welwei, *RhM* 110, 1967, 306f.

15. Polybios 2.54.1–5.

16. Polybios 2.54.6f.; Plutarch, *Aratos* 45.8–9.

17. Because of Polybios 2.54.3 the creation of the Hellenic League is usually placed in winter 224/23 (e.g. Schmitt, *StV* 3,507). This could indeed be right, but in Polybios 2.54.3 it is only the Achaians who vote

Antigonos' position, which is not evidence on which the founding of the league can be based. Moreover, in 223 the only allies mentioned are Macedonia and Achaia, and since the league was allegedly created to fight against Kleomenes, that is remarkable; hence 223/22 seems rather more probable.

18. Sources and discussion of formal aspects are in *StV* 3,507.

19. The main source is Polybios 2.65f., cf. Walbank, *Commentary* 1.272–87.

20. Tacitus, *Annales* 3.43.4 (Denthalietis); Polybios 4.24.4–8 (Sparta perhaps in Hellenic League); Polybios 2.70.1, with Walbank, *Commentary* 1.287–88, cf. Oliva, *Sparta*, 263f.

21. Polybios 28.19.3, 30.29.3; Plutarch, *Kleomenes* 16.7 (Antigoneia), cf. Polybios 2.70.5, 5.9.10; Plutarch, *Aratos* 45.3; *IG* 4².1,589 = *ISE* 1,46 (Epidauros); *IG* 5.1,1122 (Geronthrai); *IG* 5.2,299 (cf. *SEG* 11, 1089) (Mantineia).

22. Polybios 4.6.4, cf. 87.8.

23. Polybios 2.70.6–7; Plutarch, *Kleomenes* 30.

24. Plutarch, *Aratos* 46.2–3.

25. Polybios 4.87.7–8.

26. Polybios 7.11.8.

27. Justin 29.1.10; Polybios 4.29, 66, 5.97.

28. Crampa, *Labraunda*, vol. 3, pt. 1. nos. 5, 7 (Karia); Polybios 4.5.8 (Messenia).

29. Polybios 4.25, cf. Fine, *AJPh* 61, 1940, 129f.; Will, *Histoire politique* 2²,69f.

30. Polybios 4.29f., cf. Walbank, *Philip V*, 22f.

31. Polybios 2.65.4 (Sellasia); 4.19.7 (220). On the Second Illyrian War see Gruen, *Hellenistic World*, 368f.

32. Polybios 5.2.1–3.

33. Polybios 5.2.8.

34. Cf. Errington, *Historia* 16, 1967, 19f.

35. Polybios 5.97.1 (Bylazora); 100.1–8 (Phthiotic Thebes); *Syll³* 543, cf. Habicht, *Archaia Makedonia* 1, 1970, 273f., for the date (Larissa); Polybios 5.101.1–2 (Skerdilaidas).

36. Polybios 5.103.7, cf. *StV* 3,520 (Peace of Naupaktos); Polybios 109.1f. (*lemboi*). A discussion with recent literature is in Will, *Histoire Politique* 2²,75f.

3. The New Activism

1. On Illyrian expansion in the third century B.C. see Dell, *Historia* 16, 1967, 344f.; Cabanes, *L'Épire*, 208f.

2. Main sources for the Illyrian Wars: Polybios 2.2–12; Appian, *Illyrike* 7 (17), 8 (22); Dio Cassius 12 frg. 49 (229); Polybios 3.16, 18–19; Appian, *Illyrike* 8 (22–24); Dio Cassius 12 frg. 53. Most recent discussion by Gruen, *Hellenistic World*, 359f.

3. Livy 22.33.3, 5.

4. Polybios 5.110.

5. The main source is Polybios 7.9.1–17, cf. *StV* 3,528.

6. Livy 24.40.

7. Polybios 3.19.9.

8. Livy 27.30.13, 29.12.13 (Atintanes); Livy 29.12.3, 13 (Parthinoi and Dimallon); Polybios 8.13–14 (Lissos); Polybios 8.14b (Dassaretis).

9. Sources are in *StV* 3,536; most recent discussion is in Gruen, *Hellenistic World*, 17f.

10. Livy 26.25.1–3, 8, 15. The site of the Dardanian town Sintia, which he took, is not known. Perhaps the text is corrupt; cf. Papazoglu, *Central Balkan Tribes*, 152.

11. Livy 27.32.10–33.1, cf. Justin 29.4.6 (209); Livy 28.8.14 (208).

12. Sources are in *StV* 3,543.

13. Polybios 15.21.3–23 (Kios, Chalkedon, Lysimacheia); Strabo 12.6.3 (Myrleia); Polybios 15.24.1–3 (Thasos), 18.2.4 (Perinthos); Livy 31.29.4 (Aitolians and Rome).

14. So Polybios 15.23.6.

15. On Krete see Effenterre, *La Crète*, 221f.; Holleaux, *Études*,4,124f.; Errington, *Philopoemen*, 27f.

16. Cf. Will, *Histoire politique*, 2^2,112f.

17. Polybios 16.18–19, 22a, 39; Josephos, *Jewish Antiquities*, 12.130f.; Justin 31.1–2; Jerome, *In Danielem* 11.13f., cf. Will, *Histoire politique* 2^2,118–19.

18. Habicht, *AM* 72, 1957, 253f. no. 64; Polybios 16.2.9 (Samos), 16.15.5–6 (Miletos); Livy 31.16.4 (Maroneia and Ainos). The question of the so-called Secret Treaty against Ptolemy is one of the most disputed problems of hellenistic history: see Schmitt, *Antiochos III*, 237f.; against the treaty see Errington, *Athenaeum* 49, 1971, 336f.; idem, *Epigraphica Anatolica* 8, 1986, 5; also Will, *Histoire politique*, 2^2,114f.; Gruen, *Hellenistic World*, 387f.

19. Polybios 16.2–9 (Chios), 16.10.1, 15 (Lade), 16.1 (Pergamon), 24 (Bargylia). The order of events is very uncertain; cf. Walbank, *Commentary* 2,497f.

20. Polybios 18.44.4, cf. Walbank, *Commentary* 2,611 (Lemnos). Of the other islands we can name Andros, Paros, Kythnos (Livy 31.15.8) and perhaps Imbros (cf. Livy 33.30.11).

21. Polybios 16.34.5, 18.6.2.

22. Polybios 16.12, 24.1, 18.44.4 (Iasos, Euromos, Pedasa, Bargylia); Livy 33.18.22; Polybios 30.31.6, cf. Walbank, *Commentary* 3, 457–58. (Stratonikeia); Errington, *Epigraphica Anatolica* 8, 1986, 1f. (renaming of Euromos).

23. Polybios 16.11.1; Polyainos 4.18 (Knidos and Prinassos); *Syll*^{3} 572 (Nisyros), cf. Livy 33.18, from which further Macedonian attacks on Rhodian possessions may be assumed.

24. Polybios 16.24.

25. Polybios 16.29–34; Livy 31.16.3–18.9.

26. Livy 31.2.3.

27. Livy 31.6–8.6, 14.2.

28. Polybios 16.27.2–5.

29. Livy 31.15.6f. On Athens at this time see Habicht, *Studien*, 142f.

30. Pausanias 1.36.5f.; *ISE* 1,33.

31. Livy's phrase *dum etiam Romanos haberent* (31.15.4) can be understood in this way.

32. Livy 30.26.3–4, 42.2, 31.3.3f.; Polybios 18.1.14.

33. Polybios 16.27.2–5.
34. Polybios 18.44 gives the main points.
35. *StV* 3,548.
36. Explicitly in the case of Achaia: Livy 32.19f. (autumn 198).
37. On the events of the war the main sources are: Polybios 18; Livy 31.22.4–47.3, 32.4.1–6, 9.6–25.12, 32–40, 33.1–21.5, 24–25, 27f.
38. Cf. Polybios 18.44 with Walbank, *Commentary* 2, 609–12.
39. Polybios 18.37.8–9.
40. On the disputed question of whether the conditions of peace were extended by a treaty of alliance see Gruen, *CSCA* 6, 1973, 123f., who rejects this possibility.

4. IN THE SHADOW OF ROME

1. On Antiochus in Asia Minor see Schmitt, *Antiochus III*, 262f.; on his and the Aitolians' relationship with Rome see Badian, *Studies*, 112f.; one new general account is in *CAH²* vol. 7, pt. 2.
2. Polybios 18.48.3–4; cf. Livy 33.35.2–6. On this advice see Gruen, *CSCA* 6, 1973, 123f.
3. Livy 34.26.10.
4. Livy 35.12.10–14, 39.28.6.
5. Livy 35.31.5f.
6. Livy 36.10.10, 39.23.10.
7. Details are in e.g. Walbank, *Philip V*, 219.
8. Livy 39.24–26.
9. Livy 39.27.10 (189); 23.13, 24.9 (186/85), 27–29.2 (Thessalonike), 33.4, 34 (184); Polybios 23.3; Livy 39.53.10 (183).
10. Livy 33.19.1–5 (197), 31.28.1–3 (200), 33f.
11. Livy 37.7.8–16 (190), 38.40–41, esp. 40.8 (Vulso); Polybios 22.13 (Maroneia).
12. Livy 39.27.10.
13. Polybios 22.14.12; Livy 39.35.4 (Amadokos); Diodoros 32.15.5 (Teres: the date is uncertain, but the marriage fits Philip's policies better than Perseus'; for the opposite view see Seibert, *Historische Beiträge*, 44); Livy 39.24.3–4; Polybios 23.10.4–5, cf. Livy 40.3.3–4 (population policy); Polybios 23.8.3–7; Livy 39.53.12–16 (campaign of 183); Livy 40.21–22 (campaign of 181).
14. Polybios 21.13.3.
15. Livy 40.57–58 (attack); 40.5.10 (Perseus).
16. This interpretation colours the whole of Polybios' account and that of those writers who follow him (in particular Livy). It is rejected almost unanimously by modern historians.
17. Polybios 23.10.9–10, cf. 5.9.4.
18. Cf. Livy 41.24.4–5.
19. Polybios 23.1–2, 3.4–9 (Demetrios in Rome); Livy 40.5f., 20.3f. (later developments). A classic discussion is by Edson, *HSPh* 46, 1935, 191f.; a more probable reconstruction is by Gruen, *GRBS* 15, 1974, 221f.
20. Livy 40.58.9.
21. Polybios 22.18.2–3; Livy 42.13.5, 40.5, 41.11; cf. Meloni, *Perseo* 61f.

(Abrupolis); Livy 42.29.12, 51.10; Polybios 30.17 (Kotys); Livy 42.67.4f. (Autlesbis).

22. Polybios 25.6.2–6; Livy 41.19.4–11.

23. Livy 41.23.12, whose statement is clearly tendentious against Perseus.

24. *Syll*[3] 636, cf. Daux, *Delphes*, 303f.; Giovannini, *Archaia Makedonia* 1, 1970, 147f.

25. Polybios 25.3.

26. Polybios 25.4.8–10; Livy 42.12.3–4.

27. Livy 41.23–24.

28. Livy 41.22.4–8 (Dolopia and Delphi), 42.12.5 (Boiotia).

29. Livy 42.11–13; Appian, *Makedonike* 11.1–2.

30. Livy 42.10.11.

31. The outbreak of the Third Macedonian War is controversial. It seems certain that Perseus did not seek war (see e.g. Gruen, *Hellenistic World*, 403f.), but the fundamental character of the Roman decision suggests that less lofty and honourable motives were decisive than Gruen in the end chooses. Cf. Harris, *War and Imperialism*, 227f., whose view here seems more realistic.

32. At least Chalkis, Athens and Abdera suffered under C. Lucretius Gallus and L. Hortensius: Livy 43.7.5–11 (Chalkis), 6.1–3 (Athens), 4.5–13 (Abdera), cf. 43.17.2.

33. Livy 44.33–46, 45.4–8; Plutarch, *Aemilius Paullus* 12–27.

5. AFTER THE STORM

1. Livy 45.18.

2. Diodoros 31.40a, 32.15; Zonaras 9.28; Livy, *Periochae* 48–50.

3. Perhaps correctly doubted by Gruen, *Hellenistic World*, 431f.

4. A general survey is in Papazoglu, *ANRW* II, 7, 1, 302f.

VI. The Macedonian State

1. KING AND STATE

1. For pretenders other than Andriskos see Zonaras 9.28; Livy, *Periocha* 53; Eutropius 4.15; Varro, *De re rustica* 2.4.1–2.

2. On fictitious descent from the Argeadai see Errington in Badian, ed., *Alexandre le Grand*, 153f., for references and discussion. For the Ptolemies, see Robert, *Amyzon*, 1.162 n. 31.

3. Cf. Ritter, *Diadem und Königsherrschaft*. The so-called diadem that was found in grave II at Verghina is not a diadem: cf. Ritter, *AA* 1984, 105f.

4. Plutarch, *Demetrios* 41–42 (Demetrios); Diodoros 16.3.1 (Philip II); Polybios 5.27.6 (Philip V).

5. On the whole question of the army assembly see Errington, *Chiron* 8, 1978, with further literature; see also above, chap. 1.1 n. 6.

6. Demosthenes 1.4, 18. 235.

7. See below, pp. 243f.

8. Ailian, *Varia Historia* 2.20.

9. Herodotos 5.21.

10. Satyros in Athenaios 13.557d. Cf. Tronson, *JHS* 104, 1984, 116f.

11. A systematic listing of these marriages is in Seibert, *Historische Beiträge*.

12. Cf. *SEG* 12.311 (= *Syll³* 459) (Demetrios to Harpalos); *ISE* 110 (Philip V to Archippos), 111 (Andronikos), 112 (Nikolaos and Doules); see below, chap. 6.2.

13. *IG* 10.2, 1028; *ISE* 111 (Thessalonike); Plutarch, *Moralia* 178F (Philip II).

14. Herodotos 5.17 (Alexander I); Diodoros 16.8.6 (Philip II and Krenides); Livy 39.24.2 (Philip V). The study of Macedonian coins is not far advanced. Until a certain chronology has been established, a systematic historical treatment is unfortunately impossible for long periods. The ordering of the first great systematic collection, by Gaebler, *Die antiken Münzen von Makedonia und Paionia*, faces growing criticism: see e.g. Rider, *Le monnayage d'argent*, Boehringer, *Chronologie*, 99f. For the brickworks (near Florina) see Bakalakis, *Praktika* 1934, 104–13.

15. Livy 39.24.2; Ps. Aristoteles *Oikonomika* 2.22 (1350a), cf. below, p. 235.

16. *StV* 2.186 lines 22–23, 231 lines 9f.; Livy 45.29.14 (timber), cf. Meiggs, *Timber*, 126f.; Livy 45.29.11 (mines).

17. Durrbach, *Choix*, 48 (Aristoboulos), sees him, however, with the older literature, as buyer; but Macedonia was shortly afterwards (227) able to donate 100,000 bushels of grain to Rhodes (Polybios 5.89.7), and Perseus, to whom Thessaly was no longer available, had collected enormous amounts before the Third Macedonian War (Livy 42.12.8). Hence Macedonia seems likely, particularly when it controlled Thessaly as well, to have produced a sizable grain surplus. On Thessaly see *SEG* 34, 1984, 558; the text with English translation is also in *JRS* 74, 1984, 36, cf. *JRS* 75, 1985, 25.

18. Livy 45.29.4, cf. 39.24.2.

19. Plutarch, *Aemilius Paullus* 20.6.

20. Herodotos 5.22; Justin 7.2.14 (Alexander I); Solinus 9.16 (p. 65 Mommsen) (Archelaos); Diodoros 17.16.3; Arrian, *Anabasis* 1.11.1 (Dion). This festival may have been called *Basileia* in the third century B.C. under Gonatas, probably to honour Zeus Basileus: cf. *IG* 2^2 3779; Plutarch, *Alexander* 3.5; 4.5 (Philip's victories).

21. Dio Chrysostom 2.23 (Alexander); Suda s.vv. Hippokrates, Melanippides (Perdikkas); see above chap. 1.3 n. 37 (poets); Dio Chrysostom 13.30, cf. Diogenes Laertius 2.25 (Sokrates).

22. Diogenes Laertius 5.1 (Nikomachos); Athenaios 11.508e; Plato, *Epist.* 5 (Euphraios); Demosthenes 19.308 (Philip).

23. Plutarch, *Moralia* 14b, cf. Robert, *BE* 1984, 249.

24. Plutarch, *Alexander* 7.2f. (Aristoteles); on Philip see Cawkwell, *Philip*, 50f., with references.

25. Diogenes Laertius 2.141f. (Menedemos), 7.6f.; see above, chap. 5.1 n. 18.

26. Examples of Samos' epigrams are in *Anthologia Palatina* 6, 114–16; Photios, *Bibliotheka* 176, 35 = *FgrHist* 115 T 31 (Theopompos).

27. The fragments were collected by Jacoby in *FgrHist* 114 (Antipa-

tros),135–36 (the two Marsyai), 342 (Krateros), 133 (Nearchos), 139 (Aristoboulos), 154 (Hieronymos), 138 (Ptolemaios).

28. A selection of photographs of these objects is in Hatzopoulos and Loukopoulos, *Philip*; Andronikos, *Verghina*; see the exhibition catalogue, *Treasures of Ancient Macedonia* (Thessalonike); Petsas, *Lefkadhia*.

29. For references see below, chap. 7.2 n. 6.

30. SEG 12, 311 = *Syll³* 459 (Demetrios' letters); on the cult of Herakles and the Antigonids see Edson, *HSPh* 45, 1934, 213f.; Livy 42.51.2 (Athena Alkidemos).

31. *ISE* 111; on Macedonian cults in general see Baege, *De Macedonum sacris*, passim; Hammond, *History*, 2,184f.

32. Plutarch, *Alexander* 2.1 (Philip and Olympias); *Hesperia* 37, 1968, 220; *BCH* 95, 1971, 992 (Philip Arrhidaios and Alexander IV); Justin 24.3.9 (Arsinoe); Livy 44.45.15 (Perseus); *SEG* 12, 399 (Lemnos).

33. Herodotos 8.121.2 (Alexander); Solinus 9.16. (p. 65 Mommsen) (Archelaos). On the Amphiktyony in the fourth century B.C. see Roux, *L'Amphictionie*, passim; on the second century B.C. see Giovannini, *Archaia Makedonia* 1, 1970, 147f.; on Perseus see Plutarch, *Aemilius Paullus* 28.2.

34. Pausanias 5.20.8, cf. Griffith in Hammond, *History*, 2,691f. (Philippeion); Pausanias 6.16.3 (Doson and Philip V).

35. On Delos see Bruneau, *Recherches*, 545f., with complete references; on the League of the Islanders see Buraselis, *Hellenistisches Makedonien*, 60f.

36. Durrbach, *Choix*, 55; other Macedonians or Macedonian functionaries are known from Durrbach nos. 45, 47–49.

37. Lindian Temple Chronicle = *FgrHist* 532 F 38 and F 42.

38. *Die Inschriften von Stratonikeia* I (= *Inschriften griechischer Städte aus Kleinasien*, vol. 21), nos. 3 and 4.

39. Herzog-Klaffenbach, *Asylieurkunden* (Kos); Kern, *Inschr. Magnesia*, no. 47 (Magnesia); Holleaux, *Études*, 4,178f. (Teos).

40. Curtius 10.9.11–12 (Babylon); Livy 40.6.1–2 (Perseus).

41. *IG* 7.3055; on the oracle see Pausanias 9.39.5f., though his description is probably of procedures somewhat refined to suit visitors of the second century A.D.

2. ADMINISTRATION AND CITIES

1. Livy 45.29.1, 4.

2. See Giovannini, *Archaia Makedonia* 2, 1977, 465f., for the Antigonids.

3. On the Popular Assembly see Herzog and Klaffenbach, *Asylieurkunden*, no. 6 lines 22–23, from which a council can be inferred. On *epistates* and eponymous priests see Lazarides, *BCH* 85, 1961, 426f., nos. 1–3; *Syll²* 832; *Geras Keramopoullou*, 159f.; Herzog and Klaffenbach, *Asylieurkunden*, no. 6 (priest, line 20, archontes, line 32). One of the youngest documents from the period of the monarchy seems to mention a board of *politarchai* for the first time (Koukouli-Chrysanthaki, *Macedonian Studies Edson*, 229f.). Whether these extend or replace the otherwise-known officers is unclear. In the Roman period *politarchai* become the leading municipal officials in almost all cities; cf. Schuler, *CPh* 55, 1960, 90f.

4. Herzog and Klaffenbach, *Asylieurkunden*, no. 6 lines 36, 40, 43.

5. Giovannini, *Archaia Makedonia* 2, 465f., assumes the existence of a popular assembly also for Kassandreia, but only to create a parallel with a decree of Thessalonike (*IG* 10.2, 1028), which, however, shows clearly that a decision of the council claimed to represent the city; this happened also in Kassandreia: see Herzog and Klaffenbach, *Asylieurkunden*, no. 6 lines 1ff. (esp. line 8); no. 7 (Pella).

6. Amphipolis: see above, n. 5. Philippoi: unpublished fragments with excellent lettering of the fourth century B.C. were photographed and copied by Charles Edson in 1938. His notebooks are now deposited at the Institute for Advanced Study, Princeton; the fragments concerned are his numbers 585 and 588. An archon, apparently eponymous, is mentioned: see also Herzog and Klaffenbach, *Asylieurkunden*, no. 6, lines 35f. (*tamias, archon, strategoi*). Kassandreia: *Syll³* 332, 380; Herzog and Klaffenbach, *Asylieurkunden*, no. 6, lines 1ff. (priest, *strategoi, tamiai, nomophylakes*); Beroia: *ISE* 109 (priest); on the date see Errington, *Archaia Makedonia* 2, 1977, 115f. See also the Law of the Gymnasiarch, dating probably from shortly after the end of the monarchy, for other officials who probably, at least in part go back to the royal period: *SEG* 27, 261. Pella: Herzog and Klaffenbach, *Asylieurkunden*, no. 7 (priest, *tamiai*). Thessalonike: *IG* 10.2, no. 2 (priest, *tamiai*).

7. References as in n. 6 above.

8. Kassandreia and Philippoi: Herzog and Klaffenbach, *Asylieurkunden*, no. 6, lines 2, 15, 52. Beroia: *ISE* 109. Amphipolis: see n. 15 below.

9. Kassandreia and Philippoi: Herzog and Klaffenbach, *Asylieurkunden*, no. 6, lines 2, 63; Beroia: *SEG* 27, 261.

10. Livy 33.19.3.

11. Herzog and Klaffenbach, *Asylieurkunden*, no. 6, line 10, cf. 13 (Kassandreia); line 31, cf. 24–25, 30 (Amphipolis); lines 48–49, cf. 46–47; no. 7, lines 5–6, 12. Cf. Giovannini, *Archaia Makedonia* 2, 465f.

12. *SEG* 12, 311 (= *Syll³* 459).

13. *IG* 10.2, 3 = *ISE* 111.

14. *ISE* 112.

15. The earliest known *epistates* is Kallippos (*BCH* 85, 1961, 426f. no. 1), who stands alone; Spargeus is coupled with the priests Hermagoras (*Geras Keramopoullou*, 159f.) and Euainetos (*BCH* 85, 1961, 426f. no. 3). Also known are Aischylos (*Syll²* 832); Kleandros (*BCH* 85, 1961, 426f., no. 2) and Xenias, son of Orgeus (Herzog and Klaffenbach, *Asylieurkunden*, no. 6, lines 20–21).

16. *IG* 10.2 no. 2, lines 3–4, no. 3 (= *ISE* 111), line 23 (*epistates*), no. 1028 line 10 (*hypepistates*).

17. *ISE* 110.

18. Veligianni, *ZPE* 51, 1983, 105f. (= *SEG* 30, 1982). The attribution of the stone to an assumed period of rule by Ptolemaios Philadelphos over Gazoros is improbable. The stone also seems to give no reason for assuming a fully organized city-state (Veligianni, 112). No organs of a city-state are mentioned, although the rather roughly formulated text clearly tries to imitate decrees of city organs. Robert, *BE* 1984, 259, assumes that Plestis was only a private citizen.

19. Polybios 31.2.12.

20. Thrace: Alexandros of Lynkestis (Berve, *Alexanderreich*, vol. 2, no.

37); Memnon (Berve, *Alexanderreich*, vol. 2, no. 499); Zopyrion (Berve, *Alexanderreich*, vol. 2, no. 340); Onomastos (Polybios 22.13.3–7). Paionia: Didas (Livy 40.21.8).

21. Livy 39.24.2; for the fourth century B.C. see Ps. Aristoteles, *Oikonomika* 2.22 (1350a).

22. *Syll*[3] 332.

23. See n. 20 above.

24. See above, chap. 2.4, pp. 62f. (Philip and Alexander); p. 69 (Lamian War); chap. 5.2 and n. 6 (Doson).

25. *Syll*[3] 543; on the date of the first letter see Habicht, *Archaia Makedonia* 1, 1970, 273f.

26. Polybios 4.76.2.

27. See above chap. 3.4, p. 124 and chapter 4.1, p. 137 and n. 22 (Kassandros); chap. 5.1, p. 170 and n. 29 (Gonatas).

28. Plutarch, *Demetrios* 39.2.

29. Polybios 18.11.6.

3. THE MILITARY

1. See above, chap. 1.

2. Diodoros 16.3.1–2; Polyainos 4.2.10.

3. On Philip II and Alexander the Great the following modern studies are of fundamental importance: Berve, *Alexanderreich*, vol. 1 (more valuable for the collection of material than the too-systematized account); Griffith in Hammond, *History*, vol. 2; Milns in Badian, ed., *Alexandre le Grand*, 87f.

4. Diodoros 16.85.5.

5. Diodoros 17.17.3–5. For divergent sources and discussion see Berve, *Alexanderreich*, 1,177f.

6. Arrian, *Anabasis* 1.29.4.

7. Arrian, *Anabasis* 3.16.10; Diodoros 17.65.1; Curtius 5.1.40.

8. Diodoros 17.63.1.

9. Arrian, *Anabasis* 7.12.4.

10. Diodoros 18.16.11.

11. Diodoros 20.110.4.

12. Polybios 2.65.1–5; cf. Plutarch, *Aratos* 43.

13. Livy 33.4.4–5 (Kynoskephalai), 33.14.3–4 (Korinth), 33.18.9 (Karia), 33.19.3 (Dardanioi).

14. Livy 44.42.7, 42.41.3.

15. *ISE* 114 B[1] line 3.

16. *ISE* 114 B[1] lines 3–8. Polyainos 4.2.10, where, however, the sword is missing, and other names for individual items of equipment (except for sarissa and greaves [*knemides*]) are used. This could be explained either by Polyainos' using nontechnical vocabulary or by changes of name, which might reflect modifications in the equipment in the 150 years between the two references.

17. See the large collection of material by Launey, *Recherches*, 1,366f.

18. Launey, *Recherches*, 1,633f.

19. *StV* 3.498, 501, 502. On Kretan mercenaries see Launey, *Recherches*, 1,248f.

20. Polybios 4.53–55, 7.11.9.
21. Sources are in Berve, *Alexanderreich*, 1,104f. and 112f., who assumes a general division according to regions; but see Griffith in Hammond, *History*, 2,357f., 411f., 426f. who argues that regional units in the strict sense existed only for the cavalry.
22. Arrian, *Anabasis* 3.16.11.
23. Frontinus, *Strategemata* 4.1.6 (Philip); Polybios 12.19.6, cf. Arrian, *Anabasis* 7.23.3–4 (Alexander).
24. Arrian, *Anabasis* 2.10.2, 3.9.6, cf. Milns, *Historia* 20, 1971, 194; Griffith in Hammond, *History*, 2,419f.
25. This structure emerges from the army regulations from Amphipolis: *ISE* 114, where further literature, with interpretations which in part vary from mine, may be found. The new-style *lochoi* are not mentioned in the document, but in Philip V's letter to Archippos from 181 (*ISE* 110) the *tetrarchos* seems to be the immediate superior of the *lochagos*. The letter concerns some soldiers who were organized in a "first *lochos*."
26. Griffith's valuable research (in Hammond, *History*, 2,408f. and 705f.) has uncovered this development in the Macedonian army. It is not wholly certain but seems the most probable solution to an extremely difficult source problem. See also Milns in Badian, ed., *Alexandre le Grand*, 137f.
27. See above, chap. 3.
28. Esp. Plutarch, *Eumenes* 16.6, 18.2, cf. Launey, *Recherches*, 1,297f.
29. Polybios 2.66.5, 4.67.6; Livy 44.41.2; Plutarch, *Aemilius Paullus* 18.8. The purely descriptive name was also used in other hellenistic armies: Polybios 5.91.7 (Megalopolis), 30.25.5 (Antiochos IV); Plutarch, *Sulla* 19.4 (Pontos).
30. *ISE* 114 A^2 line 3, 110 line 13; Polybios 18.33.2.
31. On the development see Polybios 2.65.2–3 with Walbank, *Commentary*, 1,274–75.
32. Polybios 4.87.8.
33. Kougeas, *Hellenika* 7, 1934, 177f.; more accessible in Welles, *AJA* 42, 1938, 252f.
34. Arrian, *Anabasis* 7.23.3.
35. For the Seleukids see Cohen, *Seleucid Colonies*; for the Ptolemies Uebel, *Kleruchen Ägyptens*.
36. See Hauben, *Ancient Society* 6, 1975, 51f. (Philip); idem, *Ancient Society* 7, 1976, 79f. (Alexander).
37. Diodoros 19.69.4, cf. Hauben, *Ancient Society* 9, 1978, 47f.
38. Plutarch, *Demetrios* 43.
39. Cf. Buraselis, *Hellenistisches Makedonien*, 107f.; Walbank in Adams and Borza, *Philip II*, 213f.
40. Polybios 5.109.3; Livy 24.40.
41. Polybios 16.2.9.
42. Polybios 18.44.6.
43. Plutarch, *Aemilius Paullus* 9.3; Livy 44.28–29.

The Most Important Sources

Before the time of Philip II nobody had tried to write a history of Macedonia or even a history in which Macedonia played a central part. For the early period the modern historian of Macedonia is therefore forced to rely on casual mentions by ancient authors, whose main interests lay in quite other things—for instance Herodotos, who was writing about the struggle between Greeks and Persians in the fifth century B.C., or Thukydides, who mentions Macedonia in his *History of the Peloponnesian War*, or his continuator Xenophon in his *Hellenika*. Under the influence of the enormous Macedonian surge to power under Philip II historians began to show more interest. The first outsider to do so was probably Theopompos of Chios, a contemporary of Philip's, who constructed his *Philippika* as a broad account of Greek affairs but gave it a clear Macedonian emphasis, as the title suggests. Anaximenes of Lampsakos, also a contemporary of the first really important Macedonian ruler, wrote another *Philippika*. The earliest known historical work from Macedonia itself is the account Antipatros wrote of the Illyrian campaign of Perdikkas II; then came, perhaps under Alexander, the *History of Macedonia* by Marsyas of Pella, possibly imitating the model of Theopompos. Unfortunately these works are lost, and there is no way of telling precisely how much influence—if any—they had on surviving accounts, most of which were written much later.

Philip II and Alexander's spectacular expedition pushed Macedonia into the centre of attention in the Greek world, and this was reflected in the historiography. Alexander employed Aristotle's nephew Kallisthenes to interpret his achievements in a way that would suit the literary and historical tastes of the Greeks until Kallisthenes felt he could do so no longer. But also a mass of other participants in the expedition wrote histories, reports and memoirs, which flooded the Greek world in the years after 323. All these are now lost, but they shaped the accounts of the later writers, Arrian, Plutarch, Curtius Rufus, Diodoros and Justin, which have survived. Interest in things Macedonian did not slacken in the next generation. The history of the successors was written in particular by Hieronymos of Kardia, who himself participated in, or was present at, many of the events associated with Eumenes, Antigonos, Demetrios and Gonatas. His history, which sadly is lost, took a line friendly to the Antigonids and served as the main source for this part of the history of Diodoros and the relevant *Lives* of Plutarch. Probably in the third century B.C. one Marsyas of Philippoi also wrote a Macedonian history.

The middle years of the third century B.C. are a historical ruin, the only narrative source being the short and careless work of Justin, written in the third century A.D. From 220 B.C. on, however, the main source is Polybios of Megalopolis, who also included occasional retrospects on the preceding period. His main subject is Rome's rise to world power, which he himself experienced; but because Macedonian affairs made up a significant part of his main subject, he treated them in substantial detail. Where Polybios' work is only known in later excerpts (after book 5), we can use Livy, who made extensive use of Polybios, including sections no longer extant.

Literary sources dating from a much later period than the events themselves thus play a large part in reconstructing Macedonian history since the contemporary sources that once existed are largely lost. The universal historian Diodoros of Agyrion in Sicily, who lived around the middle of the first century B.C. and whose account until 301 B.C. is extant, provides an irreplaceable framework of facts and events for the fifth and fourth centuries, which relies on contemporary historians. Shortly after Diodoros Livy began to write his monumental history of Rome, in which he used Polybios extensively for eastern affairs; probably in the first century A.D. Quintus Curtius wrote his *History of Alexander* and used many contemporary sources, which are now lost; a little later Plutarch wrote his moralizing *Lives*, for which he had read extremely widely, several of which make a major contribution to Macedonian history. In the second century A.D. Arrian wrote his *History of Alexander*, which was based on the works of Ptolemaios, Aristoboulos and Nearchos; and in the third century A.D. Justin wrote his trivializing *Historia Philippica*, which is an abridgement of the *Philippica* of Pompeius Trogus, who wrote in the first cen-

tury B.C. Trogus had certainly made use of a number of sources
that are now lost, but Justin has so abbreviated and reorganized
the work, without himself being familiar with the sources, that
his book—which for many periods, especially the middle years
of the third century B.C., is sadly the only surviving literary
source—is often of doubtful reliability.

In addition to the literary sources there are some contemporary
documents. Royal letters or decrees, decisions of city assemblies,
some dedications—all these preserved in the form of inscriptions
on stone—as well as the archaeological finds, like the "royal
tombs" at Verghina or the big houses at Pella, can support and
extend the picture won from the literary sources, which are often
so inadequate. The surviving speeches and pamphlets of the Athenian politicians and publicists of the fourth century B.C., Demosthenes and Aeschines above all, should also be classified as
documents. The historical characteristic of these writings is their
partisan concentration on Athenian affairs and the Athenian point
of view, which has coloured the remaining sources for this period
(which made use of them) and has especially influenced modern
writing on these topics. The historian of Macedonia must make
a conscious attempt to eradicate this partisan one-sidedness. Nevertheless, the treatment of political speeches and pamphlets, in
particular where only an inadequate parallel tradition exists, is
not easy and in the last resort unsatisfactory since subjective
judgements inevitably play too great a part.

Bibliography

Included in this bibliography are works mentioned in abbreviated form in the notes or which otherwise might be useful to the reader. No attempt has been made to be comprehensive.

Accame, S. *La lega ateniese del sec. IV. a. C.* Rome, 1941.

Adams, W. L., and E. N. Borza, eds. *Philip II, Alexander the Great and the Macedonian Heritage.* Washington, 1982.

Albini, U. *Erode Attico. Peri Politeias.* Florence, 1968.

Andronikos, M. "Verghina, the Prehistoric Necropolis and the Hellenistic Palace." *Studies in Mediterranean Archaeology* 13, 1964.

———. *Verghina.* Athens, 1984.

Andronikos, M., Ch. Makaronas, N. Moutsopoulos, and G. Bakalakis. *To Anaktoro tes Verghinas.* Athens, 1961.

Aucello, E. "La politica dei diadochi e l'ultimatum del 314 av. Cr." *RFIC* 85, 1957, 382f.

Badian, E. "Harpalos," *JHS* 81, 1961, 16f.

———. *Studies in Greek and Roman History.* Oxford/New York, 1964.

———. "Agis III." *Hermes* 95, 1967, 170f.

———. "Alexander the Great and the Greeks of Asia." In *Ancient Society and Institutions: Studies Presented to Victor Ehrenberg on His 75th Birthday,* 37f. Oxford, 1967.

———. "A King's Notebooks." *HSPh* 72, 1968, 183f.

Badian, E., ed. *Alexandre le Grand: image et réalité.* Entretiens du Fondation Hardt, 22, 1976.

Baege, W. *De Macedonum Sacris.* Halle, 1913.

Bagnall, R. S. *The Administration of the Ptolemaic Possessions Outside Egypt.* Leiden, 1976.

Bayer, E. *Demetrios Phalereus der Athener.* Stuttgart/Berlin, 1942.

Beloch, K. J. *Griechische Geschichte.* 4 vols. Strassburg/Berlin/Leipzig, 1912–27^2.

Berve, H. *Das Alexanderreich auf prosopographischer Grundlage.* 2 vols. Munich, 1926.

Boehringer, Chr. *Zur Chronologie der mittelhellenistischen Münzserien 220–160 v. Chr.* Antike Münzen und geschnittene Steine, 5, 1972.

Bohec, S. le. "Phthia mère de Philippe V., examen critique des sources." *REG* 94, 1981, 34f.

Borza, E. N. "The Macedonian Royal Tombs at Vergina: Some Cautionary Notes." *Archaeological News* 10, 4, 1981, 73f.

———. "Athenians, Macedonians, and the Origins of the Macedonian Royal House." *Hesperia,* Supplement 19, 1982, 7f.

————. "The Royal Macedonian Tombs and the Paraphernalia of Alexander the Great." *Phoenix* 41, 105–121.

Bosworth, B. "Philip II and Upper Macedonia." *CQ* 21, 1971, 93f.

————. "Errors in Arrian." *CQ* 26, 1976, 117f.

————. *A Historical Commentary on Arrian's History of Alexander I.* Oxford, 1980.

Bruneau, Ph. *Recherches sur les cultes de Délos à l'époque hellénistique et à l'époque impériale.* Paris, 1970.

Buckler, J. *The Theban Hegemony 371–362* B.C. Cambridge, Mass., 1980.

Buraselis, K. *Das hellenistische Makedonien und die Ägäis,* Münchener Beiträge zur Papyrusforschung und antiken Rechtsgeschichte, 73, 1982.

Cabanes, P. *L'Épire de la mort de Pyrrhos à la conquête romaine, 272–167 av. J.C.* Paris, 1976.

————. "Problèmes de géographie administrative et politique dans l'Épire du IVᵉ siècle av. J.-C." In *La géographie administrative et politique d'Alexandre à Mohamet.* Actes du colloque de Strasbourg, 14–16 Juin, 1979. Leiden, n.d., 19f.

Cargill, J. *The Second Athenian League: Empire or Free Alliance?* Berkeley/Los Angeles, 1981.

Castritius, H. "Die Okkupation Thrakiens durch die Perser und der Sturz des athenischen Tyrannen Hippias." *Chiron* 2, 1972, 1f.

Cawkwell, G. L. "The Defence of Olynthus." *CQ,* n.s., 12, 1962, 122f.

————. "Demosthenes' Policy After the Peace of Philocrates." *CQ,* n.s., 13, 1963, 120f. and 200f.

————. *Philip of Macedon.* London/Boston, 1978.

Chambers, M. "The First Regnal Year of Antigonos Gonatas." *AJPh* 75, 1954, 385f.

Charneux, P. "Liste argienne de théarodoques." *BCH* 90, 1966, 156f. and 710f.

Cohen, G. M. *The Seleucid Colonies: Studies in Founding, Administration and Organization.* Historia Einzelschriften, 30, 1978.

Cormack, J. M. "The Gymnasiarchal Law of Beroea." *Archaia Makedonia* 2, 1977, 139f.

Crampa, J. *Labraunda.* Vol. 3, pt. 1, *The Greek Inscriptions.* Lund, 1969.

Danov, C. M. "Die Thraker auf dem Ostbalkan von der hellenistischen Zeit bis zur Gründung Konstantinopels." *ANRW* II, 7, 1, 21f.

Daux, G. *Delphes au IIᵉ siècle.* Paris, 1936.

Dell, H. J. "The Origin and Nature of Illyrian Piracy." *Historia* 16, 1967, 344f.

Dow, S., and C. F. Edson, Jr. "Chryseis." *HSPh* 28, 1937, 127f.

Durrbach, F. *Choix d'inscriptions de Délos.* Paris, 1921–22.

Edson, C. F. "The Antigonids, Heracles, and Beroea." *HSPh* 45, 1934, 213f.

————. "Perseus and Demetrius." *HSPh* 46, 1935, 191f.

Effenterre, H. van. *La Crète et le monde grec de Platon à Polybe.* Paris, 1948.
Ellis, J. R. "Amyntas III, Illyria and Olynthos 393/2–380/79." *Makedonika* 9, 1969, 1f.
_____. "The Step-brothers of Philip II." *Historia* 22, 1973, 350f.
_____. *Philip II and Macedonian Imperialism.* London, 1976.
Errington, R. M. "Philip V, Aratus, and the 'Conspiracy of Apelles.' " *Historia* 16, 1967, 19f.
_____. *Philopoemen.* Oxford, 1969.
_____. "From Babylon to Triparadeisos: 323–320 B.C." *JHS* 90, 1970, 49f.
_____. "The Alleged Syro-Macedonian Pact and the Origins of the Second Macedonian War." *Athenaeum* 49, 1971, 336f.
_____. "Macedonian 'Royal Style' and Its Historical Significance." *JHS* 94, 1974, 20f.
_____. "Samos and the Lamian War." *Chiron* 5, 1975, 51f.
_____. "Arybbas the Molossian." *GRBS* 16, 1975, 41f.
_____. "Alexander in the Hellenistic World." In Badian, ed., *Alexandre le Grand*, 1976, 137f.
_____. "An Inscription from Beroea and the Alleged Co-rule of Demetrius II." *Archaia Makedonia* 2, 1977, 115f.
_____. "Diodorus Siculus and the Chronology of the Early Diadochoi, 320–311 B.C." *Hermes* 105, 1977, 478f.
_____. "The Nature of the Macedonian State Under the Monarchy." *Chiron* 8, 1978, 77f.
_____. "Alexander the Philhellene and Persia." In *Ancient Macedonian Studies in Honor of Charles F. Edson*, 139f. Thessaloniki, 1981.
_____. "Antiochos III, Zeuxis und Euromos." *Epigraphica Anatolica* 8, 1986, 1f.
_____. "Review-Discussion: Four Interpretations of Philipp II." *American Journal of Ancient History* 6, 1981, 69f.
Fears, J. R. "Pausanias, the Assassin of Philip." *Athenaeum* 53, 1975, 111f.
Fine, J. V. A. "The Problem of Macedonian Holdings in Epirus and Thessaly in 221." *TAPhA* 58, 1932, 126f.
_____. The Background of the Social War of 220–17 B.C." *AJPh* 61, 1940, 129f.
Flacelière, R. *Les Aitoliens à Delphes.* Paris, 1937.
Franke, P. R. *Alt-Epirus und das Königtum de Molosser.* Kallmünz-Oberpfalz, 1955.
Fredericksmeyer, E. A. "On the Final Aims of Philip II." In Adams and Borza, eds., *Macedonian Heritage*, 1982, 85f.
Gaebler, H. *Die antiken Münzen Nordgriechenlands.* Vol. 3, pts. 1–2. Berlin, 1907, 1935.
Gallis, K. "Epigrafai ek Larises (Ἐπιγράφαι ἐκ Λαρίσης)," *AAA* 5, 1972, 275f.

Gehrke, H.-J. "Das Verhältnis von Politik und Philosophie im Wirken des Demetrios von Phaleron." *Chiron* 8, 1978, 149f.

Geyer, F. *Makedonien bis zur Thronbesteigung Philipps II.* Historische Zeitschrift, Beiheft 19. Munich/Berlin, 1930.

Giovannini, A. "Philipp V., Perseus und die delphische Amphiktyonie." *Archaia Makedonia* 1, 1970, 147f.

―――. "Le statut des cités de Macédoine sous les Antigonides." *Archaia Makedonia* 2, 1977, 465f.

Gomme, A. W., A. Andrewes, K. J. Dover. *A Historical Commentary on Thucydides*. Oxford, 1945–70.

Goukowski, P. *Essai sur les origines du mythe d'Alexandre*. 2 vols. Nancy, 1978, 1981.

Granier, F. *Die makedonische Heeresversammlung*. Munich, 1931.

Green, P. "The Royal Tombs at Vergina: A Historical Analysis." In Adams and Borza, eds., *Macedonian Heritage*, 1982, 129f.

Gruen, E. S. "The Supposed Alliance Between Rome and Philip V of Macedon." *CSCA* 6, 1973, 123f.

―――. "The Last Years of Philip V." *GRBS* 16, 1974, 221f.

✓ ―――. *The Hellenistic World and the Coming of Rome*. Berkeley/Los Angeles, 1984.

Gullath, B. *Untersuchungen zur Geschichte Boiotiens in der Zeit Alexanders und der Diadochen*. Europäische Hochschulschriften 3, Bd. 169. Frankfurt/Bern, 1982.

Habicht, Ch. "Samische Volksbeschlüsse der hellenistischen Zeit." *AM* 72, 1957, 152f.

―――. "Epigraphische Zeugnisse zur Geschichte Thessaliens unter der makedonischen Herrschaft." *Archaia Makedonia* 1, 1970, 265f.

―――. "Literarische und epigraphische Überlieferung zur Geschichte Alexanders und seiner ersten Nachfolger." In *Akten des VI. int. Kongr. für griech. und lat. Epigraphik*. Vestigia, 17, 367f. Munich, 1973.

―――. "Der Beitrag Spartas zur Restitution von Samos während des Lamischen Krieges (Ps. Aristoteles Ökonomik II.2,9)" *Chiron* 5, 1975, 45f.

―――. *Untersuchungen zur politischen Geschichte Athens im 3. Jahrhundert v. Chr.* Vestigia, 30. Munich, 1979.

―――. *Studien zur Geschichte Athens in hellenistischer Zeit*. Hypomnemata, 73. Göttingen, 1982.

Hamilton, J. R. *Alexander the Great*. London, 1973.

Hammond, N. G. L. "Diodorus' Narrative of the Sacred War." *JHS* 57, 1937, 44f. Reprinted in his *Studies in Greek History*. Oxford, 1973, 486f.

―――. "The Kingdoms in Illyria circa 400–167 B.C.", *BSA* 61, 1966, 239f.

―――. *Epirus*. Oxford, 1967.

―――. *A History of Macedonia*. 3 vols. Vol. 1, Oxford, 1972. Vol. 2 (with G. T. Griffith), Oxford, 1979. Vol. 3 (with F. W. Walbank), Oxford, 1988.

―――. *Alexander the Great*. London, 1982.

Hampl, F. *Der König der Makedonen*. Diss. Leipzig, 1934.

Harris, W. V. *War and Imperialism in Republican Rome 327–70 B.C.* Oxford, 1979.

Hatzopoulos, M. B. "The Oliveni Inscription and the Dates of Philip II's reign." In Adams and Borza, eds., *Macedonian Heritage,* 1982, 21f.

Hatzopoulos, M. B., and L. M. Loukopoulos, eds. *Philip of Macedon.* Athens, 1980.

Hauben, H. "Philippe II, fondateur de la marine macédonienne." *Ancient Society* 6, 1975, 51f.

―――. "The Expansion of Macedonian Sea-power under Alexander the Great." *Ancient Society* 7, 1976, 79f.

―――. "The Ships of the Pydnaeans: Remarks on Kassandros' Naval Situation in 314/313 B.C." *Ancient Society* 9, 1978, 47f.

Heinen, H. *Untersuchungen zur hellenistischen Geschichte des 3. Jahrhunderts v. Chr. Zur Geschichte der Zeit des Ptolemaios Keraunos und zum Chremonideischen Krieg,* Historia, Einzelschriften 20. Wiesbaden, 1972.

Heisserer, A. J. *Alexander the Great and the Greeks.* Norman, Okla., 1980.

Herzog, R., and G. Klaffenbach. "Asylieurkunden aus Kos." *Abhandlungen der Deutschen Akademie der Wissenschaften zu Berlin. Klasse für Sprachen, Literatur und Kunst,* 1952, no. 1. Berlin, 1952.

Holleaux, M. *Études d'épigraphie et d'histoire grecques.* 6 vols. Paris, 1938–68.

Hornblower, J. *Hieronymus of Cardia.* Oxford, 1981.

Jaschinski, S. *Alexander und Griechenland unter dem Eindruck der Flucht des Harpalos.* Bonn, 1981.

Kagan, D. *The Outbreak of the Peloponnesian War.* Ithaca, N.Y., 1969.

―――. *The Archidamian War.* Ithaca, N.Y., 1974.

Kalleris, J. N. *Les anciens Macédoniens.* Vol. 1. Athens, 1954.

Kienast, D. "Philipp II. von Makedonien und das Reich der Achaimeniden." *Abh. d. Marburger Gelehrtengesellschaft,* 1971, no. 6. Munich, 1973.

Kindstrand, J. F. *Bion of Borysthenes.* Uppsala, 1976.

Kougeas, S. "Diagramma stratiotikes oikonomias ton makedonikon chronon ek Chalkidos (Διάγραμμα Στρατιωτικῆς Οἰκονομίας τῶν Μακεδονικῶν χρόνων ἐκ Χαλκίδος)." *Hellenika* 7, 1934, 177f.

Koukouli-Chrysanthaki, Ch. "Politarchs in a New Inscription from Amphipolis." In *Ancient Macedonian Studies in Honor of Charles Edson,* 229f. Thessaloniki, 1981.

✓ Lane-Fox, R. *Alexander the Great.* London, 1973.

Lauffer, S. *Alexander der Große.* Munich, 1978.

Launey, M. *Recherches sur les armées hellénistiques.* 2 vols. Paris, 1950.

Lazarides, D. "Epigrafe ex Amphipoleos (Ἐπιγραφὴ ἐξ Ἀμφιπολέως)." In *Geras Antoniou Keramopoullou,* 159f. Athens, 1953.

―――. "Trois nouveaux contrats de vente à Amphipolis." *BCH* 85, 1961, 426f.

Lévêque, P. *Pyrrhos.* Paris, 1957.

Longega, G. *Arsinoe II.* Rome, 1968.

Maier, F. G. *Griechische Mauerbauinschriften*. Vestigia, 1. Heidelberg, 1959.
Marek, Ch. *Die Proxenie*. Frankfurt/Bern, 1984.
Martin, T. R. *Sovereignty and Coinage in Classical Greece*. Princeton, 1985.
Meiggs, R. *The Athenian Empire*. Oxford, 1972.
———. *Trees and Timber in the Ancient Mediterranean World*. Oxford, 1982.
Meloni, P. *Perseo e la fine della monarchia macedonica*. Rome, 1953.
Merkelbach, R. "Ein Zeugnis aus Tralles über Pleistarchos." *ZPE* 16, 1975, 163f.
Merker, I. "The Ancient Kingdom of Paionia." *Balkan Studies* 6, 1965, 35f.
Meyer, E. *Theopomps Hellenika*. Halle, 1909.
Milns, R. D. "The Hypaspists of Alexander III: Some Problems." *Historia* 20, 1971, 194f.
———. "The Army of Alexander the Great." In Badian, ed., *Alexandre le Grand*, 1976, 87f.
Mooren, L. "The Nature of the Hellenistic Monarchy." In *Egypt and the Hellenistic World*, 205f. Studia Hellenistica, 27. Louvain, 1983.
Nachtergael, G., *Les Galates en Grèce et les Sôteria de Delphes*. Académie royale de Belgique. Mémoires de la classe des lettres. Coll. in 8°, 2ᵉ sér., vol. 63, fasc. 1. Brussels, 1977.
Oliva, P. *Sparta and Her Social Problems*. Prague/Amsterdam, 1971.
Pandermalis, D. *Dion*. Society for Macedonian Studies Abroad. N.p., n.d.
Papazoglu, F. *The Central Balkan Tribes in Pre-Roman Times*. Amsterdam, 1978.
———. "Quelques aspects de l'histoire de la province de Macédoine." *ANRW* II, 7, 1, 302f.
Petsas, P. M. *Ho Taphos ton Levkadion*. Athens, 1966.
———. *Pella*. Thessalonike, 1978.
Piraino, M. T. "Antigono Dosone re di Macedonia." *Atti dell' Accad. Palermo* 13, 1952–53, 301f.
Pohlenz, M. "Philipps Schreiben an Athen." *Hermes* 64, 1929, 41f.
Pouilloux, J. *Recherches sur l'histoire et les cultes de Thasos*. Vol. 1. Paris, 1954.
Prag, A. J. N. W., J. A. Musgrave, R. A. H. Neave. "The Skull from Tomb II at Verghina: King Philip II of Macedon." *JHS* 104, 1984, 60f.
Raymond, D. *Macedonian Royal Coinage to 413 B.C.* Numismatic Notes and Monographs, no. 126. New York, 1953.
Rider, G. le. *Le monnayage d'argent et d'or de Philippe II frappé en Macédoine de 359 à 294*. Paris, 1977.
Ritter, H. W. *Diadem und Königsherrschaft*. Vestigia, 7. Munich, 1967.
———. "Zum sogenannten Diadem des Philippsgrabes." *AA*, 1984, 105f.
Robert, J., and L. Robert. *Fouilles d'Amyzon en Carie*. Vol. 1. Paris, 1983.
Robert, L. *Le sanctuaire de Sinuri près de Mylasa*. Paris, 1945.
———. "Une épigramme d' Automédon et Athènes au début de l'empire". *REG* 94, 1981, 359 no. 101.
Robinson, D. M. "Inscriptions from Macedonia." *TAPhA* 69, 1938, 43f.
Roebuck, C. "The Settlements of Philip II with the Greek States in 338 B.C." *CPh* 43, 1948, 73f.

Roesch, P. *Études Béotiennes*. Paris, 1982.

Rosen, K. "Die Gründung der makedonischen Herrschaft." *Chiron* 8, 1978, 1f.

———. "Der 'göttliche' Alexander, Athen und Samos." *Historia* 27, 1978, 20f.

Rosenberg, A. "Amyntas, der Vater Philipps II." *Hermes* 51, 1916, 499f.

Rotroff, S. I. "Spool Saltcellars in the Athenian Agora." *Hesperia* 53, 1984, 343f.

Roux, G. *L'Amphictionie, Delphes et le temple d'Apollon au IVe siècle*. Lyon/ Paris, 1979.

Ryder, T. T. G. *Koine Eirene*. Oxford, 1965.

Schachermeyr, F. *Alexander der Große*. Vienna, 1973.

Schmid, W., O. Stählin. *Griechische Literaturgeschichte*. Munich, 1921–.

Schmitt, H. H. *Untersuchungen zur Geschichte Antiochos' des Großen und seiner Zeit*. Historia, Einzelschriften 6. Wiesbaden, 1964.

Schuler, C. "The Macedonian Politarchs." *CPh* 55, 1960, 90f.

Schuller, W. *Die Herrschaft der Athener im ersten attischen Seebund*. Berlin, 1974.

Seibert, J. *Historische Beiträge zu den dynastischen Verbindungen in hellenistischer Zeit*. Historia, Einzelschriften 10. Wiesbaden, 1967.

———. *Untersuchungen zur Geschichte Ptolemaios' I*. Münchner Beiträge zur Papyrusforschung und antiken Rechtsgeschichte, 56. Munich, 1969.

———. *Alexander der Große*. Darmstadt, 1972.

———. *Die politischen Flüchtlinge und Verbannten in der griechischen Geschichte*. Darmstadt, 1979.

———. *Das Zeitalter der Diadochen*. Darmstadt, 1983.

Shear, L., Jr. *Kallias of Sphettos and the Revolt of Athens in 286 B.C.* Hesperia, Supplement 17. Princeton, 1978.

Sordi, M. *La lega tessala fino ad Alessandro magno*. Rome, 1958.

Tarn, W. W. *Antigonos Gonatas*. Oxford, 1913.

———. "Philip V and Phthia." *CQ* 18, 1924, 17f.

Tronson, A. "Satyrus and Philip II." *JHS* 104, 1984, 116f.

Tscherikower, A. *Die hellenistischen Städtegründungen von Alexander dem Großen bis auf die Römerzeit*. Philologus, Supplement 19. Leipzig, 1927.

Uebel, F. *Die Kleruchen Ägyptens unter den ersten sechs Ptolemäern*. Abh. Akad. Berlin, 3. Berlin, 1968.

Urban, R. *Wachstum und Krise des Achäischen Bundes*. Historia, Einzelschriften, 35. Wiesbaden, 1979.

Veligiani, Ch. "Ein hellenistisches Ehrendekret aus Gazoros (Ostmakedonien)." *ZPE* 51, 1983, 105f.

Wace, A. J. B., M. S. Thompson. "A Latin Inscription from Perrhaebia." *BSA* 17, 1910–11, 193f.

Walbank, F. W. *Philip V of Macedon*. Cambridge, 1940.

———. *A Historical Commentary on Polybius*. 3 vols. 1957–79.

———. "Sea-Power and the Antigonids." In Adams and Borza, eds., *Macedonian Heritage*, 1982, 213f.

Wallace, M. B. "Early Greek Proxenoi." *Phoenix* 24, 1970, 199f.

Welles, C. B. "New Texts from the Chancery of Philip V of Macedon and the Problem of the 'Diagramma.' " *AJA* 42, 1938, 252f.

Welwei, K.-W. "Das makedonische Herrschaftssystem in Griechenland und die Politik des Antigonos Doson." *RhM* 110, 1967, 306f.

Westlake, H. D. *Thessaly in the Fourth Century B.C.* London, 1935.

Wiesner, J. *Die Thraker*. Stuttgart, 1963.

Wilamowitz-Moellendorff, U. *Antigonos von Karystos*. Berlin, 1881.

Will, E. *Histoire politique du monde hellénistique*. 2 vols. Annales de l'est. Mémoire, 30, 32. Nancy, 1979, 1982².

Wirth, G. *Philipp II. Geschichte Makedoniens*. Vol. 1. Stuttgart, 1985.

Wormell, Y. "The Literary Evidence on Hermeias of Atarneus." *Yale Classical Studies* 5, 1935, 57f.

Xirotiris N. F., F. Langenscheidt. "The Cremations from the Royal Macedonian Tombs of Verghina." *Archaiologike Ephemeris* 1981, 142f.

Zahrnt, M. *Olynth und die Chalkidier*. Vestigia, 14. Munich, 1971.

———. Review of Hammond and Griffith, *A History of Macedonia*, vols. 1 and 2. *Gnomon* 55, 1983, 36f.

———. "Die Entwicklung des makedonischen Reiches bis zu den Perserkriegen." *Chiron* 14, 1984, 325f.

Index

Text: 10/13 Palatino
Display: Palatino
Compositor: Auto-Graphics, Inc.